EUROPEAN DEFENCE TECHNOLOGY IN TRANSITION

European Defence Technology in Transition

Edited by

Philip Gummett and Josephine Anne Stein

LONDON AND NEW YORK

First published 1997 by Harwood Academic Publishers

This edition published 2013 by Routledge
2 Park Square, Milton Park, Abingdon, Oxfordshire OX14 4RN
711 Third Avenue, New York, NY 10017

First issued in paperback 2016

Routledge is an imprint of the Taylor & Francis Group, an informa business

---

British Library Cataloguing in Publication Data

European defence technology in transition
1. Defensive (Military science) 2. Military research — Europe
3. Europe — Defenses
I. Gummett, Philip II. Stein, Josephine Anne
338.4'7'35507'094

ISBN 13: 978-1-138-96910-0 (pbk)
ISBN 13: 978-90-5702-149-7 (hbk)

Contents

Preface vii

Notes on Contributors xi

Introduction 1
Philip Gummett and Josephine Anne Stein

1 Belgium 25
Pierre de Vestel

2 France 51
Claude Serfati

3 Germany 85
Peter Lock and Werner Voss

4 Greece 117
Anthony Bartzokas

5 Italy 137
Giancarlo Graziola, Sergio Parazzini and Giulio Perani

6 The Netherlands 167
Ton van Oosterhout and Wim Smit

7 Spain 197
Jordi Molas-Gallart

8 Sweden 219
Björn Hagelin

9 United Kingdom 261
Philip Gummett

Index 289

Preface

Serious European academic research into issues concerning defence science, technology and industrial policy is of relatively recent origin. A major impetus was given by the UK Economic and Social Research Council (ESRC) which, in the late 1980s and early 1990s, funded a programme of work on the subject, with contributory funding from the British Ministry of Defence. The programme was originated and managed by the Science Policy Support Group (SPSG) in London, led first by John Ziman, and then by Peter Healey

As that work proceeded, two things happened. First, the implications of the end of the Cold War began to become clearer. Far from having the effect, as some at first thought, of rendering this subject irrelevant, in fact the opposite proved to be the case. Adjusting defence science and technology to the post-Cold War world has been a complex business. It entailed reducing and re-orienting national efforts on the one hand, while considering, on the other, how best to use the resources released by this process. It raised important issues of comparison between East and West. It has generated fresh concerns about the problems of controlling the international flow of militarily-relevant technology, as defence users have increasingly begun to draw upon civil sources for new technology. It has also posed questions about the ability of defence technological and industrial capabilities on the European scale to survive, especially under the conditions of intensified competition with the USA that have occured in recent years. All this has expanded, rather than reduced, the research agenda.

The second development emerged naturally from the first. It concerned the realisation that an isolated programme of *British* research on this subject made little sense, for two reasons. First, it became evident that there was much to be gained from comparative study of policy and practice in the countries of Europe. Second, the subject under examination itself increasingly demanded in any case to be studied on a European scale, as governments and firms began to search for Europe-wide solutions to the dilemmas that faced them.

Accordingly, towards the end of the ESRC-funded research programme, a decision was made to try to build a European network of researchers active in this field, and formal contact was established with experienced researchers in all the main European countries with defence interests. Hence, in 1991, the CREDIT network was set up. CREDIT — *Capacity for Research on European Defence and Industrial Technology* — became an SPSG International Study Group, with initial funding from the ESRC for a study of European Defence

Technology in Transition, with special reference to lessons for the UK. From that beginning, the current 10-country network was established, the 10 countries being the nine represented in this book plus Denmark.

The book itself has emerged gradually from the continuing work of the CREDIT network, with successive versions of chapters being developed and presented at meetings in London, Milan and Rome, in the latter cases being presented to parliamentarians, government officials and industrialists, as well as academics.

In addition, DG XII of the Commission of the European Communities, with its particular interest in research and technology development policy, and in dual-use technologies, offered further valuable support for a seminar in Brussels in January 1995. This seminar, on *Defence-Related Research and Technology in Transition: Issues for Europe*, attracted the participation of over 100 industrialists, officials and academics from all over Europe, and from the USA, as well as from the Commission itself. It provided an important platform for the authors to test their ideas against a knowledgeable and informed audience, to receive constructive criticism, and generally to benefit from a stimulating exchange of ideas. Some of the material presented by others at that meeting has been incorporated into this volume.

This book is the result, therefore, of a lengthy gestation, and one, to mix the metaphor, which has been beset by particular problems of chasing a moving target, such has been the rate of change in its field. Its authors owe considerable debts to numerous organisations and individuals, among whom the following, at least, should be gratefully acknowledged:

- the UK Economic and Social Research Council;
- the UK Ministry of Defence;
- Messrs Giancarlo Chevallard, Jean-Pierre Contzen, Richard Escritt, Robert Magnaval, Isi Saragossi, and their colleagues, at DG XII of the European Commission;
- secretarial support staff in PREST, and the Department of Government, University of Manchester, especially Christine Brown and Jane Harden;
- Shahnaz Holder, Department of Government, and staff of the Computer Support Unit, Faculty of Economic and Social Studies, University of Manchester, and Edward Gummett, for overcoming problems of incompatibility among the many software systems used by our authors;
- Tiffany Tyler, PREST, University of Manchester, for the English translation of the chapter on France;
- John Ziman, Peter Healey, Carlye Honig, and secretarial support staff, at SPSG;

- other members of the CREDIT network, who have contributed indirectly to this volume through their participation at various meetings.

To all these, our warm thanks. The authors and editors, of course, remain responsible for the final product.

Notes on Contributors

Dr Anthony Bartzokas wrote his PhD on the Greek defence industry at the Science Policy Research Unit, University of Sussex, UK. He has since held posts at the United Nations University in The Netherlands and the University of Athens, Greece, and has held a NATO Fellowship.

Giancarlo Graziola is professor of Economics at the Universita Cattolica, Milan, Italy, where he directs the Centre for Studies of Armament and Disarmament. He has written widely on Italian defence industrial affairs.

Philip Gummett is professor of Government and Technology Policy at the University of Manchester, UK, where he is head of the Department of Government and a director of the Programme of Policy Research in Engineering, Science and Technology (PREST). He is academic co-ordinator of the CREDIT network, and is an adviser to the Foreign Affairs Commissioner in the European Commission. His research interests lie in defence technology policy and in British science policy.

Dr Björn Hagelin, PhLic, was born in 1947, and received a BA in political science and international politics from Stockholm University, Sweden, in 1970. After more than 10 years as a defence and security analyst with the national Defence Research Establishment in Stockholm, he became a research fellow at the Department of Peace and Conflict Research, University of Upsalla, in 1987. There he received Sweden's first academic degree in peace and conflict research, in 1989.

Dr Peter Lock is a researcher associated with the European Association for Research on Transformation, and is co-ordinator of its 'Permanent (Economic) Workshop' in Moscow. He is an advisor to the UN Department for Crime Prevention and Criminal Justice on the international gun control study, and is formerly editor-in-chief of *Militärpolitik Dokumentation*, and assistant professor (international relations) at the University of Hamburg. His research interests include defence economics, arms transfers, civil-military relations and changing characteristics of warfare.

Dr Jordi Molas-Gallart is a research fellow at the Science Policy Research Unit, University of Sussex, UK. He is author of *Military Production and Innovation in Spain*, published by Harwood Academic Publishers, and of more than 20 articles and book chapters on topics including Spanish defence industrial policy, the relationship between military and civilian technologies, conversion and diversification strategies, technology policy, and electronic commerce.

Ton van Oosterhout is a PhD student at the University of Twente, The Netherlands. He is writing his thesis on technology development in the Dutch Navy.

Dr Sergio Parazzini is an economist at the Universita Cattolica, Milan, Italy, where he works in the Centre for Studies of Armament and Disarmament. He has also held a post at the Centre for Defence Economics, University of York, UK.

Giulio Perani is director of the Military Spending and Arms Production Project at the Archivio Disarmo in Rome, Italy. He is currently a NATO research fellow, studying military technology policies in NATO countries. He has recently carried out a research report for the Italian Ministry of Defence on *Competitivity of the defence industry and the dual-use problem.*

Dr Claude Serfati is a *Maître de conférences* and member of the C3ED at the University of Versailles-Saint-Quentin, France. He has written extensively on the arms industry, with particular reference to industrial performance, and science and technological policy.

Dr Wim Smit is associate professor of Science, Technology and Society at the University of Twente, The Netherlands. He has published on such issues as nuclear proliferation, assessment and dynamics of military technological developments, assessment of nuclear technology, and risk assessment. His current interest is in socio-technical networks of military and dual-use technology.

Dr Josephine Anne Stein is a senior research fellow in Policy Research in Engineering, Science and Technology (PREST), University of Manchester, UK, and manager of PREST's London Office. Her main research interests are in international research collaboration and management, human resources for science and technology, technology assessment, and military research and technology policy.

Pierre de Vestel is a political scientist who is currently a research associate at the Institute for European Studies of the Free University of Brussels — ULB — Belgium. His chapter was written when he was researcher at GRIP-Brussels and he has since written numerous articles on defence economic and industrial affairs.

Werner Voss is a project director at ISA Consult GmbH, Germany, a consultancy specialising in advice on the introduction of new technologies and labour market policies. He graduated from the Economics Department of the University of Bremen and he has published widely on arms production and conversion questions.

Introduction

Philip Gummett and Josephine Anne Stein

The Context

The six-nation European Community was conceived in the aftermath of World War II with the aim of making future war in Europe inconceivable. But after the failure of plans to establish a European Defence Community, the goal of military security was to be achieved indirectly, through non-military forms of cooperation. Thus, the Common Market, and the agreements to cooperate in the three industries of coal, steel and atomic energy, were seen not as ends in themselves but as the means of binding the member states into a form of union within which war could have no part. As the Community expanded to 12, and then 15 member states, the same approach has been followed. The resulting taboo on direct involvement with defence issues has, however, inhibited a common European approach to defence, and hence also to our subject, defence technology policy.

Article 223 of the 1957 Treaty of Rome formalised the European Community's exclusion of defence from its joint responsibilities.[1] Only in cases where trade in dual-use items distorted the operation of the civil common market could the European Commission step in, and even then reluctantly because of the sensitivity attached by member states to this area.

The picture changed somewhat with the Maastricht Treaty on European Union of 1992. The Treaty established a commitment to move towards a common foreign and security policy (CFSP), raising the prospect of 'the eventual framing of a common defence policy, which might in time lead to a common defence'. However, the same article of the Treaty (article J.4) called not on the institutions of the EU but on the Western European Union (WEU), which had been resurrected in the 1990s to act as a bridge between the EU and NATO, 'to elaborate and implement decisions and actions of the Union which shall have defence implications'. Military matters thus remained outside the area of supranational activities, being kept firmly at the inter-governmental level. (Gummett, 1996).

These (deliberate) constraints notwithstanding, various forces and circumstances are raising ever more prominently the question of the formation of defence technology policy in Europe. First, the Maastricht Treaty stipulated that the Council of Ministers should report to the European Council in 1996 on progress with the CFSP, with a view to formulating the next steps. The 1996 Inter-Governmental Conference offers, therefore, an occasion for further possible development in this field, since movement towards a CFSP implies closer defence, and therefore, defence equipment, harmonisation. Moreover, in 1998 the WEU aims to complete the planned revision of its 1948 Brussels Treaty, which will present a further occasion to re-evaluate the EC-WEU relationship.

To these developments must be added another, but on a different plane. As observed by J.P. Contzen, a senior European Commission official responsible for the Joint Research Centre, new technologies today are increasingly 'the combination of several technologies'. They are, he suggests, 'super-technologies', and he goes on to conclude that future product or process innovation, be it civilian or military, will require the 'simultaneous mastering of several technological sectors' (Contzen, 1995). In addition, as the balance of demand for advanced technologies has shifted over the years more and more towards the civil sector, so leadership in technical change has also shifted increasingly to the civil sector.

Hence, although relatively isolated from each other in the 1950s and 1960s, technologies of civil and military origin have since gradually become more inter-dependent, as civil technologies have gained in strength and, in some cases, outstripped their military counterparts. In certain key fields, such as micro-electronics, firms began to source globally, and to build international alliances that reinforced their access to necessary components and markets.

At the regional level, the establishment of the Single European Market reinforced this trend, and began to alter the context of European governmental and industrial behaviour in the field of defence technology. Companies with high technology civil interests have been internationalising their activities in response to the twin pressures of the Single Market and the greater liberalisation of global trade. The increasingly blurred distinction between civil and military technology has made it harder for these processes not to spill over into the defence sector.

Another byproduct of the Single Market is the progressive reduction of border controls. While the provisions governing the movement of weapons and military technologies continue to differ from those for civil goods and technologies, the logic of the Single Market drives towards free movement inside Europe, and towards a 'common European fence' regulating imports and exports — that is, the same regulations, applied to equal standards, throughout Europe. The growing salience of dual use technologies intensifies this problem.

Yet another strand of argument emerges from the long-established practice of European cooperation in defence technology. This has begun, albeit on a very small scale, to move upstream into the research field, with the EUCLID (European Cooperation for the Long-term In Defence) programme. At the development and production levels, the four-nation *Eurofighter 2000* programme is but the most prominent current example of the imperatives driving governments and firms to pool resources of finance, expertise and markets, in order to achieve economies of scale that offer some prospect of competing on price and quality with the considerably larger US firms and US market

Overcapacity in the defence sector, even before the arrival of Mr Gorbachev, has also raised questions about how best to capture the investment made by each country in military technology and in skilled researchers, designers and engineers. In one sense, the decline of the European defence industry can be seen as analogous to decline in other industrial sectors, such as those on which the early Community was based, namely, coal and steel. Local, national and European programmes can thus be envisaged to support retraining and regeneration of areas affected by declining military production. KONVER, the EU's programme to aid defence conversion, operates in this sense just like any other sectoral policy.

In other respects, however, defence differs from other industrial sectors. Its scale and, often, geographical location, is the direct or indirect result of past decisions made by governments, who play a crucial role as the only customer in the so-called defence 'market'. This may be thought to confer on them a special responsibility in managing the effects of declining defence demand. The nature of its products, and the skills available within it, render it subject to special controls. In addition, the importance of its products to governments gives it a special political status. It is this that tempts governments to try to retain indigenous capability even when the technological and economic odds may be stacked against them.

The end of the Cold War brought all these questions into sharp and urgent focus. Global defence spending fell from $1.2 trillion in 1987 to $850 billion in 1994 (in 1994 dollars). Over that same period, defence spending in the US fell to 76% of its 1987 level, and in NATO Europe to 89%. Spending on procurement fell even faster, dropping by as early as 1992 to 73% of its 1987 value in the US, and to 72% in NATO Europe. Job losses in the US military aerospace and missile sector alone fell between 1990 and 1995 from 627,000 to 326,000; while in Western Europe over the same period total defence industrial employment fell from 1.6 million to 900,000. In Russia, employment on military production and research and development (R&D) in 1993 was down to 40% of its 1991 level, and falling. (IISS, 1996; SIPRI, 1995).

From a West European perspective, the structure of the industry, especially in terms of the comparison between the US and Europe, continues to be unfavourable. The European defence industry as a whole remains oversized (although it has shrunk faster in some countries than others), and the number of prime contractors (and variety of products flowing from their factories), remains far in excess of those found in the world's largest defence market, the United States.

With a market twice the size of western Europe combined, yet only one prime contractor for main battle tanks (Europe has 4), one for submarines (Europe has 5) and three for combat aircraft (Europe has 4, including the Eurofighter consortium), US firms enjoy production runs two to five times larger than their European competitors, with corresponding economies of scale and commonality of equipment for the armed forces. US firms have also been undergoing concentration faster and more decisively than European firms which, beyond a certain level of national concentration, encounter the difficulties of international mergers, acquisitions or joint ventures in a sector which is still treated as politically sensitive, and in which differences in state-industry relations and in production costs remain significant. (Figures from GIFAS, the French aerospace industry association, quoted in *Aviation Week*, 22 April 1996, p. 54, suggest that France, for example, has average labour costs in the aerospace sector that are 35% higher than in the US and 45% higher than in the UK. Even if only approximately accurate, such disparities are somewhat inconvenient for negotiations over international restructuring). The world's largest defence firm in 1995, Lockheed-Martin, was the product of just such a US merger. Its annual turnover exceeded the defence procurement budget of the UK or France, giving it enormous resources with which to compete with European firms either in Europe itself or in the global export market. With the addition of Loral in 1996, the new company's annual turnover will equal the sum of annual procurement spending by France and the UK.

Nor are there easy escape routes into defence exports. First, the volume of global arms exports fell from a high of $60 billion in 1987 to $22 billion in 1993, and this despite most exporting countries altering their policies to facilitate exports (IISS, 1996). Second, from a European perspective, the character of competition with US firms has altered. Whereas European firms have long depended on exports for about a third of their business, US firms, with their much larger home market, have been much less dependent, although still sufficiently so to have held prime place in the export league. Now, however, with the US domestic market shrinking, and doing so faster than the European one, the pressure on US firms to export, both to Europe and to Europe's own export markets, has grown. Hence, France, for example, has seen its arms deliveries fall from FF39 billion in 1990 to FF17 billion in 1994. At the same time, the US share of the reduced world market grew from 35% in 1990 to 55% in 1995. In a clear sign of the changed times, in the years 1996–2000, US firms are expected to produce about four times as many combat aircraft for export as for domestic purchase (Forsberg, 1994, Appendix Table 2).

If European states wish to retain a defence industrial capacity (rather than buy American), the choice appears to be between paying a high economic price for national independence, or finding some common European solution. At the same time, internationalisation of development, design and production of defence equipment, together with changes in the technological basis of defence capabilities, complicates the task of controlling the international flow of militarily-relevant technologies. As we have indicated, however, there is already a good deal of European level policymaking going on in this field, despite the historical inhibitions. In addition, the 1996 Inter-Governmental Conference, not to mention the issue of enlargement of the EU to the east, cannot avoid addressing fundamental questions about the security basis of the overall European project.

This book, focusing more narrowly on defence technological and industrial issues, aims to provide information about current policy and practice in those countries of the EU which have the most significant defence industries, and to contribute to the evolving policy debate. The remainder of this introduction is devoted to introducing various developments and issues which will recur, and receive more specific treatment, in the country chapters that follow.

Defence Industrial and Technology Policy

Until the late 1980s, the size and shape of European defence activities reflected the specific geopolitical circumstances of the Cold War. As these circumstances changed, the defence sector suffered not just a loss of demand, but a loss of coherence. The military strategies and force structures pertinent to defending against massed attacks from the East lost their relevance. It became less clear how to organise military forces in response to the more diffuse set of risks that have emerged. This is true in relation both to the possibilities of threats from weapons of mass destruction, and to the use of national armed forces in multinational coalitions, such as the burgeoning United Nations interventions. Defence planning has become extremely difficult.

The difficulty that all countries face is that of identifying requirements in a coherent fashion, and then of finding the necessary funds at a time of public pressure for cuts. When 'the threat' came clearly from the Soviet Union, it was possible to plan fairly straightforwardly. Moreover, because of the scale of forces assembled to deal with that threat, lesser defence problems could be managed with some configuration of forces drawn from the large total. But the single large threat has now been replaced by multiple smaller, but less clearcut, 'risks'. Not only is it difficult to know what to plan for, but the forces available will be much smaller than in the past, thus reducing the scope for withdrawing elements of the total to meet particular eventualities. If it could be safely assumed by each country that it would meet all conceivable eventualities in the company of the same fixed set of allies, then a division of labour might be agreed. But even this seems implausible at present. Hence the profound uncertainty that has been gripping defence planners and, by extension, those responsible for planning defence R&D. Details are given in the chapters that follow, while Table 1 gives an overview of the relative scales of expenditure by western European states on military and civil R&D, and military equipment expenditure.

Table 1: Data on Military R&D and Equipment Expenditure, 1994

Country	**Government R&D Expenditure** millions 1994 ECU	**Military R&D** millions 1994 ECU	**Military R&D as percentage of Govt. exp.**	**Military Equipment Expenditure** millions 1994 ECU
Belgium	1,213	2	0.2	260
France	13,690	4,433	32.4	6,345
Germany	16,510	1,393	8.4	3,339
Greece	176	3	1.7	891
Italy	5,378	478	8.9	2,675
Netherlands	2,194	76	3.4	2,182
Spain	1,884	214	11.3	1,214
Sweden	980	172	17.5	678
UK	7,150	3,182	44.5	7,140

Sources: EUROSTAT, except for final column, which is NATO.
Notes:
- Swedish figures are for 1992.
- French equipment expenditure, which is not declared to NATO, is taken from the *Projet de loi de finances pour 1994*, Paris: Imprimerie nationale, 1993.
- Table prepared by Pierre de Vestel.

What is striking about the various responses to the post-Cold War uncertainty, however, is how little difference they are making to the shape of the inventory of new equipment requirements. There are important exceptions, such as the new emphasis on C^3I, space surveillance and communications, and defences against weapons of mass destruction, offset by some reductions in nuclear weapons programmes, more so in France than in Britain. But most major programmes are being kept in place, albeit stretched out in time and often with a reduced number of units.

At the level of R&D, and especially 'R', European governments responded initially to the post-Cold War conditions by asserting the importance of maintaining high levels of technological competence, if not necessarily pushing this through into finished products. The position was similar in the USA where the ratio in 1985 of $1 spent on R&D for every $3 on procurement was expected to change by 1995 to a ratio of less than one to two (Van Atta, 1994).

The overall turbulence of defence policy has been making it difficult for clear lines of R&D policy to emerge. In addition, various indequacies of statistics, such as the very limited projections which most countries are prepared to publish, uncertainty in various countries over the extent to which published figures correspond to the Frascati definitions of R&D, lack of information about industrial spending, and difficulties of accounting for dual-use projects, also complicate the task of analysis. Nevertheless, it does seem that European governments have been protecting their defence research, at least relative to the rate of reduction of defence budgets in general (GRIP, 1993).

International Collaboration in Defence Research

While continuing with these levels of national defence research activity, the various European countries are also pursuing international collaboration whenever it fits their national priorities. As well as various bilateral and trilateral programmes, a pan-European initiative was launched in 1990 by the then Independent European Programme Group (IEPG). This comprises the European members of NATO, including France but minus Iceland, and has since been put under the aegis of the Western European Union and renamed the Western European Armaments Group (WEAG).

The 1990 initiative was to establish a joint research programme called EUCLID (European Cooperation for the Long-term in Defence) (Chauvot de Beauchene, 1991). A memorandum of understanding was signed by the 13 nations in November 1990, and 11 areas for research, rising later to 15, were agreed.[2] Countries may elect to join à la carte. EUCLID, however, got off to a rather slow start, and the sums of money committed so far are small. By the summer of 1993, the contracts signed amounted to only about 30 million ecus, or about one-twentieth of British defence research spending alone. Whether, in what clearly remains a highly nationalistic arena, the EUCLID budget could rise to even 10% of expenditure on European military research seems doubtful at present.

One development that could in time change the position arises from the French proposal, launched at the Maastricht summit in December 1991, for an Armaments Agency under the aegis of the Western European Union. (Sillard, 1991; Teisseire, 1991; Borderas, 1994). The functions of this Agency, it was suggested, could evolve over time from simply housing the project offices of collaborative projects, to managing R&D and equipment projects on behalf of member states, and even to becoming the procurement arm of the WEU as a whole. One clear early task could be to assume the responsibility for EUCLID.

Having made little progress, this plan was relaunched in December 1993 as a specifically Franco-German agency, to be concerned initially with the management of joint French/German defence equipment projects. After objections by other states that this idea appeared to cut across that for a WEU Armaments

Agency, France and Germany quickly offered to put their agency under the aegis of the WEU, and to represent it as the embryo of a WEU Agency, arguing at the same time that they had particular reasons for wanting to get started and not wait for agreement by the other member states.

Subsequently, the November 1994 Noordwijk meeting of the WEU Council of Ministers, 'took note' of further work on the idea of an Armaments Agency, and agreed that further discussions would continue, while also 'recognising that conditions do not currently exist for the creation of an agency conducting the full range of procurement activities on behalf of member nations'. (WEU Noordwijk Declaration, 14 November 1994). The more ambitious plans for the Agency having thus been laid to rest, Britain then began actively to consider participation, even raising the possibility that management of such major projects as Eurofighter 2000, the Horizon frigate programme, and a new European armoured car could pass to the Agency (*Financial Times*, 28 March 1995). However, in raising this prospect, the then Defence Procurement Minister, Mr Roger Freeman, spoke of the Agency as starting 'as a buying agency with delegated powers of management. In due course, it might move on to discuss long-term operational needs, research and development'. Clearly, a number of different, though not necessarily incompatible, visions exist of how the Agency might develop. At the time of writing, the status of the Agency remained unclear: France and Germany had expressed a firm intention to proceed, and the UK had expressed enthusiasm to join, but the scope and modus operandi of the Agency remained to be settled.[3]

Industrial Developments

The future European capability in defence technology depends not only on the policies of governments but also on the decisions of companies. This is not because of industry's role as a sponsor of defence technology, where it plays a minor part compared to governments, but rather because in every country it is in industry rather than government that most of the *physical* capability is to be found.

Industry responds to different pressures than those operating on governments. Accordingly, while European governments have been gradually revising their defence policies over the past several years, defence industrial companies have been moving ahead more rapidly in order to try to maintain their own viability. These developments are important to the future of European foreign and security policy, at both national and EU levels:

- they influence the defence capability of Europe as a whole, as well as that of individual states;

- they affect the economic security of states, both in terms of direct effects (such as jobs) and by altering the general attractiveness of a country, or of regions of a country, for high technology investments, according to the 'cluster' theory of Porter (1990), and the arguments of Reich (1990) over the importance of maintaining a skilled workforce as a magnet for such investments;
- for both political and economic reasons, therefore, the protection of national defence industries is a natural concern of most governments, but this concern runs against those currents in European politics that are flowing towards greater integration;
- they influence the scope for shifting the balance of European technological capabilities more in the direction of dual-use technologies, as discussed further below.

As already mentioned, Europe's defence companies are engaged in major restructuring, within and across borders, which is likely to accelerate still further (Wulf, 1993; Sandström and Wilén, 1993; Brzoska and Lock, 1992; Hébert, 1991). Skilled people are being displaced from their jobs, and there is a considerable risk that they will find little comparable work to go to. While there would clearly be little point in maintaining capabilities for which there is no demand, the abruptness and (often) geographical concentration of defence cuts can mean that there is little chance of any alternative demand manifesting itself within a short time period.

It deserves emphasis that *international* restructuring has come to the defence sector later than to the rest of industry, with defence still today being regarded as a sector of unusual strategic significance by governments, who therefore actively scrutinise foreign interventions. International restructuring has, nevertheless, been particularly evident in the electronics and aerospace sectors, with the warship and land equipment industries lagging behind.

Two main patterns of activity can be observed. One pattern has been of major defence contractors taking over second tier firms in other countries. Of greater significance, however, have been the moves to establish international joint ventures between the major players on the European scene, particularly between British and French, and French and German, firms. These present the prospect of radical reshaping of the industry, which might result in the formation of a few large multinational 'clusters' of fixed composition (Steinberg, 1992), but more probably perhaps will take the form of fluid coalitions of opportunity between divisions of the main defence firms (Walker and Gummett, 1989 and 1993).

These developments will affect not only the size and distribution of Europe's defence industrial capabilities, but also the balance of technological power within Europe and its competitiveness vis-à-vis the USA and Japan. Hence, they are of broad significance for the future of European foreign and security policy.

Defence Technology Policy

The scale of national capacities in defence technology varies considerably across Europe, with France and the UK, followed by Germany, at one extreme, and Belgium and Greece at the other. The capacity of these countries to formulate more or less comprehensive policies for the acquisition of defence technologies has to reflect these realities. And even among the larger ones, significant differences in practice can be observed. For example, in France only about 30% of defence *research* (as distinct from development) is done in establishments under the whole or partial control of the Ministry of Defence (MoD), compared with more than double that figure in the UK. The proportions done in industry vary correspondingly. On the other hand, the concentration of technical expertise within the French MoD in the hands of the Délégation Générale pour l'Armement (DGA), whose key staff come from a specialist, permanent corps of armaments engineers, gives these specialists a greater say in determining the content of the defence research (and development and production) programme than do technical specialists in, say, the British MoD.

All countries, however, have been facing the challenge of having to do more with less. Their specific responses are described in the following chapters. Here we focus on the key general problem of how they are trying to maintain adequate technological dynamism within Europe under the twin pressures of diminishing budgets and increasing American competition.

One response seen in some countries has been to think in terms of the establishment of lists of 'critical technologies' as a key instrument of defence technology policy. Such an approach can be seen in France, Italy and Sweden, for example, as well as in the United States. Branscomb (1994), however, warns that the concept of critical technologies, especially when used as the basis for policy towards supposedly commercially important technologies, is a slippery one. His main point is that the sense in which something is critical is highly context dependent, that is, that much is in the eye of the beholder. This has been the traditional position in the UK, where there has been resistance to the publication of lists of defence critical technologies, partly on grounds of the difficulty of defining them in any meaningful way, and partly because they give a hostage to fortune because they implicitly encourage companies to lobby for support for *their* contribution to an item on the list. Others, however, have felt that there is value in trying, as in the exercise by the French Groupe de stratégie industrielle

(Commissariat général du plan, 1993; and see chapter on France) to identify which technologies must be retained under national control, which can be developed in a pool with allies, and which can be bought on the open market. And even in the UK, the discussions of research plans in various official statements in 1994 (Ministry of Defence, 1994b; Cabinet Office, 1994) showed that the UK MoD clearly did have a sense of future requirements, and this has been confirmed by subsequent moves to define a defence technology strategy, and make it known to industry.

More fundamental, however, has been the challenge of responding to the important changes that have occurred on the technological plane. The post-second world war presumption that military technology sets the pace for technological change, leading from time to time to spin-off to the civil sector, has increasingly been called into question. This has been most evident in the electronics and computing fields, where the balance of demand between military and commercial customers has altered dramatically in recent decades, placing the main driver of technical advance today firmly in the civil sector. In addition, innovations in production processes, such as the concept of lean engineering, together with increasingly globalised sourcing of components, have given rise to what can be called a new technological paradigm. Improvements in the quality of technologies produced for civil purposes, coupled with reduced funding for defence research, development and procurement, have also caused defence agencies to look with greater interest to the civil sector as a supplier (Gummett and Reppy (eds) 1988; Smit 1992).

This is the framework within which interest has grown in recent years in the concepts of dual-use technology, and of civil-military integration, the latter, following the Office of Technology Assessment (1994), being divisible into issues concerning the technology itself, production processes, and supplier-user networks.

There has already been extensive discussion of the dual-use concept in the USA (see Alic *et al.*, 1992). With the election of President Clinton, the concept moved from the level of analysis to become a central pillar of defence technology policy (Van Atta 1995; Gansler 1993). The 1995 Department of Defense budget contained over $2 billion for work of this type, much of it under the Technology Reinvestment Program (TRP).

The other important context for this debate is Japan, which is now the paradigm case for the application of the dual-use concept. In his detailed account of what he terms Japan's 'technonationalism', Samuels (1994) shows how Japan has embedded a defence production capability within a civilian economy. When, by the 1970s, the relations between technologies of civil and military origin began to change, Japan found itself in an exceptionally strong position. As the world leader in the introduction of advanced electronics into a huge variety of products, and in the development of advanced manufacturing capabilities, Japan assembled an impressive commercial technology base which could be applied to military purposes, while continuing to reinforce it with work arising from military funding. To give but one example: the Japanese claim that their air-to-surface missile performs better than the US missile on which it is based because it has better gyrocompass technology. The reason, they say, is that the Japanese bearings have smoother surfaces than their US counterpart, because they were first produced for the demanding purchasers of videotape recorders.

For Samuels, the fundamental lesson from the Japanese experience is that a full-spectrum commercial capability helps defence production as much as do focused defense industrial policies. But the relationship is reciprocal. Each of the pieces, up and downstream, meshes together, resulting in a diverse commercial economy that is a huge 'knowledge generator' for society as a whole.

Such thinking has now taken root in Europe. Thus, Britain, after earlier reluctance to discuss together the development of civil and military technologies (Council for Science and Society, 1986), is becoming increasingly active on this subject. Industry is pressing strongly for a greater national effort in the development of dual-use technologies, notably through the programme operating under this title, sponsored by the Confederation of British Industry on the initiative of British Aerospace, and through the government's Technology Foresight exercise (Coghlan, 1994; Cabinet Office, 1995). The MoD, through its research arm, the Defence Evaluation and Research Agency (DERA), is acting to develop new Dual Use Technology Centres, and related initiatives which will align the programmes of the DERA more closely with those of industry (House of Lords, 1994; Ministry of Defence, 1995).

A similar debate has also been underway for some time in France, but, at least initially, in a more positive tone than in the UK. For several years there have existed large annual meetings to draw together defence and civil scientists (so-called 'Entretiens science et défense'). Civil agencies, such as the national space agency (CNES) are much more closely involved with defence programmes than would be the case in, say, the UK. The tone of the French outlook was well shown in an editorial in the house journal of the French DGA, in introducing in 1991 a special issue on *Les Technologies Duales*, which argued that the time is past when one could think of defence research in isolation from civil, adding that today's economic and technological conditions require constant attention to the issue of duality in research and development (*L'Armement*, 1991). The willingness to place defence interests firmly in the forefront of wider national technological development is a theme that was continued, and much developed, in the highly detailed 1993 report of the Groupe de stratégie industrielle of the French Planning Commission (Commissariat général du plan, 1993), while also being criticised by some in terms of its overall effect on French technological and economic development (Chesnais, 1993; and chapter on France).

Different again, at least in modality, is the German case. The most powerful economy in Europe is also one of the most heavily constrained politically in terms of defence equipment spending, relative to its size. Hence, it has already been policy since 1985 to draw on civilian-developed technology as far as possible (see chapter on Germany). Moreover, in contrast to the USA and UK, Germany has not maintained large state-owned defence research establishments. Instead, it makes heavy use of other research institutions with primarily civil interests (such as the Deutsche Forschunganstalt für Luft-und Raumfahrt, and the Fraunhofer Gesellschaft), and of private companies. These are on the whole less militarily dependent than their British or French counterparts, and in that sense much more like Japanese defence producers.

Smaller countries, such as Belgium, have also sought for some time to encourage companies to operate across the defence-civil interface, through support of Airbus and the European Space Agency, and through encouraging civil electronics firms to tender for defence electronics equipment by specifying aircraft display units, for example, that were 'mil-tailored' rather than 'mil-spec'. In the Netherlands, likewise, about one-third of the defence R&D budget is actually spent in what are primarily civil organisations.

It remains to be seen how these initiatives will evolve, and whether the interest in 'duality' will amount in the end to any more than an attempt to support defence activity from the civil base, rather than to seek a more genuine integration of the two. It is evident that a certain political opportunism has sometimes attended the use of the concept. Thus, in the US, the rush to attach the label 'dual-use' to defence projects in order to qualify under TRP backfired when the Congress elected in November 1994 turned against the TRP — with the outcome that a new Dual Use Applications Program (DUAP) has been announced, but which will consider only technologies that can be used by the military, unlike TRP which also sought to transfer technologies of defence origin to the civil sector. Similarly, in France, Serfati has pointed to the rhetorical freight carried by the term, observing that in practice it tends to be applied only to technologies that can be used in the military sector (Serfati 1995, p. 94; and chapter on France).

Despite these rhetorical uses, however, there can be little doubt that a real change has occurred in the technological base of defence production. This has implications, as yet indistinct in detail, for the ways in which the development, design and production of defence equipment will be conducted, and for the control of the international flow of defence-related technology. As Contzen has observed, the requirements for civil and military technologies will remain in many cases different, and the markets they create for future technologies will never be fully unified. The question is:

> Will the resulting separate 'market pull' components induce separate technological developments or will the technological base resulting from the combination of 'science push' and 'market pull' be sufficiently broad to meet both demands? (Contzen, 1995)

Despite these uncertainties, Contzen remains confident that the development of modern technology requires a broadening of its own technological base, and the formation of strategic alliances in order to access technology held by other organisations; and that these trends apply to both the civil and military fields. He further argues that 'most of the demands of the military market could be met by using civilian driven technological developments provided the pull from the civilian market is sufficiently ambitious and demanding'. Hence, as a matter of policy, Europe should be moving towards a common military-civil science base, and should seek more cross-demand between the two sectors.

Policies Towards Exports of Arms and Dual-Use Technologies

A problem faced by all states, but one which can only be managed at the international level, is how to control the international diffusion of weapons technologies, and to do so in a way that is coherent and equitable. This problem is made harder by the new emphasis upon dual-use technologies. Attempts to improve control regimes, notably for dual-use technologies but also for arms transfers, within the framework of the European Union and the Single European Market (the need, in other words, for a 'Common European Fence') have moved slowly, the problems lying more in the detail of lists and criteria than in any lack of agreement about the importance of the goal.

We must recognise, moreover, that the very attempt to harmonise European procedures on this subject carries the risk of arousing suspicion by importing countries that defence reasons are being used to disguise the maintenance of commercial advantage by supplier countries. We may also note that, at the level of common foreign and security policy, it may be at least as important to explore ways of reducing demand for these technologies at source, as to attempt to plug holes in control regimes. Nor, of course, are all the sources of supply under the control of western states.

The states in our study are formal members of, or behave in conformity with, all the more important arms export control agreements and fora, including the Australia Group, COCOM (until its demise at the end of March 1994), the

Chemical Weapons Convention, the Missile Technology Control Regime, the Nuclear Non-Proliferation Treaty, and the Nuclear Suppliers Group. Those within the G-7 also participate in that Group's informal working group on the harmonisation of export controls on dual-use goods.

Despite this apparent unanimity of purpose, important rivalries remain. National governments face a dilemma over balancing support for exporters against restricting the proliferation of weapons systems and technology. These conflicting economic and security objectives are often reflected in governmental arrangements for export promotion and control, and hence in the difficulties over reaching agreement on European-level regulations. Several countries (including Belgium, France, Italy, Sweden and the UK) have recently experienced controversy over the export of military and military-related equipment to Iraq as their governments were caught up in the conflicting objectives of export promotion and nonproliferation. In Britain, the Scott Report (1996) into the sale of arms to Iraq provided ample evidence of the room for manoeuvre that can exist even within well-codified 'guidelines', and in the face of a supposedly reasonably efficient implementation machinery.

Differing interests affect the detailed policies of countries. For France and Britain, arms exports are an indispensable means to create economies of scale and are also seen as legitimate instruments of foreign policy. In Italy and Spain, also, the economic importance of arms exports is emphasised. Germany and the Netherlands, however, have distanced themselves from using arms exports as instruments of foreign policy, and operate more restrictive export policies. Greece is more concerned about imports than exports, but has a particular interest in monitoring arms sales to the Balkans. Moreover, although all the EU countries adhere in principle to the Nuclear Suppliers Group guidelines and the former COCOM list, in practice the only EU country whose own national list of restricted items contains all 72 items required by these two international lists is Ireland: Germany, the Netherlands and the UK lack one item each; Italy seven; France 14; Belgium 20; and Spain 24 (Saferworld, 1994, p. 5).

Despite the renewed emphasis that was given to arms export controls after the Gulf crisis, relatively little progress has actually been made at the international level. The only notable initiative has been the establishment of the UN Arms Register (Chalmers and Greene, 1995), but even this is a confidence building measure rather than an export control mechanism.

At the regional level, efforts have been made by the European Commission to establish common export controls on both arms and dual-use goods and technologies (Müller *et al.*, 1994). Progress has, however, been slow. The European Council has taken the first step towards a common approach on arms exports by adopting, in 1991 and 1992, eight criteria which the member states should apply when deciding on issuing a licence for a specific export, but this remains far from being uniformly implemented. On dual-use goods and technologies, agreement was reached in 1994 to introduce, from 1995, effective controls, based on common standards, by all member states. The key features of the system are a common list of dual-use goods and technologies subject to export control, a list of destination countries deemed to be unproblematic, and common criteria to be applied by all member states when determining whether or not to authorise exports from the Community. Here too, however, progress is expected only in stages, with a transition period to strengthen, where necessary, national control systems, to reinforce administrative cooperation between the relevant authorities, and to reduce, and ultimately eliminate, policy differences between member states.

An interesting paradox of the present emphasis upon national control mechanisms is that most countries (and especially their firms) perceive themselves as having a more restrictive arms export control policy than their neighbours, and so harbour suspicions that competitors are gaining market advantage by promoting exports and adopting lax controls. International agreements may need to focus as much on how to build confidence among allies as on how to prevent proliferation. Certainly, without that confidence they will not succeed, partly because countries will not allow their own industry to labour under a disadvantage, and partly because governments will be reluctant to place sensitive information at the disposal of a control regime if they believe that action by themselves alone would be more effective than action by the regime.

Policies Towards Defence Conversion

As for the prospects for policy towards conversion, the European experience offers only limited encouragement. In fact, it is exceptional to find unambiguous examples of pure conversion. Those that can be identified are in most cases commercial failures, often attributable to the inexperience of military manufacturers in operating in a commercial market environment. Knowing this, companies more often adopt other means to capitalise on their investment in facilities, equipment and skilled labour as the declining defence market leaves them with surplus capacity.

It is not unusual for firms to recruit new management from the commercial world (there are examples in Germany, Greece and Spain). Other companies spin off divisions to manufacture civil products under new company and new brand names. Still others acquire smaller, civil companies as a nucleus for developing commercial business. Although civil investment, skills and technology contribute to this process, to some extent it represents the redeployment of military manufacturing capacity and could be considered a form of conversion.

In countries such as France, Greece and Spain, in which the defence industry is mostly state-owned, it is also difficult to decouple business decisions from national or regional policies. National or regional subsidies for diversification or conversion can be obscured quite easily. In addition, privately-owned military manufacturers may in practice have such close ties to national governments that, in effect, governments *de facto* subsidise diversification or conversion. One such example is Belgium, where support for civil aerospace has come to the rescue of vulnerable predominantly military aerospace firms. In another example, the German Länd of Schleswig-Holstein supported the creation of two new civil technological foundations in the vicinity of defence industries in difficulty.

Initiatives by Public Authorities

There are few national or European programmes specifically aimed at conversion. To a first approximation, most governments in Europe have considered conversion a commercial matter that should be left to the firms themselves.

For example, the German federal government stated in 1985 that it did not wish to assume responsibility for the defence industry, and that while it tried to keep indispensable defence capacities continuously occupied, it was unable to give any guarantees on employment and military equipment orders. More recently, in 1991, although the federal government had not changed its policy, the individual Länder most affected by defence cuts argued for sectoral support. Both sides were able to claim a victory in the form of a tax regime which, although not explicitly directed at the declining defence industries, happened to benefit those Länder most affected. In Britain likewise, where company-initiated defence cuts began on a significant scale earlier than in most other European countries, the government's position has been almost entirely one of non-intervention, save for some advisory services.

The Netherlands considers any sectoral industrial policy economically counterproductive, as well as being counter to the objective of European free trade. Nevertheless, the Ministers of Defence and of Economic Affairs have said that preferential treatment will be given to companies applying to the Ministry of Economic Affairs for conversion assistance.

The situation in Sweden is similar. National policy has been to sustain a high level of military equipment development. Support was given to Saab and Volvo Flygmotor in 1980 for participation in civil aviation projects with the USA. However, this was intended to maintain the industry during a lull in military orders rather than as conversion assistance. Most recently, Sweden has decided to support dual-use technology, but again in order to preserve 'remobilisation capacity' rather than to promote conversion.

Italy's BPD Difesa e Spazio, like its Belgian counterparts in the aerospace industry, has increased its focus on government-supported civil space activities. Other Italian programmes in the early 1980s supported specific civil technological projects based on military technology. In both Italy and Sweden, a number of parliamentary initiatives to support conversion have been introduced and debated, without being adopted. But in 1993 Italy did pass a law that both financed industrial activities in the defence sector and created a 5-year, £200 million conversion fund. The conversion fund provides grants and loans to military firms expanding their civil business, and also provides co-finance for regional assistance to areas affected by declining defence industrial activity.

In France, where the government remains committed to high levels of defence spending, conversion planning thus far has been confined to small and medium sized enterprises (SMEs), for which the Ministry of Defence created a *Delegation for Restructuring* in 1991, to manage a fund of about 160 million FF (about £20 million) per year. Whether the scope of this activity will expand as a result of the deep defence cuts announced in 1995 and 1996 remains to be seen.

In the 1980s, the Greek government came to the assistance of an ailing domestic industry with a massive programme of subsidies and military orders, resulting in considerable overcapacity in the defence sector. More recently, however, the government decided against either an enhanced procurement programme or additional investment to maintain the defence industry. Instead, Greece has opted for privatisation of some firms in areas of dual use technological capabilities, such as trucks and heavy vehicles, shipbuilding, and electronics, to give companies the maximum flexibility to implement conversion or diversification strategies, without an explicit commitment to either.

The responsibility for meeting the social and economic costs of declining defence industry employment usually falls to more general structural measures applied by states and the European Union. One exception is the EU's KONVER programme, which is specifically targeted at companies vulnerable to downturns in military production, and offers support for the development of alternative, civil products. Like other structural assistance programmes of the European Union, the European Commission assesses the extent to which a country is eligible for support according to standard, purely economic criteria. The KONVER funding must be matched by some combination of local, regional and national support, plus private investment, and the programme is meant to be administered on a regional basis. In practice, KONVER funds usually go to those companies or regions which actively seek the support.

It is up to each country to formulate a national programme for administering the aid in accordance with the stated EU objectives. This is easier said than done. Many countries have different objectives to those of the EU. Italy's first proposal for KONVER funding was rejected on the basis that the companies slated to receive the aid were large military manufacturers with adequate capital to undertake their own conversion projects. A modified proposal, tied more closely to regional development projects and aid for newly established companies, was approved in December 1993.

Spain promotes dual-use technology development in order to encourage firms to have the greatest possible flexibility. Rather than encouraging conversion, this has had the effect of drawing civil firms into the military sphere. Spanish military manufacturing companies did not take an interest in KONVER, and the government neglected even to submit a proposal.

More typically, countries conform to KONVER requirements by combining European Union funding with regional and/or national support. For example, France is using KONVER funding in the Bourges region. In this region, heavily dependent on arms manufacturing, there has been a 20% cut in the number of jobs in large military companies since 1986.

The Länd of Bremen in Germany approved a conversion programme in 1992 as part of a comprehensive economic policy for the region. In 1993, Bremen appointed a state Commissioner for Conversion and an Advisory Committee to oversee the state conversion programme. Bremen intends to make use of KONVER and other European Union Structural Fund programmes to support new technological projects such as sewage treatment, and for vocational training. Nord Rhine-Westphalia, though less dependent on military industry, also uses KONVER support, for retraining programmes.

Company Initiatives

The lack of strong government policies on conversion and diversification leaves the responsibility for action with companies and, in some countries, research institutes. This seems to be equally true whether the companies are state-owned or private, although obviously the precise nature of the relations between a firm and its government influences the scope for action by the firm.

Faced with the same broad problem right across western Europe, individual firms and research institutes are, however, responding in a variety of ways. Some are seeking to tighten their grip on the diminished defence sector. Others are simply cutting back surplus staff. But others have attempted to alter the basis of their activities. These, however, have found that the difficulties in shifting emphasis are compounded by the economic recession and lack of demand for civil products and services.

Dutch companies have been partially successful at diversifying or converting their military capacity. Delft Instruments, for example, which manufactures night vision equipment and laser range finders, has greatly reduced its dependence on the military market. Eurometaal, an ammunitions manufacturer, was able to compensate for lost military orders by increasing its civilian turnover from Dfl 2 million to Dfl 37 million. In order to do so, it acquired existing civil companies, and also had to lay off hundreds of employees. De Kruithoorn, another ammunitions manufacturer specialising in armour piercing penetrators, has used its expertise in metallurgy to develop a new civil metal injection moulding system. Even TNO-DO, the state-owned research institute where most Dutch military R&D is done, has increased its proportion of civil work from 6% in 1986 to 14% in 1992.

Some small-scale successes have been achieved by military manufacturers developing new civil products in areas closely derived from military products. The Italian aerospace firm BPD Difesa e Spazio has used military technology to develop civil products for forest fire-fighting and rapidly-inflatable automobile air bags. On the other hand, FN, a Belgian arms manufacturer, tried unsuccessfully to diversify into civilian engines and sports equipment as a way to cushion the company from the cyclical nature of military equipment orders. Some of the civil business was sold or spun off, but the only clearly successful civil products have been hunting weapons and fishing equipment.

In the light of cutbacks in both military orders and civil aerospace programmes, Deutsche Aerospace (DASA) has implemented an 'intrapreneurship' programme to foster the redeployment of in-house facilities, skills, and resources. If successful, as in the case of an agricultural machinery business in Flensburg, DASA spins off the division to form a separate company. DASA also has undertaken a search for new, civil products in-house. Even though DASA has had some instances of success, the company has been forced to close down facilities and make thousands of workers redundant. Another approach has been that of the Krauss-Maffei tank manufacturing company in Munich, which recognised the declining tank market early enough to completely restructure and reorient the company. The company was sold to new owners, reconstituted in legal terms more favourable to commercial enterprise, and new lines of business were opened. However, although the company was able to maintain its aggregate level of employment, only 30% of the defence workers could be retained; the remainder of the workforce had to be recruited from outside the company.

Afterword

At the heart of the debate about construction, conversion and control of European defence technological capabilities lies the question of what defence policy countries, singly and collectively, wish to pursue, and what resources they are prepared or able to devote to this purpose. This question raises, therefore, the issue of what the countries of Europe see as their role in the world, and with whom they expect to play that role. Only if these issues were resolved (or at least clarified, for they could never be ultimately settled) would it be possible to settle on a rational basis the questions of how much to spend, what development and production capabilities to retain, what to maintain in association with partners, and so on.

So fundamental a question exceeds the scope of this study. But it is at least worth noting that while European states continue to debate the relative merits of a strong trans-Atlantic orientation, coupled with a determination to be as independent as possible in the supply and management of defence resources, versus closer European integration, events are moving on. Not only is the defence industry internationalising, but developments at governmental level also threaten to create a two-tier defence community in Europe. The governmental and industrial structures within which choices are made about European defence technological capabilities could look quite different within a further five to ten years.

We should not exaggerate the prospects for such change. Neither, however, against the backdrop of the extraordinary developments in international relations since about 1988, should we under-estimate the possible rate of change. The aim of this book is to make a contribution to informed debate about the choices that lie ahead.

References

Alic, J. *et al.* 1992, *Beyond Spinoff: military and commercial technologies in a changing world,* Boston, Mass.: Harvard Business School Press.

Borderas, Mr., 1994, rapporteur, Assembly of the Western European Union, *The European armaments agency — reply to the thirty-ninth annual report of the Council,* Paris: WEU, document 1219.

Branscomb, L., 1994, 'Targeting Critical Technologies', in OECD, *STI Review,* No. 14, pp. 33–57, Paris: OECD.

Brzoska, M., Lock, P. (eds), 1992, *Restructuring of Arms Production in Western Europe*, Oxford: Oxford University Press for SIPRI.

Cabinet Office, UK, 1994, *Forward Look of Government-funded Science, Engineering and Technology 1994,* London: HMSO, April

Cabinet Office, UK, 1995, *Report of the Technology Foresight Panel on Defence and Aerospace*, London: HMSO, ISBN 0-11-430126-3.

Chalmers, M. and Greene, O., 1995, *Taking Stock: The UN Register After Two Years*, Bradford Arms Register Studies No. 5. Westview Press.

Chauvot de Beauchene, 1991, 'EUCLID: une initiative européene de cooperation en matière de recherche et de technologie intéressant la Défense',

L'Armement: Revue de la Délégation Générale pour l'Armement, Paris, No. 30, December, 40–54.

Chesnais, F., 1993, 'Commissariat général du Plan: un rapport critique ... critiqué', *Damoclès*, No. 49, pp. 30–31.

Coghlan, A., 1994, 'Stony ground for Britain's ploughshares', *New Scientist*, 22 January, pp. 12–13.

Commissariat général du plan, France, 1993, *L'avenir des industries liées à la defense*, produced by the Groupe de stratégie industrielle, Paris: La Documentation Francaise.

Contzen, J.P., 1995, 'How to ensure in the future a broader common base for civilian and military technologies?', paper given to CREDIT Seminar, Brussels, 24 January.

Council for Science and Society, 1986, *UK Military R&D,* Oxford: Oxford University Press.

Forsberg, R., (ed.), 1994, *The Arms Production Dilemma: Contraction and Restraint in the World Combat Aircraft Industry*, Cambridge, Mass.: MIT Press, CSIA Studies in International Security.

Gansler, J., 1993, 'Transforming the US Defence Industrial Base', *Survival*, vol. 35, No. 4, pp. 130–146.

GRIP, 1993, *European Armaments Industry: Research, Technological Development and Conversion*, Final Report for European Parliament/ STOA, Luxembourg: European Parliament, Directorate General for Research.

Gummett, P., 1996, 'Foreign, Defence and Security Policy', in P. Heywood, M. Rhodes and V. Wright (eds), *Developments in West European Politics,* London: Macmillan.

Gummett, P. and Reppy, J., (eds), 1988, *The Relations Between Defence and Civil Technologies,* Dordrecht: Kluwer.

Hébert, J-P., 1991, *Stratégie Francaise et Industrie d'Armement,* Paris: Fondation pour les études de défense nationale.

House of Lords, UK, 1994, Select Committee on Science and Technology, *Defence Research Agency,* London: HMSO, HL Paper 24, session 1993–94.

International Institute for Strategic Studies (IISS), 1996, *Strategic Survey 1995/96,* Oxford: Oxford University Press.

L'Armement: Revue de la Délégation Générale pour l'Armement, 1991, Paris, no. 29.

Ministry of Defence, UK, 1994a, Memorandum of evidence submitted to *House of Lords Select Committee on Science and Technology, Report on the Defence Research Agency*, London: HMSO, HL Paper 24-i, session 1993–94.

Ministry of Defence, UK, 1994b, *Statement on the Defence Estimates 1994,* London: HMSO, April.

Ministry of Defence, UK, 1995, *Statement on the Defence Estimates 1995*, London: HMSO.

Müller, H., *et al.* 1994, Peace Research Institute Frankfurt, *From Black Sheep to White Angel? The New German Export Control Policy*, Frankfurt: PRIF Reports No. 32.

Office of Technology Assessment, U.S. Congress, 1994, *Assessing the Potential for Civil-Military Integration: Technologies, Processes and Practices*, OTA-ISS-611, Washington, D.C.: U.S. Government Printing Office.

Porter, M., 1990, *The Competitive Advantage of Nations*, London: Macmillan.

Reich, R., 1990, 'Who is US?', *Harvard Business Review*, January.

Saferworld, 1994, *Briefing: Arms & Dual-Use Export Controls: Priorities for the European Union*, Bristol: Saferworld.

Samuels, R., 1994, *'Rich Nation Strong Army': National Security and the Technological Transformation of Japan,* Ithaca, NY: Cornell University Press.

Sandström, M. and Wilén, C., 1993, *A changing European defence industry: the trend towards internationalisation in the defence industry of western Europe*, Stockholm: National Defence Research Establishment, FOA Report A 10054-1.3.

Scott Report, 1996, *Report of the Inquiry into the Export of Defence Equipment and Dual-Use Goods to Iraq and Related Prosecutions*, London, HMSO.

Serfati, C., 1995, *Production d'armes, croissance et innovation,* Paris: Economica.

Sillard, Y., 1991, 'Vers l'Europe de la défense', *L'Armement: Revue de la Délégation Générale pour l'Armement*, no. 30, December, pp. 4–5.

SIPRI, 1995, *SIPRI Yearbook 1995: Armaments, Disarmament and International Security*, Oxford: Oxford University Press.

Smit, W. *et al.* (eds), 1992, *Military Technological Innovation and Stability in a Changing World*, Amsterdam: VU Press.

Steinberg, J., 1992, *The Transformation of the European Defense Industry: Emerging Trends and Prospects for Future US-European Competition and Collaboration*, Santa Monica: The RAND Corporation.

Teisseire, L., 1991, 'Quelles institutions pour l'Europe de l'armement?', *L'Armement: Revue de la Délégation Générale pour l'Armement*, no. 30, December, pp. 32–38.

Van Atta, R., 1994, 'US Dual Use Technology Policy', presentation by the Special Assistant for Dual Use Technology Policy, Office of the Assistant Secretary of Defense, USA, to the Foundation for Science and Technology, London, 16 February.

Van Atta, R., 1995, 'The US Department of Defense Dual Use Technology Policy', presentation to the International Seminar on the Relationship between Civilian and Military R&D: General Trends and Regional Patterns, ISPE/CNR, Rome, 26 May.

Walker, W. and Gummett, P., 1989, 'Britain and the European Armaments Market', *International Affairs*, vol. 65, pp. 419–442.

Walker, W. and Gummett, P., 1993, *Nationalism, Internationalism and the European Defence Market*, Paris: WEU Institute for Security Studies, Chaillot Papers, No. 9.

Wulf, H. (ed.), 1993, *Arms Industry Limited*, Oxford: Oxford University Press for SIPRI.

Endnotes

1 This reads: 'Any Member State may take such measures as it considers necessary for the protection of the essential interests of its security which are connected with the production of or trade in arms, munitions and war material; such measures shall not adversely affect the conditions of competition in the common market regarding products which are not intended for specifically military purposes.'

2 The 15 areas are: modern radar technology; silicon microelectronics; composite structures; modular avionics; electromagnetic gun; artificial intelligence; signature manipulation; optoelectronic devices; satellite surveillance technology; underwater detection and related technologies; human factors, including simulation for training purposes; aerothermodynamics; NBC defence; energetic materials; and guided weapon technology.

3 While this book was in production, the position moved on, with the formation in mid-November 1996 of the Joint Armaments Cooperation Organisation (JACO — known in France as OCCAR — Organisation conjointe de coopération en matière d'armement). Its founding members are France, Germany, Italy and the UK. Other members may join in due course. It will be located in Bonn, with a French director and German deputy, and an initial staff of 15. It will be responsible for the management of existing Franco-German programmes such as the Milan and Hot anti-tank missiles, the Roland air defence missile and the Tiger attack helicopter. It will take over responsibility for a range of multilateral collaborative programmes, including the new family of wheeled infantry combat vehicles (known as VBCI in France, MRAV in UK, and GTK in Germany). The members have agreed to implement several basic principles in defence procurement: obtaining greater cost-effectiveness by rationalising procurement procedures and programme management; improving industrial competitiveness by lowering costs; and replacing the principle of 'juste retour' by a more flexible, multi-year and multi-programme approach to ensuring reciprocal industrial benefits. The founding document is reported to have avoided language which would tie the partners to a 'Buy-European' policy, while committing them instead to 'preferring, when meeting the requirements of their armed forces, products in whose development they have participated'. This new agency is not to be confused with the establishment, a few days later, of the Western European Armaments Organisation (WEAO), whose initial remit will be confined to cooperative research projects. The WEAO has been established under the auspices of the WEU. Hence, discussions to set up a European Armaments Agency have, at the end of 1996, resulted in the establishment of two organisations. JACO/OCCAR, being an agency with four members, set up to manage major collaborative equipment programmes, and WEAO, being an organisation open to all WEU members, with a remit that initially is confined to management of collaborative research projects.

(Sources: *Defense News*, 18.11.96, pp. 4, 24, 32. *Financial Times*, 12.11.96. *Le Figaro*, 13.11.96; *La Tribune de l'Expansion*, 13.11.96).

Chapter 1
Belgium

Pierre De Vestel

Introduction

The Belgian defence industry represents only 2% of Europe's total military production. Yet most of the equipment purchased by the Ministry of National Defence (MND) is produced in Belgium, either under license, through international collaboration, or entirely by the national defence firms themselves.

Most Belgian defence firms fall into one of two categories. Some are relatively low-technology manufacturers which are almost exclusively dependent upon military production. At the high-technology end of the spectrum, military equipment producers are typically civilian enterprises employing dual-use technology in specific niches within the military market.

The structure of Belgian defence industry is closely linked to two distinct markets. The first is domestic, and consists of equipment purchases by the MND. The second, primarily export market, is for low-technology small arms and munitions. These two very different markets account for the bi-modal development of the Belgian defence industry.

The design, production and sale of military matériel in Belgium systematically combines military, economic and technological dimensions. In effect, the Federal Ministry of Economic Affairs, in association with the corresponding regional ministries, has a hand in all contracts placed by the MND. This situation arises from the vital importance for the Belgian defence firms of a system of economic and technological assistance schemes tied to military sales.

Investments in military R&D are largely geared to meet the immediate needs of the MND. Strictly speaking, there is no defence technology policy; no long-term strategy has been maintained for the past 40 years. Most military R&D in Belgium is carried out by the manufacturing companies. Only a few small-scale research laboratories in universities or at the Royal Military Academy perform military research. A certain amount of research is also carried out internationally, for example through NATO, EUCLID or under specific multilateral agreements.

Belgian military finance is quite complex due to the country's federal structure, in place since the 1980s[1]. Estimates of military R&D spending are also made difficult by the lack of available statistics. Officially, 0.2% of total public

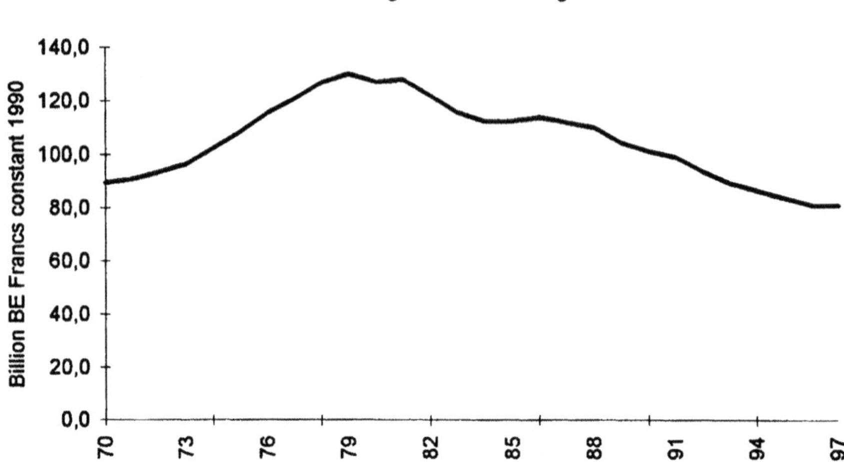

Figure 1: Belgian Defence Budget 1970–1997.
Source: A. Dumoulin, 'La restructuration des forces armées', *Courrier hebdomadaire*, No. 1383–84, Brussels: CRISP, 1992, p. 40.

spending on R&D was devoted to defence purposes in 1993. A more detailed analysis of military programmes, however, reveals that the actual figure was between 3 and 6%.

An Industry Completing Its Restructuring

While the 1970s saw a clear increase in MND equipment purchases as part of several major re-equipment programmes (including the F-16, Armoured Infantry Fighting Vehicle, and artillery), the 1980s saw a steady reduction. Total MND expenditure on equipment and related services, (including spare parts, maintenance and ammunition), fell by 48% in real terms between 1980 (BF 43.8 billion) and 1992 (BF 22.6 billion)[2].

The Ministry of National Defence's equipment purchases in 1992 accounted for 60% of Belgian defence enterprises' total turnover. However, in July of that year, the Defence Minister, L. Delcroix, announced further long-term cuts in defence spending (see Figure 1, which shows substantial growth until 1979, followed by decreases arising mainly from a public sector financial crisis in the 1980s), and reductions in the size and equipment base of the armed forces by 1997 (Table 1).

Table 1: Changes in the Belgian Armed Forces 1991–1997

	1991	**After the Delcroix plan**	**Date of implementation**
Military Service	10/12 months	abandoned	1994
Military personnel			
– conscripts	30,000	0	
– professionals	50,000	40,000	
Total	80,000	40,000	1996
Budget	102	84	1997
(billions FB constant 1991)			
Brigades	6	4	1996
Battalions: active	23	+/–13	1996
Battalions: reserve	18	?	?
Troops in Germany	22,000	3,500	1996
Combat aircraft	144	72	1993
Transport aircraft	14	14	1997
Helicopters	–	46	1993
Ships	22	15	1993
Battle tanks	334	132	1993

Source: Based on 'Note de politique générale', MDN, Brussels, 3 July 1992.

The 1992 restructuring plan accelerated this trend. In addition to substantial troop cuts, the plan provides for large-scale reductions in armaments. This will inevitably have an impact on maintenance and purchases of spare parts as well as on modernisation. The upgrading of 60 Mirage V aircrafts was cancelled (the MND aims to sell them second-hand) and only one-third of the Leopard I tanks and 48 F-16 fighters (out of 116) are to be modernised.

Budget cuts and additional costs associated with the professionalisation of the army will not offer many opportunities for equipment purchases until at least 1997. Taking into account budget forecasts, equipment purchases are expected to be reduced by 3% to 4% a year over this period. These cuts can be expected to affect the electronics and telecommunications industries less than aerospace companies and mechanical engineering firms (manufacturing armoured vehicles). The '1993–97 medium-term investment plan' places priority on telecommunications equipment, where the greatest need is now felt, following a period from 1970 to 1990, when purchases of combat equipment dominated the budget.

Belgian Military Equipment Exports

Exports of Belgian armaments were fairly steady at the beginning of the 1970s, but then increased to BF 26 billion in 1970 and reached an historic peak of BF 31 billion in 1983. After that, arms exports decreased by 20% a year and effectively collapsed in 1990. The sharp drop in exports can be explained by a combination of a fall in demand from the third world and competition from new small weapons and munitions producers.

Belgian arms exports entered into a deep crisis in 1985 marked by the bankruptcy of the main artillery munitions producer, 'les Poudreries Réunies de Belgique' as well as by major restructuring in most of the other exporting firms. Like other manufacturing sectors with low levels of technological added value, and with a workforce dominated by low-skilled labour, the Belgian arms exporters faced challenges from new producers, mostly from the newly industrialised countries (such as Singapore, Taiwan, South Korea, Brazil) and also from Israel and South Africa.

Arms exports rose again sharply in 1991 and once more in 1992, as shown in Table 2, following orders consequent to the Gulf War. The export recovery since 1991 is mostly due to a few sizeable contracts with Saudi Arabia. Overall, Belgian arms exports are still strongly dependent on Third World markets, which accounted for 89% of all arms exports in 1981. Although the proportion fell to 70% in 1987, it has recovered to between 75 and 80%.

The three main exporting companies (FNNH, MECAR and Forges de Zeebrugge) are banking on their past restructuring efforts (both modernisation and major employment cuts, entailing the loss of 80% (11,000) direct jobs in the small arms and ammunition sector alone between 1983 and 1992) as well as on their key position in certain fields (small arms, munitions and rockets) to ensure their survival in the years to come.

A Dual Industry

The Belgian defence industry can be divided into two distinct groups. One group depends almost entirely on exports of small arms and munitions; the other on economic assistance agreements tied to sales of equipment to the MND. Table 3, which shows the ten largest Belgian defence firms by military turnover, displays this dichotomy well. On the one hand, we see a group of small arms and munitions firms, who are highly defence dependent *and* export oriented; on the other, aeronautical and telecommunications firms, who are less defence dependent (with one exception) and who also depend on the Belgian market rather than on exports.[3]

Table 2: Trends and Distribution of Belgian Arms Exports (Billions of BF)

	Arms Exports		To Europe and North America	To the Third World	Arms exports as % total Belgian exports
	(current prices)	(constant prices 1986)			
1970	3.934	11.339			0.68%
1971	2.916	8.079			0.47%
1972	2.946	7.714			0.42%
1973	2.808	6.875			0.32%
1974	5.411	11.756			0.49%
1975	9.036	17.409			0.85%
1976	12.520	22.096			0.49%
1977	15.877	26.163			1.18%
1978	14.073	22.187	22 %	78 %	0.99%
1979	13.071	19.748	19 %	81 %	0.79%
1980	12.985	18.374	13 %	87 %	0.69%
1981	17.361	22.825	11 %	89 %	0.84%
1982	15.961	19.300	14 %	86 %	0.66%
1983	27.686	31.094	14 %	86 %	1.04%
1984	24.537	26.048	21 %	79 %	0.82%
1985	19.420	19.660	16 %	84 %	0.62%
1986	13.495	13.495	25 %	75 %	0.44%
1987	13.500	13.340	30 %	70 %	0.37%
1988	12.000	11.681	n.a.	n.a.	0.30%
1989	10.000	9.441	n.a.	n.a.	0.22%
1990	7.500	6.844	n.a.	n.a.	0.16%
1991	11.200	9.880	20–25%	75–80%	0.23%
1992	13.900	12.270	20–25%	75–80%	n.a.

Sources: 197C to 1985: official statistics. 1986 to 1992: author's estimates, based on data supplied by arms exporting companies.

Table 3: The Ten Leading Belgian Defence Firms in 1992 (turnover in BF millions, Employment in Absolute Numbers)

Company	Turnover 1992 (1)	Employment	% turnover in defence	Type of dependence (3)	Type of production
FNNH	8,824	1,328	100	Exp.	Light arms and ammunitions
MECAR	4,152	352	100	Exp.	Ammunitions, ordnance
SABCA	5,800	1,846	65	IM	Aerospace (airframe)
TECHSPACE AERO	6,100	1,168	33	IM	Engines
SONACA	3,469	1,399	40	IM	Aerospace (airframe)
FORGES DE ZEEBRUGGE	1,125	204	100	Exp.	Rockets
THOMSON-CSF ELECTRONIC BELGIUM	724	199	100	IM	Telecommunication
CMI	8,363	1,539	10(2)	Exp.	Armoured vehicles
ALCATEL BELL-SDT	2,523	672	20	IM	Telecommunication
SAIT-RADIO HOLLAND	10,100	1,933	5(2)	IM	Telecommunication-radar

Source: company balance sheets and reports.
(1) In BF millions; (2) Estimates; (3) Oriented mainly towards exports (Exp.) or the internal market (IM).

The industry has been dominated by several long-established enterprises, such as FN, a private company set up in 1889 in Liège under the name of Fabrique Nationale d'armes de guerre. This company, Belgium's leading armaments firm, built its reputation on light weapons production — assault and machine guns and munitions — which were exported all over the world. In 1970, more than sixty countries were using FN assault guns. New enterprises were established one by one; les Poudreries Réunies de Belgique (PRB) and a few aeronautical enterprises were founded as far back as the 1920s and 1930s.

However, the real boom in armaments production occurred at the end of the 1960s and especially in the 1970s. Before the 1960s, there were almost no armaments enterprises apart from FN, PRB and a few aircraft companies, mostly working for export. The Belgian Army had been supplied with most of its equipment by the United States for free after the Second World War as part of the rebuilding of western armies.

It was only at the end of the 1960s, and especially between 1972 and 1980, that a long series of contracts was signed between the MND and Belgian or foreign enterprises in order to proceed with the modernisation of heavy military equipment that had become obsolete (aircraft, armoured vehicles, warships). This was how enterprises which had hitherto been exclusively involved with civilian activities branched out into armaments production. Some companies were created specifically for that purpose, such as BMF, whose entire production consisted of assembling one thousand armoured vehicles. The enterprise was left dormant when production ended in 1988.

The crisis in the Belgian defence industry preceded that affecting most other European arms-producing countries by several years. The collapse of the export market, beginning in 1984, and the downturn in MND equipment purchases three years later affected both categories of Belgian companies: low-tech small arms exporters and high-tech manufacturers.

Table 4 shows the evolution of the defence industrial sector as a whole and the pattern of decline. For example, in 1983, 44,000 people were employed in the industry, but by 1992, only 16,000 remained, a fall of 65% in just one decade.

As far as aerospace, electronics and telecommunications enterprises are concerned, Belgian participation in the European Space Programme (dating from 1971) and in the Airbus consortium (since 1979) will somewhat offset the decline in military business. For the traditional defence firms, on the other hand, the government has taken no particular action to assist their adaptation to the new circumstances, other than some steps to ameliorate the social consequences of the major restructuring of the 1980s. The medium-term prospects for the industry are also gloomy. The national defence budget has been frozen at its

Table 4: The Belgian Defence Industry: Turnover, Employment, Exports, 1980–1992 (in billions of constant 1990 BF or ECU, employment in absolute numbers)

Year	Defence Budget (BBF)	Defence budget (BECU)	Equipment procurement (BBF) (a)	Exports (BBF) (b)	Imports (BBF) (c)	Turnover		Employment		
						(a + b – c)	BECU	total	direct	percent of industrial workforce*
1980	126.8	2.99	43.8	20.3	7.8	56.3	1.33	45,000	30,000	5.5%
1981	127.7	3.01	42.0	25.1	6.5	60.5	1.43	45,235	30,738	5.5%
1982	121.7	2.87	39.7	21.3	7.3	53.7	1.27	36,921	25,102	4.7%
1983	115.6	2.73	39.0	34.3	8.5	64.7	1.53	44,267	30,048	5.7%
1984	112.2	2.64	37.4	28.5	7.9	58.0	1.37	39,127	27,988	5.1%
1985	112.4	2.65	37.9	21.5	7.0	52.4	1.23	33,263	22,376	4.4%
1986	113.7	2.68	38.1	14.8	6.4	46.6	1.10	28,204	20,054	3.8%
1987	111.8	2.63	35.9	14.6	6.6	43.9	1.04	25,780	17,913	3.6%
1988	110.0	2.59	34.9	12.8	5.7	42.0	0.99	22,869	17,092	3.2%
1989	104.2	2.46	31.7	10.3	4.8	37.2	0.88	19,657	14,538	2.7%
1990	101.2	2.39	30.6	7.5	4.5	33.6	0.79	17,200	10,320	2.4%
1991	99.0	2.33	27.8	10.8	3.9	34.7	0.82	17,286	10,371	2.4%
1992	93.6	2.21	22.6	13.0	2.8	32.9	0.77	15,903	9,542	2.2%

Sources: Various defence budgets. Exports, for 1980–87 official dates and after estimations using the information given by the enterprises. Imports, 1980–87.
AGDA informations, after estimations. Employment calculated using an input-output method.
* direct employment as percentage of total Belgian industrial employment.

Table 5: Major Shareholders of Belgian Defence Enterprises

Company	Percentage	Owner	Country
FNNH	90%	GIAT	France
MECAR	100%	Allied Research Association	USA
SABCA	53%	Dassault	France
	43%	Fokker	Holland
Techspace Aero	51%	SNECMA	France
	30%	Région Wallonne	Belgium
	19%	Pratt & Whitney	USA
SONACA	90%	Région Wallonne	Belgium
Forges de Zeebruges	100%	Thomson Brandt Armement	France
Thomson-CSF Electron. Belgium	100%	Thomson-CSF	France
CMI	100%	Région Wallonne	Belgium
Alcatel Bell-SDT	55%	Alcatel Bell Téléphone	France
SAIT-Radio Holland	100%	Various Banks	Belgium

Sources: 1992 annual reports of the companies.

1994 level until 1997, which meant a cut of 8 to 10% overall, with a larger cut still in equipment purchases. As for arms exports, we can note an increase in 1991, 1992 and probably 1993 flowing from orders from the Middle East after the Gulf War.[4] But this situation is unlikely to continue beyond 1996–97, and a further reduction could hit the exporting firms.

One other significant feature of the Belgian defence industry is the extent of foreign ownership of companies, the majority of which belong to foreign entities or groups. Indeed, the restructurings of the 1980s were often accompanied by takeovers by foreign, mainly French, interests (see Table 5).

At present, about 70% of military equipment production is controlled by foreign industrial groups. This makes the Belgian defence industry one of the most internationalised in the world. There are two principal explanations for this. In the 1960s, several firms were taken over by foreign groups in order to get privileged access to the fast-growing Belgian military market. At that time, for example, Dassault took over the main Belgian aerospace company (SABCA).

A second wave of foreign takeovers occurred at the beginning of the 1990s, when la Société Générale de Belgique sold its armaments companies (FN, PRB and Forges de Zeebrugge being virtually bankrupt). GIAT, SNECMA and Thomson Brandt Armement seized the opportunity to take over enterprises depleted of their excess staff and offered at a low price[5].

Defence R&D in Belgium

According to data provided by the Ministry of Scientific Research and its successor (since 1988)[6], public expenditure on defence R&D in Belgium is low. The proportion of the R&D budget devoted to defence, according to official sources, reached a maximum of 1.5% in 1985, declined to 0.4% in 1990 and declined still further, to 0.2%, in 1993[7]. The sharp drop in military R&D expenditure since 1986 is partly a consequence of the overall public financial crisis facing the federal State (in 1993 interest payments on the public debt accounted for one third of total federal expenses). The decline in military R&D spending at the national level also reflects the 'federalisation' of the Belgian State and the progressive transfer of a series of competences and associated budgets to the Regions and linguistic Communities.

Political responsibility for scientific research has been divided between six different authorities: the federal State, the Flemish Region and Community, the French Community, the Walloon Region and the Region of Brussels and its environs. If one considers that three federal ministries can also intervene in defence R&D policy (National Defence, Economic Affairs and Scientific Policy), one can see the difficulties in coordinating and communicating a coherent scientific and technological policy[8].

Since the 1988 constitutional reforms, the regional authorities have not offset the cuts in federal spending on military R&D. Thus, in the Walloon Region, where about 60% of Belgian military production is performed, the regional authorities have expressed an intent to participate in the EUCLID programme. However, the extent of Walloon's direct financial commitment either to EUCLID or to other military R&D is not known at this time. The Walloon Region also provides indirect support to defence enterprises via capital-sharing, refundable-in-advance payments and other grants, though the total is thought not to exceed several tens of millions BF a year. In Flanders, in contrast, the authorities decided not to finance military research.

Defence R&D spending reported by the Ministry of Scientific Research through 1988, and thereafter by the Commission of Federal Cooperation, only covers expenditure by two federal Ministries: Economic Affairs and Scientific Research. These finance two types of projects: prototype R&D (for example a 15 mm machine gun in the 1980s, a failed project to develop an electrically-powered armoured infantry fighting vehicle, a minesweeper constructed of composite materials, the RITA communications system, and part of the Belgian participation in the International Frigat programme); and research projects (for example on a kinetic energy gun, night vision goggles and gas mask design).

Table 6: Belgian Defence Expenditure and Military R&D, 1985–1993 (BF billion, constant 1990)

Year	Defence budget	Defence equipment purchases (1)	public defence R/D spending (2)	Total public R/D spending (GBAORD) (3)	Civil industrial R/D spending (BERD) (4)
1985	112.4	37.9	0.492	32.4	62.2
1986	113.7	38.1	0.501	31.2	64.7
1987	111.8	35.9	0.330	31.0	65.4
1988	110.0	34.9	0.206	31.1	69.3
1989	104.2	31.7	0.203	40.1	69.4
1990	101.2	30.6	0.147	38.9	73.8
1991	99.0	27.8	0.083	39.9	76.3
1992	93.6	22.6	0.079	39.4	n/a
1993	89.3	n/a	0.077	42.5	n/a

Source: Research and Development Expenditure, Basic Science and Technology Statistics, OECD, Paris, 1991, p. 56. After 1988, the R&D figures are extracted from the 'Apercu des dépenses de R/D par les autorités belges', Commission Coopération fédérale, SPPS, December 1993, p. 18.

(1) Including equipment, spares, maintenance and ammunition. (2) Government Budget Appropriation for defence R&D, not outlays. (3) GBAORD Government Budget Appropriations (not outlays) for R/D. The sharp increase between 1988 and 1989 is due to a change of methodology. (4) BERD Business Enterprise Expenditure on R&D.

Official Data and Hidden Realities

The officially reported expenditure on military R&D is, however, only a small part of the money that is actually involved. Public spending on defence R&D is likely to be far higher, in part because MND accountancy practice does not systematically differentiate between expenditure on R&D and on production.

Thus, in the three main Belgian military programmes (Future Large Aircraft (FLA), Mid-Life Update (MLU) on the F-16 fighter, and Minesweeper), R&D spending may account for up to 20% for the MLU and the FLA, and up to 40% for the Minesweeper programme in the near-term, but these costs are not disaggregated from the total cost of the programmes in the official statistics. Military R&D spending on these three projects is estimated at many hundreds of millions of francs, most of which would be spent in the contractor companies.[9]

A rough estimate[10] suggests that in the 1980s, a total of BF 1 to 2 billion was spent per year on military R&D (mainly development) associated with

Table 7: The Ten Largest Military Programmes, 1994–2005

Programme	Estimated cost (BF million, 1993)	Duration (1)
Future Large Aircraft	55,583	1993–2015
Minesweeper	12,600	1993–2002
Mid-life update F-16	10,835	1993–2001
Trigat ATK Missile (2)	7,838	1996–2005
Air to Air Missile (2)	5,000	1996–2001
Light truck	5,160	1994–2000
ECM F-16 (2)	4,700	1994–?
RITA Upgrating	4,569	1993–2001
Mistral Missile (2)	3,522	1996–2001
Command and Control Information System CCIS	2,116	1997–?

(1) Year of first order; the final year is only indicative and subject to change.
(2) Programmes subject to modifications or depending on defence budget opportunities.
Source: 'Plan à moyen terme du Ministère de la Défense Nationale 1993–1997', Ministère de la Défense Nationale, 2 July 1993.

MND equipment purchases. Thus, the extent of publicly-funded military R&D in Belgium greatly exceeds what is claimed in the official statistics.[11] For example, in 1985, spending on military R&D probably comprised between 3 and 6% of total government R&D spending, between 2 and 4 times the amount given in official documents.

This position is likely to have continued to the present. Moreover, the Belgian defence R&D effort is expected to increase in the near future, as seven out of the ten main armaments programmes of the 1990s (shown in Table 7) will involve substantial R&D input. This situation differs from that of the 1980s, when the majority of equipment programmes involved production under license of equipment already developed abroad (such as the F16, AIFV M 113, and the Augusta helicopter A 109).

In parallel with the national technological and industrial projects, often specialised within fields such as telecommunications or minesweeping technology, Belgium participates strongly in international programmes. This strategy allows for synergies, gives Belgium access to foreign capital and technology, and amplifies the impact of national R&D investment. Belgium's commitment to the Europeanisation of defence cooperation and defence procurement is profound in terms both of politics and of overall outlook.

Belgium's European Commitment

During the Belgian chairmanship of the Independent European Programme Group (IEPG) between 1991 and 1992, Guy Coëme, then Defence Minister, restated Belgium's commitment to European cooperation in defence. It was under the Belgian chairmanship that regular contacts between the IEPG, the European Community institutions and the general Secretary of the WEU were established.[12] These contacts led to the incorporation of the IEPG into the WEU under the new name of Western European Armaments Group in 1993.

The Belgian IEPG chairmanship also gave impetus to the establishment of a number of R&D projects in the EUCLID programme. Belgian enterprises take part in eight of the 22 EUCLID R&D projects. In 1992, the Belgian federal authorities asked the Regions to take part in the EUCLID programme, but only the Walloon Region gave a positive, if still not fully clear, response.

The MND also participates in certain common NATO R&D projects and in the cooperative effort to upgrade the F16 (radar, avionics). Belgian participation in these projects is usually minor, and confined to components development and production. The most recent major programme in which Belgium could play a significant part was the tripartite mine hunter. Together with France and the Netherlands, Belgium took part in the design and production of 28 mine hunters in the 1970s and the first half of the 1980s.

In addition to participating in inter-governmental programmes, Belgian enterprises have gone into partnerships, some of which are quite close, with other European enterprises on R&D and production programmes. Among the most important is the RITA programme with Thomson-CSF in which Belgium has a 12.5% share. However, Belgian authorities have never sacrificed equipment quality nor economic spin-off effects linked to contracts on the altar of a 'European preference'. The purchase of American F-16 fighter bombers in 1974 was mainly dictated by the technological superiority of this aircraft in comparison with the Mirage F-1 offered by Dassault.

Belgium has an ambivalent attitude towards a possible abrogation of Article 223 of the Treaty of Rome. Small arms and munitions producers, as well as dual-use equipment and technologies producers, accustomed to competitive markets, support opening up European defence equipment procurement (so long as 'fair play' is observed, avoiding the conferring of advantage to the largest suppliers). On the other hand, firms heavily dependent on MND orders disagree.

A study carried out in 1992 by the Central Economic Council, the highest economic and social authority in Belgium, could not reach a conclusion on the question of Article 223 (CEC, 1992, pp. 29–30). Other public authorities seem to share the same ambivalence. The prospect of being marginalised by the big

European countries counter-balances the *Communautaire* impulses natural to Belgium in most other areas. The ten major armaments programmes of the 1990s nevertheless show that Belgian authorities rely on a very progressive integration of the defence markets in Europe through multi-national development and production programmes.

A Defence Technology Policy?

Belgium has never had an explicit defence technology policy, according to a report prepared by Ghent University as part of the study for the Central Economic Council, mentioned above (Debackere, 1992, p. 24). There has never been any debate on this matter in Belgium, nor has any official document ever been published on the subject. Rather, Belgian defence procurement policy has always been marked by pragmatism. The main selection criterion, alongside operational and cost considerations, has always been the question of industrial and technological benefits. Thus, the evolution of the defence technology base in Belgium is primarily the result of market pull rather than technology push (Debackere, 1992, pp. 51–64).

The lack of a defence technology policy explains why, in contrast to The Netherlands, Sweden or Switzerland, Belgium's defence industry has not specialised in technological niches other than those low-technology areas used to produce infantry weapons and ammunition.

The development of the Belgian defence industry in aerospace and armoured vehicles, reflects those firms' high degree of dependency on technological and economic benefits resulting from big armaments contracts with foreign firms. Belgium has been a specialist in offset agreements for more than 30 years, these agreements involving both production offsets and also inward technology transfers.

Economic Offset Mechanisms

The system for economic offsets related to defence procurement is managed by the (federal) Ministry of Economic Affairs with the aim of stimulating the Belgian economy. A distinction is made between direct, semi-direct and indirect offsets.

Direct Offsets

Direct offsets consist of payment to Belgian companies for production, assembly, delivery, maintenance and services linked to equipment orders for the Belgian Army. It includes orders for elements and subsystems which are assembled in Belgium, along with foreign components. Usually, sectors are favoured in which small batches (linked to the small scale of Belgian orders) can easily be incorporated in a standard process of production, such as for aerospace, mechanical, electrical or electronical applications. As a rule, this kind of activity requires only limited involvement by Belgian firms in R&D (most of the development having already been done abroad). Most of the time they have to be content simply with acquiring equipment and a certain amount of 'know-how'. However, Belgian companies are then well placed to participate in the subsequent modernisation programmes of these weapons systems.

Semi-Direct Offsets

This type of support consists of offsets directly linked to a military contract. Belgian companies produce arms components for export either to the country of origin (the producer of the full military system) or to other countries ordering the same equipment. The most significant example is the production of certain F-16 components exported to the United States, Israel, Turkey and Pakistan.

Offsets are usually considered as economically beneficial when they lead to 'single source' contracts in which Belgium becomes the only supplier of a particular component.

Indirect Offsets

Indirect offsets are orders aimed at production, works and services, which are *a priori* independent of military contracts. Only some such orders have a high technological content. Indirect offsets orders are only considered important when they lead to further commercial possibilities or expose a firm to new technologies; those involving technology transfer can benefit the national industrial base whether in the military or civil sector[13].

In December 1993, the Minister of Defence stated that national defence should be less dependent on a system of economic compensation,[14] which according to some, greatly increases the unit price of military equipment[15]. This desire to cut costs is, however, viewed by others with circumspection. Thus, as long as Article 223 remains in force, military orders are one of the last instruments public authorities have to implement a (limited) industrial and technological policy. In the current gloomy economic climate, pressure from regional authorities, unions and enterprises dependent on military contracts leaves the MND with little room to manoeuvre.

In all probability, the industrial and technological offsets which foreign orders offer will remain the main selection criterion. A study of the ten major armaments programmes for the years 1993–1997 by the Minister of Defence suggests that the economic offsets system will remain important, if not decisive, in determining the extent of Belgian involvement with foreign customers (Ministry of National Defence, 1993).

One State, Two Regions

While few changes in policy are foreseen at the federal level, diverging developments have been taking place at the regional level since the Regions inherited part of the federal State's responsibilities for economic and technological affairs.

In the Flanders Region, where PRB conducted two-thirds of its manufacturing until the company closed in 1991, there have since been no companies exclusively devoted to defence. Some civil high technology firms in Flanders accept military contracts on a selective basis. Other civil enterprises (telecommunications, electronics) do contract work for the military on a regular basis and enjoy the ongoing support of regional authorities in securing these contracts.

The position is different in Wallonia. This region is the cradle of the traditional defence industry of Belgium, as well as of the main aerospace firms. Between 50 and 60% of Belgian defence jobs are located there, compared with 10% in Brussels and 30–40% in Flanders. Although defence accounted for only about 5,000 jobs in 1992 (where there had been 17,000 at the start of the 1980s), nevertheless, in a region that is suffering severe industrial decline, these jobs assumed particular importance (Adam *et al.*, 1991b). The regional authorities have adopted different policies to those in Flanders, emphasising capital subsidies and finance of research programmes, together with support for exports. That support provoked a major political crisis in September 1991, as we discuss later.

A Dual-Use Policy?

Alongside the policies adopted with respect to defence industry and technology which, it should be recalled, are characterised more by economic pragmatism than by long-term vision, the federal and regional authorities have developed since the mid-1970s some relatively purposeful policies in the civil aerospace sector, with respect notably to Airbus and the European Space Agency. Belgium participates in these two major cooperative programmes to the tune of 2.8% of Airbus and 5% of ESA. These are major commitments by the standards of Belgian R&D, with the R&D funds devoted to space activities alone amounting to 19% of total public funds for R&D in 1993 (Commission de cooperation fédérale, 1993, p. 18). This support, moreover, served the important purpose of enabling a number of companies that had been dependent on defence contracts to diversify their activities.

The decision to support the aerospace industry in this way was based in part on political considerations (support for European projects), in part simply as support to Belgian industry, and also as a way to promote technological strengthening of the industry (by integrating firms into high technology programmes from the outset). It proved judicious. There is almost no doubt that the two main Belgian aerospace companies would have failed at the beginning of the 1990s without this increased support for Airbus and the European space programme.

In addition, various smaller initiatives have been taken such as financing by the Walloon Region for the participation of Belgium's only aero-engine manufacturer (Techspace Aero) in the CFM56 civil engine programme. This support enabled Techspace Aero to diversify its portfolio on the brink of a sharp fall in military production.

More generally, most aerospace enterprises (both airframe and engines) adopted this strategy from the end of the 1970s, taking part in the Airbus programme or forging alliances with large foreign groups to develop civilian products. A survey carried out in 1991 in the Walloon Region showed that defence-related employment declined from 6,400 jobs in 1983 to 3,026 in 1990, whereas jobs in civil aerospace increased from 600 to 2,507 during the same period (Adam *et al.*, 1991b, p. 70).

How successful, from a technological point of view, has this diversification been? No systematic studies have been done of the companies' redeployment of equipment, labour and other technological assets, but some hypotheses can be advanced. The low R&D capacity of companies that manufacture arms only under license to foreign firms makes it unlikely that they have become integrated into the most advanced civilian technological fields. However, infrastructure and personnel inherited from military programmes have, without doubt, been used in a number of cases.

A major difficulty facing the typical defence manufacturer is adaptation to the realities of the civilian market. Managers long accustomed to a protected defence market are ill equipped to cope with competition rules, competitiveness issues, marketing, financial risk taking and managing shareholder equity. One of the keys to success in diversification, and even to corporate survival, lies in the ability to break economic habits and to adapt to an increasingly competitive civilian market.

The Belgian experience of diversification has followed three distinct patterns related to the type of company concerned.

A Spectacular Failure of Diversification

An example of the first kind is a failure which hit the most important Belgian military manufacturer. The company FN was created in 1889 under the name of 'Fabrique nationale d'armes de guerre'. It has always been involved in civilian activities along with the production of small arms and munitions. In the 1960s, it began building military aircraft engines. About ten years later, it went into the production and marketing of sports equipment, of which some products, such as hunting and fishing equipment and surf boards, are technologically closely related to light military equipment. In 1978, FN took over the Browning sales network, with 10,000 points of sale in the United States. At the beginning of the 1980s, new industrial processes were developed, particularly in robotics.

In 1975, the defence and security division accounted for 60% of FN's turnover. However, by 1985, defence turnover had declined to 37%. From the end of the 1970s, FN organised its production in four divisions: defence and security, engines, sport and leisure, and goods and services. At that time, the company's aerospace business was 90% dependent on military production (the F-16's F-100 engine). Handling equipment, waste processing and other engineering accounted for a maximum of 4% of FN's turnover.

The FN diversification aimed to free the company from dependency on highly cyclical and volatile military business. For instance, in 1982 and 1983 FN faced serious problems from the decrease in Third World demand, and 15,000 workers engaged in armaments production, some 60% of the total labour force, were made redundant.

Moreover, from the end of the 1970s, the scale of FN's handling equipment and sport and leisure investment was already too ambitious in comparison with expected sales. However, the company borrowed money to finance further investment and marketing in these areas, such that by 1986, servicing the debt required nearly 10% of the company's turnover. Diversification was therefore curbed, first in 1984, and then much more strongly in 1988, following a restructuring plan devised by the Société Générale de Belgique.

FN's industrial goods and services division was cut back, and the handling equipment division was taken over by the French company SNECMA in 1989. The Browning division (sport and entertainment) become a subsidiary, but products such as tennis rackets, golf equipment and wind surfers are no longer manufactured. The production of hunting weapons and fishing equipment is now the only remnant of FN's successive diversification efforts. FN itself was taken over by the French GIAT in 1991. It was renamed 'Fabrique Nationale Nouvelle Herstal' and is now concentrating on core business activity, manufacturing infantry weapons and munitions. In 1993, the company employed less than 1,300 people, compared to 9,500 in 1982.

A confused attempt at diversification with no consistent industrial and technological strategy can partially account for this failure. The FN group, specialising in defence, entertainment, aerospace, and industrial equipment at the beginning of the 1980s, was in effect an incoherent business. Numerous commentators have questioned the management's ability, in particular as regards marketing, to implement new, competitive strategies geared to a civilian market very different in character to the military market.

From One Type of Dependence to Another

Other enterprises — mainly in aerospace — diversified their activities more successfully than FN, taking fewer risks. In the 1980s, when the F-16 fighter bomber production was at its highest (160 units produced), military activity dominated the aerospace sector. In 1987, military orders accounted for 61% of aerospace business; by 1992 this had fallen to 46%, and in 1995 to less than 30%.

These same, mainly military, aerospace companies benefited from massive public spending on ESA and Airbus, which began in 1976 and 1979, respectively. It is hard to say how far the technological and industrial capacities which the firms acquired in the course of military work has been applied to these civilian programmes. Some of the workforce *has* been transferred successfully from one side to the other. On the other hand, in the international context, these companies, relatively small and often subcontractors, could not expect to play a decisive technological role.

As a consequence of public spending on these two civil aerospace programmes, the four main Belgian aerospace companies were able to reverse their dependency on military business between 1987 and 1990. At present, civil business accounts for more than half of their aggregate turnover. In terms of employment, the 3,374 military-related jobs that were lost between 1983 and 1990 were partially offset by 1,907 civilian jobs created in the same enterprises (Adam *et al.*, 1991b, pp. 41–2). However, although these companies have managed to survive relatively intact, this was achieved only by substituting dependency on 'protected' European aerospace programmes for dependency on military orders from government. Needless to say, both sides of the business are dependent on public finance, which has come under increasing pressure in Belgium.

From Mil-Spec to Mil-Tailored Production

Belgium offers the example, in a third type of diversification, of a firm that has built a capability in the military market by supplying materials that meet military needs, but at prices much lower than those of its competitors. Barco Electronics, specialising in electronic and liquid crystal displays, has been described in the trade press as able to adapt technologies of civil origin to military ends. Thus, its military aircraft displays are 'mil-tailored' rather than mil-spec. That is, Barco engineers have designed a more affordable, but equally effective, product by tailoring a generic design to meet the military's specific requirements, rather than following a design strategy based purely upon conformance with broader military specifications. This approach has also made it possible to manufacture commercial and military displays on the same production line.[16]

Originally, Barco was a television equipment manufacturer. It became involved in the F-16 programme and, owing to a particularly daring R&D policy, managed to lay claim to several promising technological niches. It specialised in the production of electronic displays, both for commercial markets such as television studios, air traffic control and civil aviation, and in ruggedised form (to meet the specific requirements of the military environment: temperature, shock, electromagnetic impulses, etc), or mil-tailored for a series of military clients.

Barco's flexibility extends to adapting its technological skills and capacities (infrastructure, assembly lines) for military customers outside Belgium. The company supplies flat panel displays for fighter aircraft (F-16 and Rafale) and for the US Air Force Missile Army Center (Cheyenne Mountain).[17] Barco has been developing continuously since 1987; it has set up subsidiaries in several countries including the United States. Other Belgian electronics or telecommunications enterprises have tried to follow Barco's example, although with somewhat less success.

Dual-Use and Military Technology Export Controls

In July 1991, Belgium adopted a new law on the import, export and transit of weapons, munitions, materiël specially designed for military use, and related materiël, in the wake of the discovery of numerous illegal arms exports to countries under embargo such as Iraq and Iran. However, the issue aroused markedly different political sensibilities in the Flemish part of the country — where the last ammunition exporting enterprise had already gone bankrupt — and in the Walloon Region, where several companies were struggling to survive. There was active debate in Belgium concerning numerous applications for arms export licences to Middle-East countries at the end of the Gulf war. Diverging assessments and interests ultimately led to the fall of the federal government in September 1991.

The political problem was dealt with by redistributing the power to grant export licences to the Flemish, Brussels and Walloon regional governments. Since then, Belgian arms exports have increased each year, from BF 7.5 billion in

1990, to BF 11.8 billion in 1991, BF 14.9 billion in 1992, and probably to more than BF 20 billion in 1993. Wallonian firms account for most of the increase.

The federal government does not publish any systematic information on the nature or destinations of arms exports, nor of possible restrictions placed on arms exports. According to information obtained directly from the manufacturers and reported in the press, there seems to have been no change, in practice, in the arms export regime. Most exports still go to Saudi Arabia and more generally to the Middle East, to Turkey and, to a lesser extent, to Africa.[18]

As far as controls on dual-use and military technology are concerned, one must distinguish between conventional and nuclear technology. Belgium has never been an important exporter of conventional weapons technology because of its relatively low level of military technological development; in fact, many of these technologies are imported. In most cases, foreign companies or states transferring technology to Belgium impose strict re-export restrictions. For example, Belgian industry produces almost the entire F-16 aircraft, but the United States prohibits sub-systems export except through negotiated offset agreements.

The situation regarding dual-use nuclear technologies is more complex. Here, Belgium plays an important technological and industrial role in Europe. She builds nuclear plants, develops nuclear waste reprocessing technology and trains numerous nuclear specialists. In order of importance, the Belgian nuclear industry ranks fourth in Europe after France, the United Kingdom and Germany.

The Belgian authorities' stance towards the enforcement of non-proliferation procedures revealed a certain ambiguity during the 1980s — not surprisingly, considering the great economic stakes facing the Belgian nuclear industry. Officially, Belgium has supported the efforts made by the International Atomic Energy Agency, the former COCOM and the European Community to control the diffusion of nuclear and dual-use technology (Verbeek, 1992). But according to some sources, Belgium is not among the strictest countries in observing non-proliferation controls. Of the 72 dual-use items found in the Nuclear Suppliers Group List and in the former COCOM Nuclear list (to which Belgium has nominally adhered), 20 are not proscribed under national legislation (Müller, 1993, p. 12). Fears that the political will to enforce non-proliferation policy is inadequate have been reinforced by the welcoming of Pakistani nuclear scientists to the Mol nuclear research centre in the north of Belgium.

Belgian authorities appear to be willing to strengthen controls on dual-use products and technology transfer only insofar as all exporting countries adopt a similar attitude (Verbeek, 1992, p. 183). The same approach is used within the framework of negotiations aimed at harmonising arms export legislation at the European level.

Conclusion: A Japanese Model in the Heart of Europe?

The Belgian defence industry has undergone massive and painful changes in the past decade. Turnover was cut by one half between 1983 and 1992, and 28,000 jobs (out of a total of 44,000 in 1983) were lost. However, despite the lack of a long-term defence technology policy, or even of medium-term management of military R&D, the various initiatives taken by public authorities, both federal and regional, have nevertheless had the effect of mitigating the decline in military business.

It is paradoxical that a system of distributed responsibility for industrial and technology policy amongst three federal ministries and three regional ministries should produce a relatively consistent overall policy. This is probably a result of traditional Belgian economic and social pragmatism dominating over party political and cultural considerations. However, while pragmatism evidently has been useful to certain enterprises, it has also had long-term drawbacks: this kind of short-term market-pull technology policy has not given Belgian defence industry the opportunity to develop technological capacities equivalent to those of, for instance, Swiss or Swedish industries.

Three types of company faced the crisis in demand for military equipment in different ways. Small arms and munitions producers have suffered from a decline in sales to the third world as well as the emergence of new competitors. Faced with these difficulties and confronted with enterprises highly specialised in military 'low-tech' production, public authorities could only act to curb the social consequences of industrial restructuring and job losses. In Wallonia, the most affected region, the authorities in the end provided financial and political support to relaunch the surviving enterprises.

The aerospace industries were cushioned by some domestic military orders and by the system of industrial and technological offsets attached to foreign military orders. Some of these enterprises could not have survived the 1970s without these orders and the associated technology transfers. Public finance of Belgian participation in the European Space Programme and in the Airbus consortium also mitigated the effects of the decline in military business, while enabling also the redeployment of their skilled labour and part of their technological capability.

Thirdly, those civilian high technology enterprises which took part in military programmes by integrating military and civil manufacturing developed and put into practice the concepts of ruggedised and mil-tailored production.

To speak of a 'Japanese model' of civilian and military production integration in Belgium would be presumptuous. The expression as such is never used in Belgium. Nevertheless, certain comparisons can be drawn between the two countries, bearing in mind the important difference in scale between the two economies. Belgium, like Japan, imports most of its military technology and its major weapons systems. Also, military production is commonly done under license by predominantly civil, successful manufacturing companies. Military production is done in small batches, drawing upon the firms' existing technological capacity.

For the future, a large proportion of planned equipment programmes of the Belgian Army (telecommunications, modernisation and perhaps the Future Large Aircraft) can be accommodated by integrating development and production into existing civilian or dual-use technology facilities. In the medium term, it seems that the public authorities can utilise existing civilian and dual-use high technology enterprises capable of integrating the occasional military equipment orders, preferably by incorporating civilian technologies and production processes so as to reduce the costs. As far as strictly military enterprises are concerned, on the other hand, their future would appear to lie in the uncertain world of foreign markets.

Endnotes

1. Several constitutional amendments (in 1980, 1988 and 1993) have reorganised Belgium into three levels of power. The federal state has responsibility for areas of general interest (defence, public order, social security, etc.). Moreover, Belgium is divided into three linguistic Communities consisting of 5.5 million Flemish speakers, 4.5 million French speakers and a German-speaking minority of 30,000. These three Communities are mainly responsible for education and culture, and along with the three Regions (Flanders, Brussels-capital and Wallonie), are responsible for the economy, technology and infrastructure. The different aspects of defence policy cut across these three levels of power.

2. Exchange rate: approximately BF 60 = £1 sterling in 1990, and 50 in 1995.

3. Some enterprises significantly involved in military markets do not provide sufficiently precise information on military turnover and are therefore omitted from this classification.

4. Belgian authorities do not provide any official figures on arms exports. We have therefore calculated the amount by adding up military exports included in company balance sheets and other communications.

5. The British enterprise ASTRA firstly took over les Poudreries Réunies de Belgique and then, wary of the high liabilities, rapidly withdrew.

6. The Ministry of Scientific Research was replaced by the Service of Scientific Policy Planning, reporting directly to the Prime Minister, after the 1988 constitutional amendments.

7. According to the institution responsible for collecting R&D statistics in Belgium, the figures it provides correspond to the public funding of R&D as defined in the Frascati handbook and therefore these figures only represent the appropriations and not the actual outlays. See Commission de Cooperation fédérale, 1993, pp. 6–7.

8. To face this complexity the authorities had to set up a new structure, 'The Commission for Federal Cooperation of the Interministerial Conference on Science Policy', whose main task is to collect statistical information on R&D from the different federal authorities, Communities and Regions in an attempt to coordinate policies.

9. For instance, in 1989 the defence budget released BF 608 million in R&D investment credits for the Trigat programme alone. That same year, the Federal Commission reported to the OECD that *total* military R&D spending in Belgium amounted to BF 196 million.

10. This estimate could be refined by systematically analysing the different military programmes, but this has not been possible within the framework of the present study.

11. To illustrate the lack of credibility of official statistics, two studies were carried out in 1992 by the universities of Gand (Ghent) and Louvain (Leuven) on technological aspects of the defence industry, at the request of the Central Economic Council (CCE). The findings provide no statistics on military R&D spending in Belgium! See Debacker, 1992; and Sleuwaegen, 1992.

12. Interview with G. Coëme, IEPG Chairman, in *Avianews International*, no. 198, July–August 1991.

13. The Ministry of Economic Affairs is responsible for assessing proposed offsets and enforces, sometimes over the course of several decades (F-16), compliance with contractual agreements. Financial penalties can be imposed in cases of non-compliance.

14. *Le Soir*, 'Le MDN veut acheter mieux et moins cher', 3 September 1993.

15. According to an estimate made in a study by the Free University of Brussels, Belgium is said to have paid 34% more for the first 116 F-16s produced in Belgium than if it purchased them off the shelf (van Brusselen, 1992, p. 57).

16. 'Belgium's Barco foresees growing demand for large high-resolution colour displays', *Aviation Week and Space Technology*, 18 May 1992, p. 59.

17. The company proposed ruggedised or mil-tailored flat screens for a price 2–6 times cheaper than that of a screen designed and produced according to standard military criteria. Source: Barco lecture on 'Dual-use Products' given to the 'Centre de Recherche et d'Etudes de Défense'.

18. *De Morgen*, 'Belgisch-waalse wapenuitvoer: business as usual', 29 December 1993, p. 2.

References

Adam, B., 1989, *La production d'armes en Belgique*, Brussels: GRIP, Notes et Documents no. 139.

Adam, B., De Vestel, P. and Zaks, A., 1991a, *Perspectives d'harmonisation des réglementations et politiques d'exportations d'armes au sein de la Communauté Européenne*, Brussels: GRIP, Notes et documents no. 157–58.

Adam, B., De Vestel, P. and Zaks, A., 1991b, *Contexte et perspectives de restructuration de l'industrie de l'armement en Wallonie*, Brussels: GRIP, Notes et Documents no. 161–162.

Commission de Coopération fédérale de la Conférence interministérielle de la Politique scientifique, 1993, 'Apercu des dépenses de R&D par les autorités belges 1989–1993', Brussels, December.

Central Economic Council, 1992, 'Perspectives du marché de défence', synthesis report, Brussels: CCE, April.

Delhauteur, D., 1991, *La coopération européenne dans le domaine des équipements militaire: la relance du GEIP*, Brussels: GRIP, Notes et Documents no. 159.

Dehousse, F., *et al.* 1992, 'Aspects juridiques, institutionnels et politiques des perspectives du marché de défense', Université de Liège, CCE, 1992/299.

Debacker, K., *et al.* 1992, 'Onderzoek naar de technologische toekomst van de belgische defensie industrie', Rijksuniversiteit Gent, CCE 1992/300.

De Vestel, P., 1995, *Defence Markets and Industries: Time for Political Decisions?* Paris: Western European Union, Institute for Security Studies, Chaillot Paper no. 21.

De Vestel, P., *et al.* 1993, *European armaments industry: research technological development and conversion*', Luxembourg: European Parliament — Scientific and Technological Options Assessment.

De Vestel, P. and Fohn, R., 1993, 'Les données macro-économiques de la défense en Europe' in *Memento défense-désarmement 1993*, Brussels: GRIP, pp. 337–390.

Dumoulin, A., 1992, 'La restructuration des forces armées', *Courrier hebdomadaire*, no. 1383–1984, Brussels: CRISP.

'Guide de la recherche scientifique', 1991, Brussels: Service de la programmation de la politique scientifique.

Ministry of National Defence, 1993, *Plan à moyen terme du Ministère de la Défense Nationale 1993–1997*, Brussels: MND.

Müller, H., 1993, 'The export control debate in the "New" European Community', *Arms Control Today,* Vol. 23, (2).

OECD, 1992, *Main science and technology indicators*, Paris: OECD.

Sleuwaegen, L., *et al.* 1992, 'De toekomst van de belgische defensie-industrie: industriel, strategische aspecten' Catholic University of Leuven, CCE 1992/303.

Van Brusselen, P., *et al.* 1992, 'Pespectives du marché de la défense en Belgique: études des aspects macroéconomiques de l'industrie belge de la défense', Université Libre de Bruxelles, CCE 1992/302.

Verbeek, P., 1992, 'Belgium', in H. Müller *et al. The European non-proliferation policy 88–92*, Brussels: Inter-university Press, pp. 175–184.

Zaks, A., 1992, *Diversification et reconversion de l'industrie d'armement*, Brussels: GRIP, Notes et Documents no. 165.

Chapter 2
France

Claude Serfati[1]

Introduction

The French armaments industry faces today considerable difficulties. The economic and political conditions in which it developed in the 1960s and 1970s have changed profoundly. The production of a wide range of nuclear and conventional weapons required to maintain 'strategic independence' has absorbed vast financial means, mobilised scarce technological resources and subjugated certain crucial industrial branches (especially electronics, and certain types of specialised equipment suppliers) to 'exotic' uses.

This strategy of independence, the limits of which were shown in the Gulf War, where the French armed forces played an auxiliary role in the American intervention, became increasingly difficult to defend in economic terms. The spiralling costs of improving weapons performance have been an ever-increasing burden, aggravating the budget deficit. Moreover, France lacks the means to bring to maturity on its own those technologies which are essential to remaining in the race for military innovation. In some fields, she is already dependent on foreign suppliers (electronic components, materials, composites).

This chapter outlines the particular framework in which French armaments decisions are taken. It discusses the central role of the Délégation Générale pour l'Armement (DGA) which, as the key military institution in the armaments field, structures the system of arms production by acting as the hub of a tight network of relationships between the large enterprises, their sub-contractors, and the public research laboratories. It indicates the scale of resources devoted to military technologies, estimating the R&D expenditures of companies working in the defence sector to represent about 30% of total industrial R&D expenditure. It suggests that the concept of military R&D is both qualitatively and quantitatively different from the traditional concept of R&D. We outline the recent introduction by the DGA of the concept of 'dual use' technologies, showing, on the one hand, how this notion has been used to draw up a list of 'critical technologies' for the armaments industry and, on the other, how it has been used to try to reinforce the links within and between the military-industrial and the civilian systems of innovation. We shall see also how the concept has been used to propose an increased role for the DGA in the formulation and implementation of

French technology policy. Finally, we discuss the issue of conversion. We conclude that the DGA does not envisage undertaking conversion measures. Indeed, in the period 1982–1993, the number of jobs in the arms industry fell from 310,000 to 230,000 despite a rise of 16% in real terms in equipment expenditure, and at least a further 64,000 jobs are expected to go in the next few years, even though, at least until mid-1995, equipment expenditure had been expected to remain steady. While the DGA does speak of diversification, it considers that the general state budget (and not its own) should foot the bill, although under the direction of the Minister of Defence.

Basic Information

The Organisational Context

The organisation of the defence industry and defence research is profoundly influenced by the DGA. Its head holds the same rank as the commander-in-chief of the armed forces. But its importance can be better seen by its position at every point along the interface between decisions over French military needs and over their industrial fulfilment. Through its various divisions, the DGA is involved in every step in the life of an equipment programme, from establishment of operational requirements, through feasibility definition, and on through development, production, acquisition, subsequent maintenance and modifications, and export (Playe, 1983). If a comparison of broad equipment acquisition procedures between France, the UK and Germany shows few fundamental differences (Huffschmid and Voss, 1991), it is nonetheless probable that the role played by the DGA has no near equivalent in either of those two countries.

This role is reinforced by the fact that the DGA has two missions: a *policy mission* (general orientations, elaboration of concepts, followed by specification and oversight of armaments programmes, etc.) and an *industrial mission*, in the sense that a significant part of defence research, production and maintenance is conducted within its own establishments. The policy mission draws upon over 20,000 staff, while the industrial mission is essentially concentrated in the Directorate for Naval Construction (DCN); in contrast, aircraft work lies in the hands of private or state-owned firms, while land equipment production was transferred from direct DGA control when it was reconstituted as GIAT-industries.

The DGA is the key to the organisation of French arms production (Chesnais and Serfati, 1992; Serfati 1992, and 1995, Hébert 1995). The production of armaments is organised into a network defined by the market and nonmarket relations among the large companies, the publicly-funded dedicated military research laboratories (CEA, ONERA) and the DGA, the last being at the centre by virtue of the power at its disposal. *Armaments Engineers*, who form one of the *grands corps* of the Ecole Polytechnique and run the DGA, reinforce the cohesion of this network by their ubiquitous presence at the head of all of the large defence companies. This ensemble constitutes a subsystem (or *meso-system*) of the national production system itself. For more than 30 years the defence meso-system has had rules and procedures which distinguish it clearly from the civilian sector. The reproduction of this meso-system, beyond any form of public accountability, is facilitated by this mode of functioning, reinforced by the status of military institutions in general in French society.

Formally speaking, the State is able to control the arms industry because it controls the majority — and often the totality — of the capital of most of the arms producing firms. State-owned companies (where the majority of capital is under state control) are responsible for about 80% of production and employ 100,000 workers. In practice, however, the proposed privatisation of these companies, which for some of them would simply represent a return to the *status quo ante* their nationalisation in 1981 (following the election of Francois Mitterrand), would not change the depth or the cohesion of the meso-system, nor the close links of these companies with the DGA. In any case, by the time of writing, no military companies had yet been firmly presented for privatisation, partly perhaps because some of them (eg, SNECMA, Aérospatiale) are in financial difficulties.

Since the start of 1995, the DGA began to undergo reorganisation, in order better to deal with the radical changes in the arms market and the need to achieve substantial economies in the arms budget, which became even more acute with the cuts announced in June 1995 by the Juppé government, and a clear expectation that much more was to come as the new government set about its economic programme and planned reforms of the armed services. The reorganisation hinges on the DGA distinguishing more sharply its responsibilities for formulating armaments policy from those for managing the industrial implementation of those policies. These latter are in any case decreasing. Not only have the DGA's former land-systems activities been transferred to GIAT, but a reorganisation of the activities of the Directorate for Naval Construction is also underway. Nevertheless, the DGA will aim to profit from this reorganisation to reinforce its role of 'industrial architect' of major arms programmes (Info-DGA, 1994). Perhaps one of the more striking changes, at least in symbolic terms, was the appointment of an industrialist, rather than a career *ingenieur d'armement*, as head of the DGA from early 1996.

Some Data on the Arms Industry

In 1994, the turnover of the French armaments industry stood at FF 97 billion, or 2% of GDP, down from FF 103 billion in 1993, and FF 113 billion in 1992. Exports accounted for 20% of this turnover. Table 1 shows that the turnover increased in both real and current values between 1982 and 1990, and subsequently fell slightly (by 3.5% between 1990 and 1992). Exports have continued to drop from their peak in 1985.

According to DGA estimates, the number of employees in the sector also began to fall dramatically from 1985. As of January 1993, the arms industry (including the policy-making staff of the DGA) directly employed 230,000 people (80,000 fewer than in 1982), of whom 189,000 worked to supply national orders and 41,000 on exports (CGP 1993). This represents approximately 5% of national industrial employment. Estimates indicate (CGP 1993) that one indirect job is provided for every 2.5 direct jobs, which gives an estimated 330,000 people employed directly or indirectly in arms production. This number can be expected to continue to fall in the light of more recent defence cutbacks.

The main arms firms, and their specialisations, are listed in Table 2. (See also Table 7 for further data).

It is evident from Table 7 that exports are extremely important to the industry, a subject we return to later. Here, though, let us note that in order to export within Europe, French companies have increasingly had to enter into agreements with military contractors in the importing countries, especially as market conditions have become increasingly more difficult and the costs of development and production have risen. The Dassault group is an exception: despite strong export activities, it has always refused any form of cooperation with foreign firms.[2]

French firms have developed two types of general strategy for these purposes:

- creation of joint venture companies (GIE — Economic Interest Groups in the French legal terminology), or similar forms of partnership. The capital of the new company is shared (equally or not) among its parents, with the result that government oversight of firm strategy and accounts becomes more difficult.
- assumption of a majority share holding in the foreign firm by the French firm.

The choice of strategy depends on the histories of the firms, their corporate cultures, and their degree of overlap in products. Some examples are given in Table 3.

Both *Aérospatiale* and *Matra* generally prefer the first solution. *Aérospatiale*, a fully nationalised enterprise (though listed now for eventual privatisation), is

Table 1: Sales of French Arms Industry, 1982–1993, Billions of Current and Constant (1991) Francs

	1982	1983	1984	1985	1986	1987	1988	1989	1990	1991	1992	1993	1994
FF billion, current													
In France	46.6	53.1	56.4	60.5	65.3	72.9	78.0	82.9	85.9	86.5	84.7	82.5	80.2
Exports	28.9	33.0	41.9	43.9	43.1	34.1	38.2	37.3	38.6	29.1	28.3	20.6	16.7
TOTAL	75.5	86.1	98.3	104.4	108.4	107.0	116.2	120.2	124.5	115.6	113	103.1	96.9
FF billion, constant 1991													
In France	71.6	74.4	73.7	74.5	76.3	82.5	85.5	88.1	88.6	86.5	81.7	79.3	77.1
Exports	44.4	46.3	54.8	54.1	50.3	38.6	41.9	39.7	39.8	29.1	27.3	19.9	16.1
TOTAL	116.0	120.7	128.5	128.5	126.6	121.2	127.4	127.8	128.4	115.6	109.0	99.2	93.2

Source: Adapted from CGP (1993).

Table 2: Specialisms of the Principal Arms Firms

GROUPS*	MAIN MILITARY PRODUCTS	Military as % of Total Turnover 1993
Aérospatiale	Aerospace: military aviation (helicopters, transport aircraft), missiles (long range), space (observation satellites)	30
Thomson-CSF	Electronic systems: aeronautical (radar, opto-electronic, displays), communication, control and detection (land, air and sea), missiles (air defence)	70
Matra-Hachette	Electronic systems: missiles (air-air, ground-air), information and control systems	10
Dassault-Aviation**	Aircraft: combat, patrol, maritime	80
Dassault-Electronique**	Electronic systems: guidance systems, onboard computers, detection, electronic warfare	91
GIAT-industries	Land equipment: tanks, armoured vehicles, weapons and munitions	93
SNPE	Chemicals: rocket motors, explosives, decoys, reactive armour	42
SAGEM	Electronic systems: navigation, inertial guidance, opto-electronic equipment (thermal imaging, guidance, aerial reconnaissance)	26
Labinal	Aircraft: engines (for aircraft, helicopters, missiles), and related equipment	45
SNECMA	Aircraft: engines, landing gear, brake systems, power transmission systems, reverse thrusters	46

Source: Company annual reports.

Notes:

* The term 'group' denotes a consolidated company, which might include other subsidiary companies (as in the case of Aérospatiale, which includes its joint venture, Eurocopter, with the German firm Daimler Aerospace.

** Dassault-Aviation and Dassault-Electronique are companies within the Dassault-Aviation Group. In these cases the relevant information is published at company rather than group level.

Table 3: Examples of Foreign Operations of 4 French Industrial Groups

French Firm	Operations with Foreign Firms	Type
Thomson-CSF	Defence division of Philips (NL) (1990)	Acquisition
	Link-miles (USA) (1990)	Acquisition
	Ferranti (UK) (1990)	Acquisition of 50% of sonar division
	Pilkington (UK)	Acquisition of 50% of optronics division
	SAES (Spain)	49% share holding
	Short Brothers (UK) (1993)	Joint venture
GIAT-Industries	Herstal SA (Belgium)	Acquisition
Aérospatiale	MBB (Germany) (1991)	Creation with MBB of Eurocopter (30% MBB, 70% Aérospatiale)
	Alenia (Italy) DASA (Germany)	Joint venture for satellites
	Euromissile	Joint venture with DASA
Matra	GEC Marconi (UK)	Joint venture, Matra-Marconi-Espace
	British Aerospace Dynamics	Joint venture on missiles (planned from 1993)

Source: Author, drawing on specialist press.

under strong state control: it is the monopoly supplier of nuclear missiles, and maintains close ties with the DGA. Since the 1960s, at the behest of the public authorities, Aérospatiale has developed a policy of very close cooperation with MBB (now Daimler Benz Aerospace) in both military (Euromissile) and civilian domains (Airbus Industrie), in which Aérospatiale retains de facto operational management and technological leadership (although in planned further cooperation in space activities, the leadership role will be reversed). The French group realises 60% of its turnover in cooperation with the German firm.[3] There have, however, been modifications in the work share since the end of the 1980s in the light of the growing strength of MBB within the Daimler Benz group, and its desire to gain leadership in the civilian sphere, while leaving the dominant military role to Aérospatiale (Serfati 1992). Today, Aérospatiale's chief executive envisages transforming the group into a holding company which would manage the group participants in joint companies (Marx, 1993).

Matra is one of the rare large military contractors in which the majority shareholders are private. This company has developed a strategy of cooperation with European and US firms because of its relatively secondary role in military electronics, far behind industry leader Thomson, a long-standing favourite of the DGA. In addition, the company's wish to develop its abilities in civil space has led it to develop a strategy of cooperation which is indispensable in that sector.

Thomson and *GIAT-industries* (since its transformation from the status of a state arsenal in 1990) more often choose the second solution, that of taking majority control. For more than twenty years, Thomson's strategy within France has been to take a dominant position, preferably a monopoly, in the field of military electronics. Through a series of takeovers of state companies in the 1980s, it thus became the 'national champion' in the electronics industry. Following the same strategy internationally, Thomson is attempting to strengthen its hold on the larger European market. It has even ventured into the US market, but its attempt to acquire the missile division of LTV met not only opposition from the Department of Defence (DoD), but also strong reservations from Aérospatiale and the DGA. The attempt to form in 1991 a 50–50 joint venture with British Aerospace for the production of missiles also failed.

Major Programmes Currently in Development

Table 4 shows the ten largest military programmes currently underway in France. The six largest of these will cost a minimum of FF 500 billion in current year terms, of which FF 350 billion remain to be spent within the next 8 to 10 years. These substantial sums mean that these six programmes alone will account for some 40% of annual equipment expenditures (so-called 'Title 5' in the terminology of the defence budget) (Paecht, 1993).

Spending on Military Equipment and Military R&D

There has been a steady reduction in recent years in the proportion of GNP devoted to defence, falling from 4.08% in 1983 to 3.13% in 1993. Over the same time period, the proportion of defence spending allocated to equipment (Title 5), as opposed to operating costs, grew from 45.7% in 1983 to 53.02% in 1991, falling slightly in the two years after that.

Table 5 shows a continuous rise until the 1990s in military R&D expenditure, and a significant change between the 1970s and 1980s, sustained into the 1990s, in its importance relative to the overall equipment budget. The equipment budget itself enjoyed substantial growth over the past three decades: +10.5% per annum in current francs and +2.5% in constant francs between 1965 and 1990. These

Table 4: Major Programmes in Development

Programmes	**Cost (FF billions 1992)**	**Duration**	**Principal firms**
Rafale	197	1986–2015	Dassault-Aviation (35%), SNECMA (30%) Thomson-CSF (13%)
Ballistic missile launching nuclear submarines (SNLE NG)	89	1986–2005	Directions des constructions navales (DCN): 51%, ECN Indret (12%), Thomson-CSF (6%)
Mirage 2000 (D, DA)	80	1976–2002	Dassault-Aviation (26%), SNECMA (27%), Thomson-CSF (12%)
Submarine launched ballistic missile (M4 and M5 MSBS)	71	1983–2011	Aérospatiale (55%), SEP (17%), SNPE (8%)
AMX Leclerc Tank	42	1982–2007	GIAT-industries (50%), SAGEM (20%), SACMM (11%)
Helicopters HAP/HAC (Tigre and Gerfault)	35	1987–2010	Eurocopter (78%), Turbomeca (8%), MTU (8%)
Helicopter NH 90	35	1991–2011	Eurocopter, Agusta, Fokker
Nuclear powered aircraft carrier (PAN)	27	1986–2007	Directions des constructions navales (DCN) 51%, ECN Indret (21%), Thomson-CSF (23%)
Long range air-ground missile (ASLP)	28	1991–2007	Aérospatiale (ND)
Maritime patrol aircraft (Atlantique 2)	24	1977–2002	Dassault-Aviation (20%), Thomson-CSF (19%), Aérospatiale (14%)

Sources: DGA, and Boucheron (1992).

Table 5: Military R&D Expenditure 1971–94 (Billions of Current Francs)

Year	Military R&D spending (a) (FF billions)	Defence spending (b) (FF billions)	Ratio a/b (%)
1971	3.90	14.14	27.6
1972	3.90	15.34	25.4
1973	4.35	16.38	26.6
1974	4.65	18.48	25.2
1975	5.05	20.44	24.7
1976	5.60	22.84	24.5
1977	6.10	24.21	25.2
1978	7.55	25.58	29.5
1979	9.35	31.23	29.9
1980	11.35	36.06	31.5
1981	17.67	44.61	39.6
1982	17.86	51.09	35.0
1983	20.31	55.48	36.6
1984	22.98	66.64	34.5
1985	23.60	71.64	32.9
1986	24.60	75.68	32.5
1987	26.62	85.81	31.0
1988	32.41	90.85	35.7
1989	32.98	98.00	33.7
1990	34.69	103.10	33.6
1991	33	102.93	32
1992	32	102.90	30.9
1993	30	96	31.2
1994	29	94.9	30.5

Source: Author, drawing on parliamentary reports and data from the Ministry of Research and Technology.
Note: There is a discontinuity between 1981 and 1982 due to a redefinition of the financing of military R&D in 1981.

rates of increase exceeded those for budget provision for major state-funded civilian infrastructure programmes (hospitals and roads, for example) over the same period. Moreover, in the period 1962–1990, defence equipment spending rose faster than GNP (excluding non-profit state turnover). Military equipment alone accounts for almost half of total annual state capital expenditure (47.5% in 1993).

Military R&D and procurement spending is regulated by *Military Programme Laws* (Lois de programmation militaires) which were introduced in 1960. Their goal is to establish an intermediate temporal horizon between *planning*, that is, formal reflections by the Ministry of Defence on its military capabilities and long term missions (15–20 years), and *finance laws,* voted every year, which permit the undertaking of expenditures based on the voted budget allocations.[4] The objectives set for equipment expenditures in the seven military programme laws between 1960 and 1994 were rarely met precisely, and the differences between those objectives and credits voted in the annual finance law became wider under the military programme law of 1987–1991 (named, after the then defence minister, the 'Giraud' law).

Nonetheless, it has been emphasised (Schmidt 1992) that the military programme laws have enabled a rise in equipment expenditures and have eventually ensured the completion of the basic armaments programmes, even if at the cost of a delay in their timetable. By and large, since 1977 the ratio of planned to realised expenditures has been over 93%. Hitherto, therefore, Programme laws have maintained their status as a guiding framework. Whether the same will apply to the 1995–2000 military programme law, in view of the cuts announced in mid-1995 (see below), seems much less certain.

In 1992 the Ministry of Defence adopted a new method of presenting its budget. Where formerly the budget was broken down by branches of the military services[5], the new presentation is made by *module* (that is, is more project-based). The MoD considers that this reform will allow better inter-service management of resources, since many arms programmes have the potential to be used by more than one service (Rafale and the NH 90, for example, will be used by both the land- and sea-based forces). The reform will also enable better account to be kept of expenditures on space, intelligence gathering and research. It should be noted, however, that this sanguine view was contested by the chairman of the Defence Committee of the Parliament who, in analysing the budget for 1993, argued that the new procedures will mean that 'control of the credits will become more difficult' (Hollande, 1993, p. 114).

A new Programme Law (1995–2000) was voted by the Parliament in spring 1994. Under this law, equipment spending would be FF 613 billion in 1994, of which FF 162 billion (26%) would be devoted to research and development. Equipment expenditure was voted to increase by 0.5% per annum until 1997, from when it could rise to 1.5% per annum 'if the economic situation permits' (MoD, 1994). The main programmes are (cf. again Table 4): Rafale (FF 198 billion in 1994), SNLE (FF 77 billion), Leclerc (FF 42 billion), Tigre (FF 41 billion), and NH 90 (FF 40 billion). No major programme was cancelled, but the M5 missile programme was delayed until 2010.

From the outset, however, it was clear that this budget could not realistically sustain all the programmes that were under development. It was widely expected that some of them (perhaps Rafale) would be reduced in scale, and others (the

NH 90 helicopter?) even cancelled. Even so, against a background of determined efforts by the Balladur government to control public spending, a budget that projected growth was remarkable. It was, therefore, not too surprising when the Juppé government announced in June 1995 a reduction of 8.5% in 1995 defence equipment spending, with more to follow. The implications of such a step, however, against the background of the inadequate provision in the 1995–2000 Programme Law for the programmes under development, led to considerable industrial and parliamentary concern. Over 70 conservative legislators, all members of the parliamentary defence committee, abstained from voting in July 1995 when the government presented a supplementary bill to cut the planned defence budget. (*Defense News*, 17 July 1995; *Jane's Defence Weekly*, 29 July 1995), but without much prospect of reversing the cuts.

Arms Exports

As we saw in Table 1, arms exports are a major component of the turnover of the armaments industry. Indeed, this has been true since the 1960s, in terms of the importance of arms exports both to the economy as a whole (with arms exports being the leading surplus category in the 1992 balance of payments) and to the arms companies. Nevertheless, their net macro-economic effects remain unclear, not least because of taxpayer contributions, amounting sometimes to the entire cost of non-payments, as happened over Iraq in 1990 for armaments totalling several billion francs (Fontanel and Ward, 1990).

Military R&D

The Ministry of Defence plays a major role not merely as the prime source of funds for defence R&D, but also as the principal provider of public R&D funds to companies.

Before proceeding, we should note that there are considerable methodological difficulties with using French defence R&D statistics. This is because data are presented according to different conventions by different official bodies. These differ in the categories used, on what counts as R&D, and on such questions as whether or not to include value-added tax. In recent years, the Ministry of Research and Higher Education (MRES) has had the responsibility of reconciling figures from different sources, and of bringing them into line with the OECD's Frascati convention. Just to illustrate, this process required the amendment of the MoD's figure for R&D spending in 1988, from FF 32 billion to FF 25 billion (MRES, 1990). We use MRES figures as far as possible below.

Table 6: Export Orders, by Category of Matériel

	1977	1978	1979	1980	1981	1982	1983	1984	1985	1986	1987	1988	1989	1990	1991	1992	1993	1994
Land systems	8.6	8.0	4.4	11.2	18.1	9.3	5.6	43.6	11.6	8.5	7.9	13.5	7.1	17.4	10.1	–	–	–
Sea systems	1.9	2.3	1.7	15.1	3.9	4.0	1.5	2.3	4.8	2.4	5.5	4.2	2.5	4.6	16.7	–	–	–
Air systems	16.9	11.4	18.9	11.0	11.8	28.3	22.0	15.9	28.1	14.4	15.5	19.8	10.4	11.4	7.4	–	–	–
Total	27.4	21.7	25.0	37.3	33.8	41.3	29.1	61.8	44.5	25.3	28.9	37.5	20.0	33.4	34.2	45.7*	38.9	31.7

* Rapport d'information, Commission de la défense nationale et forces armées, Assemblée nationale.

Source: Ministry of Defence.

In 1994, the R&D expenditure of the MoD amounted to FF 29 billion. This broke down thus: 52% to companies, 44% to laboratories under the MoD (ONERA, Institut Saint-Louis, DGA experimental centres, and Atomic Energy Commission (CEA) military research, etc.), and 3% to public laboratories and universities. Of the public laboratory money, the majority goes to the CEA for civilian research and to the National Centre for Space Studies (CNES).

Expenditures for military R&D represented 31% of total allocations for public research (FF 95 billion in 1994) (MRES, 1995). But if we focus on public funding of R&D in companies, the significance of the MoD rises sharply: it provides nearly 70% of the total public funding for research available to companies. This funding, moreover, is concentrated in a very small number of firms (cf. Table 7), with 92% of it going to firms employing more than 2000 workers. These enterprises, in addition, often belong to larger groups, and it is estimated that the ten largest contractor groups receive 70% of the total military R&D budget. The aerospace sector is the largest beneficiary of military R&D expenditure (57% of total), followed by electronics (34%). These two sectors thus capture more than 90% of the total public expenditures for military R&D.

In addition to MoD-funded R&D done by firms, the question arises of how much defence R&D firms themselves fund. There being no official statistics on this matter, we have made an estimate based on a direct survey of the principal arms groups (Table 7). This suggests that self-financed R&D was about FF 15 billion francs in 1992. Adding the R&D funds supplied by the DGA, we estimate that in 1992 French arms groups spent approximately FF 30 billion on R&D, representing nearly 30% of total 1992 R&D expenditures by French companies. The military-oriented groups also figure prominently among the largest French industrial groups, and come high in the rankings of groups according to R&D expenditure (8 of the top 25 French firms, on this indicator, being arms firms). When ranked by R&D expenditures, the top five French industrial groups all have military activities,[6] while 11 of the top 25 firms in terms of patents are also military oriented. The concentrated distribution of DGA funds has, therefore, important implications for the overall innovative effort of French firms.

Relative to equipment spending, public spending on military R&D will probably increase moderately, but steadily, in the next few years. In particular, strong growth is expected in the space sector, at the expense of nuclear R&D. This change results from the realisation of the military and strategic importance of space-based assets, especially since the Gulf War, and more recent concerns over Iraqi troop movements, and from the willingness of the MoD to be the focus of the efforts to regroup European military space activities, thanks to the guiding role of the French space industry in the civilian realm. The 'upstream' research (roughly equivalent to basic and strategic research, in Frascati terms)

Table 7: Leading French Arms Companies (Excluding DGA and CEA), in Order of Armaments Turnover, 1993

Company	Total turnover (FF millions)	Armaments turnover (FF millions)	Armaments as % total turnover	Total R&D (FF millions)	Self-financed R&D (FF millions)	Arms Exports (FF millions)	Personnel (Persons)
Thomson-CSF	34,300	23,940	70	8,100	2,600	18,000	48,900
Aérospatiale	50,850	15,050	30	15,600	4,300	7,400	43,900
Dassault-Aviation	11,315	9,030	80	2,800	1,211	1,850	10,250
SNECMA	19,556	9,000	46	3,452	2,278	1,700 (d)	12,240
Matra-Hachette	53,900	5,500 (a)	10	6,000	NA	3,000	41,900
GIAT-industries	5,500	5,115	93	1,160	334	1,700	11,600
Labinal	8,540	3,840 (b)	45	900	NA	1,600	16,200
SAGEM	13,038	3,400 (c)	26	NA	NA	NA	14,500
Dassault-Electronique	2,770	2,520	91	1,643	316	518	2,888
SNPE	4,160	1,760 (a)	42	700	150	116	6,150
SFIM	1,661	1,080	65	405	98	316	2,451
Alcatel Espace Défense	1,885	660	35	330	NA	0	1,304
Compagnie des Signaux	2,073	632	30	NA	86	156	2,873
Inter-technique	1,249	437	35	NA	152	412	2,150

Notes: NA: not available.
a) Space/Defence Branch; b) Defence aeronautical branch; c) Navigation, optronic, defence branch; d) Engines only.

Source: Annual reports, and data collected from the firms, 1995.

devoted to military space activities exceeded FF 200 million in 1991 and nearly FF 800 million in 1994. However, despite this shift, nuclear continues to be funded about four times more heavily than space research (Paecht, 1993).

Another significant development in the pattern of funding of military research was the announcement in 1994 that FF 2 billion were to be allocated for 'dual use' aeronautical and nuclear research.

Current Thinking on Defence and 'Dual Use' Technologies

The Future of Defence Technology Capabilities

Before proceeding further, it is important to recall the particular role and position of the DGA within the French system, as described earlier. The apparent absence, or late publication, of official policy positions does not in any way imply that the officials of the DGA have been inactive in researching the problems concerned with the planning of new technology and arms systems: on the contrary. This is why we will draw heavily here on a report published in 1993 by a working group of the Commissariat Général du Plan (CGP, 1993), charged with examining the future of the defence industries. Such a report does not bind the government to its recommendations, yet the very strong representation on the working group of the DGA, and of other elements of the armaments meso-system, means that the report can be safely taken to represent their thinking.

In addition to its interest as a demonstration of how French policy-making works in this field, there is another reason for dwelling upon this report. This is that the report is one of the most explicit and systematic treatments of the issue of dual-use technologies to be found anywhere in Europe, and this alone makes it worthy of attention.

We should note, however, that this report was published in advance of the reformulation of French defence policy following the dramatic changes in the international situation at the end of the 1980s. That reformulation began in the *Livre blanc sur la défense* (February 1994) and continued in the 1995–2000 Programme law (June 1994), and thereafter.

In these documents, six types of crisis are envisaged, in which France might be involved. From the nuclear level (e.g., a 'regional crisis' in which a nuclear-armed Middle Eastern country might be involved), through threats to overseas departments and territories, or the possibility of a major threat to any Western European country, the same theme emerges: the scale and complexity of the threats requires France to keep her military budget at a high level and, if need be, to increase it. All existing major equipment programmes were to be maintained, even though some of them, such as the Leclerc tank, Rafale, and the Charles de Gaulle aircraft carrier, had been conceived in the very different climate of the early 1980s. In recognition, however, of the disparity between the costs of such programmes and the available resources, renewed emphasis was placed upon European cooperation.

Of course, we should also recall that the domestic political environment within which these documents were produced has itself since changed significantly, following the 1995 presidential elections and the new defence cuts subsequently announced by prime minister Juppé. Further changes are in train, most notably the moves towards a smaller but wholly professional army announced in early 1996. Nevertheless, at the time of writing the documents referred to above remain the principal statements of official thinking about the future of French defence industrial and technological capabilities.

The Issue of Dual-Use Technologies

Appendix 5 of the CGP report merits special attention. Dealing specifically with 'technological aspects,' and comprising the most complete official statement to date on the issue of dual-use technologies, it was prepared by a group headed by V. Marcais, former head of the Direction des recherches, études et techniques (DRET) in the DGA.

At the outset, we can observe that the concept of 'dual-use' technologies proves to be very elastic in the usage of the report. Methodologically, it is as poorly founded as the idea of 'spin-off' which preceded it in the vocabulary of the chiefs of the military-industrial complex (Serfati, 1993). Consequently, the notion of 'dual-use' technologies can be employed for numerous policy purposes. Appendix 5 of the CGP report uses it in two particular ways.

First, the term is used as a constituent, if subordinate, element in an analysis which establishes a list of 'critical technologies' (see Table 8). Second, it is presented as a significant new feature of the technological landscape in order both to advocate a tightening of the relations within the process of innovation between the civilian and the military sectors, and to propose a larger role for the DGA in the planning and implementation of overall French technology policy.

Dual-Use Technologies and the Idea of Critical Technologies

The CGP report defines critical technologies as 'those which condition the future of defence industries in terms, first, of their military components, but also of their increasingly important civilian applications' (p. 168). The report goes on

Table 3: Critical Technologies, as defined in CGP (1993)

Key:

Dual character:

– Technology uniquely defence	O
– Technology weakly dual	X
– Technology medium dual	XX
– Technology strongly dual	XXX
– Technology totally dual	XXXX

Degree of dependence acceptable:

– Technology of which France wishes to keep total mastery, rejecting all dependence and all cooperation	F
– Technology that France is willing to share in more or less extended partnership with WEU countries, while keeping a certain national capacity	E
– Technology that France will share on a wider scale, or acquire via licenses, taking account of the existence of several suppliers globally	M

Very high military technology:

– Technology particularly sensitive to risk of proliferation of certain armaments	X

Priority A (Highest)

Critical Technologies	Comments	Dual character	Degree of dependence acceptable	Very high military technology
Nuclear technologies	Nuclear armaments	O	F	X
Structural new materials (including composites) and associated processes for their development and application	Taking into account the totality of mechanical constraints (including vibratory, acoustic and thermal), as well as fatigue, vulnerability and problems of maintenance …	XXX	Materials: E* Fibres: M Processes: E	
	Taking into account 2 fields in particular:			
	– corrosion, surface treatments	XXXX		
	– thermostructural materials	XXX	F	X
Micro/nano electronics (for systems and sub-systems)	Specific electronics	XXX	E	X
	Hardening	O	F	X
Propulsion systems	Aircraft engines	XXX	E	X
	Land and sea diesel engines	XXX	E	
	Motors and propellants for tactical missiles	O	E	
	Motors and propellants for strategic missiles	X**	F	X
	Nuclear reactors	XX	F	X
Navigation equipment	Automatic, piloted, guidance	XX	E	X
Detection equipment (sensors, receivers) and signal processing	Electromagnetic, acoustic, optic	XX	E	X
	Submarine acoustic	XX	E	X
	Data fusion	XXX	E	
	Electronic warfare	O	F	X
Control of signatures and technologies relevant to stealth	Understanding of phenomena, development of computer codes, mastery of stealth materials, distributed antennae	O	E	X
Mastery of complex systems	Conception, integration	XXX	F	X
	Architecture tools (infomatic, software)	XXXX	M	
	Modelling and simulation	XXXX	E	

* Except Fibres.

** Some duality with space launchers.

Priority B (Intermediate)

Critical Technologies	**Comments**	**Dual character**	**Degree of dependence acceptable**	**Very high military technology**
Advanced computer codes	Modelling of complex physical phenomena in the fields of: – aerothermodynamics – structural analysis – high speed dynamics – hydrodynamics – cavitation phenomena – meteorology – electromagnetic phenomena	XXX	E	
Software engineering for information systems		XXX	M	
Artificial intelligence and neural networks		XXXX	M	
Electronic module architecture	Especially for aircraft	XXX	M	
Energetic and detonating materials	Ammunition	X	E	X
	Liquid rocket fuels			
	Explosives			
Advanced computers	For massively parallel computing	XXX	E	X
Telecommunications matériel and networks	On the ground, sea, air and in space, for voice, written and image transmission	XXXX	E	
	Interconnections			
Optical and optronic devices		XX	E	X
Directed energy devices	Lasers	X	E	X
	Micro-waves	O	F	X
Power generators. Electricity storage and processing devices	For electrical propulsion and electrical weapons	XXX	E	

Priority C (Lowest)

Critical technologies	Comments	Dual character	Degree of dependence acceptable	Very high military technology
Industrial production systems	Including automatic and robotic	XXXX	M	
Shaping and processing of conventional materials		XXXX	M	
Control systems		XXX	E	
Ergonomics and neurosciences	Including cognitive sciences	XXXX	E	
Technologies and methods supporting security of weapons systems and matériel		XXXX	M	
Impact of weapons systems and matériel on the environment		XXXX	M	

to propose that, in order to avoid the trap of too open-ended a list of critical technologies, these technologies can be usefully classified according to:

- the extent to which they have dual 'civil-military' character;
- the level of dependency vis-à-vis foreign countries which France is prepared to accept in each case;
- their sensitivity with respect to arms proliferation.

They develop the first of these criteria by proposing that each technology can be classified on a scale running from solely for defence purposes, to weakly, moderately, strongly, and, finally, totally dual-use.

The second criterion is elaborated in terms of whether France:

- wishes to maintain total mastery of the technology, rejecting all dependency and cooperation;
- would be willing to share the technology with the members of the Western European Union, while maintaining a certain level of technological capability within France;
- would consent either to engage in partnerships on an even wider scale, or to acquire the technology by license agreement or purchase of matériel, taking into account numerous global sources of supply.

Finally, the criterion concerning proliferation implications would be an absolute one, turning upon whether or not a technology belongs to the group of the most sensitive military technologies. In such a case, the technology should not be diffused outside France, except perhaps to a very limited number of reliable partners.

Using these three criteria, the appendix lists a total of 24 technological domains critical to the future of the arms industry (Table 8). Eight of these domains were given the highest priority (group A), nine were given an intermediate priority (group B), and seven were given a lesser priority (group C). No great surprises emerge. Broadly speaking, the list corresponds very closely with the critical technologies list of the US Department of Defense (DoD).

The composition of group A, does, however, confirm the ever-present nuclear and aerospace priorities of the French armaments meso-system. Included within this group are nuclear technology; new structural materials; micro- and nano-electronic components, propulsion systems; detection and signal processing equipment; stealth technologies; and systems integration.

Dual-Use Technologies and the Tightening of the Network Linked to Innovation

It has been documented elsewhere how the French national innovation system as a whole (Chesnais, 1992), and the constituent sub-sections of the arms meso-system (Chesnais and Serfati, 1992), display systemic relations which are rather more extensive than those found in most other industrialised states. Nonetheless, the DGA and the other authors of Appendix 5 of the CGP report propose yet further tightening in both civilian-defence synergy and in the military innovation system itself.

Underlying this preoccupation is concern over American competition in the domain of dual use high technology and the evolution that the appendix authors foresaw in the GATT process. They considered the GATT negotiations to be 'very important for the future of the defence-linked industries which for the most part now also hold, or will hold, civilian high technology capabilities which will be the focus of relentless competition, notably between France and the United States. The clear American objective is to regain technological and commercial leadership in such sectors as aeronautics and space, where France and the rest of Europe have seized important market shares, and in materials and electronics, where Japan has taken market leadership.' (p. 157).

According to the DGA and their co-authors, the Americans would seek to impose their 'national model' of industry support. This model of support would include:

- no subsidy or loans for developing a commercial product;
- only *indirect* state support, that is, upstream of the products, including research support, exploratory development and support for demonstrator projects;
- no limitation on this last support, or if there must be one, it should be proportional to the turnover in the area in question, which gives advantage in the majority of cases to the American industry, whose vast domestic market assures them of supremacy.

In this event, the central issue for high technology French firms would be 'to augment civilian and military support for research and technological development — a route heavily exploited by the Americans.' More importantly: 'as demonstrated by the Americans, it has become fundamental to have the *political will*, manifested in a *closing of ranks* at the national level, and also at the European level, to form a more efficient 'alliance' among the diverse actors in research and technology. It is also essential to recognise the inherent difficulty that the European Economic Community (EEC) has competence only for civilian research, and that we lack, at the European level, a collaborative framework for military research'. (CGP, 1993, p. 157. Emphases in original).

The Tightening of the Network Linked to Military Innovation

Regardless of the subsequent actual outcome of the Uruguay Round, these observations remain important as an indication of French official thinking on this subject. It lead them to the conclusion that they can count only on their own strength. Thus, they wrote of the need for *concentration* of activities between the DGA, the chiefs of staff, research institutes and laboratories, and industry, at the levels of systems and sub-systems firms and equipment manufacturers. Using the current terminology of the economics of technical change, they explain that 'these organisations constitute a *network* within which must be organised a harmonisation, permitting the necessary *synthesis*, updated periodically, in such a way as to support the establishment of '*technological plans of action*' optimised with respect to estimated needs.' (CGP, 1993, p. 148).

The appendix makes detailed proposals for such harmonising of technological plans of action, including the establishment of a compulsory annual meeting of the different institutions within the network, and the formation of new coordinating structures. For these, it suggests:

- technology groups drawn from the DGA and armed services, industry, and the research laboratories, to focus on specific critical technologies; and
- a consultative committee representing all elements of the network, charged with preparing an annual synthesis of technology plans for each sector in order to make them homogeneous. It would also oversee their consistency with the results of national 'prospective' (foresight) analyses.

The perceived need to keep abreast of the US technological competition also lead the authors to press for further financial support. They argued that whereas in France the division between research, exploratory development and final development has remained fairly steady over the last decade, in the USA the research share of the procurement budget has similarly remained steady, whereas that allocated to exploratory development and demonstrator programme has increased, at the expense of final development and production. While, say the authors, it would be difficult for France to follow suit in the short to medium term, given current budgetary projections and equipment plans, it is essential at least to maintain the current level of research and technology support

Increasing the Role of the DGA in Civilian Technology Policy

The DGA and its allies do not restrict themselves to presenting recommendations for the internal strengthening of the defence meso-system, but also take aim at the organisation of French technology policy itself. Hence, they observe that there is a large domain of science and of generic technologies that is of interest to both civil and military interests, and is amenable to stronger coordination. They note with approval the concerted policies for stimulating such fields as advanced materials and processes, manufacturing techniques, and electronic components in countries such as Germany and Japan. They do not hesitate themselves to criticise the traditional French emphasis (in which they themselves had, of course, played no small part) on vertical integration via 'grands programmes' which, they say, no longer corresponds with today's requirements for the diffusion of new technologies (CGP, 1993, pp. 158–9).

From this analysis, they proceed to argue for closer coordination of the research and technology programmes of civil ministries and of the Ministry of Defence. Thus, they ask, 'Taking account of the current and future economic competition, should not the Ministry of Defence involve itself more in national technology policy?'. In a reversal of the current liberal economic discourse on the 'retreat of the state', they suggest that civil ministries would also find advantage in a better definition and coordination of techno-economic strategies for industry and the economy more generally. Hence, they call for the establishment of some 'grands programmes génériques technologiques', and for the creation of a new organisation, a 'direction de la technologie autonome', to define these programmes. (CGP, 1993, pp. 159–160)

In this respect, the recent history of the National Centre for Space Studies (CNES) illustrates this new thinking at work. The CNES, created in 1962, was the only major technologically-oriented French government agency not under the auspices of the Ministry of Defence. The crucial role of space in military strategy, underlined in the Gulf War, has since led the MoD to strengthen the ties between the space agency and the DGA. An important step was taken in August 1991 with the creation of a joint committee of the CNES and the DGA charged with harmonising civil and military space R&D (CNES, 1992). This tightening of institutional links was described by the heads of the CNES as, 'very original from the point of view of what is done in other places, notably the United States, and very well-suited to French strengths … (It is) of immense importance to the future' (CNES, 1992). The 'co-tutelage' thus introduced defines a new stage in relations between these organisations.

International Collaboration in R&D by French Companies

Both the *Livre blanc* and the CGP report emphasised the need for increased international defence technological cooperation. In practice, cooperative R&D programmes at the level of French companies are very limited in scope. The annual amounts invested in this area are only a few hundred million francs (MF): 100MF with Germany, 70MF with the United Kingdom, 60MF within EUCLID. These sums represent barely 1% of the military R&D budget. It is interesting to note in passing that, insofar as this was its aim, the EUCLID programme has had difficulty in 'federalising' European military R&D: thus, the French investment is less than that devoted to cooperation with Germany or the UK.

In view of the ever-rising costs of R&D, the DGA advocates a strengthening of European cooperation, both East and West. With the countries of Western Europe, a special effort is being made to integrate testing facilities[7] (cf. also the UK chapter, this volume), and in a more general sense, to establish joint exploratory development programmes. With the countries of Eastern Europe, efforts are concentrated on the development of intensive contacts with high-level scientific researchers (De Saint-Germain, 1993). There could be as many as 150 cooperation agreements with the countries of the East for a total of 50 million francs (*Les Echos*, 28 April 1993).

The DGA also favours strengthening cooperation in research and technology among the member states of the WEU. In this respect, it has taken the lead in the formation of a joint Armaments Agency with Germany and others (see Introduction), intended in due course to operate with wider membership under the auspices of the WEU. The DGA seeks, likewise, to involve itself more closely in the formulation of research proposals by French industry for participation in the EUREKA programme; believing that some EUREKA programmes have dual-use characteristics that could benefit the MoD.

Conversion and Diversification

To conclude, we offer a few words on the subjects of policy on defence conversion and diversification, and on controlling the diffusion of defence-related technologies.

There has been great stability over two decades in the list of leading French defence contractors, and correspondingly little interest in conversion to civil production. In the 1980s, however, certain highly specialised military firms began to develop a degree of diversification based on the technical expertise derived from their military activities. This was the case within the aerospace industry, particularly with Aérospatiale and SNECMA. The electronics groups, on the other hand, have had more limited success with diversification, the difficulties being pronounced at Thomson, and to a lesser extent at SAGEM and Dassault-Electronique. The Matra group (defence electronics) has diversified, not by transfer of military technology to civil purposes, but mostly by acquisition of other firms, including space activities and, far removed from its high technology activities, also publishing interests.

More recently, the defence cutbacks have led the public authorities to consider the problems facing military specialist companies. But this has not resulted in any thorough-going policy of defence conversion. At the most, it has resulted in consideration of a few proposals for assisting diversification, and mainly of small and medium enterprises (SME).

To help these SMEs, the MoD created in 1991 a *Delegation for Restructuring* (DAR) whose objective was to help the restructuring of the armed forces and the arms industry. The DAR manages the *Fund for Reconstruction and Employment in Defence*, which was awarded FF 100 million in 1992, and FF 160 million in 1993 and 1994.

MoD officials are not optimistic about the possibilities for diversification of SMEs. They believe that most arms companies which intend to will already have diversified their activities, and that further possibilities will be limited. (CGP, 1993, p. 206). Moreover, the officials charged with these questions are sceptical about the technological and commercial capacities of SMEs, estimating that only one company in three is capable of successful conversion. According to DGA estimates, this conversion could take from 18 to 36 months (*Les Echos Industries*, 28 April 1993). Nevertheless, these same officials argue that diversification issues do fall within the purview of the State and should be supported, but by funds allocated by other ministries (CGP, 1993, p. 224). The disbursement of these funds, however, in their view, should still be directed by the MoD.

Overall, therefore, we see no French organisations or institutions proposing wholesale conversion of their military activities. On the political level, all of the major parties (those represented in Parliament) support the continued existence of a strong arms industry (though some favour reducing the nuclear emphasis). Thus, the Rafale programme, with an estimated cost of FF 200 billion, is supported by all the political parties, all the unions, and by a wider public.

While diversification activities can be played out on the micro-economic level, measures dealing with defence conversion demand an ensemble of macro-economic measures. There is little sign of these emerging, even with the more substantial recent defence cuts. Essentially, the armaments meso-system has embedded itself firmly in the national economy, and constitutes a type of enclave which thus far has proved very difficult to dislodge.

Controlling the Diffusion of Defence Technologies

The official regulations regarding the export of arms are very rigorous. The decree-law of 18 April 1938 is the basis for the control of exports. In principle, all exports of armaments are forbidden[8] but the state can nonetheless authorise exports according to very strict rules. For example, each sale of war matériel, and of equipment for its construction, is subject, prior to the decision of the prime minister, to the opinion of the Interministerial Commission for the Study of Exports of War Matériel (CIEEMG). Arms leave the country only after the Minister of Finance has delivered an Authorisation for the Export of War Matériel (AEMG). Additionally, in the past COCOM controlled the export of military goods or dual use goods (Ferrier, 1991).

Other documents have been written to support this law in principle. France adheres to the guidelines of the Australia Group, created in 1984, which in 1992 published the first export control list of 'dual use' materials related to chemical and biological weapons (Daguzan, 1993). France has also ratified the Missile Technology Control Regime (MTCR).

Nonetheless, the government has been wary of proposals from the US government since the Gulf War aimed at restricting arms exports. The French see these proposals as linked to the unprecedented effort from the Bush and then the Clinton Administration to increase the market share of American producers and force the French and the British out of markets where they had previously dominated. Moreover, as we have seen, the French arms industry, and economy, depend to an important extent on arms exports. All the official reports of the last few years emphasise this point, and express concern over the decline of exports since the end of the 1980s. The reports suggest that, in the face of the aggressive stance of American producers on the export markets, the French government should engage more strongly in the support of French exporters. Thus, a 1993 parliamentary report (Galy-Dejean, 1993) argued that political activities must come into line with efforts to conquer markets, and should no longer work at cross-purposes to them.

Despite the implication in these reports that arms and technology export regulations are hampering French industry, it is clear that, at least in the past (e.g., Kolodziej, 1987), arms sales have often bypassed diplomatic channels and made a mockery of the allegedly strict rules. Hence, while the government is clearly concerned to prevent exports to certain countries, in general there is strong pressure in favour of arms exports (Serfati and Chesnais, 1995).

With respect to the control of dual use goods and technologies, a licensing system aimed at what is termed *control of final destination* is applied by the Ministry of Industry. That is to say, judgements about the issuing of authority to export depend not only on the technology (a list of controlled materials and sensitive technologies being published in the *Journal Officiel*), but also on the purchaser and on the country in which the technology will finally be used.

The control of technology exports is also affected by Interministerial Instruction 486. This instruction was established by the Secretary General for National Defence (SGDN) in 1982 to protect French scientific and technological property within international exchanges. Certain of its measures[9] are specifically oriented towards military and dual use technologies. Thus, the DGA has the right of oversight on all patent registrations, including those not directly relevant to the military industry, and the DGA can prohibit or delay the granting of a patent if the technology could enhance national security[10].

In addition, the new penal code, as reformed in July 1992, makes the transgression of rules regarding technology transfer punishable as an attack on the fundamental interests of the nation[11].

In terms of internationally agreed controls, France seeks complementary relations between the EU and other control regimes. As regards the European Commission's attempts to introduce dual use controls, there has been considerable debate over how to resolve differences over whether certain items should be classified as dual use or as military goods, with the French government often taking the tougher view. (Ferrier, 1991). As for the discussion over a successor to COCOM, France has been reserved on the idea of a 'Super-COCOM', that is, a body to regulate north-south as well as the traditional east-west trade, preferring instead better enforcement and strengthening of established systems.[12]

Conclusion

France is today still the leading European country in terms of defence equipment expenditure and general determination to maintain an independent capability in this sector. Behind this present position lies a long and deeply embedded tradition, though one whose consequences for overall French industrial and technological development can be questioned. At the same time, there is now a clear political appreciation that the budget levels of the past can no longer be sustained; that significant restructuring of the industry is required; and that industrial and technological capabilities must increasingly be achieved on a European, rather than a national, basis.

The French arms industry, built as a 'meso-system' at the end of the 1950s, is today facing its greatest change in 40 years, with the nature of any new equilibrium point still far from clear. Some argue that the current changes could be so dramatic as to lead to an '*implosion*' or '*mutation*' of the system (Hébert,

1995). Alternatively, the deepening cuts in the workforce, the privatisation of the major companies, the increase in European collaboration, and the streamlining of the DGA can be seen simply as a major reshuffling of the elements of the system, in an attempt to maintain its essential character (Serfati 1995).

Endnotes

1 F. Chesnais contributed to parts of this chapter. We thank Tiffany Tyler for the translation.

2 An important exception is Dassault-Systems, which produces large-scale, integrated software solutions for mechanical design and manufacturing (Computer Assisted Design and Manufacturing (CAD-CAM)). Dassault-Systems has links with IBM, which owns 10% of the company.

3 According to its chief executive, cf. *Le Monde,* 8 June 1993.

4 Within each annual budget (finance law), the parliament also includes *programme authorisations*, which are elements of expenditure for equipment programmes which go beyond a specified time period. But only those *payment authorisations* which are written into the finance law may actually be spent.

5 There were 5 budgetary sections: land, sea and air forces, national guard, and common (which includes nuclear expenditures).

6 These are Aérospatiale, Alcatel-Alsthom, Thomson, SNECMA, Matra-Hachette.

7 cf. P.I. de Saint-Germain, then head of DRET (Research Directorate of the DGA): 'Each time an investment exceeds 5 million ECUs, we act in concert [with the Germans and the British, C.S.] to eliminate duplication of facilities,' *Les Echos*, 28 April 1993.

8 Article 13 of 18 April 1938 stipulates: 'The exportation through any customs administration whatsoever, without authorisation, of war equipment or equivalent goods, is prohibited.'

9 These measures define procedures concerning scientific and technical cooperations and those concerning visits and internships, as well as rules concerning foreign nationals wishing to work in 'sensitive' installations and rules for French nationals living abroad.

10 Interview with a DGA official.

11 According to Article 410.1, 'The fundamental interests of the nation are understood to mean its independence, its territorial integrity, its security, the republican form of its institutions, its means of defence and diplomacy, the safety of its population within France and abroad, the defence of its "natural situation" and environment and the essential interests of *its scientific and economic potential*, and of its cultural patrimony.'

12 Cf. Annie Kahn, *Le Monde,* 30 April 1993.

References

Bensadoun, M., 1990, 'Politique de recherche des industries d'armement', *L'Armement,* no. 25.

Bérégovoy, P., 1992, *Projet de loi de programmation militaire pour les années 1992–1994*, Paris: Assemblée Nationale, 1 July.

Boucheron, M., 1992, *Rapport relatif à l'équipement militaire et aux effectifs de la défense pour les années 1992–1994*, Paris: Assemblée Nationale, no. 2935, 7 October.

Chesnais, F., 1992, in R. Nelson, *National Innovation Systems: Comparative Analysis*, Oxford: Oxford University Press.

Chesnais, F. and Serfati, C., 1992, *L'industrie française d'armement: genèse, ampleur et coût d'une industrie,* Paris: CIRCA Nathan.

Chesnais, F., (ed.), 1990, *Compétitivité internationale et dépenses militaires,* Paris: Economica.

Commissariat Général du Plan, 1993, *L'avenir des industries liées à la défense,* Paris: La Documentation française.

Conze, H., 1994, Délégué général pour l'Armement, Interview, *La Tribune Desfossés,* 13 January.

Curien, H., 1993, Ministre de la recherche, communication, *Conseil des ministres,* 12 February.

Daguzan, J-F., 1993, 'Diffusion de la technologie et détournement, communication aux journées d'études du SGDN', *Sécurité collective et crises internationales,* Toulon 9 and 10 September.

De Saint-Germain, P-I., 1993, 'Politique scientifique et technique du ministère de la défense', *Les recherches de défense 1993,* Paris: DGA-DRET.

DGA, 1993, dossier 'La DGA et la préparation de l'avenir', *Armées d'aujourd'hui,* no. 185, November.

DGA, 1994, 'Réorganisation de la DGA: ce qui va changer', *Info-DGA*, no. 60, January.

DGA-DRET, 1993, *Les recherches de défense 1993,* Paris: DGA, 1993.

Ferrier, M., 1991, 'Le contrôle à l'exportation des matériels sensibles', *L'Armement*, no. 26, February/March.

Fontanel, J. and Ward, M.D., 1990, 'Les exportations d'armes et la croissance économique', *ARES*, vol. 12.

Galy-Dejean, 1993, *Rapport d'information, La crise des industries de défense*, Paris: Assemblée Nationale, no. 552, October.

Gras, O., 1987, 'Les composants électroniques dans la défense', *L'Armement,* December.

Hébert, J-P., 1995, *Production d'armement: Mutation du système francais,* Paris: La documentation française.

Hollande, F., 1993, *Rapport sur le projet de loi des finances pour 1993, annexe no. 39, Défense*, Paris: Assemblé Nationale, no. 2945, October.

Huffschmid, J. and Voss, W., 1991, *Defence Procurement, the Arms Trade and the Conversion of the Armaments Industry in the Community*, Bremen: Progress-Institut für Wirtschaftsforschung GmbH, May.

Javelot, M., 1993, 'Point de vue', *Défense et Technologie,* no. 12, March.

Kolodziej, E.A., 1987, *Making and Marketing Arms, The French Experience and its Implications for the International System,* New Jersey: Princeton University Press.

Labbé, M-H., 1993, 'Le contrôle à l'exportation des technologies de pointe, communication au colloque de I'IRIS', *L'avenir de l'industrie de défense,* Paris, 9 June.

Les Echos industries (Dossier), 1993, 'La difficile reconversion de I'industrie d'armement, *Les Echos,* 28 April.

Marx, P., 1993, 'Gallois oriente Aérospatiale vers un holding industriel', *La Tribune Desfossés,* June.

Ministère de la Défense (1994), *Loi de programmation militaire 1995–2000,* Paris: Imprimerie Nationale.

Ministère de la recherche et de l'enseignement supérieur (MRES), 1990 and 1995, *Etat de la recherche et du développement technologique*, Paris: Imprimerie Nationale.

Müller, H., 1993, 'The Export Controls Debate in the "New" European Community, *Arms Control Today,* vol. 23, November.

Paecht, A., 1994, *Rapport sur le projet de loi de finances pour 1994, annexe no. 39, Défense*, Paris: Assemblée Nationale, no. 580, October.

Paecht, A. and Balkany, P., 1993, *Rapport d'information sur la politique militaire de la France et son financement*, Paris: Assemblée Nationale, no. 452, September.

Perrin, P., 1992, 'Interopérabilité', *DGA Science et Défense,* Paris: Dunod, vol. 2.

Playe, 1983, 'La DGA et la définition des armements', *L'Armement,* October.

Pouplard, J.P., Zigmann, R. and Sandt, F., 1992, 'La dualité en vision pour la robotique mobile', *DGA Science et Défense,* Paris: Dunod, vol. 1.

Schmidt, C., 1992, 'La portée économique des lois de programmation militaire', *Défense Nationale,* March.

Senges, G., 1991, L'Aérospatiale se donne des allures de holding, Les *Echos,* 10 June.

Serfati, C., 1990, 'L'économie francaise et le fardeau des dépenses militaires', *Les Temps Modernes,* no. 524, March.

Serfati, C., 1990, 'Stratégie et contraintes d'un groupe francais à spécialisation: l'exemple de Thomson", in Chesnais, 1990.

Serfati, C., 1991, 'Primauté des technologies militaires, faiblesse des retombées civiles et déclin de compétitivité: le cas de l'industrie électronique francaise', *Communication au Colloque international "Maîtrise sociale de la technologie',* Lyon (MSHR) September.

Serfati, C., 1992, 'Le méso-système de l'armement et son impact sur le système productif de la France', *ARES,* vol. 13.

Serfati, C., 1993, 'L'emprise coûteuse des technologies militaires', *Mondes en développement,* 3rd trimester.

Serfati, C. and Messisi-Lavorel, L., 1995, 'L'innovation militaire et l'industrie des biens d'equipement en France: quelques hypothèses de travail', *Innovation,* (L'Harmattan), no. 2.

Serfati, C., 1995, *Production d'armes, croissance et innovation,* Paris: Economica.

Serfati, C. and Chesnais, F., 1995, 'Imperieuses et coûteuses exportations d'armes', *Observatoire des transferts d'armement, Rapport 1995,* Lyon.

Southwood, P., 1991, *Disarming Military Industries: Turning an Outbreak of Peace into an Enduring Legacy,* Houndmills and London: Macmillan.

Chapter 3
Germany

Peter Lock and Werner Voss

Introduction

The impact of the radical political changes in defence and security policy since the later 1980s has been far more pronounced in Germany than in other parts of Western Europe, for several reasons.

First, and quite unexpectedly, Germany became reunited. The National People's Army (NVA) of the former GDR was partially integrated into the Bundeswehr before its dissolution. The internationally agreed ceiling of 370,000 soldiers to be achieved by the end of 1994 was to be approximately half the manpower of the two armies before unification. By late summer 1994 more than half a million persons belonging to the Soviet Red Army were withdrawn from the territory of the former GDR. The troops of NATO allies stationed in the former FRG also saw considerable cuts. Thus, 853,000 soldiers will have disappeared from German soil, a reduction of 62%.

The dissolution of the NVA and the ensuing extensive restructuring of the remaining resources continues to absorb virtually all available planning resources of the German Ministry of Defence. The employment consequences of winding down the armed forces in Germany elicit wide-spread local and regional opposition which impedes the on-going redeployment of units. Nevertheless, additional cuts were proposed by the minister of defence in April 1994 and March 1995 because the available financial resources did not suffice to support a modern army of 370,000.

Second, Germany has had to cope with the huge costs of reunification. So far, the net transfers absorbed annually by the new Länder have been in the range of DM 150 billion, with a steady upward trend. By the end of 1994 the diverse 'hidden budgets' were expected to accumulate liabilities of well above DM 500 billion (for a detailed analysis of the costs see: Hoffmann 1993). This volume of debt severely restricts the financial flexibility of the government for the years to come and limits such policy options as an active industrial policy, for example.

Third, Germany fulfilled its CFE obligations to reduce its armour mainly by eliminating heavy weapons that it had inherited from the former GDR. The stocks of defence matériel which came to be administered by the Bundeswehr were beyond the imagination of western intelligence. They included 52,000 trucks, 25,000 trailers, 1,500 motorbikes, 295,000 tons of ammunition, 1.2 million hand guns, 4,500 tons of liquid fuel for missiles, 760,000 items of clothing and 600,000 pieces of personal equipment. The government managed to sell at bargain prices or donate most of this unwanted surplus matériel, but a lot remained to be dismantled and disposed of at considerable cost. However, this disposal activity did at least provide a new market niche for the ailing ammunition industry.

Fourth, the new international circumstances provoked controversy concerning German participation in military missions out of area. The positions taken ranged from contending that all conceivable actions were permissible under Germany's Basic Law, to the view that any activity of men in uniform outside the NATO-mandate violated the Basic Law. The first position was confirmed by the Federal Constitutional Council on 12 July 1994, but the constitutional court ruled later that German participation in international peace preserving operations is a feasible option of German foreign policy. It also emphasised the role in such matters of the United Nations and ruled that the government cannot act on its own; it must seek an absolute majority of all members of parliament.

Finally, under long-standing NATO arrangements, Germany has supported Turkey, Greece and Portugal with military equipment by heavily subsidising the purchase of equipment or by 'cascading' refurbished equipment in large quantities. In the wake of severe budget restrictions, German defence industrial, naval construction and tank production in particular will be affected, as this 'military godparent' regime is not likely to be continued.

Basic Data

The Organisational Context

Reflecting historical experience, the military in Germany are clearly subordinated to civilian control. The institutional framework of arms procurement reflects this deliberate policy. Requests for weapon systems are formulated by a military hierarchy within the Ministry of Defence, but their implementation is the responsibility of the Armaments Division in cooperation with the Federal Office for Defence Technology and Procurement (BWB — Bundesamt für Wehrtechnik und Beschaffung). The BWB was established in 1957, clearly separated from the ministry, with the legal status of a 'supreme federal authority'. It runs several test centres (Wehrtechnische Dienststellen) and laboratories (Wehrwissenschaftliche Dienststellen) as well as arsenals. Its headquarters are located in Koblenz, while the other agencies are widely dispersed throughout the former FRG.

In addition, the MoD is required to coordinate its defence programmes with the Federal Ministry of Economics. This puts it under tighter control than non-military state procurement activity (e.g., railways or mail) which has traditionally been conducted under the sole control of the relevant authority (Bontrup, 1986, p. 53).

In response to the recent costly reduction of the armed forces, an assumed expansion of tasks and the severe budget limitations, the MoD is determined to cut costs radically wherever possible. Struggling against bureaucratic inertia and entrenched interests, it envisages a profound rationalisation of its procedures at every level (*Wehrtechnik*, No. 1/1994, p. 5).

As a first step, more precise job descriptions were introduced in order to eliminate high levels of duplication. The BWB is targeted to cut 4,000 of its present 17,000 employees by the year 2000. At the same time, major responsibilities pertaining to the procurement process were transferred from the MoD to the BWB, including that for the Research and Technology Programme (RTP, on which more below). The share of procurement orders administered by the BWB will increase beyond the present level of 70%.

The enhanced duties of the BWB include:

- management of complex projects
- systems technology (integration of technical devices into complex systems)
- systems technology within preliminary phases
- other tasks in the field of research and technology not assigned to MoD
- procurement
- major technical tasks including checking of quality
- major economic tasks (contract monitoring and assessing prices)
- major administrative tasks and control.

The existing parallel capacities of the test centres and laboratories will be amalgamated into single institutions. Furthermore, the departments of weapons and ammunition technology and the department of missiles were merged in 1994. The responsibilities of the division for communications technology and electronics underwent a major reorganisation at the end of 1994 whereby its mandate for procurement was reduced. This change reflects the rapid technological progress in the field of communications and data processing, which today is determined by innovation in the civilian markets and not by extensive military research. The MoD intends to take advantage of off-the-shelf civilian technology, in order both to reduce costs and to improve the quality of procurement.

In contrast to the USA, the former USSR, the UK and France, the FRG abstained from creating large state-owned military laboratories. Instead, about two-thirds of the military R&D budget is designated as 'applied research'. It involves close connection with the development of specific weapon systems such as fighter aircraft, naval ships and tanks. The bulk of contracts is awarded either to private companies or so-called 'supporting institutions', mostly independent non-profit general research institutions.

Extensive (though unwarranted) secrecy concerning R&D prevents us from specifying the distribution by sectors and companies, but rough estimates indicate that the lion's share of the thousand contracts awarded annually goes to only a few companies. The various defence producers, now concentrated under the roof of Daimler Benz, were reported to receive 25% of total military R&D expenditures in 1987. Siemens is another major contractor. Both receive an equally large share of civilian R&D funds.

While industry receives more than half of the military R&D budget, about one third is allocated to publicly funded research institutes. The rest goes into applied research in universities, two of which actually belong to the MoD, and other institutions.

The Publicly Funded Research Infrastructure in Germany

Funding for public research institutions comes from both the federal and state (Länder) governments — directed basically at four types of institution.

A. *Großforschungseinrichtungen (GFE)*

16 different GFEs carry out research in fields which were considered central to the strategic competitiveness of German industry at the time of their creation. Their activities are typically long-term and they have invested heavily in large research facilities. Total manpower in 1992 was 24,000, and the budget was DM 3.5 billion. The fields covered include (nuclear) energy, environmental problems, space and aeronautics, and bio-technology.

The German Research Institute for Aviation and Space Technology (DLR — Deutsche Forschungsanstalt für Luft-und Raumfahrt) is by far the largest engineering research institution in the FRG, with a budget of over DM 800 million (1992), more than 4,000 staff, and seven (geographically dispersed) major facilities. Major fields of research are flight engineering/flight control, aerodynamics, materials/construction, communications technology, reconnaissance and energetics. The relevance of the research for military aircraft technology is obvious, though MoD contracts cover only a portion of the DLR budget.

B. *The Max Planck Society (MPG)*

Founded in 1911 as the Kaiser Wilhelm Society, the MPG comprises over 60 research institutes which perform basic scientific research, most of which is in the natural sciences. The linkages to the MoD are negligible.

C. Institutes of the Blue List

The Institutes of the Blue List comprise a wide range of independent research organisations, jointly funded by federal and state governments. They work in such disparate fields as social science, economics, medicine, biology, history, and scientific museums. Although the overall budget of these institutes is almost 1 billion DM, there are no visible linkages to the MoD.

D. The Fraunhofer Society (FhG)

The Fraunhofer Society is mandated to transfer research results into industrial use with particular emphasis on innovation in products and production technology. In 1993, the FhG budget was one billion DM. Its staff totalled 7,800, of which 2,600 were scientists and engineers as well as roughly 1,000 graduate or doctoral students. It is structured into 47 independent institutes, working in a wide variety of fields. Five institutes work exclusively for the MoD, while others have absolutely no defence connection. Defence research funding at the FhG in 1993 totalled DM 66 million, of which DM 55 million came directly from the MoD. The balance came from industry on the basis of MoD contracts they were carrying out, together with one joint project with the Ministry for Science and Technology.

The FhG was created in the early 1950s by the state of Bavaria in support of its regional industrial policy. The broadening of its sponsorship was relatively slow and it was only in the early 1960s when the MoD began to award demanding, medium range contracts, that the FhG consolidated its existence. When the liberal/social-democratic government took over in 1969, the FhG was chosen to carry out a large portion of the greatly expanded industrial policy the federal government was undertaking. This big push laid the foundation for its present structure. Most FhG institutes receive research contracts from industry. On average, one third of the budget derives from contracts awarded by industry and one third governmental research projects, including contracts with the MoD.

With its apogee of military research in the 1960s, the FhG is typical of the institutional path of military R&D in Germany. (Interestingly, data in the 1993 Annual Report suggested that the average age of defence scientists in the FhG is markedly higher than for scientists in the former FRG as a whole, confirming the idea that the defence institutions reached their peak in the 1960s.) The relatively small size of the individual units and the built-in competition for research contracts from industry and government agencies have allowed an unusual flexibility. Thus, institutes are used to reorienting their focus. Even fully military-oriented institutes have taken the initiative to move into civilian applications of their research. The Institute for Applied Materials Science (Institut für angewandte Materialwissenschaften) is one example. This Bremen-based institute has been diversifying since the beginning of the 1990s, for which purpose it entered into formal cooperation with the University of Bremen.

E. Other

Some other arrangements outside this general institutional framework must also be mentioned. One is the Research Institute for Water, Sonar and Geophysics operating under the direct control of the MoD. The Research Society for Applied Natural Sciences (Forschungsgesellschaft für angewandte Naturwissenschaften) carries out research on high frequency physics, data processing, optics, sensor data in particular and electronic warfare. Wholly financed by the MoD, in 1993 its budget was DM 45 million and the staff totalled almost 350.

The Industrieanlagen Betriebsgesellschaft GmbH (IABG) was established in 1961 at the MoD's initiative to provide research facilities for the evolving aerospace industry. Its mandate gradually expanded into systems analysis, simulation, project management and the application of operations research. Most of its revenue came either directly from the MoD or via industrial research contracts related to military projects. From 1990 onwards, the IABG faced a sharp reduction of military orders, to below 50% of its income. However, public sector orders still represent 80% of its turnover, because the IABG successfully entered the field of monitoring the environmental damage caused by military activities on German territory, especially in the former GDR, where the Soviet troops left a heritage of environmental damage. But with a clear, finite time associated with this particular diversification activity, the future of this establishment is insecure. The government failed to interest a German or European consortium in taking it over, and IABG was finally taken over by the US company BDM. It had 1,500 employees and recorded a turnover of DM 350 million in 1993.

Finally, dating back to the early 1950s, there is a joint Franco-German research institute in Saint Louis. It employs 500 people in military research (aerodynamics, ballistics and measurement). The German contribution was almost DM 40 million in 1993.

This short overview of the institutional framework and trends in military R&D in Germany reveals a strong tendency towards decentralisation and towards further privatisation of activities. The MoD has also taken steps to give civilian innovation an important role in procurement. While most of these changes reflect a secular trend dating back to well before the end of the Cold War, overcoming the inertia of the system has been greatly assisted by sharp defence budget cuts. The cost of German reunification has clearly been the most important factor in a major restructuring of the defence sector. The present trend tends to increase the structural differences between Germany on the one hand and the UK and France on the other. The rhetoric of centralising procurement, and by implication, R&D at a European level, is clearly contradicted by this rapid restructuring in Germany.

German Defence Industry

With respect to military procurement, turnover and employment in the defence industrial sector, Germany belongs to the 'Big Three' in Western Europe. The German defence industry is comparable to its French and British counterparts as far as conventional weapons are concerned. This is particularly evident in the case of naval shipbuilding, which gained larger shares of the international market during the last decade (Voß, 1993), and for tank construction. New technological developments like the development of a vehicle with a single all-electric propulsion system may even gain a competitive edge in international markets (*Wehrtechnik* 11/1993, p. 56). Certain components like diesel engines, 120 mm guns and gear boxes have already gained dominant positions in international markets, notwithstanding national procurement policies. These positions are related to civilian synergies or reflect an implicit know-how gained in almost one hundred years of specialisation.

The standing of the German aerospace industry is more ambiguous. In the design of military fighter aircraft, France and the UK clearly dominate. So far, there has always been political support for keeping the German aircraft manufacturers as partners in European co-production projects, even at high costs, the declared aim being to catch up and to maintain a production base for fighter aircraft. This political decision put Deutsche Aerospace in a relatively fragile position with respect to military aircraft production. While the corporate strategy of its parent, Daimler Benz, focuses on global markets — still civilian by definition — the envisaged production of the Eurofighter neither offers significant military-civilian synergies nor contributes to a strategic expansion of markets, in the former Soviet Union in particular. The equipment industry, on the other hand, claims to be fully competitive in several important areas. The huge merger of the aerospace industry under the aegis of Daimler Benz provides it with strategic financial resources, but also subordinates it to the corporate logic of its parent on questions of restructuring and efficiency.

However, the production of defence matériel is only a small part of German industry. According to the respected IFO-Institut, the number of jobs directly or indirectly depending on defence production in 1991 was 280,000 (IFO 1991), or 1.1% of the total work force. Decreasing procurement reduced employment, so that by late 1994, only 130,000 jobs — directly or indirectly dependent on defence orders — were left, a reduction of more than 50% within 4 years. Quasi-official estimates anticipate a further reduction that could amount to as much as another 50,000 jobs lost in the next three to four years. (*Kieler Nachrichten*, 29 October 1994).

The German defence industry is characterised by the dominance of the private sector and its relatively high concentration. These features were reinforced by a profound restructuring of the defence sector throughout the 1980s. The result of this restructuring is reflected in the ranking of companies by turnover (Table 1). Daimler Benz moved from position 18 in 1983 to the top position after successively taking over MTU, AEG (TST), Dornier and MBB. Its dominant position was further strengthened by acquiring the Dutch company Fokker. Siemens AG, ranking second, also internationalised its defence business by purchasing part of Plessey (UK), although defence production remains below 2% of its turnover and is strategically negligible. In contrast, Rheinmetall AG, Diehl GmbH & Co, as well as the Bremer Vulkan Group, expanded their defence businesses by purchasing German defence companies, while Rheinmetall and Bremer Vulkan also diversified, by acquiring civilian companies. Hence, in spite of their military acquisitions, they reduced the share of defence in total production. However, there are no signs so far of an international network in defence production beyond strategic alliances.

Nor is there an international network in naval shipbuilding. One of the major strategies that shipyards pursued in the aftermath of the crisis of merchant shipbuilding in 1975 was to shift towards naval export markets. Indeed, the export of naval ships became an important asset in their survival strategies. Their success was based on technological innovation (modularisation) and systematic international sourcing of subsystems and components.

The ten largest defence research and procurement projects are shown in Table 2, from which the dominance of the Eurofighter project can be clearly seen.

Nominal military expenditures have declined, but only slowly, since 1990. However, this apparently low rate of reduction conceals more than it reveals, since a considerable share of the defence outlays have gone to cover the high costs of partially integrating the former NVA into the Bundeswehr, and extending the military infrastructure to cover the whole territory of the reunited Germany. Since personnel expenditures are not flexible in the short term, the consequences of these reductions have fallen mostly on investments (meaning equipment procurement plus spending on physical infrastructure such as bases, barracks, etc.). However, in a pre-election speech in 1994, Chancellor Kohl promised that the military could plan on the basis that the budget has bottomed out at DM 48 billion, and that the armed forces could expect increases in line with inflation.

Table 1: The Main Defence Corporations in Germany

Rank 1983	Rank 1991	Corporation	Arms products	Arms turn over in 1983 (Mn DM)	Arms turn over in 1991 (Mn DM)	Arms share of turn-over in 1991 (%)	Total employment 1991
18		Daimler Benz	V, A, H, M, EL,	320	6550	7	379250
18		– *Mercedes Benz*	E, V	320	490	1	237442
n.a.		– *DASA , of which*	A, H, M, EL, E	n.a.	6060	49	56465
		– *MBB*	A, H, M, EL	>3290	2450	51	20730
		– *Telefunken System*	EL	<1926	1130	83	8846
		Technik	E	1133	1950	32	17052
11		– *MTU*	A, EL, M	640	530	45	9527
		– *Dornier*					
		Siemens	EL	2000	1500	2	402000
12		Diehl	EL, I, M	582	1326	44	15529
15		– *Bodenseewerke*	M	>440	190(a)	67(a)	n.a.
n.a.		Bremer Vulkan	WS, EL	100	1300	39	15021
n.a.		– *Systemtechnik-Nord*	EL	n.a.	710	75	2441
15		– *Atlas Elektronik*	EL	215	474	59	4259
		Rheinmetall	O, I	936	1280	37	13661
		– *MAK System Gesellschalt*	V, OT	<828	n.a.	n.a.	n.a.
		Thyssen	V, WS	729	1280	4	148557
10		– *Blohm & Voss*	WS, V	781	660	49	5758
12		– *Nordseewerke*	WS	236	320	64	2084
13		– *Henschel*	V	493	300	22	3976

Table : *continued*

Rank 1983	Rank 1991	Corporation	Arms products	Arms turn over in 1983 (Mn DM)	Arms turn over in 1991 (Mn DM)	Arms share of turn-over in 1991 (%)	Total employment 1991
n.a.		Mannesmann	V	>0	657	3	125188
		– *Krauss-Maffei*	V	1880	657	46	5004
11		Lurssen	WS	279	640(a)	81(a)	1080(a)
16	10	HDW	WS	1000	490	42	4866
n.a.	n.a.	MAN	V, WS	n.a.	385	2	64170
n.a.	n.a.	Mainz Industries	V, OT	n.a.	350	100	2700
n.a.	n.a.	Dynamit Nobel	IOT	n.a.	320	18	8646(a)
n.a.	n.a.	Bosch	EL	n.a	250	1	181498
n.a.	n.a.	IABG	OT	n.a.	145	51	1650
n.a.	n.a.	IWKA	0	n.a.	152	8	8539
n.a.	n.a.	Krupp	V	n.a.	n.a.	n.a.	n.a.
n.a.	n.a.	SEL	EL	n.a.	n.a.	n.a.	n.a.
n.a.	n.a.	Wegmann	V	n.a.	n.a.	n.a.	n.a.
n.a.	n.a.	Rhode & Schwartz	EL	n.a.	n.a.	n.a.	n.a.

(a) = data from 1990.

Sources: SIPRI company data bank; Grundmann and Matthies (1993).

Arms products: A = aircrafts, E = engines, EL = electronics, H = helicopters, I = infantry weapons, M = missiles, O = ordnance, OT = others, V = vehicles, WS = war ships.

Table 2: The Ten Largest Defence Projects

Weapon system	Numbers planned	Costs of research and procurement (in billion DM)
Support Helicopter (UHU)	360	17
NATO Helicopter 90 (NH-90)	272	>10
Eurofighter 2000	140	>22
Tactical Air-Defence System (TVLS)		
Air Independent Submarine	4	3.5
Frigate 124	4	3.5
Supplier EVG 702	2	0.5
Corvette	6	
Reconnaissance Vehicle Zobel	262	
Modernisation of Leopard 2-tanks	252	

Sources: M. Martin and P. Schafer, 'Die Bundeswehr als Instrument deutscher Machtprojektion', *Blatter für Deutsche und Internationale Politik*, No. 1 (1994), p. 44; and various issues of *Wehrdienst*.

Expenditures for military research and development fell more slowly to a level of DM 2.5 billion by 1993 (see Table 3). This figure compares with a total of approximately DM 80 billion for all research and development in Germany. It should be noted that the reunification process has been associated with a relative increase of the governmental share of R&D relative to private industry (OECD *Science and Technology Statistics*, 1993).

Policy Towards Defence and Dual-Use Technology

Initially, the FRG relied on the private sector to carry out military R&D and did not create institutions within the public domain. The military orders were believed to enhance the competitiveness of the German manufacturing sector. It would also have been a demanding task to create a public research infrastructure while the defence bureaucracy itself was still in the process of formation.

Table 3: Development of Certain Sections of the Einzelplan 14 (in billion DM)

Year	Einzelplan 14	of which			
		expenses on personnel	expenses on investments	expenses on procurement	expenses on research and technology
1985	48.872	20.616	16.640	11.605	2.461
1986	50.188	21.33	17.468	12.254	2.487
1987	51.089	22.009	17.383	11.970	2.812
1988	51.223	22.447	16.828	11.610	2.759
1989	52.524	23.116	17.093	11.367	3.030
1990	53.366	23.871	17.013	10.833	3.296
1991	53.605	26.825	14.420	9.115	3.055
1992	52.107	25.949	13.149	7.790	2.994
1993*	49.600	26.300	11.1	6.6	2.5
1994**	48.481	24.991	10.6	5.870	2.2

* preliminary information.
** planned outlays.
Sources: Information supplied by the Ministry of Defence, 1992 and 1994.

A few sectors, aerospace in particular, were developed with massive government support and direct intervention. While proclaiming straightforward market economics as its guiding principle, the Ministry of Economics explained the interventionist policy practised in this sector in terms of the limited number of manufacturers able to integrate systems, as well as the unique characteristics of the international market for large civilian aircraft.

Another example where the procurement of military equipment served as an instrument of interventionist economic policy, in this case stabilisation of the shipbuilding industry in a specific region, was the construction of a series of frigates (F-122) which was spread across five different shipyards.

The concentration of the aerospace sector in 1989 under Daimler Benz was only possible because the Minister of Economics overruled a decision of the Federal Cartel Office, which had opposed the mergers on the grounds that they turned Daimler Benz into the largest defence producer in Germany. The MoE argued that only the resolute leadership of a globally-oriented company like

Daimler Benz would be capable of correcting the profound deformation of the German aerospace sector caused by three decades of political intervention by federal and state (Länder) agents. Daimler Benz was apparently seeking synergies between the aerospace and automotive sectors.

Government Policy Statements on the Future of the National Defence Technology Base

In anticipation of sharp defence cuts, preliminary studies on the future of the German defence industry had begun as early as 1992. Five working groups were set up within official circles, with the aim of establishing the thresholds of indispensable industrial capacities needed in order to preserve the technological capabilities of the different branches of the defence sector. They aimed first to reach provisional conclusions, and then to review these by the spring of 1995.

The five working groups focused on:

(1) tank construction
(2) aerospace and astronautics (military aircraft, helicopters, missiles)
(3) ammunition
(4) shipbuilding
(5) information technology/electronics

Although the recommendations were not officially published, they were leaked in a lobby newsletter at the end of 1993 and again in the spring of 1995. As might be expected of a bureaucratic-industrial panel, the outcome basically sought the preservation of the minimum capacities across the whole spectrum of military manufacturing. The recommendations covered a wide range of issues:

- further reduction and (cross-border, if necessary) concentration of industry, together with reduced scope for competition;
- restructuring of procurement by integrating the phases of research and development;
- reorganisation of programme timespans;
- introduction of support programmes;
- EC-based harmonisation of regulations for the export of armaments and their application;
- reasonable compensation in the case of foreign procurement.

Confronted with tight budgets for the foreseeable future, industry demanded that the preservation of the key technological and economic areas of armament should become an integral part of Bundeswehr planning. The defence industry considered it indispensable to increase the proportion of procurement expenditure within the defence budget, while pursuing all possibilities to rationalise further and to seek additional support.

All working groups concurred with the demand to preserve national capabilities for the development and integration of state-of-the-art weapon systems and main sub-systems (system capability), and for the production of critical components (component capability).

According to the MoD, support for the maintenance of the national research and development base is indispensable because (Heyden 1992, p. 13):

- The credibility and acceptability of the national defence policy presupposes a capacity to contribute to the NATO defence technology base, and in particular to verification technology.
- There is an international consensus that active participation in the formulation of security policy presupposes a sufficiently developed technology base.
- Advancing Germany's security strategy also demands a sufficient scientific base for independent evaluation.
- The participation of Germany in cooperative development and production involves risks that should be minimised by the use of carefully tested components and modules. In order to improve control of time and costs, the early (more research-oriented) phase of system design should be extended.
- In an environment of decreasing budgets, the growing complexity of future weapon systems will require international cooperation to start earlier, at the concept evaluation stage, as opposed to the present development stage.
- The role of research and technology during the present phase of arms reduction is ambivalent. As technological capabilities are difficult to assess, only quantitative reductions can be relied upon. It is therefore of increasing importance to rely on the autonomous ability of a country to respond fast, and with flexibility, to changing scenarios with the appropriate defence technology.

Additionally the following issues were emphasised by the MoD:

- minimising dependence on foreign countries;
- minimising the risk of buying obsolete products;
- preservation of national state-of-the-art technology;
- maintaining sensitivity with respect to certain product areas;
- difficulties involved in the eventual reconstruction of a particular industrial capacity once it had been abandoned.

The detailed list of technological capabilities which the working groups concluded should be maintained in the national domain is reproduced in Appendix 1.

This joint report of MoD and the defence industrial sector reflects the traditional pattern of military development and procurement policy. Virtually all basic fields of technology are given priority, though it is questionable whether all these capacities can in fact be maintained, as the government has refused to support the defence sector in addition to placing normal procurement contracts. The IABG is a case in point. While the preservation of this company was considered to be indispensable to an independent national capacity in systems analysis and risk evaluation in the field of artillery, the government nevertheless consented to its take-over by an American company.

At the same time, more radical thinking is also gaining ground. In 1993, the chairman of Rheinmetall — a major traditional arms manufacturer (smooth bore guns, machine guns, anti-aircraft artillery) — gave a talk about developments in the field of defence technology at the annual meeting of 'Wehrtechnische Gesellschaft'. His views of the future of defence technology reflect the interrelationship between general economic development, industrial innovation in particular and military security. Whereas the MoD/defence industry prescriptions do not take account of the industrial and economic parameters of future defence production, this manager attempted to draw a realistic picture of the development of the defence industry, saying:

> An important element of the defence industry within the new framework seems to be the design of production for the future equipment of the army. I am talking about the intensity of armament specialisation concerning the structure of production of defence matériel. As far as I am concerned, we had already reached the point from whence expenditures in time and money — compatible with success — for the development of defence matériel were no longer appropriate. We have asked ourselves for many years why, for example, electronic gun fire-control equipment had to be developed anew when state-of-the-art equipment useful for this purpose is already developed by the civil industry.
>
> ... If the defence industry intends to stay competitive, supplying the army against the background of a decreasing budget, the appropriate strategy would be to cut back the intensity of armament specialisation of the products in order to reduce the requirements for development and to lower the costs of production.
>
> In the future, the proportion of civil components used for defence matériel has to be markedly increased. Only the level of product integration should be militarised ...
>
> ... Looking at the problem from a technological point of view, the fact that spin-ins from the civil industry already outweigh spin-offs from the defence industry shows the strategy of lessening the intensity of specialisation of armament products to be realistic.
>
> ... Scientists in the defence industry will have to concentrate hard on creating new systems by reducing the intensity of defence specialisation of the product.' (Manuscript of the speech)

While there is hardly any commonality between the proposals of the five working groups and this view by a defence industry manager, it seems certain that the severe financial drain of German reunification will influence political decisions towards more economical forms of defence procurement in the way the defence manager suggested, rather than by following the maximal demands of the MoD working groups. A selective approach concerning the preservation of capacities is inevitable. Priorities are not likely to be chosen on a strategic basis; rather, case by case decisions will lead to an implicit selection.

Budgetary Trends

The strategy of using, for military purposes, technologies which emerge from civilian activity was already part of the 'Research and Technology Programme' (RTP), initiated by the current conservative-liberal government as early as 1985. This strategy is based on recommendations by the 'Commission for the Long-term Planning of the Armed Forces' (Kommission für die Langzeitplanung der Bundeswehr). Within the framework of the Planning Concept of the Armed Forces, the RTP is produced, with the aim, *inter alia*, of guaranteeing that technological developments in civilian areas are also considered for military purposes. The RTP is formulated in joint working groups of the service branches and the Armaments Division. R&D targets are discussed in detail with industry and military-oriented research institutes. Only after these extensive deliberations are research projects proposed to the Secretary of Defence for approval.

The RTP is evaluated and updated every year. This procedure ensures that in accordance with changes of military concepts, any necessary reorientation of the development of advanced defence technology is integrated into the planning process (*Wehrtechnik* no. 12/1990, p. 81).

This new emphasis is reflected in the defence budget. In 1991, DM 766.2 million were divided between:

- the field of 'military research' (Wehrtechnische Forschung) with DM 265 million;
- a sub-section called 'technology of the future' with DM 324.5 million; and
- 'systems technology' with DM 176.4 million.

In 1993, the plan for the Armed Forces made provision for research funding to rise steadily from DM 550 million in 1993 to DM 690 million in 1999 (*Wehrdienst* No. 1304, p. 2). Because, however, of substantial changes in the MoD's planning procedures, these numbers give only a rough indication of the future volume of defence research.

The broader context of these trends is that, from 1987, the budget for defence research and technology began to decrease, with the cuts falling mainly on the industrial contractors. By 1991, the volume of contracts awarded annually to industry had fallen nominally by DM 172 million compared to 1987, and its share of all military R&D contracts from 49% to 43% (Heyden, op. cited, p. 14). The military oriented research institutes fared slightly better and at least saw their relative share increasing.

In the 'Bundeswehrplanung' 1993, freezing the budgets at current prices (thereby making reductions in real terms) established a new trend. Thus, the research institutes Deutsche Forschungsanstalt für Luft-und Raumfahrt, Fraunhofer Gesellschaft, Forschungsgesellschaft für Angewandte Naturwissenschaften and the Franco-German Institut St. Louis were set to receive DM 203 million in 1993, and DM 202 million in the years to follow.

This financial stagnation has entailed a reduction of personnel at these institutes. The Fraunhofer Institut für angewandte Materialforschung has been transferred from the MoD to the BMFT (Federal Ministry of Research and Technology) with a concurrent reduction in personnel. Another Fraunhofer Institut specialising in hydro-acoustics was closed down in 1993. Further drastic personnel reductions are under consideration, especially at institutes in Göttingen (DFLR/aerodynamics), Braunschweig (DFLR/aerospace) and Freiburg (FhG/Ernst-Mach-Institut).

Developments in Institutions

The apparent impact of the on-going reorientation of military policy on research policy, particularly as regards dual-use technology, is minimal. The project orientation of military research in Germany has, however, put the various institutions on permanent alert to look for new projects, either military or civilian (Burton/Hansen 1993, p. 37).

The approach taken by the TZN research and technology centre in Lower Saxony (Technologiezentrum Nord), created in 1986, is an example of such a strategy. Officially, the TZN is a joint initiative by the state of Lower Saxony and Rheinmetall. Lower Saxony's contribution to the foundation of the 'high-tech' institute was a DM 100 million loan. Additionally, local companies have formed a society in support of the TZN.

TZN, situated next to the premises of Rheinmetall in Unterlüß, received administrative support from the company. In mid-1992, TZN had 86 employees, working on sensors, lasers, microelectronics, test and installation methods, computer-aided simulation and computer networks.

The contracts TZN secured in 1990 and 1991 were half military, half civilian. The proclaimed aim of the institute is to achieve a 2:1 ratio in favour of civilian orders, with the focus on aerospace and astronautics, robots, production automatisation and conservation technology. Rheinmetall managers have stated, however, that progress towards diversification has been much slower than expected, mainly, they suggest, because of the economic recession.

Participation in International Collaborative Defence Research Projects

The Government of the FRG has always emphasised the need for international cooperation among the countries of both Western Europe and North America in the development and production of arms. Over 70% (or DM 4 billion) of its main projects are based on international cooperation, (letter from the MoD, 4 March 1993). Thus, the 1985 Defence White Paper formulated the goals of 'political, military, economic and technological' cooperation as follows (White Paper 1985, pp. 360–361):

> The political aim is the still closer integration of the (NATO) Alliance.... The military aim is the standardisation of equipment and procedures. Where standardisation cannot be attained, the member states should at least aim at interoperability of equipment. The economic aim is to make more effective use of national public funds for defence...
>
> The technological aim is an increased exchange of technological and scientific know-how. This interchange of experience and knowledge increases the capability of national industries, as military systems are technologically most demanding devices.

In addition, efforts to achieve intensified international competition (such as the initiatives of the IEPG) have been consistently supported by the FRG.

Major International Corporate Joint Ventures

Given the size of the US arms market in contrast to the 'small' and nationally fragmented Western European markets, the large German manufacturers give priority to the creation of large, transnationally operating units capable of facing the American competition. Only a single consolidated European procurement market will secure the conditions which would stimulate the restructuring and rationalisation of the European arms industries, they contend. Thus, the then chairman of DASA, and later chairman of Daimler Benz, has called for the formulation of a joint European export policy, and the completion of the privatisation of state-owned or state-controlled defence industries as a prerequisite for the formation of enterprise alliances and transnational groups in defence production (Schrempp 1994).

German defence firms consider themselves equal to their West European counterparts and, in certain product ranges, even superior. The use of German engines and gear boxes for the Leclerc tank and naval shipbuilding are examples of particular technological excellence. Industry constantly criticises German export regulations for discriminating against German manufacturers.

Furthermore, the dominant manufacturers pursue a strategy of focusing on certain product ranges, and being prepared to shed others. The transfer of its helicopter development capability to Aérospatiale illustrates this approach by DASA. The emerging global alliance to build a 'very large commercial transport aircraft' confirms the corporate long-term strategy. At the same time, though, DASA has lobbied jointly with other European companies for the funding of the military future large aircraft (FLA) (Schrempp 1994).

In the FRG, military technology is mostly incorporated into the general innovation system. This explains why so few changes have been made thus far to adjust the system of military development and procurement to the new post-Cold War scenario. It may, however, also be the case that the MoD is too weak to impose fast and far-reaching changes against the vested company and regional interests. So far, the MoD appears to be geared towards 'a preservation of existing structures', although it is safe to predict that the financial situation in Germany will generate a transformation of the defence industrial sector towards further specialisation, and increasingly, the adoption of dual-use technologies.

While the defence industry seems set for an aggressive European strategy, all serious political attention to far-reaching decisions was suspended for a period prior to the 1994 parliamentary election. It was noticeable during the election campaign that there was no significant opposition to the Chancellor's pledge concerning stability in the defence budget. Since the election, the opposition has been in agreement with the government regarding appropriate and stable defence expenditures.

Policy Towards Conversion

Past Experience

The political and analytical debate about the restructuring of defence resources reached its climax in the mid-1980s (Grundmann/Matthies, 1993, p. 12). One part of the debate focused on the situation of the work force in the defence industry. Declining defence orders had begun to threaten the traditional job security in the sector. Conversion was conceived as a formula to mitigate the negative employment consequences of procurement cycles, to reduce the pressure from the industry for an expansion of arms exports, and to compensate for the reduction of defence orders following the emerging conclusion of arms control agreements.

The discussion was also oriented towards qualitative concepts of economic development. The social utility of potential alternative production became a focus of discussion. The resources tied to the production of armaments were to be transferred to areas of social deficit, such as social and environmental programmes, as well as foreign aid. Alternative non-military production was not to be oriented towards existing civilian markets, but to satisfy social and ecological needs. In a number of enterprises, union-oriented employees established task forces for the development of alternative production, modelled on the initiative by shop stewards of Lucas Aerospace in the UK.

Short-term interests at the enterprise level were to be replaced by a long-term orientation towards social and global interests. However, the supporters of this strategy were unable to convert their preferences into operational concepts either at the enterprise level or through the political process. Financial constraints and other claims on public funds prevailed, and the federal government refused even to launch a pilot programme for conversion.

Political pressure in favour of conversion came mainly from the unions and, in a broader sense, from a left-wing, union-oriented and peace-committed public. Politicians at the federal level and company management hardly reacted to the pressure from below because they either remained committed to the continuity of the Cold War pattern (a perception greatly reinforced by the arms drive of the Reagan administration) or were committed to corporate diversification within the prevailing market structures, as opposed to a potential market of politically-regulated demand. As a consequence, the federal government was not prepared to define an explicit policy on restructuring the resources of the defence industry:

> The federal government neither can nor wants to assume responsibility for the defence industry. It tries to keep indispensable defence capacities continuously employed, although it is unable to give any guarantee on employment and orders. This can also be applied to essential changes of structure and size of defence capacities that result from varying priorities of the Bundeswehr planning, putting increasing stress on essential parts of systems like ammunition and command systems (White Paper 1985, p. 369).

The disarmament processes between 1990 and 1992 significantly changed the situation. The question of defence restructuring reappeared inescapably on the public agenda. But this time, the spectrum of discussion was much broader. The dramatic reductions of troops stationed in Germany created profound economic problems at regional levels. However, the ensuing debate focused on the closure of bases, and did not give comparable attention to the problem of converting industrial plants.

Current Government Policy Towards Industrial Conversion

After the end of the Cold War, several reports on the defence industrial sector concluded that disarmament, defence cuts, and industrial conversion did not pose serious challenges for Germany's industrial economy. Compared to the

USA, the UK and France, German companies have generally been less dependent on military spending. For example, the IFO-Institute for economic research in Munich rejected the idea of a nation-wide programme for conversion in its report *Produktion von Wehrgütern in der Bundesrepublik Deutschland* (IFO 1991) for the Ministry of Economics. According to the IFO:

> Since there is no resistance to expect either at the national economic, or at the sectoral level that could possibly overtax the mechanism of free enterprise adaptation, there is no need for governmental support of the defence industry. Regions being affected by large-scale dismissals are entitled to draw on support from regional economic programmes, as well as on resources provided by the Law on Employment Promotion.

While the Federal Government concurred with the IFO's position, those Länder mostly affected by the reduction of troops and defence orders demanded that a programme of support be launched by the Federal Government. Thus, the issue of conversion was discussed at the level of the Fachminister, both from the Länder and the Federal Government, within the framework of the Conference of the Ministries of Economics in 1991. Agreement on a basic commitment for a regionally and structurally oriented programme for conversion was achieved. However there are major disagreements among the Länder, and between the Federal Government and the Länder, concerning the time frame, the criteria for applicability of the programme, and who was to pay for it, which remain unresolved.

In December 1991, the issue was withdrawn from the agenda of the Fachminister conferences, and resolved instead through the mechanism of mediation between the Länder and the Federal Government over the distribution of tax revenue in 1992. In practical terms, this meant that the funds were to be distributed in order to cope with a broad range of problems. Restructuring of the defence industry was clearly not a top priority.

Some Länder decided to institute their own schemes. One such was Bremen, one of the major centres of the defence industry in Germany. For centuries, the Free Hanseatic City of Bremen has served as an international port and a centre for all types of shipbuilding. Naval shipbuilding promoted the growth of a maritime and naval electronics sector through upstream linkages. The local aircraft industry is also partly military. In 1990, about 13,000 jobs were directly or indirectly dependent on defence orders (almost 14% of all industrial jobs in Bremen). Some companies were as much as 75% defence dependent (BAW 1990, 1991; and Elsner 1993). According to EEC data, Bremen is the third highest Defence Industry Dependent Region in western Europe, behind the UK regions of Cumbria and Essex (EEC 1992).

To complicate matters further, the Bremen economy is structurally weak, even apart from the defence industry. This is because of structural shocks, mainly in shipbuilding, fisheries and steel, in the 1970s and 1980s. For example, in the shipbuilding sector, the work force decreased from 21,000 in 1975 to about 6,500 by 1992. The decline of the shipbuilding sector initiated an on-going debate on regional restructuring. Defence conversion is therefore but one aspect in this discourse.

Bremen's state government commissioned a study which produced *A Report on the Consequence of Demilitarisation for Bremen and on Possible Actions* (BAW 1991). This report concluded that 4,500 industrial jobs were in danger from procurement cuts expected through 1996, constituting one in three of the region's defence jobs. Since the regional economy could not offer alternative employment the report recommended conversion within the existing facilities.

The State of Bremen initiated and coordinated discussions among experts, the public, companies and unions. As a result, a state conversion programme, an integral part of a comprehensive economic policy programme for the region, was approved by the state parliament in 1992. The prime objectives were supplying subsidies for pilot projects in defence-oriented enterprises and for conversion investment, providing risk capital for newly founded firms, and developing the R&D infrastructure in Bremen.

A regional conversion fund was established in 1993 with almost DM 10 million, including a contribution from the EU PERIFRA programme. Bremen planned to spend DM 10 million in 1994 and in 1995; DM 15 million were ear-marked for 1996. The long-term plan proposes annual increases of the conversion fund until the year 2004. A further contribution to this strategy arises from Bremen's success in being funded by the EU KONVER programme until 1998, to the tune of DM 18 million.

Each company applying for conversion subsidies is requested to submit a corporate medium-term conversion plan, containing articulated goals for reducing defence dependence, for transforming specific military know-how into civilian know-how, and for training employees to meet future civil market requirements. The programme is coordinated by a Commissioner for Conversion, supported and reviewed by a wide-ranging advisory committee.

This conversion programme combines an economically acceptable restructuring framework with transparency, cooperation and political participation. Using these measures, it appears feasible to overcome ambiguous short-run 'market' signals, as well as to support calculated and coordinated projects which speed the necessary transformation of industry, in a way that reduces the risk of further job losses.

In contrast to the situation in Bremen, the labour market in other Länder is more affected by the reduction of troops and the closure of military bases. Therefore the emphasis of conversion programmes elsewhere is on reinforcing the regional economy, and not the support of specific industrial enterprises.

In some of the Länder, defence enterprises receive support from foundations created to promote technological innovation. In some cases the Fraunhofer Gesellschaft is involved in advising on restructuring, and many regional and local authorities offer the services of technology transfer departments. A particularly interesting case is the technology foundation in Schleswig-Holstein created in 1992. The sale of government shares of HDW, a major shipyard in Kiel engaging in naval production, provided the funds. The aims of the foundation explicitly include the support of enterprises engaged in converting their military production. Some success stories of small enterprises are attributed to the support the foundation gave in down-stream fields like market exploration, product selection and marketing.

Mention of these activities should not obscure the fact that very little government subsidy is available for these conversion programmes, and the companies concerned have to rely mainly on their own resources.

Controlling the Diffusion of Defence Technologies

Arms exports have long been a politically sensitive issue in Germany. Article 26 of the Basic Law reflects German history, and tries to draw lessons from Germany's role in two world wars. In the early post-second world war years, all activities relating to German production and sale of armaments were controlled by the Allied High Commission. In time, however, Germany became a full member of all the major arms export control regimes. The Law on Foreign Economic Relations (Aussenwirtschaftsgesetz — AWG) of 1961 served to regulate foreign trade, particularly under the COCOM agreements. A regulation appended to the law (Aussenwirtschaftsverordnung — AWV) contains a list of commodities covering weapons of war and strategic goods which the government had pledged to control under the COCOM agreements.

The early controls imposed upon it meant that the German defence industry was never allowed to compete fully in the Arab oil-producing countries, even though Kuwait was a major shareholder in, among others, Daimler Benz (about 10%). A special relationship with Israel largely confined the German role in Arab countries to co-production, where the partner nation nominally figured as exporter.

As industrial pressure for a free hand in arms exports began to mount, the government chose to grant export licences by stretching its own regulations to extremes. After the global crisis in shipbuilding in 1975, the government decided to license virtually all naval exports (although a large Taiwanese naval order was denied by the government, strategic trade interests in China having prevailed). Even clearly aggressive dictatorships became eligible for naval exports. Commenting on one such favourable decision, a Social Democrat

Minister of Defence argued that at least submarines could not be used against domestic opposition parties.

In trying to accommodate the increasing pressure arising from an arms industry that was suffering from cyclical procurement and a lack of entrepreneurial initiative, as well as a politically vocal peace-oriented general public, the Liberal/Social Democrat government formulated and published new guidelines for the export of armaments in 1982. The successor Conservative government maintained these guidelines. The government also relinquished its veto against exports in all cooperative production schemes within NATO, insisting only that recipients of German weapons outside NATO should not be in an 'area of tension', a criterion that turned out to be of limited significance in practice.

The export of defence technology as such has never been particularly important to the German economy, in sharp contrast to exports of machine tools and construction of industrial installations abroad. In practice, therefore, recent years have seen the export of, in effect, dual use capabilities that have been used to develop arms capabilities. Successive German governments failed to exert diligent controls and accepted most civilian applications stated in the licence applications at face value. Germany hence became the preferred supplier of any country that aspired to establish its own arms industry (like Libya, Iran and Iraq), or (like South Africa) was under an mandatory arms embargo.

These practices came under political scrutiny only after the delivery of a poison gas factory was discovered in Libya, at the same time as disclosures concerning the export of sensitive technology to Iraq. Faced with these events, a major review was undertaken of the law to control weapons of war (Kriegswaffenkontrollgesetz). In general, the government showed an unprecedented eagerness to support all international control regimes. Most significantly, a list was appended to the law, with a set of countries whose trade would be monitored with particular care.

Exporters are now required to make a declaration that, to the best of their knowledge, the exported item will not be used for 'the establishment or the operation of an installation for the exclusive or partial manufacture, modernisation or servicing of weapons, munition or military matériel'. In addition, the management is held legally responsible for all export activities concerning its company; courts do not have to prove its active involvement. This clause is a reaction to the increased sophistication of potential buyers of sensitive technology who try to disguise their aim by deliberately splitting their orders. The participation of German specialists in weapons production and missile projects outside the OECD countries was also brought under the export controls.

The AWG and AWV now provide tighter controls over the final destination of commodities with respect to both export and import. (Imports also came under scrutiny because Germany was found to have served as a transit country for sensitive transfers: a case in point was heavy water from Norway to India in the 1960s). The requirements of the various international regimes were translated into different lists of commodities which require a licence. Even when COCOM reached a consensus to reduce considerably the list of items to be monitored or excluded from export to former Communist countries, the German government did not correspondingly reduce the lists of the AWV because, by then, the geographical focus of trade to be monitored had shifted.

Politically, therefore, the government has in recent years displayed an unprecedented resolve to bring sensitive trade under control. The export control administration has been restructured and its personnel tripled, the customs authorities have been reinforced, and the protection of personal privacy can now be temporarily lifted if there is reason to suspect an infringement of export regulations. Nevertheless, the vigorous export orientation of German manufacturing industry must be recalled in order to put these controls into perspective. The control of exports is a truly Herculean task, with 18 million separate transactions to be monitored annually.

German export controls today, in comparison to their state at the end of the Gulf War, have improved considerably. Given the profound damage to the image of German industry which the spectacular cases of illegal exports of military technology for the manufacture of weapons of mass destruction had caused, there was initially a broad consensus, including the powerful Association of German Industrialists (BDI), that the inconvenience and commercial disadvantages of strengthening export controls was in the best interest of all parties involved.

More recently, however, industry has begun to lobby for a reduction of existing controls, claiming that present German practice seriously disadvantages both German exports and the international cooperative prospects of German companies. The strong national consensus behind the tightening of controls had perhaps been helped by the expectation of the arms industry that the integrated European market would soon come into effect, providing less stringent European export controls. During 1993, it became evident that a European solution would take some time to evolve and that its likely configuration would pose problems for the special situation of Germany. The continuation of the tightened German controls has led to the arms industry resuming its criticisms of them.

The campaign of the Association of German Industrialists, and the arms industry, has prompted rapid government action. The government decreed a reduction in the list of sensitive countries to twenty countries, with a further reduction to only eight or nine projected for the spring of 1995. Hence, while on paper the regulations continue to look tight, their geographical scope is in the process of being considerably reduced.

This outcome suggests that the dichotomy reflected in Germany's post-war foreign economic policy between Article 26 of the Basic Law, which embodies Germany's political role in the first half of the century, and the free trade philosophy pressed by specific industrial interests, is shifting away from 'moral' restraints on exports. Reunification may have tipped the balance. On the other hand, we should also note that, in comparison with Britain, the structure of German industry as a whole gives military-industrial interests a more limited voice.

If the defence sector does follow the path of the rapidly globalising civilian industry, the leading German players in the global economy can be expected to exert pressure for abandoning Germany's historical position in this field. Thus, we may hypothesise that the strong pressure of the BDI anticipates the rapidly increasing share of civilian components in the total of value added in future military production as well as the ensuing internationalisation of military manufacturing. The Japanese, for example, do not export weapons, yet their products are embodied in every modern weapon system produced in the United States, a position that German players in the global economy would like to emulate.

The German Arms Industry in a European Context

Harsh political decisions (including the decision over procurement of the EF 2000) were postponed until 1995 and the assumption of office by the new government, and even then not all were decisively resolved. The European political context will have a major impact on these decisions or, to put the point conversely, these decisions will be a test of the viability of continued political integration of Europe.

Several mutually exclusive scenarios have their respective lobbies. Some scenarios require the renewed creation of an ideological consensus as a necessary precondition for increasing defence expenditures considerably. Another option, in order not to depend on superior American military technology, would be to introduce a European-wide 'peace tax' (rather than a peace dividend). Pre-1995 French budgetary decisions heralded this option, though Europe as a whole moved in the opposite direction.

Other options require a new geo-strategic orientation, aiming at integrating Eastern Europe, including Russia, into the European commonwealth of democratic and highly industrialised nations. This option presupposes an integration of the military-industrial and research and development capacities of Russia and Western Europe. For the time being, this is beyond the horizon of the establishments entrenched in the German MoD and defence industries. Neither are the relevant actors in Russia mentally prepared to envision such an option. All other options involve confrontation and renewed armaments development, production and marketing, possibly even less regulated than during the Cold War.

In the absence of a broad new pro-defence consensus in Western Europe, the economic realities are likely to impose profound and deeply unwelcome changes onto the dominant national defence establishments. The relentless globalisation of production and markets is rapidly taking root in Eastern Europe as well. The German economy, being more directly exposed than other industrial nations, is likely to spearhead such developments. It is a difficult task, though, given the historical apprehension of its neighbours, especially concerning German relations with Russia.

Though the agenda of procurement issues still reflects bureaucratic inertia and projects launched years ago, the Eurofighter being the most visible example, the future European defence equation will emerge in the context of these new political and geo-strategic options involving hitherto unknown complexities. The future course of the German defence industry and its stance towards international cooperation will be an important element in this equation.

The rhetoric of integration, cooperation, co-production, and interoperability has dominated the discussion for at least two decades within NATO, and more recently within the revived WEU as well. The institutional web of intended cooperation contrasts with the reality of entrenched national military-industrial interests, which have successfully fended off rationalisation, internationalisation, division of labour, and the formulation of a European military doctrine. As a result, there are few viable transnational corporations capable of generating civil-military synergies, and of assimilating the huge potential of civilian innovations into weapon systems and their manufacture. The European defence industry is still not part of the thriving global networks which dominate the civilian economy.

The first manifestations of rapid restructuring have, however, begun to emerge in Germany. Nowhere else in Europe is the defence industry quite as integrated into the dynamics of the global civilian markets. Moreover, Russia's economy with its over-sized military-industrial complex is about to enter the global stage, yet Russia's comparative advantages are already being integrated into the global production networks of corporations like Daimler Benz and Siemens. Given, finally, the change of technological paradigm, whereby civilian industry sets the pace of technological innovation, will a strict separation of civilian and military activities still be a viable strategy within the production networks of these large global corporations, of the type which now controls the core of the defence industry in Germany?

Whatever the preferences of the industrial actors involved, it is unlikely, that Germany can pursue a scenario of its own liking. The burden of history limits the parameters of independent German action without creating severe dissonance among its Western partners. Here, however, our analysis would have to return to the structural differences at both governmental and industrial levels that bedevil attempts at integration of the European defence sector. How this European quagmire of contradictory defence-industrial interests will eventually evolve is difficult to predict. Radical changes are in the offing, but their pace and direction will result from a complex political equation, as entrenched actors attempt to pursue their own interests in the guise of national interest.

Appendix

Key Technology Areas

The following areas were listed by the working groups of the MoD as potential national preserves to be protected by future defence planning (cited in: *Wehrdienst* no. 49, 6.12. 1993, p. 2):

Working Group on the Construction of Tanks

- tank protection
- tracks and suspensions
- hull and turret

Working Group on Cannons and Ammunition

- tank cannons and ordnance
- automatic guns
- ammunition of tanks and artillery
- smart ammunition for cannons
- propellants
- anti-personnel and anti-tank mines
- smoke and decoy mines/ammunition

Working Group on Aerospace and Astronautics/Military Aircraft

*system management firms

- capability of realising research in the field of definition and development in a cooperative manner
- physics of aviation, friend-foe identification
- highly stressed, highly integrated and camouflage constructions (stealth)
- landing gear and integration, hydraulics

*engine construction firms

- capability of realising cooperative research in the field of definition and development
- development of components
- engine control systems
- testing

*key areas of equipment

- flight control and engine control systems
- process data computer including software
- communications, navigation
- displays
- mission avionics

Working Group on Aerospace and Astronautics/Drones

*system management firms

- capability of realising cooperative research in the field of definition and development
- carrier and airframe technology
- air navigation
- processing sensor data and information, transmission of information, mission planning
- test and flight experiments

*equipment industry

- FLIR, static-free data transfer, radar warhead
- engine, gyropilot

Working Group on Aerospace and Astronautics/Helicopters

- development of high technology components (for instance, rotor and rotor control)
  verification through simulation projects

Working Group on Missiles

- homing warheads
- radar homing warheads

- infrared homing warheads
- combination of fuse/warheads
- engine

Working Group on Naval Shipbuilding/Naval Technology

- anti-ship warfare, air defence and anti-submarine warfare with sensors and data processing
- dissimulation through signature management and air independent propulsion
- anti-mine sensors, anti-mine simulation and clearing technology as well as remote control and data transmission technology used by anti-mine drones
- task and cost optimised platforms and their components
- reconnaissance instruments, signal intelligence and code instruments, ECM installations and databases

Working Group on Information Technology/Electronics

* data processing/information systems

  - command information systems
  - combat and operational weapon systems
  - combat command technology
  - simulation technology

* communications technology

  - communication networks
  - radio
  - cryptography
  - navigation (except aeronautical navigation)
  - identification

* reconnaissance technology/fire control technology

  - radar technology
  - optronics/optics
  - other sensor technologies (multi-sensors, sonar technology)

* electronic warfare
  - signal intelligence
  - electronic countermeasures
  - supportive measures

References

Arbeitsgemeinschaft Schiffbau/IG Metall, 1993, Bezirk Küste, Kurzfassung der VSM-Studie Roland Berger & Partner GmbH, *Perspektiven der Wettbewerbsfähigkeit der deutschen Schiffbauindustrie*, Hamburg.

BAW 1990: Heinrich Gräber and Gerd Voss: 'Zur Rüstungsabhängigkeit des Landes Bremen: Analyse und wirtschaftspolitische Schlußfolgerungen'; BAW-Monatsbericht 3–4.

BAW 1991: Wolfram Elsner und Gerd Voss, 'Bericht zu den Abrüstungsfolgen für das Land Bremen und zu den Handlungsmöglichkeiten', in *Regionalwirtschaftliche Studien* No. 9, Bremen: BAW.

Bontrup, H-J., 1986, *Preisbildung bei Rüstungsgütern*, Köln.

Brixle, M., 1993, *Neue Geschäftsfelder und Konversionsstrategien, Probleme, Lösungen und Fallbeispiele*, München.

Brückl, S., 1994, 'Krauss-Maffei — Pionier ökologisch orientierter Konversion?' in: S. Brückl, A. Burger, R. Erben, E. Petri, M. Simon (ed.), *Betriebliche Konversion, Erfahrungen — Probleme — Perspektiven*, Münster.

Brzoska, M., 1986, *Rüstungsexportpolitik*, Frankfurt.

Burton, D.F. and Hansen, K.M., 1993, 'German Technology Policy: Incentive for industrial innovation', *Challenge*, January/February.

EEC, 1992: Commission of the European Communities, Directorate General for Regional Policies, *The economic and social impact of reductions in defence spending and military forces on the regions of the Community* (Study prepared by Economists Advisory Group in conjunction with the Centre for Defence Economics, University of York), Brussels/ Luxembourg.

Elsner, W., 1993, 'Industrial Defence Conversion: Guiding the Market at the Regional Level', paper presented at the annual ASSA/AFEE-meetings, Anaheim, CA, January.

Fock, H., 1993, 'Zur Zukunft des europäischen Schiffbaus', *Wehrtechnik* no. 1/1993.

Grundmann, M. and Matthies, M., 1993, *Kleinere Bundeswehr und weniger Rüstungsproduktion: Konversion als regionale und betriebliche Gestaltung*, Münster/Hamburg.

Heyden, J., 1992, 'Forschung und Technologie im Rüstungsbereich', *Wehrtechnik* no. 4/1992.

Hoffmann, L., 1991, *Warten auf den Aufschwung*, Regensburg.

IFO, 1991: Ifo-Institut für Wirtschaftsforschung, M. Berger, W. Gerstenberger *et al.*, *Produktion von Wehrgütern in der Bundesrepublik Deutschland*, Munich.

Mey, H.M., 1993, *Die Zukunft der deutschen wehrtechnischen Industrie*, IAP-Dienst, no. 19–20, Bonn.

Pfeifer, S., Voß, W., Wilke, P. and Wulf, H., 1993, *Rüstung und Abrüstung in Deutschland — Perspektiven für Rüstungsindustrie und Rüstungskonversion*, ISA Schriftenreihe No. 5, Hamburg/Bochum.

Pottmeyer, K., 1991, *Kriegswaffenkontrollgesetz*, Kommentar, Köln.

Schrempp, J.E., 1994, '"Partnerschaft für den Frieden" heißt mehr denn je "wirtschaftliche Partnerschaft" ', *Handelsblatt* no. 29, February 10.

Voß, W., 1992, *Die Rüstungsindustrie vor unsicheren Zeiten. Strategien und Diversifikationsbemühungen rüstungs-orientierter Unternehmen*, Bremen.

Voß, W., 1993, *Langfristige Entwicklungen und Trends im deutschen Marineschiffbau*, Bremen.

White Paper, 1985, Federal Ministry of Defence, *White Paper 1985*, Bonn.

White Paper, 1994, Federal Ministry of Defence, *White Paper 1994*, Bonn.

Wulf, H., 1991, 'The Federal Republic of Germany', in I. Anthony (ed.), *Arms Export Regulations*, Oxford University Press, for SIPRI.

Chapter 4
Greece

Anthony Bartzokas

Introduction

The European defence market is in unprecedented flux. Demand is falling and shifting in composition, governments are reviewing the regulation of internal and external markets, and industries are reorganising within and across frontiers. How to manage effectively defence technology and procurement needs without distorting the civilian economy, have therefore become acute problems for advanced Western European countries. The R&D costs imposed by the development of defence technological capabilities on these countries' economies, and thus eventually on their geopolitical standing, provide one reason for their interest in reducing the burden of military expenditure, and in finding more efficient ways of organising the domestic defence industrial base. There are other, even stronger, pressures to change the relationships between states and defence industries and the policies that underpin them. They are coming in particular from revolutionary changes in technology, not least because these changes are mainly initiated in civil industry sectors; and from changes in the perceptions and realities of international security.

Until the events of 1989, there was a broadly common view of security and military strategy in Western Europe. There were, of course, many differences of opinion, even amounting on occasion to serious conflict. However, the broad strategic paradigm of the Cold War remained intact. It resulted in a rather stable force structure, leading to broad agreement on the quantity and type of equipment that was needed. It also involved acceptance of the different roles and stances taken by European countries. The defence industries regarded the future levels of demand for military equipment as relatively predictable.

These certainties no longer exist. With the passing of the US-Soviet dominated geopolitical order, the international situation has become extremely complex and confused. The Southern European region, in particular, finds itself in a peculiar strategic position. On the one side it participates in the European balance, while on the other it borders upon North Africa and the Middle East. In the evolving security environment, a new area of regional threat has emerged in the Balkans. Different political systems, economic disparities and religious discord have exacerbated regional instability. Emerging risks from the Southern European region and the continuing Greek-Turkish problems make the Greek perception of indigenous arms production remarkably different from that in other European nations.

Greek Defence Market and Defence Industry

The decision to develop the Greek military industry was first of all a response to fears of regional conflict with Turkey. It was also a way of achieving independence from foreign weapons suppliers. Similar intentions were developed later in the area of military manufacturing technology. A large-scale investment programme of technology transfer was implemented in an attempt to establish links with diverse sources of foreign military technology.

In the defence literature and among policy makers, military industrialisation has been understood as a simple import-substitution process: the transfer of procurement programmes from foreign suppliers to local firms. The development of the Greek armament sector was strongly influenced by such perceptions. It was believed that the size of the market would be sufficient to occupy the installed military manufacturing capacity. Investment in arms production was part of the national defence policy and therefore a broad consensus could be expected. However, both arguments had their weak points. The Greek market was not large when set against the huge modernisation programme which was under way. And what of the longer-term future? The assumption was made that roughly the same volume of orders could be sustained for the future.

Table 1 provides information on the size of Greek defence spending since 1970. The increasing level of defence expenditures was the outcome of the major modernisation programme for the Air Force and the Navy which started in

Table 1: Defence Expenditures and Equipment Procurement (1970–1994)

US $ million, constant 1985 prices

	1970	**1975**	**1980**	**1985**	**1990**	**1991**	**1992**	**1993**	**1994**
Defence Expenditure	939	1727	1774	2332	2101	2025	2122	2094	2125
% of Gross Domestic Product	4.7	6.7	6.6	6.2	5.8	5.4	5.6	5.5	5.6
Equipment Expenditure	77.0	333.3	308.7	424.4	449.6	411.1	496.5	517.2	518.5
% of Defence Expenditure	8.2	19.3	17.4	18.2	21.4	20.3	23.4	24.7	24.4

Source: *NATO Review*, various years.

Table 2: Greek Defence Market and Loan Repayment, 1990–1994

million US$, current prices

	1990	1991	1992	1993	1994*
Defence procurement	1087	1119	1411	1373	1604
Loan payments	726 (66.8%)	644 (57.5%)	884 (62.6%)	900 (65.5%)	1149 (71.6%)
Total defence spending	2727	2776	3168	2956	3058

*: Estimates.
Source: Author's calculations based on data provided by the Ministry of Economics.

the mid-1970s and expanded rapidly until the early 1990s. These aggregate data, however, provide limited information on the scale of contracts allocated to domestic firms. A closer look at recent trends in the Greek defence budget reveals that a large share of annual defence spending goes to loan payments, for the increasing debt on Foreign Military Sales loans provided by the US Government to the Greek Ministry of Defence (see Table 2). Of the orders for equipment-related procurement, many contracts go to foreign suppliers, especially in the case of advanced weapon systems. Therefore, for a country like Greece, with high import penetration in its domestic defence market, we should distinguish between aggregate defence procurement and new orders available for the domestic defence industrial base.

The Greek defence industry comprises state enterprises and small private companies, with between them approximately 20,000 employees in total. The defence manufacturing base is largely state controlled. The state controls the major Greek military firms and is the source of 70% of total fixed capital. In terms of employment the share of the private sector is 20%. The state-owned firms are modern capital-intensive plants; the private sector includes many small, labour intensive firms and a few dynamic firms specialised in metal parts and electronic equipment manufacturing. Military arsenals cover maintenance needs with a total workforce of around 10,000. They are part of the armed force's management structure. The privatisation programme of the two major shipyards is changing the existing ownership structure.

Military manufacturing capabilities have been established in six product areas: tanks and military vehicles, aircraft maintenance and parts manufacturing, naval shipbuilding, electronic equipment, arms and ammunition, and spare parts. The degree of indigenous technological capabilities is limited. Most of Greece's military firms have concentrated on mass production, repairs and manufacturing of parts of low technological complexity. Only the two major state-owned defence companies (HAI and EVO) have been involved in advanced production activities.

HAI is a state company located near Athens, which was founded in 1979. It is a supporting and maintenance centre, mainly for Hellenic Air Force aircraft and helicopters. HAI has invested heavily in facilities, based on foreign technology, for parts manufacturing and electronic equipment. Involvement in maintenance and retrofitting has become a well-established corporate activity. In comparison, manufacturing of aircraft equipment remains heavily subsidised. Since 1991, foreign personnel (US Lockheed's staff) took over HAI's management in an attempt to strengthen management capabilities needed to implement a major reconstruction programme in HAI.

EVO is a state company with four plants: small arms and medium calibre cannons, heavy and precision engineering, foundry and ammunition. EVO experienced rapid growth during the 1980s by expanding its mass production lines for rifles and ammunition. However, the ambitious plan to become a systems manufacturing centre was less successful. The company is kept operating with state subsidies and, recently, the Greek Government decided to support EVO with new orders for indigenously designed products.

PYRKAL remains a traditional ammunition manufacturer, established in 1894, with a wide range of capabilities in the production of infantry projectiles. Facing a shrinking export market, PYRKAL also produces for only a small fraction of the domestic demand for ammunition. Its manufacturing equipment is obsolescent and the prospects for modernisation investment are limited. The government is pursuing a plan for the merger of PYRKAL with EVO.

ELVO is a state company with a minor private shareholder. It was established in the early 1970s as a joint venture between the Austrian company Steyr Daimler Puch and Greek state-owned banks. Initially, it represented an attempt to establish an assembly plant for military vehicles and tractors in a well-protected market. The Greek Government assumed management control in 1983, and tried to increase corporate efficiency, technical capabilities and the degree of local value added. However, the transformation of an assembly plant to an independent manufacturing centre proved to be difficult. ELVO improved its manufacturing capacity but its product development capabilities remained rather narrow. In 1993, the Greek Government announced its intention to privatise ELVO by selling forty per cent of its portfolio to the private sector. The advertisement received limited attention among foreign investors and, after continuous pressure from unions and regional authorities, a major policy reversal took place in 1994 and the programme was cancelled.

Eleusis and Hellenic Shipyards are the two major Greek shipyards. In the early 1980s they failed to diversify when the tanker market collapsed. Naval procurement has been part of a state-coordinated effort to keep them operating. Since 1985, naval orders have comprised the major part of their new shipbuilding work, representing a new area of activity for these yards. The shift from tankers and bulk carriers to naval ships required new investments in machinery, training and more man-hours of production work. Because of serious delays in the implementation process, this programme did not in the event help the shipyards very much, and their debts increased. Eleusis (the smaller yard) has been privatised and Hellenic Shipyard (Skaramanga) has been on the privatisation list for some time. The privatisation of Skaramanga proved, however, to be very complicated. From one side there was growing pressure from the European Commission to stop the increasing flow of subsidies provided by the Greek government to the yard. From the other side, investors were reluctant to invest in a shipyard with such large liabilities. Privatisation has also been under increasing pressure from the unions. In March 1995, a bill was passed by the Greek Government which wrote off all liabilities and allowed a radical reduction of the yard's personnel. Under the new rules of the game, negotiations went ahead between the Greek government and foreign investors and the final outcome was expected in 1995.

A large part of the Greek defence industry's capacity is dedicated to maintenance, repairs, upgrading and retrofits. Military facilities and naval yards covering these needs have been involved in the modernisation of military equipment. The installed machinery is typically old, needing extensive repairs. Only a few military arsenals have modernised their own inventory.

The presence of private companies in the Greek defence industry has been rather limited. They participate in the production of ammunition, electronic equipment and metal manufacturing. State companies have established subcontracting networks with a few small private manufacturers. For example, a small group of dynamic medium-sized firms has been involved in spare parts and electronic components production. The majority of these firms have invested in advanced manufacturing equipment in an attempt to produce according to high quality standards and military specifications. With constant defence orders and easy access to investment loans, they have managed to improve their technological capabilities.

The Greek defence industrial base expanded in three directions with quite different objectives. The first was the continuation of maintenance and mass production activities for internal defence needs and the production of simple weapon platforms with assembly and mature manufacturing technologies. Initially, the Ministry of Defence allocated resources to these areas in an attempt to assure the future viability of these military firms. Later, disputes emerged on the size of future orders and the increasing production costs of local manufacturers.

The second direction led to increasing military manufacturing capacity. A significant share of the domestic defence market constituted, in effect, an indirect state subsidy, to firms involved in heavy engineering activities. In most of them, state-controlled banks assumed managerial control. These projects were essentially part of the state's industrial policy and their links with national security objectives were slight. The defence procurement agencies of the Greek armed forces supported them only when additional funds were allocated.

The third direction taken was the involvement of the more advanced state-owned military firms in indigenous product development and systems design. Corporate plans for rapid expansion and government ambition for technological modernisation were the driving forces behind these programmes. However, the implementation of specific projects required additional funds and subsidies, and the armed forces opposed the re-allocation of their resources to this end. During the expansion phase, the policy towards defence industrialisation became less clearly defined. First, it proved difficult to reconcile defence and industrial policy objectives. Also, control over the defence industrial base became an area of dispute between the government and the armed forces.

Developments along this third direction resulted in various failures, themselves the result of both policy errors and structural defects in the interplay of the institutions involved. Technical inefficiency was also a factor. The entry into production of weapon platforms began with many expectations for in-depth defence industrialisation and ambitious targets for the domestic defence industry. In comparison with the technical requirements of simple defence equipment and maintenance, the scale of investment was larger and these projects needed imports of product technology and systems integration knowledge. Systems integration is an industrial activity with complex technical requirements but it provides limited value added to the assembly plant which puts together imported sub-systems (electronic equipment, weapons). At the same time, orders from the domestic defence market could hardly provide enough work to pay for the installed manufacturing capacity. In addition, the increasing number of technical faults and delays in assembly work caused serious conflicts between military firms and their customers. Other side-effects were the expansion of military technology imports and the increasing investment cost of new military manufacturing projects.

Another problem was the excessive optimism of corporate and official forecasts of the future of military firms. The interpretation of occasional successes in arms exports as a clear indication of future demand, and the belief that there were increasing prospects for beneficial cooperation with military firms from allied countries, were among the assumptions on which investment programmes were based. Finally, Greek access to foreign markets proved difficult, whereas firms from other Western countries followed a policy of market penetration through technology transfer to Greek firms.

During the expansion phase, the first major problem was the re-allocation of orders from imports to domestic military firms. Institutional malfunction led to excess manufacturing capacity, the absence of a realistic strategy for the domestic defence industry and its interrelations with foreign firms, and disputes between the local defence market and military firms. Technical difficulties during the transition to the production of weapon platforms and other advanced military manufacturing projects caused delays and dissatisfaction. The credibility of the optimistic views on indigenous defence industrialisation was seriously affected. In the end, the two main objectives adopted by the state and military firms — defence procurement as a form of industrial policy and investment in systems technologies — were abandoned.

The defence industry became an enclave manufacturing system working for the monopsonistic defence market while the broad industrial base was facing fierce competition from foreign firms, especially in downstream engineering activities (e.g., shipbuilding, foundries, metal processing, assembly). Military specialised firms made new investments on the assumption that the domestic defence market was going to provide a stream of future contracts. Their manufacturing process was organised according to preferences defined by the defence market. In so doing, production management gave priority to product reliability and special-purpose machinery. Other factors like efficiency and cost effectiveness on the shop floor received less attention. Even quite small contracts could become the basis for new investments in manufacturing capacity and technology imports without serious consideration being given to other options such as the adaptation of existing capacity and diversification of other military firms. After only a few years, however, domestic demand proved unable to continue to support local defence firms in this process of expansion through new orders and subsidies. Thus, an overcapacity problem emerged for the Greek defence industrial base. Additionally, the heavy burden of loan repayments decreased the availability of funds for new orders from domestic defence firms.

The Greek defence industry is not comparable to those of the advanced European nations. The links between the defence and the civilian sectors of industry are minimal, and the defence firms are not part of an integrated industrial infrastructure. Since the 1950s, it has been a receiver rather than a generator of military technology, whether when obtaining used military equipment through military grants, importing weapon systems, buying military manufacturing technology, or selling to play an active role in current European attempts to create an integrated European defence market and/or force structure. The pressure for efficient management of the defence industrial bases that has become increasingly important in many other states in the 1990s has still not really materialised in Greece. Its defence industry is isolated from broader economic activities, and national planners are willing to subsidise arms production because they expect thereby to gain greater independence and to introduce technologies that could be spread to other sectors of the national industrial base. Economic activity within the military sector is being conducted in a regulatory environment that has been largely autonomous, and that has enjoyed its own distinctive rules and procedures.

Defence Technology Capabilities

The defence industrial base in Greece developed as a system of manufacturing activities closely linked to defence procurement but isolated from the broad manufacturing sector. When the decision to develop the defence industry was taken in the mid-1970s, the manufacturing sector was facing serious structural problems. The domestic industry was unable to carry out defence production without additional state support for modernisation. However, the evolution of the defence industrial base was also determined by the formulation of a defence industrialisation strategy which gave priority to the development of 'military specialised' firms in every category of defence needs — from simple items to weapon systems. Defence planners maintained that this form of investment could safeguard discipline and efficiency in the emerging Greek armament sector, avoiding at the same time the presence of private monopolies in the defence market.

Among the Greek government's expectations was that investment in defence manufacturing could provide technological benefits for the broad domestic industry. But general trends in the Greek economy undermined this strategy. In the 1980s, the gap between defence industrialisation priorities and declining domestic engineering capabilities increased. Resources were poured into the defence area when the domestic industry was in decline. Heavy engineering plants shifted to the defence market trying to secure orders and state subsidies. The enclave character of the defence sector further compounded the problem.

Nevertheless, the strategy of developing 'military specialised' plants worked fairly well for a time. During the first phase of import-substitution (the 'easy' phase), all the internal actors (government, armed forces, corporate management) supported the indigenisation of maintenance and the local production of simple defence equipment. The size of the contracts and the export demand arising from Iran-Iraq war were sufficient to support the installed capacity in the new plants. Also, technological requirements were relatively modest. Most of the plants were using mass production or standardised maintenance techniques, which were both high value-added manufacturing activities. With imported technical assistance, a manufacturing system was established based on embodied technology and strictly defined specifications. The Greek personnel proved efficient in assimilating process technology and the military firms managed to respond to the defence market's technical requirements.

The initial objective of the Greek programme as regards defence industrialisation was clear. Taking into account defence needs, available financial resources, access to foreign technology, and indigenous technological capabilities, defence planners had to decide the form of foreign technology transfer and of specific investment programmes in military manufacturing. However, institutional malfunction and competing interests amongst the actors involved caused problems during the implementation of these projects. But as the general objectives were clearly defined, investments were carried out with some success.

Later, however, things became more complicated. New issues such as the objectives of the defence sector and the future control of military firms emerged. The armed forces wanted to preserve their control over the defence industrial base. The government developed similar intentions. And naturally, corporate management of military firms sought more independence. Ill-conceived objectives and plans for the future of military firms were a constant source of difficulties. While for all the involved actors the defence industrial base was a strategic asset, their specific proposals for its development were often contradictory. Different roles within the defence industrial system underpinned different interests (and priorities). The armed forces supported programmes linked to security, while the government introduced broader objectives into the defence industrialisation strategy. The heterogeneity of proposals on the future of the domestic defence sector became a difficult problem to handle.

In the Greek case, the local defence manufacturing base was successfully developed in the areas of maintenance and production of simple defence items. The move into more sophisticated weapon platforms was thwarted by technical problems and institutional malfunction amongst local agents involved in the defence industrialisation process. Corporate performance has been better in process technologies than in design, product development and systems integration. Comparing different areas of technological achievements, metal processing techniques have been absorbed relatively efficiently, while in the case of military electronics, domestic production has been limited to simple products.

Technology acquisition and development by state-owned and private military firms has been 'demand-led' and so aligned with specific procurement objectives. The most common practice is to import or copy the basic idea, and sometimes even the detailed design, from abroad. As Table 3 shows (columns E–J), the Greek military technology system operates in close co-operation with foreign companies and research centres. Laboratory equipment and scientific instruments are imported.

Specialised studies, tests, and experiments are another type of foreign input. Greek military firms have concentrated on the development of laboratory prototypes of relatively simple defence items. In such cases, foreign companies have been involved in the supply of sub-systems and problem-solving services for

Table 3: Greek Defence Industry: Areas of Technological Collaboration and Endogenous Capabilities

Firm	**Source of technology**									
	A	B	C	D	E	F	G	H	I	J
HAI (aerospace: maintenance and parts manufacturing)		*		*	*	*	*	*		
EVO (arms, artillery, and ammunition)	*	*			*	*		*	*	*
ELVO (military trucks and LAVs)					*	*				
Hellenic (shipbuilding)					*		*	*		
Eleusis (shipbuilding)										
Military arsenals (maintenance)					*	*				
Private firms (metal parts, electronics)		*			*	*				
Military research centres	*						*	*	*	*

Notes: A = Firm's own research & development; B = Firm's engineering experience; C = Purchasing domestic patents; D = Joint research with domestic research centres; E = Importing technical data packages; F = Purchasing the entire production line; G = Foreign technology participants; H = Foreign consultancy imports; I = Copying products of other countries; J = Improving products of other countries.

Source: A. Bartzokas (1992a), p. 154, updated in January 1994 with telephone interviews.

prototype development, which requires extensive technical expertise for the successful integration of parts and sub-systems. The form of co-operation during this initial phase can determine the shape of commitment in long term co-production programmes.

There has, however, been some attempt at the development of a Greek military R&D system. The military research infrastructure began to be established in the 1970s when major programmes for setting up laboratories and general infrastructure were undertaken by the Armed Forces. Table 4 provides an indication of the limited scale of investment in military R&D since 1981.

We should emphasise, however, that this infrastructure is not dedicated exclusively to product development. The scientific personnel also provide calibration services, weapon operational studies, technical assistance for manufacturing process and other services. According to rough estimates. Only an estimated 27% of the scientific personnel working in military research centres participate in true development projects. The capacity of this R&D infrastructure to promote innovation has remained small compared to that of foreign suppliers.

Foreign companies' engagement in technical cooperation with Greek firms has been a clear part of their marketing strategies. The transfer of technology to the Greek military industry has helped them to export parts, sub-systems and other final products to the Greek market. Their prime concern, however, has been to establish preferential access in the host defence market and not to create permanent sub-contracting networks in Greece. For the Greek firms, access to

Table 4: Government R&D Appropriations for Defence, 1981 to 1993

(million US$, current prices)

Year	**1981**	**1982**	**1983**	**1984**	**1985**	**1986**	**1987**
Defence R&D **% of Government-funded R&D**	1.3 2.2	1.2 2.0	1.2 1.4	2.8 3.5	2.4 2.9	2.6 2.7	2.9 2.3
Year	**1988**	**1989**	**1990**	**1991**	**1992**	**1993***	
Defence R&D **% of Government-funded R&D**	3.2 2.2	3.6 2.0	2.1 1.4	4.4 1.5	2.7 1.5	2.4 1.4	

*Estimates.

Source: Data provided by the Greek Secretariat for Science and Technology (figures correspond to OECD Frascati definitions).

technology in oligopolistic markets (e.g., aircraft technology) was linked to the development of close relations with major Western firms. A similar strong influence during the importation of mature manufacturing technologies was exercised through direct management control of the Greek plant for the Leonidas project. In these cases, technology transfer was carried out on a turn-key basis. Foreign suppliers provided process technology, technical assistance and instructions for equipment purchases in 'package' form. The Greek government and the armed forces expected to import reliable production technology for specific defence equipment needs. However, fulfilment of this objective encountered two problems. Firstly, the government and the Ministry of Defence failed to control the process of technology transfer. Secondly, technology was imported without realistic consideration of future demand. The expiry of domestic orders created idle capacity and financial problems.

In projects with less advanced technical requirements, Greek firms tried to develop indigenous product development policies (e.g., Artemis anti-aircraft system, landing craft). The extent of technology transfer was decided by the local firms. Successful implementation of these projects required not only process technology but also design and systems engineering skills. In the meantime, the promotion of 'great expectations' for future achievements became, for these firms, a way to secure new orders. The manufacturing process itself, however, was another matter. Firms engaged in the production of indigenously designed defence equipment faced serious technical problems in their manufacturing work and, in some cases, declining support from the domestic defence market. The armed forces had doubts about the expansion of Greek military firms into complex manufacturing projects. In most cases, the initiative was taken by the corporate management of military firms and by the government. New investments were primarily the result of the proliferation in the objectives of the defence industrialisation strategy (support of declining industries and technological modernisation) rather than on defence requirements.

Field research by the author in five different case studies has provided a basis for comparative analysis of the accumulation of defence technological capabilities in the Greek defence industry (Bartzokas 1992a). *Aircraft maintenance* work was found to have been undertaken in a protected market which provided a constant stream of orders. A gradual process of accelerating improvements in manufacturing work and production management led to a sufficient degree of specialisation in maintenance services. The introduction of mature manufacturing technologies in *vehicle production* lines and *naval shipbuilding*, however, has produced more equivocal results. Technological requirements were relatively modest and manufacturing work was carried out successfully, at least in terms of product reliability. But the scale of the projects and managerial inefficiency proved obstacles to technological benefits and financial gains. The remaining case studies were either of investments in *advanced manufacturing equipment* required for sub-contracting work (aircraft manufacturing) or on the development of *systems integration* capabilities.

Military firms tended to underestimate technical requirements and the complexity of manufacturing work in these projects. Their industrial inefficiency caused delays and increasing product development cost. Their expansion into more advanced programmes was based on state subsidies. When the link with the domestic defence market became weak, military firms were unable to self-finance their projects or to gain orders in competitive markets. Thus, while the import of process technologies and large defence contracts created favourable initial conditions for local military firms, to which they responded with enthusiasm, the move into weapon platforms became problematic either as a result of institutional malfunction and limited domestic demand or due to technical inefficiency in product development and manufacturing work.

Declining Demand and Changing Policy in the Defence Manufacturing Base

By the early 1990s, the decline of demand had led to the following structural problems in the Greek defence industry:

- Declining demand for new procurement contracts;
- Increasing debt from Foreign Military Sales Loans;
- Lack of financial resources needed to maintain employment levels and to finance new development projects;
- Declining credibility of technical capabilities;
- Cheap imports of second-hand military equipment from allied countries;
- Cuts in R&D support provided by the Ministry of Defence for development projects by state-owned military firms.

For these reasons, Greek participation in international military research programmes such as EUCLID remained marginal, and engagement in European research programmes such as ESPRIT and BRITE declined.

The reaction to these problems at the firm level was to cut existing levels of employment and R&D budgets. The collective reduction of military R&D expenditures by EVO, PYRKAL and HAI, arms, artillery and aerospace respectively, in the years 1986–91, is shown in Table 5.

Table 5: Defence Industrial R&D Spending in EVO, PYRKAL and HAI

(million US$, current prices)

SECTOR	1986	1989	1991
Arms and Ammunition	4.7	8.6	1.2
Aerospace	0.2	0.4	0.4

Source: Data provided by the Greek Secretariat for Science and Technology (figures correspond to OECD Frascati definitions).

In the meantime, loans from state-owned banks helped state-owned military firms to run their plant with idle capacity. Skilled personnel moved to dynamic private firms in areas such as consulting, electronics and software.

Government policy shifted to privatisation in areas of dual use capabilities such as military truck and heavy vehicles, shipbuilding and electronic equipment manufacturing. The production of arms, artillery, ammunition, and the aerospace plant, however, remained under state control. This privatisation programme was intended to cope with the heavy financial burden of state-owned military firms without offering a clear conversion strategy to transfer existing technological capabilities to the local manufacturing base. Additionally, the privatisation programme encountered many delays as a result of the huge financial liabilities accumulated in military firms. Moreover, the attempt to transfer technological capabilities from defence firms to civil coincided with the decline of the local manufacturing industry as it struggled to find a viable position in the competitive environment of the EEC.

The Greek government financed projects and gave subsidies to the defence industry in the belief that it provided significant externalities to the domestic civil manufacturing sector. Training effects, the development of sub-contracting networks in high value-added activities and the development of technologically sophisticated industries in Greece were the prime examples of spillovers that were anticipated. The experience of attempts to achieve conversion into civil manufacturing activities suggests that it is unlikely that these benefits can be realised.

Greek military firms have responded to declining demand in different ways.

HAI: In 1991, the Greek Government hired foreign management (Lockheed staff) to reorganise HAI. Financial problems were the first priority for the new management. The Greek Air Force subsidised HAI through overpricing maintenance services. The accumulated debt and lack of previous experience in collaboration programmes undermined corporate plans for active involvement in commercial and competitive markets. Corporate plans failed to cope with problems emerging from the co-existence of cost-plus maintenance activities and manufacturing/product development activities. To address the problem of idle capacity, HAI tried to increase exports to foreign maintenance markets and to increase its participation in subcontracting networks. In the domestic market, HAI's management has suggested diversification into the local telecommunications equipment market. However, HAI faces competition from well-established Greek private firms. HAI introduced a programme of prototype development in electronic and telecommunications equipment with limited success.

EVO and PYRKAL: The Greek Government considers the production of arms, artillery and ammunition to be the core of domestic defence manufacturing capabilities, and keeps it under state control for national security reasons. The response to declining demand was to reduce employment by 30 per cent and increase efficiency through the merger of the two firms. The experience so far is an attempt to develop, on a smaller scale, a defence industrial system linked to the domestic defence market on the principles of the Greek defence industrialisation programme in the early 1980s. However, the environment is different because the Armed Forces are reluctant to finance future defence manufacturing projects. Further development of endogenous technological capabilities received limited financial support and all the major product development projects have been cancelled. Imported technology and technical assistance became the main source of military technology. Capable R&D personnel moved to the private sector. The implementation of across-the-board cost reduction without a clearly defined corporate plan for the deployment of the workforce is putting accumulated technological capabilities in jeopardy. Declining credibility of existing manufacturing capabilities, import penetration and shortage of financial resources for new purchases of defence equipment created increasing difficulties to EVO and PYRKAL. Production lines have been closed with harmful effects on accumulated experience and technological capabilities.

ELVO: ELVO is a firm with significant technological capabilities in the assembly of heavy trucks and other vehicles. The corporate response to declining demand was a reduction of the labour force and discussions with foreign firms on the local production of trucks and other vehicles. ELVO is a typical example of a dual-use plant with skilled personnel and significant technological capabilities. Since 1990, delays in the implementation of the privatisation programme have undermined plans for corporate restructuring. The government cancelled plans to privatise ELVO in 1994. The Ministry of Defence then decided to support ELVO with a major contract for the production of armoured personnel vehicles.

ELEUSIS: Eleusis was sold to one of the leading expatriate Greek ship owners (Peratikos). Under the new management, Eleusis is carrying out a major programme for the construction of landing craft for the Greek Navy. At the same time, it has developed a growing interest in public procurement projects such as water supply and big environmental projects in the Attiki (Athens) region. Since 1993, the ship-repair division has increased its turnover. The factors underlining the success of Eleusis' diversification programme are the previous experience of the new management in shipping services, the availability of financial resources provided to Eleusis by the Peratikos group of companies, and corporate assets, including dual use infrastructure and its privileged geographical position in the Piraeus port. Contacts with the local public procurement market will determine future market prospects for Eleusis.

Skaramanga: Skaramanga is the major Greek shipyard, where construction of frigates for the Greek Navy is taking place with German technical assistance. Its poor performances and declining defence sales have, however, led to an increasing debt to Greek banks. Private interests are proving reluctant to get involved in the ownership of a firm with huge financial liabilities, while the Greek Navy prefers in any case to keep the yard under public control, at least until the frigate programme is completed. From December 1993, however, the European Union put increased pressure on the Greek Government to end subsidies to Skaramanga.

Private Firms: A small group of private firms invested in advanced manufacturing capabilities during the expansion of the Greek defence industry in the mid-1980s. They responded to declining demand with successful export promotion programmes for modernisation and increasing involvement in the domestic public procurement market. The expansion of R&D activities in private firms has benefited from their participation in European and national science and technology projects. Recruitment of engineers and research personnel from state-owned military firms stimulated the initial development of their technological capabilities. The majority of small private firms failed to keep operating in the domestic defence market following the decline of new orders and the elimination of subsidies and financial support. The diversification of private firms has, however, had mixed success. It has tended to depend on their contacts in the international market, established during the participation in offset programmes, and on engineering product integration capabilities accumulated in defence manufacturing projects.

The defence industry does not appear to be a particularly appropriate or effective development instrument for pulling the Greek manufacturing base towards technological modernisation. Training effects and other learning externalities, though occasionally important for individual careers, could hardly justify the outlays involved in the expansion phase of the industry. Training effects can only be considered externalities if, during the implementation of a conversion programme, labour is eventually released and employed again, making full use of learned skills in other activities. Weapon systems design and fabrication, however, demand specialised skills that in countries like Greece, with a weak manufacturing base, are unlikely to be efficiently used in alternative sources of employment. From the Greek experience, it appears that successful transfer of skills has taken place only from state-owned military firms to small private firms, and in the area of general purpose engineering and product integration technological capabilities.

Export Controls

In the early 1990s, the defence industries of the Balkans gained renewed significance. For example, the capabilities of the domestic military industry supported Serbian military strategy in Bosnia-Herzegovina. In other small Balkan countries, the evolution of military strategies depends, to a large extent, on the weapons they can produce or import. In a region with strong tensions, the introduction of offensive conventional weapons poses a fundamental challenge to the stability of the military balance. Furthermore, were indigenous technological capabilities to be used to achieve 'breakthroughs' that permitted qualitative leaps in the type and quantity of weapon systems deployed in the region, they could complicate the regional security system upon which a fragile stability has in the past been based.

The Greek Ministry of Foreign Affairs has put forward a proposal for the limitation of arms trade in the Balkan peninsula, covering all types of weapons of mass destruction and close monitoring of other military sales in the region. This idea seems particularly beneficial for a region with historical experience of deep-seated local arms races.

The problem of non-proliferation, however, is always a problem of the relationship between civilian and military applications of relevant technologies. If, in establishing a regime to prevent the proliferation of this or that type of weapon, we also limit the peaceful economic and technological development of countries, we will create a regime that can hardly endure. Thus, the analysis of policies for the peaceful use of technology and scientific cooperation must be included when exploring the foundations of a regional non-proliferation regime.

Conclusions

In recent decades, economic activity within the Greek military sector has been conducted within a regulatory framework that has been largely autonomous, and has had its own distinctive rules and procedures. In the US and Western Europe, the pressures for efficient management of the defence industrial base call for greater constraint on the exports of weapons and on the transfer of weapons manufacturing capabilities. These pressures are likely to become even more compelling in the late 1990s. However, this is not the case in Greece. Military-industrial complexes there have been isolated from broader economic activities, and national planners have designed strategies with strong emphases on defence needs.

In the Greek defence industrialisation programme, the shift from large-scale production runs to smaller orders for weapon platforms requiring advanced product and process technologies created many difficulties. In recent years, increasing financial problems in state-owned military firms forced the Greek Government to change its policy in favour of the privatisation of dual-use state-owned plants. The Government asked some of the main state military companies to convert their activities to the production of civil goods. For the Greek defence planners, the response to the privatisation programme from European and US firms was disappointing, with the notable exception of the aerospace industry. In this case, DASA and major US defence firms have expressed interest in HAI. Discussions are continuing over the form of collaboration with foreign partners in aerospace.

A deputy minister responsible for the defence industry was appointed in November 1993 and the Ministry of Defence expressed its intention to re-examine its policy for the local defence industry. Policy-makers in the Ministry of Defence have emphasised the need for efficient management in the defence manufacturing system, with increasing emphasis being placed on the mobilisation of existing technological capabilities and long-term planning of demand and supply.

The current reconstruction of the West European defence and security structure is already exercising a significant influence on national procurement practices in Greece. Pressures for the adoption of 'buy European' clauses and for compensation agreements using surplus equipment have grown. In the meantime, the European defence industry faces a steep recession, with declining orders and pressure for reconstruction and adjustment to the appropriate size in the new security environment. In this rationalisation process, Greece has limited opportunities for specialisation at the low end of defence manufacturing technologies, a sector which also faces dramatic job losses, mergers and concentration in the advanced European countries. Moreover, stagnating procurement budgets could increase protectionism in defence markets right across Europe. Potential suppliers from Greece, mainly in the areas of metal parts and electronic components, will find market entry difficult. Participation in co-production programmes with advanced arms manufacturers from allied countries will remain linked to the evolution of defence cooperation in the European integration process and the degree of influence exercised by the US on Greek procurement preferences. In any case, future developments in the Greek defence industry will be shaped more by the regional situation than by general trends in European defence cooperation.

The basic prerequisite for a realistic policy for the Greek defence industry is the adoption of modest objectives for future defence manufacturing activities and the reconstruction of the local defence industrial system. The first step in this direction is to solve the problems of idle capacity and the introduction of more efficient manufacturing and managerial practices at the firm level. Hitherto, policies for these problems have revolved around the distinction between public and private control of defence firms. What remains unclear is the linkage between the privatisation programme and conversion policy. What is needed now is to find ways to preserve the existing technological capabilities in firms under privatisation and to inject them into other productive activities with the transfer of skills and the development of well-defined corporate plans approved by the Government and private investors. A quasi-public market is not always a viable solution, especially when other domestic firms have established themselves in a strong position in the local market. For the remainder of the defence industry, the challenges facing the Ministry of Defence and corporate management are twofold: to propose policies to reconcile market protection with the introduction of efficient managerial practices; and to find practical ways to modify such characteristics of the established military specialised plants as their dependence on defence orders. To respond to these challenges, state-owned firms will need to introduce well-defined restructuring programmes.

References

Note: there is very little literature on the Greek defence industry published in English. References to publications and articles in the Greek trade press can be found in the following sources, all by the present author:

— 1992a, *Military Technology Transfer and Domestic Defence Production: The Case of Greece*, Ph.D. Thesis, University of Sussex.

— 1992b, 'The Developing Arms Industries in Greece, Portugal and Turkey', in Brzoska, M. and Lock, P. (eds.) *Restructuring of Arms Production in Western Europe,* Oxford: Oxford University Press.

— (1993), *Defence Industrialisation in Greece, Portugal and Turkey (the DDIs),* Brussels: NATO Fellowship Report.

Chapter 5
Italy

Giancarlo Graziola, Sergio Parazzini, and Giulio Perani

Basic Data

Main Characteristics of Italian Weapons Procurement

Italian military planning in general, and weapons procurement in particular, is characterised by the lack of a strong centralised authority. The Chief of Defence Staff (CSD) is responsible for coordinating technical and financial plans drawn up by the Chiefs of Staff of the Army, the Navy and the Air Force. The General Secretary of Defence (GSD), as National Armaments Director (NAD), coordinates the separate service General Directorates in charge of weapons procurement. But it is these General Directorates which, acting on behalf of their service chiefs, constitute the principal 'poles' of procurement decision making. (See Figure 1). During the 1980s, successive Defence Ministers drew up draft reforms, but none of them reached the stage of parliamentary debate.

A draft law on the reform of the central organisation of defence submitted on 4 February 1993 by then Minister Salvo Andò, was passed by the Senate but was not voted on in the Chamber of Deputies. At the end of July 1994, the Council of Ministers approved a new draft. In September 1994 it also approved a draft law on the 'Restructuring of the Armed Forces and the Reorganisation of Defence Military and Civilian Personnel', which contained important innovations on such matters as the increased role of volunteers, and the enlistment of women in the Armed Forces. Neither of these draft laws has yet been discussed in Parliament. Under these reforms, the GSD would have direct responsibility for coordinating the General Directorates in charge of weapons acquisition; undertaking industrial planning in respect of both public and private industry; and directing R&D activities, production, procurement and deployment. The CSD's position would also be strengthened relative to the separate service chiefs. (Figure 1).

A second important characteristic of the Italian weapons procurement regime is that Parliamentary control of programmes for research, development, production and acquisition of major weapons systems is inadequate. This inadequacy does not arise from any lack of legislative tools; indeed, the Ministry of Defence is required by law to transmit more comprehensive information concerning its operations to the Parliament than any other Ministry.[1]

1. The present multi-polar organization

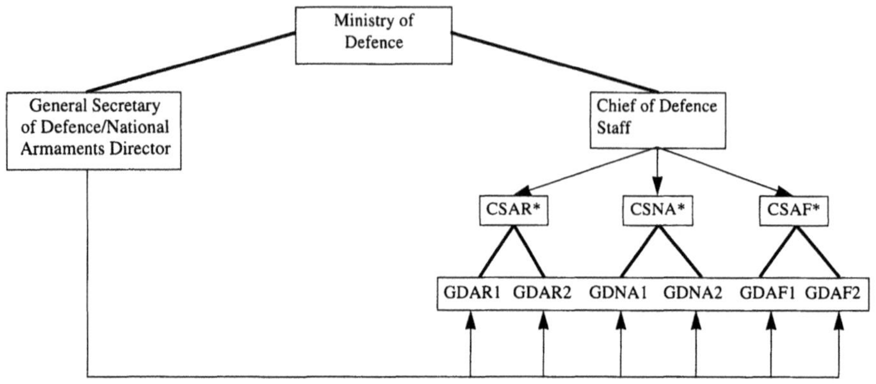

2. The proposed unipolar organization

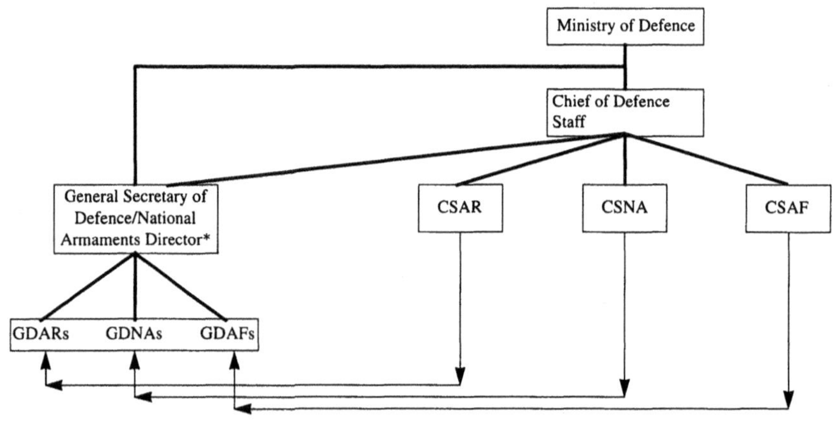

Key: * = a pole of procurement decision making; CSAR, CSNA, CSAF = Chiefs of Staff of Army, Navy, Air Force respectively; CDAR, GDNA, GDAF = General Directorates for Procurement, Army, Navy, Air Force. Thick lines = strong hierarchical link; thin lines = weak links

Figure 1: Central Organization for Weapons Procurement in Italy.

Despite the legislative powers at their disposal, members of Parliament are often ill equipped to formulate a realistic and coherent defence policy as many are unduly influenced by ideological arguments or lobbying interests. Major weapons procurement programmes are rarely subject to serious evaluation or debate. For example, the New Defence Model (NDM) presented to the Parliament by the then Minister of Defence Virginio Rognoni in November 1991, has never been debated. In the meantime, rapid political and economic changes forced the Defence Administration to prepare a second, downsized version of the NDM, submitted to the Parliament in July 1992 by Salvo Andò. A further, even more reduced, version was announced at the end of 1993. More recently, in the spring of 1995, the Chief of Staff of the Army openly complained about this lack of political attention to the NDM, and its consequences for military planning.

A third important characteristic of Italian arms procurement has been the lack of effective coordination between the Ministry of Defence and other, industrial, ministries responsible for sectors in which defence firms operate. This affects aerospace and electronics firms, whose turnover is dominated by military sales, and telecommunications and shipbuilding companies with substantial military business. Ministry of Defence spending for R&D and weapons production is basically determined by the needs of defence, and not by macro- or microeconomic considerations, such as the stabilisation of aggregate demand or the support of private R&D activities. However, given the extent of dual-use technologies and the importance of military demand in shaping the prospects of individual firms, including the market structures of the sectors in which they operate, there is an obvious need for coordination.

In August 1984, a Defence Industry Committee (DIC) was established by the Ministry of Defence, the Ministry of Industry and the Ministry of State Holdings (since abolished, in 1993) as part of a larger reorganisation of military procurement and the military technology base. In addition to drawing members from the three ministries, the DIC included representatives of the Ministry of Foreign Trade, the Ministry of Scientific Research and the defence industry. The DIC was set up to:

- coordinate the ministries involved in R&D relevant to the military;
- coordinate the R&D activities of the Ministry of Defence with those of Italian military firms;
- promote the participation of Italian defence firms in international military R&D programmes, especially under NATO; and
- coordinate the activities of ministries supporting arms sales abroad.

These aims were never actively pursued. To appreciate the full extent of what the DIC *could* have done, consider that all its tasks but the last were fully supported by the necessary legislation.[2] For example, the Ministry of Industry administers a Fund for Applied Research, established at the end of the 1960s, which could have been used to support military R&D in firms through soft loans or grants. In 1982, the Fund for Technological Development was set up,[3] providing additional money for R&D of a more basic or risky nature, which could also have been used in this way.

From 1982–87, these two Ministry of Industry funds provided industrial firms with Lit. 4.64 billion and Lit. 4.11 billion respectively. A large share of these funds was channelled to pharmaceutical, electronics, transport and telecommunications companies, among which were the principal companies involved in defence production. Roughly 90% of the funds disbursed from the Fund for Applied Research, and 75% from the Fund for Technological Development, went to large companies. In fact, almost half of the money from the Fund for Applied Research went to IRI, ENI, EFIM and FIAT (which historically have dominated the industry), together with Olivetti, Pirelli and Montedison. Because these industrial groups are typically diversified, there is a clear need to coordinate the R&D funds assigned to them from the two Ministry of Industry funds and those obtained through contracts for major weapons programmes awarded by the Ministry of Defence.

Another lost opportunity for R&D coordination between the Ministry of Defence and other ministries has been in the aerospace sector. A law passed on Christmas Eve, 1985 in support of the aeronautical industry, and the establishment of the Italian Centre for Aerospace Research (CIRA) in 1989, did not lead to any significant policy initiatives.

In contrast, Italian space policy has been very active and successful, figuring prominently in the Major Research Programmes of the Ministry of Universities and Scientific and Technological Research (MURST, established in 1989). During the 1980s, public financing of space research activities rose by a factor of seven in real terms, and is presently about Lit. 700–800 billion/year[4] (although it has fallen since 1991 due to the difficulties caused by the huge national deficit). Almost all public finance for space R&D in industry is channelled through the Italian Space Agency (ASI — *Agencia Spaziale Italiana*) established in 1988. Its activities are predominantly civil, but it would seem natural that an institution like the DIC would take account of the dual-use nature of the technologies developed under the aegis of ASI, especially with respect to the industrial sector. There are, however, no indications of any explicit coordination between military and civilian space R&D activities, apart from some modest support by the MoD for some primarily civil space programmes that also have a military aim, such as the Lit. 40 billions approved in 1995 for the Helios satellite.

Major Projects

The 1993 estimate for 'modernisation and renewal' expenditure by the Ministry of Defence was Lit. 4150 billion (see Table 1, which gives basic data on the defence budget), of which 1154 billion was allocated to the Army, 851 billion to the Navy, 1480 billion to the Air Force, and 666 billion to interservice projects run by the GSD/NAD.

Of this expenditure, Lit. 919 billion was allocated to R&D, 2769 billion for weapons procurement and 462 billion for infrastructure. The first two of these constitute the core of domestic demand for the Italian defence industry; the remainder is for the purchase of minor weapons and for maintenance activities. There are roughly 20 multiyear projects in progress in the military services at any given time.

Table 1: Italian Defence Expenditure, 1985–1995 (Lit. billions, current prices)

Year	Investment				Operation & Maintenance	Total Defence	Total MoD Budget	Total Defence Nato Definition
	Major weapons	R&D	Infra-structure	Total				
1985	—	—	—	—	—	13,001	16,380	17,767
1986	3,511	397	711	4,619	4,103	13,981	17,585	20,071
1987	3,905	522	675	5,102	4,405	15,113	19,104	22,872
1988	3,882	906	677	5,465	4,851	16,517	21,047	25,539
1989	4,356	496	535	5,387	5,055	17,977	22,905	27,342
1990	3,813	610	669	5,093	5,312	18,214a	23,155	28,007
1991	3,118	721	382	4,221	5,241	18,304	24,466	30,191
1992	3,197	1,071	510	4,778	5,416	19,568b	24,517	30,813
1993	2,766	918	465	4,150	5,114	18,136	25,560	32,364
1994	2,429	915	421	3,765	5,518	18,480	26,166	34,179
1995	2,481	904	478	3,863	5,534	18,398	25,974	—

a) During the Fiscal Year 1990, cuts were made of Lit. 286 bn (Figures after cuts: Total Invest = 4,807, Total Def. = Lit. 17,929 bn).
b) During the Fiscal Year 1992, cuts were made of Lit. 1800 bn (Figures after cuts: Total Invest = 3,577; Op&M = 4,859; Personnel = 9,332; Total Def. = Lit. 17,768 bn).
Sources: MoD, 'Nota Aggiuntiva allo Stato di presvisione per la Difesa', various years. NATO, 'Financial and Economical data relating to NATO defence', various years.

Table 2: Major Projects, and their Costs (Lit. billions)

	Total cost	1993 estimate	1994 estimate
ARMY			
Skyguard Aspide, SAM	963	150	583
Centauro, ACV	1531	260	300
Ariete 1, MBT	1453	79	1374
NAVY			
EH-101 helicopter	2238	85	1145
Two De La Penne destroyers	1373	8	9
AV-8B fighter	1403	153	937
AIR FORCE			
Eurofighter 2000	13545	520	11460
SPADA, SAM	2057	78	580
AMX tactical fighter	7636	409	1571
MRCA bomber	9330	40	2335

Note: the above figures are not directly comparable because of the differing timeframes and spending patterns associated with each project.

Major projects (costing more than Lit. 1000 billion at 1993 prices) are shown in Table 2.

The total expenditure on major projects by the Air Force, even excluding the Eurofighter 2000, is by far the largest. In fact, all the major projects except the Ariete 1 involve the aerospace industry. Three major projects, MRCA, EH-101 and Eurofighter 2000, involve European collaboration, and one, the AMX, is conducted in collaboration with Brazil. One project, the AV-8B, is based on a weapons import, with offsets in its production. A few of the major projects are expected to absorb a considerable amount of the total military equipment development expenditure in the future: the Ariete 1 will comprise almost half of the Army's share; the EH-101 and AV-8B will take 60% of the Navy's share; and the Eurofighter 2000 is expected to absorb over half of the Air Force's budget.

Policy Towards Defence and Dual-Use Technology

Policies Regarding the National Defence Technology Base

For the first time in many years, the Italian Ministry of Industry (MoI) presented, in a 1993 report entitled *A Different Future for the Italian Economy*, a statement regarding the future of the national military industry.[5] In this document, the MoI proposed 'a process of reorganisation that ... through industrial alliances either at national or international level, could maintain the (military) sector at the leading edge of advanced technology, with high skill jobs and centres of decision making preferably based in our country'. There were, however, no consequential policy changes during 1994 that strayed from the traditional approach to military procurement, technological development, defence industrial policy and conversion. Nevertheless, within that traditional framework, two trends could be discerned: 1) increasing reductions in procurement spending; and 2) concentration of military industrial and R&D activities in two industrial groupings: Finmeccanica and FIAT (the third historical grouping, EFIM, having been wound up in 1994 — see below).

Political support for increased military spending received a boost in February 1994 when the then Prime Minister, C.A. Ciampi, stated, 'we have to provide ourselves, in conjunction with our Allies, with defensive and dissuasive capacities against any possible aggression' and, as a consequence, 'to increase, within our national capabilities, the financial effort for Defence'. At the same time, he anticipated a need, after several years of spending cuts, to stabilise the military budget, pegging it to the evolution of the GDP, in order to make reliable planning possible, not least for industry.

In February 1995, the Minister of Defence, Mr Corcione, confirmed the government's commitment to sustain the Italian defence industry, saying: 'a strong financial allocation needs to be implemented as soon as possible.... time flies, and the technological gap is widening; one consequence will be a reduced capacity to spread this effort over a long period of time, while the operational capacity of the armed forces will be increasingly reduced.' (*Interarma News*, No. 3, 22 February 1995, p. 30). Nevertheless, the strict financial policy imposed by the prime minister, Mr Dini, led by the following month to a further 1% cut in the already declining defence budget. The overall financial position will make it hard in subsequent years for the government substantially to increase the military procurement budget (*Interarma News*, No. 4, 8 March 1995, p. 48).

Policies on Dual-Use Technologies

A *Three-Year Plan for Research* is published by the Ministry of University and Scientific Research (MURST) every three years which includes policies on mission oriented R&D. In the 1994–96 Plan, two major objectives are defined with respect to dual-use technologies (MURST, 1994). The first is to orient civil research towards dual-use applications; the second is to co-ordinate MoD military programmes with other, civil research programmes, especially in the so-called 'diffusive technologies' (i.e. information technologies, biotechnologies and new materials).

In the *Three-Year Plan*, MURST commits support for five priority tasks for the Italian Armed Forces, in order to acquire a national production capability for the following six classes of weapons systems:

- air defence systems (fighter aircraft, SAM missiles, ABM missiles, UAVs, etc.);
- air and space reconnaissance systems (satellites, aircraft, UAVs);
- transport aircraft;
- command, control, communication, intelligence and information systems;
- air defence radar systems (both airborne and ground-based);
- simulators for advanced training.

The technological areas underpinning these systems include artificial intelligence, robotics, optoelectronics, composite materials, laser and radar technologies. However, despite the specificity of the *Three-Year Plan*, it does not formally oblige any specific action to be taken by either public or private bodies.

Within the MoD, the definition of *critical* defence technologies is the responsibility of the General Secretary/National Armaments Director. A proposed *Military Technology Plan* by the Office of the General Secretary is due to replace a 1989 document listing 13 technological areas as priorities for national defence, but although preliminary studies have been done, a definitive text will not be released until after the New Defence Model has received parliamentary approval. There has been some overlap between these 13 areas and those considered critical by NATO, and by WEAG in its EUCLID Programme. However, according to a high-ranking MoD official, the forthcoming *Military Technology Plan* will be 'almost completely matched' with technologies being pursued under the EUCLID Programme.

At a national conference on the Italian defence industry in March 1993, Mr G. Bocchini, then President of the Advanced Technology for Defence Industries Group (RITAD), summarised the industrial perspective by saying that the

> challenge is to replace a number of national industries with a new, integrated, multinational structure, more technologically competitive and more cost-effective, but safeguarding all participants' rights.

RITAD's concern was that the Italian industry was in a weak position with respect to the larger European defence market. Bocchini thus proposed to manage carefully the integration process, saying:

> this process of transition (towards a unification of supply and demand at the European level) needs to be led [towards] a gradual rationalisation of the industrial base [while providing] for a balanced and intelligent presence of every country.

The Italian defence industry is aware that its future position in the European Union is highly dependent upon current investment in R&D. Nevertheless, this awareness is qualified, since, according to Bocchini:

nowadays there is a wide consciousness about the need to preserve research activities and more advanced production [capability]. But with a more precise definition: an increasing level of high technologies is characterising defence systems, with the *soft* component of such technology ... prevailing upon the *hard* component; such an evolution is quite obvious. But it would be a mistake ... to bet only on high tech requirements ... [based on hypothetical scenarios. One] needs, instead, to work out selection criteria based on ... *needed technologies*, promoting the development of a balanced mix of technologies, both conventional and innovative. These technologies should enable the [European] Community to maintain, with regard to autonomy and completeness, its own system of defence in the future (*Interarma News*, No. 6, 26 March 1993, p. 207).

Analysis of Military Technology Policy

The Italian Ministry of Defence is paying closer attention to industrial activity, accepting that policies for technology and procurement may not coincide with the operational needs of the Armed Forces. The *Military Technology Plan* currently in preparation appears to be, quite simply, a means to give political and financial support to firms involved in international collaborative projects. This approach, in the absence of a more general technology policy and the explicit definition of national priorities, would appear to be driven primarily by national military procurement choices.

In July 1993, there was extensive debate over the need for the Armed Forces to implement a 'buy Italian' policy. The issue was forced by the perceived need for a fighter aircraft to fill the gap before the *Eurofighter 2000* would become available (De Andreis and Perani, 1994). The debate was reinforced by the Italian aerospace industry's belief that the aging fleet of F-104 fighters needed upgrading and/or that additional AM-X tactical fighters should be purchased as air interceptors.

The Minister of Defence, Mr F. Fabbri, stated that

if the national industry were now able to supply us the aircraft we need, we would have no problem opting for a national aircraft ... [but] national firms cannot attempt to [influence decision making on] national security [by] threatening job cuts. Air defence is a priority now. We cannot update the F-104s only to sustain our industry. (*Interarma News*, No. 13, 2 July 1993, p. 463).

In the event, a procurement package was worked out whereby 24 British MRCA IDS Tornado aircraft were leased, worth Lit. 2,176 billion, and funds were provided for updating 60–70 F-104 fighters. However, only Lit. 500 billion were allocated to the United Kingdom, with industrial offsets worth Lit. 120 billion to be spent in Italy. Furthermore, Lit. 1,600 billion would be devoted to maintenance and upgrading the Tornado and F-104 aircraft by Italian firms.

According to the 1995 MoD procurement budget proposal, Lit. 1,237 billion will be spent on R&D out of a total procurement budget of about Lit. 3,300 billion. Most of this is earmarked for modernising existing equipment, such as the Tornado and F-104 aircraft, frigates and other major weapons systems, commissioning foreign technologies (a subject of some importance; see Sandri and Politi, 1994), such as the Harrier Plus AV-8B aircraft, aeroengines and radars, or for promoting and engineering new weapons systems. Very little was reserved for advanced research projects.

Military R&D Institutions

Military R&D in Italy is carried out by three main types of organisations:

- 16 technical and experimental centres of the Ministry of Defence
- private and public military firms
- universities and other research centres (as minor performers).

There are only a few military research centres in Italy:

- *Centro Ricerche Esperienze e Studi per Applicazioni Militari* (CRESAM — Centre for Military Research and Studies) based in Pisa, Tuscany. CRESAM works in four fields: nuclear energy, opto-electronics, electro-magnetic compatibility and material diagnostics.
- *Armed Forces Technical Centres* serving the Army, the Air Force and the Navy. The Air Force Air Division for Studies, Research and Experiments (DASRS) is of special interest because of its collaboration with the aerospace industry.
- *Experimental Centres and Firing Grounds* maintained by the three Armed Forces; Salto di Quirra (Sardinia), for naval experimentation, and Nettuno, for ground artillery, are the best known.

These research centres have played only a limited role in the past in developing military products; they acted mainly as testing facilities for industrial firms producing military equipment. Nonetheless, the acceleration of MoD procurement budget cuts, coupled with the need to preserve technological capabilities within military industry, will probably lead to limitations in the Armed Forces' R&D activities, and even the possible closure of some experimental and technical centres. As the Air Force Chief of Staff, Gen. Pillinini, said in March 1994, '... we cannot have both a reduced Air Force *and* a research branch, even if important and efficient, oversized with respect to requirements. The Air Force has to maintain [the] right ratio between research, experimental activity and operational activity.' (*Interarma News*, No. 4, 9 March 1993, p. 55). Consequently, even though the political emphasis is on increasing R&D spending, the Armed Services are in practice experiencing a reduction in R&D and experimental capabilities.

Participation in International R&D Programmes

The Italian share of EUCLID resources initially amounted to some 14 MECU (nearly 12% of the total), and Italy chaired the Common European Priority Area (CEPA) on Opto-electronic Devices. The Italian Ministry of Defence judged this to be the most appropriate area because its technological requirements were less advanced than some other CEPAs. A technology support group brought together some of the leading Italian defence firms (Agusta, Alenia, Elettronica, FIAT and OTO Melara) to assist the MoD in coordinating this research activity.

In 1994, Italian firms participated in 28 out of 44 Research and Technology Projects (RTPs) within EUCLID, taking a leadership role in projects on intelligent sensors, advanced space synthetic aperture radar and optical fibres for underwater acoustics (Pavone, 1994).

The Italian defence industry is also actively involved in various NATO Industrial Advisory Group (NIAG) pre-feasibility studies, including:

- Future Light Battlefield Helicopter (FLBH)
- Conventional Disarmament Verification Technologies
- Very Short-Range Air Defence System for Ships
- Smoke Ammunition
- NATO Submarine Rescue System
- NIAG Study on a Technology Forecast (POST 2000)

Only a small group of leading military companies in Italy, mostly in the aerospace and electronics sectors, participate in EUREKA. Nevertheless, participation by Italian military firms in European programmes, especially EUCLID and EUREKA, is considered important for the industry. Furthermore, the Italian defence industry is increasingly turning to European Union research programmes to support both civilian and dual-use activities.

Significant Industrial Developments

Until the early 1990s, the Italian defence industry was dominated by two major public holding companies, IRI (whose defence interests were in turn concentrated within the group Finmeccanica) and EFIM. The second of these, EFIM, had been built up from the 1960s around a conglomeration of mechanical engineering interests, civil (notably, railways) as well as military. In 1973 it entered the aeronautical sector, taking over Agusta helicopters and OTO Melara (battle tanks and defence systems), among others.

In 1992, EFIM was put into liquidation, the result of a long history of operating with weak financial controls and persistent losses in many of its businesses. At the time of its liquidation, 81 of its 114 companies were running deficits. The government decided to transfer the defence and aeronautical firms to Finmeccanica, together with a recapitalisation fund of Lit. 4,068 billion. By the end of May 1994, all 28 of these firms, including Agusta, Agusta Sistemi, Officine Galileo, OTO Melara, and Breda Meccanica Bresciana had been transferred. (Ministro del Tesoro, 1994).

As a result of these developments, by early 1995 Finmeccanica controlled about three-quarters of the Italian defence industry, playing a monopoly role in aerospace, radars and defence systems, and a major role in defence electronics, as well as such technologically important civil sectors as transport, energy and automation. It ranked eighth among Italian companies in terms of consolidated sales, and third among manufacturing firms. It had already been the dominant Italian firm in several defence sectors, notably aerospace, where the merger in 1990 of Selenia and Aeritalia into Alenia gave it an aerospace firm comparable to British Aerospace, Aérospatiale and Daimler Benz Aerospace. The addition of the EFIM firms strengthened its position in this and other sectors.

After Finmeccanica, the next most important defence firm is FIAT Avio, which has been strongly involved in restructuring FIAT's defence interests during the 1990s. A specialist designer and manufacturer of aeroengine parts, from the 1980s it began diversifying into commercial aeroengines, power plant generators, and gas turbines. In the 1990s it engaged in a series of joint ventures with leading international aeroengine and power generator firms, including General Electric, Pratt and Whitney and Westinghouse (US), Rolls Royce (UK) and SNECMA (France). Another major step in this diversification process came with a commitment towards space propulsion activities, particularly from 1993–94.

Taking into account the ownership patterns that emerged by the mid-1990s, the top ten Italian defence firms, in descending order of military sales in 1992, are shown in Table 3 (see also Appendix for further details of these firms).

Sales for these firms in 1992 amounted to some Lit. 5,963 billion, accounting for 70.1% of the total gross military sales revenues of the top 55 Italian defence companies. Seven of them are in high-technology sectors (aerospace, electronics and communications). Five are state owned and, of the others, three

Table 3: The Ten Leading Italian Defence Firms, (listed in descending order of total military sales revenues in 1992)

1. Alenia (IRI/Finmeccanica), aerospace
2. OTO Melara (IRI/Finmeccanica), land warfare
3. Agusta (IRI/Finmeccanica), aerospace
4. FIAT Avio (FIAT), aerospace
5. IVECO (FIAT), transportation
6. Aermacchi (private), aerospace
7. Alenia Elsag Sistemi Navali (IRI/Finmeccanica), electronics
8. BPD Difesa e Spazio (FIAT), land warfare
9. Elettronica (private), electronics
10. Elmer (IRI/Finmeccanica), electronics

are controlled by FIAT. It should also be noted that Finmeccanica has a critical stake in both of the non-FIAT private firms, controlling 25% of Aeronautica Macchi, the parent company of Aermacchi, and 47% of Elettronica.

These ten companies are adopting different strategies to cope with the shrinking defence equipment market, a decline they see as permanent. Our analysis is based on the concept of a firm's vulnerability level, after Bitzinger's (1993) analysis of the huge, heterogeneous US defence industrial base and the work of Huffschmid and Voss (1991) in analysing 30 major arms producers in Europe for the European Parliament.

Table 4 shows that firms from the aerospace sector generally have a medium level of vulnerability (Aermacchi is an exception), and a mainly 'expansion' strategic response. These firms are opting for concentration and international cooperation, combined with a slow withdrawal from military activity by diversifying their business and laying off staff. All three electronics and communications firms are highly vulnerable, and have adopted a combination of an 'expansion' strategy, concentrating their defence activities, with a 'defensive' strategy involving layoffs. The two firms in land warfare manufacturing fall into the medium vulnerability category. However, they differ in their strategies. The state-owned OTO Melara has maintained its levels of production and employment until relatively recently, while the privately-owned BPD Difesa e Spazio has taken a number of different approaches.

Taken as a whole, the ten leading Italian defence firms would appear to have adopted a predominantly 'expansion' strategy, by concentrating and specialising their activities, and by reinforcing their position in the international market through international cooperation. However, this is not the full story, as almost all of these firms have also adopted 'withdrawal' strategies including

Table 4: Strategic Responses of the 10 Major Italian Defence Firms

Firm	**Military Dependency (%)**	**Level of Vulnerability**	**Firm Strategy**						
			Expansion			**Withdrawal defensive**		**offensive**	
			1	2	3	4	5	6	7
1. Alenia	69	Medium	+	++	++	++		++	
2. OTO Melara	100	Medium		+		+			
3. Augusta	82	Medium		+	++	++		+	
4. FIAT Avio	50	Medium	+	++	++			++	+
5. IVECO	7	Low			++			+	
6. Aermacchi	95	High	+	++	++	++		+	
7. Alenia Elsag	100	High	+	+	++			+	
8. BPD Dif. E Sp.	46	Medium		+	+	+		+	+
9. Elettronica	96	High	+	+		+		+	
10. Elmer	95	High		+		+			+

Notes: There are two main strategies: A) stabilising or extending defence activities (expansion or specialisation); B) withdrawing (slowly or rapidly) from defence activity. Further, each strategy may contemplate different options.
Strategy A, options: (1) increasing exports; (2) concentrating or reorganising military productions at a national level; (3) reinforcing firm's position at international level through international co-operation.
Strategy B, options may refer to two subsets of options: a) defensive, b) offensive. Among the defensive options: (4) downsizing production level through laying-off of employees and possibly shutting down plants; (5) selling off defence activities. Among offensive options we could find: (6) diversifying activities towards civil sector, and (7) converting military to civil activities.

diversification and downsizing. There have been no notable instances of selling off divisions or of conversion to civil production.

Firms in the high-technology sectors (aerospace, electronics and communications) are more firmly committed to an 'expansion' strategy than those in mature technology sectors (land warfare and transportation). Interestingly, there seems to be no essential difference between the strategies adopted by state-owned and private firms, except in Finmeccanica's active process of concentration through mergers and acquisitions in the aerospace and electronics sectors.

The survival strategy of the major Italian defence firms is first to maintain a certain level of production capability, taking into account expected national and international demand, but also to participate in international R&D and industrial collaboration programmes in order to develop technological strength and share risk. These firms will probably become more selective as they concentrate in critical areas. The high-technology firms in particular are committed to defence work, paring and tailoring their R&D and production facilities as required to concentrate on market niches and core technological capabilities. However, there are also some cases of successful diversification activities. For example:

- Aermacchi agreed in 1990 to join the German firm Dornier (part of Daimler Benz Aerospace) in the DO328 regional aircraft. In early 1994, when military production was flagging, this new development provided some, though insufficient, compensatory work;
- Alenia strengthened its position in regional aircraft through partnership with Aérospatiale, enlarging the successful ATR aircraft family, and through participation as a sub-contractor or minor partner in major commercial aircraft programmes such as the Boeing B767 and the McDonnell Douglas MD11;
- FIAT Avio, as already mentioned, diversified in the early 1990s through increased participation in international civil aeroengine consortia and by strengthening its space activities (eg, by development of key parts of the engine for the European Ariane launcher). It also joined with Westinghouse Electric and Mitsubishi Heavy Industries to increase its activities in industrial gas turbines.

It is in the aerospace sector that the most far-reaching efforts to diversify have occurred, and this also happens to be the sector for which collaborative R&D and industrial cooperation in Europe is most important.

Policies on International Collaboration

There is no coherent national policy on internationalisation for the Italian defence industry. In fact, extensive support for the mostly public-owned large domestic producers in Italy has had the effect of hindering the international competitiveness of the defence industry and slowing the process of industrial integration at the international level. Nevertheless, the Italian military has sponsored international programmes, including consortia established by intergovernmental Memoranda of Understanding (MoUs) and international, mainly European, development and production agreements for a weapon system or a family of weapons. This position was confirmed in February 1995 by the Minister of Defence, who argued that ever-increasing participation in international cooperative projects was vital, not least because without such nourishment the technological assets acquired through years of hard work would decay

Table 5: Main Co-operative Projects in which Italian Military Firms are Participating

PROGRAMME OR JOINT VENTURE	PARTICIPANT FIRMS
Panavia GmbH (Tornado)	Finmeccanica-Alenia (I), BAe (UK), MBB (G)
Turbo Union Ltd (engine RB 199)	FIAT Avio (I) MTU (G), Rolls Royce (UK)
Eurofighter	Finmeccanica-Alenia (I), BAe (UK) CASA (Sp) DASA (G)
Eurojet Engines GmbH (engine Eurojet 200)	FIAT Avio (I) MTU (G) Rolls Royce (UK) Sener (Sp)
GE 90 (aeroengine)	FIAT Avio (I), GE (US), SNECMA (F)
GIE Eurosam (missiles)	Finmeccanica-Alenia (I) Aérospatiale, Thomson-CSF (F)
GIE Atr (ATR 42/72 commuters)	Finmeccanica-Alenia (I), Aérospatiale (F)
Milas (anti ship missile)	OTO Melara (I), Matra (F)
Consorzio Esplosivi Compositi (explosives)	OTO Melara (I), SNPE (F)
Euroflag (transport aircraft)	Finmeccanica-Alenia (I), Aérospatiale (F), BAe (UK), CASA (Sp), DASA (G)
MIDS (Multifunctional Information Distribution System)	Computing Device (Can), INISEL (Sp) Italtel (I), Plessey (USA), Siemens (G), Thomson-CSF (F)
NIS (NATO Identification System)	Eseina (Sp), Italtel (I), Plessey (UK), Bendix, Raytheon (USA), Siemens (G), Thomson-CSF (F)
MLRS (Multiple Launch Rocket System)	Aerospatiale (F), Hunting (UK), RTO (G) BPD Difesa e Spazio (I)
Euro Hermespace	Finmeccanica-Alenia (I), Aérospatiale (F), DASA (G)
Helios (military satellite)	Finmeccanica-Alenia (I), DASA (G), Matra (F)
AM-X International (AM-X fighter)	Finmeccanica-Alenia, Aermacchi (I) Embraer (Brazil)
EH Industries (EH-101 helicopter)	Agusta (I), Westland (UK)
Regulus (booster for Ariane V)	BPD Difesa e Spazio (I), SNPE (F)

Source: S. Rolfo, 'Mutamenti dell'industria militare: la prospettiva europea' in *L'industria*, No. 4/1993.

fast, with negative consequences for civilian spin-offs. (*Interarma News*, No. 3, 22 February 1995, p. 30). Table 5 lists the main cooperative programmes in which Italian firms are participating.

Italian firms are not involved in strategic agreements or joint ventures such as Euromissile, Eurodynamics or Eurocopter. They prefer to defend their share within the domestic market or to define international collaboration on a strict *juste retour* basis. Thus, Italian firms are involved in government-guaranteed programmes such as Tornado, Eurofighter, the RB 199 and EJ 200 engines, AM-X fighter, EH-101 helicopter, MLRS, Helios satellite, Horizon frigate and the NH 90 helicopter. Italian military firms have also participated, in a limited way, in collaborative production in the civil sector. For example, BPD Difesa e Spazio is part of the European Ariane consortium, Finmeccanica is involved in the production of the ATR commuter aircraft with Aérospatiale of France, and FIAT Avio is a partner, with the US General Electric, Japanese IHI, and French SNECMA, in the development and production of the civil GE 90 aeroengine.

The attitude of Italian firms — and consequently that of the Italian government — towards either liberalisation or integration of the defence market is decidedly cool. The rhetoric, as exemplified by Mr Airaghi of Finmeccanica, is that Italian industry is offering a 'first class' contribution to international defence cooperation. However, there is an evident attempt to regulate and to slow down the integration process. As Mr Matteucci of FIAT said in 1994 at a conference in Milan, '... [we need] a cooperation policy oriented to participation in international programmes both in research and in industrial fields, but with fair qualitative and quantitative returns ... a European policy but without unilateral eagerness.' (Matteucci, 1994).

Mr Bocchini (1993), then President of RITAD, indicated at a conference in Rome in December 1993, that he would favour increasing concentration in the military industrial sector, adding, however, that

> we should avoid ... uncontrolled cartels of firms developing ahead of a related aggregation of demand. Monopolies at continental level may actually be established, reproducing, on a larger [scale], the 'national champions'... On the contrary, [there] should be: in a first phase, favoured aggregation between European firms, considering existing asymmetries, and guaranteeing a well-balanced and 'intelligent' presence of all countries; only in a second phase would established industrial groups with an adequate 'critical mass'... be able to compete at the international level, in which all qualified and efficient producers could have room. Definition of common rules will guarantee a balanced functioning of the European defence market.

The Italian defence industry clearly prefers a European market strongly controlled by national governments. The current share of Italian military industry in the European market is considered too small (about 10%) to compete in a free market with British, French and German firms. Joint ventures and strategic alliances between firms are considered to be just as much of a threat to the survival of a national military industry in Italy.

Policy on Conversion

Past Experience

Military industrial policy has traditionally been the responsibility of the Ministry of Defence, which used procurement policy to orient and sustain the productive capacity of the military industrial sector. Procurement spending directly influenced the size of military industry both in periods of rising domestic military spending (1970–1989) and in the current period of declining budgets. Between 1985 and 1989, growth in domestic procurement spending almost completely compensated (at least in financial terms) for the decrease in arms exports.

After 1989, the combined reduction in domestic and international demand for Italian military products focused attention on the need to reduce military productive capacity and to develop a policy for conversion. It has been the Parliament rather than the Government that has taken initiatives for conversion. Since 1987, ten draft bills have been presented to define several policy tools, such as a conversion fund, a monitoring unit, and financial support for regional activities in this field. Nevertheless, a comprehensive law has yet to be passed.

There have been some general laws which provided partial support for conversion or diversification activities, *inter alia*. For example, law 46/1982 supported technological innovation and applied research in Italian industry, and several projects were undertaken to produce civil items using military technologies. Similarly, law 808/1985 supported civil activities in the aerospace industry, some of which drew upon military technologies.

Current Conversion Policy

In 1993, the attitude of the Italian Government towards the military industry changed substantially. As we have seen, for the first time, the Ministry of Industry officially and publicly recognised the existence of an autonomous 'defence industrial sector', and went on to indicate its support for national and international reorganisation of this sector in order to maintain it at the leading edge of technology, and with a distinct presence in Italy.

Also in 1993, the Parliament passed a law (237/1993) creating a Conversion Fund under the administration of the Ministry of Industry, and Lit. 500 billion were appropriated for a five-year period. However, that same law also financed industrial restructuring activities in the defence sector, and the acquisition of four frigates by the Italian Navy.

The Conversion Fund consists of two main instruments for promoting 'rationalisation, restructuring and conversion of the war industry'. The Ministry of Industry may offer grants or loans to military firms willing to widen their range of civil products. The Conversion Fund may also support regional initiatives in collaboration with local governments, firms and other organisations, for developments in regions affected by declining military industrial activity and redundancies. However, the Fund has not yet been implemented. So far, the Ministry of Industry has only issued regulations dealing with 'restructuring activities', and not yet for the effective implementation of the Fund. Consequently, the Ministry regards the EU KONVER programme as the main conversion initiative currently underway in Italy.

Firms' Activities

Over the past few years, major Italian arms producers have made it a priority to explore the possibility of turning to civil production and marketing. But although a number of feasibility studies and market research exercises have been carried out, no significant conversion strategies have emerged. In some cases, subsidiaries were created to produce commercial goods. However, most of the large defence firms opted to continue producing for the Italian government, and with a preference for military over civil products.

Data in the Appendix (which are in current prices, and so do not allow for inflation) give some indication of how firms have responded to defence cutbacks. We can note that total and military sales of the four aerospace firms (Alenia, Agusta, Aermacchi and FIAT Avio) started to fall in real terms at the turn of the 1990s, even taking into account such developments as restructuring of some of their defence activity. A significant downsizing of employment came later, especially by the end of 1991 and early 1992. R&D expenditure (expressed in the Appendix as a percentage of total sales) also fell for the two state-owned firms, Alenia and Agusta, but increased for the private FIAT Avio, indicating a difference in corporate attitudes towards risk.

Firms like Elmer and Elettronica, in the electronics sector, show an upward trend in their total and military sales (in current values) and an initial, but weak, process of diversification in 1991. The demise of civil activities and the sharp increase of military sales of Alenia Elsag SN reflects the restructuring carried out by Elsag in 1990, whereby all its defence business was concentrated in the newly created Alenia Elsag Sistemi Navali. Data on R&D for these firms are available only for Elettronica, which devotes to R&D about 5% of total sales. Employment in these firms has fallen since the end of the 1980s, even if less sharply than in other defence firms.

In the case of OTO Melara, which is 100% defence-oriented, sales and employment have shown a downward trend since the mid-1980s, when its export markets began to decline. No efforts at diversification have been made. On the other hand, BPD Difesa e Spazio started in the late 1980s to cope with a declining military market by increasing efforts to diversify towards space activities, as the diverging trends for its military and civil sales confirm. Even so, a significant fall in workforce could not be avoided.

Finally, given its low military dependence, IVECO presents a different case. Its military sales have actually increased since 1991, following a sharp fall just before that, largely as a result of fluctuating domestic demand. Its total sales, on the other hand, were badly affected by the downturn in the commercial transport market, which was also the cause of the reduction in employees between 1991 and 1993.

In 1992, local authorities in the Rome region carried out a study of the reorganisation plans of military firms and found that three basic approaches were being followed:

- reduction of productive capacity and employment (by up to 40% of the 1990 level);
- widening the product range offered (military, civil and dual-use);
- reorganisation of the corporate structure. (Regione Lazio, 1992).

To produce both military and civil products more effectively, firms focused specifically on:

- strengthening R&D and design capacity;
- creating or strengthening marketing capacity;
- streamlining the production process;
- reforming the workforce, by creating a multi-faceted skills base, simplifying hierarchical structures, extending the use of information technology and introducing Just in Time and Total Quality models.

To give one specific instance of plant-level conversion, BPD Difesa e Spazio set up at one of its sites, in January 1994, a new firm called Bag, through a joint venture with two US firms. As the name might suggest, the firm was to produce automobile air bags, replacing the earlier business of manufacturing military explosives, but using for this purpose some of the firm's original explosives expertise. Further expertise came from the two US firms. Hence, a plant that would otherwise have closed continued in business, although with a reduced workforce. (*Il Sole 24 Ore*, 17 November 1994).

More recently, interesting conversion initiatives have been taken by the Regional Governments of Lombardy (Milan) and Tuscany (Florence). In Lombardy, a regional law was passed establishing a Regional Conversion Agency, to define the most effective actions for promoting defence conversion

In Tuscany, the regional government is supporting a public-private non-profit institution aimed at carrying out research activities for improving the regional scientific and technological infrastructure, and for encouraging conversion activities in high-tech military firms.

Conversion Policy and the European Union

In 1992, several Italian regions proposed a number of industrial projects to the Ministry of Industry for joint financing by national sources and the European Community's KONVER Programme. An 'Italian Defence Industry Conversion Programme' was adopted, consisting of 15 projects. Four of these were recommended for EC funding:

- a centre for executive aircraft to be based in Genoa;
- a precision casting plant in L'Aquila (Abruzzi), using a plant formerly producing missile castings;
- the production of air bags for the automobile industry in the ammunition production plant of BPD Difesa e Spazio in Colleferro, near Rome;
- a centre in Naples for design and prototyping of an amphibious aircraft using advanced composite materials.

This Conversion Programme was criticised by the European Commission for being too 'industrial' in its approach, instead of focusing on regional development, as the KONVER Programme had intended. Following amendments to the proposal, however, the Commission approved it in December 1993. In 1994, the initial phase of the programme was implemented in Italy through collaboration between the Ministry of Industry and relevant regions. After several regional conversion plans had been prepared, the Ministry submitted to the Commission in late 1994 a comprehensive National Conversion Plan which, at the time of writing, was still under examination in Brussels.

European Union Structural Funds, which *could* be used to support diversification or conversion activities, are underutilised in Italy: only 30% of the funds available are actually applied for by local government authorities and small and medium industrial firms. In part, this inefficiency is due to the lack of a tradition in collaboration between the public and the private sectors in Italy, and the associated bureaucratic difficulties. Moreover, the Structural Funds have not generally been used in Italy to promote technological development in small companies. A further problem is that European funds are not intended to support the conversion activities of large firms, in order not to distort industrial competition in Europe.

Partly as a result of this situation, the Italian defence industry has not taken an interest in promoting collaboration between the European Commission and the Italian Government in developing a conversion strategy. Instead, they have argued for strict enforcement of Article 223 of the Treaty of Rome in order to defend public support to the national military industry. In consequence, we can expect the Italian Government to prefer 'restructuring' of military industries to conversion to civil production.

Controlling the Diffusion of Defence Technologies

National Military Exports

According to SIPRI estimates, at the beginning of the 1980s, Italy was the fourth largest exporter of weapons in the world. At the end of the decade, it had dropped from the list of the ten leading arms exporters. This decline can be partially attributed to increased government controls on transfers, which were previously almost unrestricted. (For example, Italy repeatedly ignored the UN embargo on South Africa, and sold arms to countries at war, such as Iran and Iraq). Another factor has presumably been the declining technological and commercial competitiveness of the Italian arms industry.

Export regulations were initially implemented by Ministerial Decree. Then, in July 1990, a law on export controls was passed by the Parliament, and in 1992 this was followed by a law dealing specifically with the transfer of dual-use advanced technologies.

Under the 1990 law, *New rules for the control of export, import and transit of military equipment*, arms transfers are subject to state approval and must be in accordance with Italian foreign and defence policies. The law prohibits:

- the production, import and export of nuclear, chemical and biological weapons and related technologies;
- exports which are contrary to the Italian Constitution, to international obligations and to national security;
- exports to countries engaged in wars, countries embargoed by the United Nations, countries which violate human rights, and countries benefiting from Italian development aid programmes whose military expenditure exceeds that required for self-defence;
- exports when there are inadequate guarantees on the final destinations of the items concerned.

However, certain categories of arms transfers, such as sports and non-automatic weapons, the import of weapons from NATO allies, and government to government exports under a military aid programme, are exempted from these controls.

The 1990 controls list thirteen categories of weapons systems, some of which, such as missiles, torpedos and howitzers, are for military use only. Others, such as aircraft, vehicles and ships are considered dual-use items and are only subject to control if 'specifically constructed for military use'. In September 1991, a detailed list of all items included in the thirteen categories was published by the Ministry of Defence. More recently, some items have been transferred to come under the jurisdiction of the 1992 law on the transfer of military technologies (see below).

Parliament has the legal right to be informed ex-post about arms exports by a special branch of the Prime Minister's Office, through an annual report detailing the previous year's export authorisations and deliveries.

In cases of violations of the law, the Ministry of Defence can suspend a company from the National Register of exporting companies, and the Ministry of Foreign Affairs can suspend any authorisation. In addition, the law provides for penalties of up to twelve years' imprisonment and fines for false declarations of information, violations of procedure related to final destinations of weapons, and exports without authorisation.

General guidelines for export policy were initially provided by an Inter-Ministerial Committee on the Exchange of Defence Weapons. The Committee was responsible for approving major, politically-sensitive arms deals, and for defining and updating the countries to which restrictive arms sales apply. It was also the Committee's responsibility to identify exceptional cases in which a temporary suspension of sales of non-automatic weapons might be imposed. In 1994, this Committee was disbanded, and its responsibilities were reassigned to a less specific Inter-Ministerial Committee for Economic Programming.

At the international level, Italy is a member of all the main organisations involved in controlling arms exports, including the UN, EU, G-7, COCOM (until it was disbanded), MTCR, Australia Group, Nuclear Suppliers Group, OSCE, CWC and Zangger Group.

The Italian Government also aims to improve international cooperation in controlling the diffusion of military equipment and technologies, both in order to make controls more effective and to prevent Italian firms from being disadvantaged as a result of the restrictive Italian laws and regulations. Italy has contributed to the UN Arms Trade Register, the definition of common European Union criteria for limiting arms exports, a joint policy of the G-7 countries for controlling trade of 'critical' products, and the reform of the COCOM regime together with an extended partnership with East European countries.

Almost all arms export deals signed by Italian firms are linked to technology transfers or offset agreements involving mutual exchange of products and know-how. For instance, in the last decade, Agusta and Aermacchi exported aircraft to countries such as the Philippines, Australia, South Africa, Brazil and Singapore, and with them, related knowledge on assembly and maintenance. On occasion, technology is also transferred to another highly industrialised country, such as the Intermarine blueprint for building one-piece GRP mine-hunter hulls sold to the US Navy, and a license to produce the naval gun 76/62 sold by OTO Melara to the American firm FMC.

The Italian Parliament is discussing the need to institute a requirement that any high-technology product purchased by the Government abroad must be accompanied by a compensatory order to an Italian firm. The aerospace industry is pressing strongly for such a regulation, particularly since 1993 and the planned acquisition of four Canadair CL-415 fire-fighting aircraft by the Italian government without any element of industrial or technological offset. To compound the political sensitivity, this order was placed shortly after the newly-elected Canadian Government announced the cancellation of an order for 35 EH-101 anti-submarine warfare helicopters from Agusta and Westland in the UK.

Export of Dual-Use Technology

In 1992, a law was passed (222/1992) controlling the transfer of high technology products, which required checks on the final destination and use of equipment and on the potential proliferation of technologies for weapons of mass destruction. The responsibility for controlling exports of dual-use items thus passed to the Ministry of Foreign Trade.

In 1993, a Ministerial Decree was issued liberalising the export of high-technology products to industrialised countries and streamlining the license application process. The Decree allows for a 'general authorisation' to be granted to a manufacturer which obviates the need for licenses for individual exports to the European Union, Australia, Japan, Norway, Switzerland, or Turkey. Only a few items, such as supercomputers, cryptographic devices and atomic clocks, must follow the normal procedures.

In Italy, there are no known restrictions on the nationality of scientists or engineers working on international research programmes, or of those working in universities. However, researchers employed by military firms must normally be cleared for access to classified data.

Export control in Italy is motivated primarily by the desire to coordinate security policies at an international level. Issues of national security and economic and industrial considerations have only been secondary in defining export restrictions. The Italian Government is committed to define a common high-technology export policy in collaboration with its European partners, as well as the members of G-7, OSCE, NPT and other multinational fora.

The general attitude of the Italian Government towards military and dual-use exports neither favours nor restricts exports. Rather, Italy attempts to establish a link between military exports and foreign policy. In fact, one of the criticisms levelled at the old regime by the Chamber of Deputies was that the transfer and the transit of weapons had become a 'parallel foreign policy'. Consequently, the decision making authority was shifted, after the approval of law no. 185 in 1990, from the Ministries of Defence and Foreign Trade to the Ministry of Foreign Affairs. However, this transfer of power has been difficult to implement because it is not clearly set out in law, and the Ministry of Foreign Affairs has not been allocated additional funds to carry out its new responsibilities.

Conclusion

The overall approach of the Italian government towards military and dual-use technology and industry has been to seek an institutional framework in which each country maintains a negotiated and balanced trade position corresponding as much as possible to the *status quo*. Italy would not welcome greater competition within Europe, nor with the other major Western arms producers; nor is it strongly committed to conversion. Rather than confront the implications of the overall decline in demand for military equipment, Italy is defending its military industrial interests; issues of national security and more strategic economic considerations have been of secondary importance.

Endnotes

1 One particularly important law (Directions for simplifying and controlling the procedures adopted for the central procurement for Defence) was adopted on 4 October 1988. Article 1 of this law establishes that the programmes for the upkeep and modernisation of armaments systems and other defence equipment must be approved either by law (in case of extraordinary financing) or by Ministerial Decree (where ordinary budgeting applies). In the latter case, the programmes must be submitted to the relevant Parliamentary Committees for approval.

2 It was only in 1990 that the Italian Parliament passed a law on 'New Norms on the Control of Exports, Imports and Transit of War Materials'.

3 The relevant law was 'Intervention for economic sectors of national importance', 17 February 1982.

4 To put this into perspective, 1991 state R&D expenditure was estimated at Lit. 3,225 billion, of which Lit. 852 billion was allocated to defence and Lit. 733 billion to space. The amounts allocated to other objectives were much smaller.

5 'Per un futuro diverso dell'economia italiana', Ministero dell'Industria, December 1993; see *Il Sole 24 Ore*, 15/12/1993.

Appendix: Main Economic Indicators of Major Defence Firms, 1986–1993 (Lit. billion)

FINMECCANICA GROUP

ALENIA	1986	1987	1988	1989	1990	1991	1992	1993
Total Sales	1,404	1,586	1,655	2,052	3,221	3,866	3,779	n.a.
Military Sales	980	1,030	1,100	1,130	1,970	2,660	2,600	n.a.
M.S./T.S. (%)	70	65	66	55	61	69	69	n.a.
R&D (% of TS)	38	37	36	29	25	18	n.a.	n.a.
Employment (no.)	12,906	13,662	14,177	14,903	21,981	21,836	18,433	17,354

ALENIA ELSAG SISTEMI NAVALI	1986	1987	1988	1989	1990	1991	1992	1993
Total Sales	378	405	319	342	498	209	257	324
Military Sales	n.a.	162	125	101	90	209	257	324
M.S./T.S. (%)	n.a.	40	40	30	18	100	100	100
R&D (% of TS)	n.a.	n.a.	n.a.	n.a.	n.a.	n.a.	n.a.	n.a.
Employment (no.)	1,880	1,872	1,844	1,815	1,780	314	278	n.a.

Note: 1990 data refer to the Military Division of Elsag SpA.

ELMER SpA	1986	1987	1988	1989	1990	1991	1992	1993
Total Sales	n.a.	117	127	158	126	190	190	171
Military Sales	n.a.	117	127	158	126	180	180	160
M.S./T.S. (%)	n.a.	100	100	100	100	95	95	94
R&D (% of TS)	n.a.	n.a.	n.a.	n.a.	n.a.	n.a.	n.a.	n.a.
Employment (no.)	n.a.	1,024	1,054	1,066	1,060	988	927	949

AGUSTA SpA	1986	1987	1988	1989	1990	1991	1992	1993
Total Sales	688	669	777	1,127	997	864	845	827
Military Sales	550	495	536	890	790	650	690	650
M.S./T.S. (%)	80	74	72	79	79	75	82	79
R&D (% of TS)	33	37	30	22	n.a.	n.a.	n.a.	n.a.
Employment (no.)	3,612	3,629	4,285	8,426	8,117	6,998	6,990	4,943

OTO MELARA SpA	1986	1987	1988	1989	1990	1991	1992	1993
Total Sales	625	660	561	607	570	601	748	610
Military Sales	625	660	561	607	570	601	748	610
M.S./T.S. (%)	100	100	100	100	100	100	100	100
R&D (% of TS)	15	n.a.	15	14	n.a.	14	12	n.a.
Employment (no.)	2,437	2,379	2,329	2,294	2,245	2,149	1,917	1,823

FIAT GROUP

FIAT AVIO	1986	1987	1988	1989	1990	1991	1992	1993
Total Sales	490	703	1,044	938	1,007	801	899	1,039
Military Sales	343	422	424	550	560	454	449	415
M.S./T.S. (%)	70	60	41	59	56	57	50	40
R&D (% of TS)	15	12	10	13	16	24	25	n.a.
Employment (no.)	4,526	4,656	4,749	4,651	4,666	4,719	4,656	4,538

BPD DIFESA e SPAZIO	1986	1987	1988	1989	1990	1991	1992	1993
Total Sales	354	335	264	302	374	329	425	351
Military Sales	n.a.	268	210	241	190	184	197	n.a.
M.S./T.S. (%)	n.a.	80	80	80	51	56	46	n.a.
R&D (% of TS)	n.a.	n.a.	n.a.	n.a.	n.a.	n.a.	n.a.	n.a.
Employment (no.)	2,429	3,519	2,189	2,120	2,019	1,812	1,464	1,160

Note: Data until 1988 refer to BPD Difesa e Spazio Division of SNIA BPD SpA.

OTHER PRIVATE GROUPS

AERMACCHI	1986	1987	1988	1989	1990	1991	1992	1993
Total Sales	230	231	257	330	337	301	323	319
Military Sales	219	220	244	314	320	286	307	287
M.S./T.S. (%)	95	95	95	95	95	95	95	90
R&D (% of TS)	14	n.a.	n.a.	n.a.	n.a.	n.a.	14	n.a.
Employment (no.)	2,474	2,649	2,690	2,715	2,740	2,351	2,145	2,059

ELETTRONICA SpA	1986	1987	1988	1989	1990	1991	1992	1993
Total Sales	150	183	205	191	151	224	196	n.a.
Military Sales	148	183	205	190	150	220	188	215
M.S./T.S. (%)	99	100	100	99	99	98	96	n.a.
R&D (% of TS)	8	5	5	6	8	4	5	n.a.
Employment (no.)	1,485	1,319	1,344	1,368	1,363	1,330	1,445	1,217

Source: Coordinamento Nazionale degli Osservatori sull'Industria Militare in Italia, Lettere 2–6, Firm's Annual Reports.

References

De Andreis, M. and Perani, G., 1994, 'Italy's aerospace industry and the Eurofighter 2000', in R. Forsberg (ed.) *The Arms Production Dilemma*, Cambridge, Mass.: MIT Press.

Bitzinger, R.A., 1993, 'Adjusting to the Drawdown: the Transition in the Defense Industry', Washington, DC: Defense Budget Project.

Bocchini, Mr, 1993, speech to ENEA seminar on *Applicazioni 'duali'delle tecnologie militari*, Rome, December.

Huffschmid, J. and Voss, W., 1991, *Defence Procurement, the Arms Trade and the Conversion of the Armaments Industry in the Community*, Study for the Directorate-General for Research of the European Parliament.

Matteucci, Mr, 1994, speech to meeting on *Trends and Perspectives of Defence Industry in Western Europe: The firms' adjustments and the role of public policy*, Milan: Universita Cattolica.

Ministri del Tesoro, 1994, *Relazione sullo stato di attenuazione del decreto-legge 19 dicembre 1992, no. 487, recante 'Soppressione del'Ente Parteci-piazioni e Finanziamento Industria Munifattuiera-EFIM'*, Rome, 20 July.

MURST, 1994, *Ricerca e innovazione per lo sviluppo* (Research and innovation for development), Rome, April.

Pavone, G., 1994, Ricerca e sviluppo in campo militare in Italia, *Informazione della Difesa*, No. 4, 1994.

Regione Lazio, 1992, *Rapporto sulle possibilità di valorizzazione delle risorse tecnologiche del sistema dell'industria civile che opera per la Difesa nella regione Lazio*, Rapporto di Ricerca, Rome.

Sandri, S. and Politi, A., 1994 *Il problema della quantificazione di dati attendibili sull'interscambio militare/industriale fra I vari Paesi*, Rome: CeMISS.

Chapter 6
The Netherlands

Ton van Oosterhout and Wim A. Smit

Introduction

The Netherlands is a relatively small country with a small defence industry, and a defence policy aligned to NATO doctrine and strategy. The Dutch armed forces are today undergoing a substantial post-Cold War reorganisation, which affects the Army in particular. During the period 1991–2000, the Dutch Army is facing a 54% reduction to 36,000 personnel (including 10,700 civilians). The Air Force will number 13,000 personnel and the Navy 17,500 in the year 2000, both being reductions of 25% from the 1991 level. These changes are accompanied by a reduction in matériel acquisitions and a shift in defence equipment needs.

The Dutch defence industry is fully aware of these changes. Some sectors, like ship and radar construction, are relatively little affected, but others, like ammunition production, are facing problems. The major part of Dutch defence industry depends on military sales for only a modest percentage of its overall output. A few companies, however, are heavily involved in defence equipment production, and are thus more vulnerable to reductions and shifts in defence spending.

In terms of expenditure, the Dutch Armed Forces buy some 60% of their matériel needs from Dutch companies and the remaining 40% from abroad. Apart from Navy surface ships and submarines, no large weapon platforms are built in the Netherlands. Tanks and military aircraft, including helicopters, are bought abroad. The Dutch aerospace company Fokker, until its collapse in early 1996, was, however, able to produce military transport aircraft, derived from a civilian machine.

The Organisational Context

Dutch defence technology development involves the Ministries of Defence (MoD) and of Economic Affairs (MoEA). The latter's interest is confined to the limited number of areas in which the Dutch defence industry operates, and hence is narrower in scope than that of the MoD. Moreover, unlike the MoEA the MoD's interests are not confined to stimulating the development of technology and equipment by the Dutch defence industry. Rather, the MoD is interested in maintaining a broad technological base of know-how, in order to be able to operate as a knowledgeable customer. This implies the ability to evaluate and test technology and equipment offered either domestically or from abroad. In some cases, the MoD also wishes to influence the specifications of new equipment. MoD's R&D expenditures are to a great extent devoted to these latter tasks. A relatively modest sum of money is aimed at the development of new technology and new equipment, for example when the future matériel requirements of the Armed Forces involve technologies or products that are not readily available off the shelf.

The role of the MoEA is secondary as regards both the procurement of defence equipment by the MoD and the development of defence technology by Dutch industry. The MoEA is the chief Dutch actor in negotiations on offset orders for Dutch industry in cases of Dutch purchases of defence matériel from foreign companies. These offsets may be direct, such as co-production and joint development, or indirect, such as placing orders with Dutch companies in other, sometimes civil, areas. Indirect offsets may also involve opening a subsidiary in the Netherlands of the foreign company selling to the MoD. Dutch policy is that offset orders should contribute to the technological competitiveness of Dutch industry at large. At an early stage in the defence acquisition process, negotiations on the possibilities for purchasing from Dutch companies are held between the MoEA and Dutch industry (or its representative organisation NIID — see below). Sometimes, the MoEA subsidises domestic purchases to make them more attractive to the MoD. Its main aim in such cases is to help Dutch industry.

The Dutch defence industry has established an organisation, the Foundation for Dutch Industrial Participation in Defence Procurement (Stichting Nederlandse Industriële Inschakeling bij Defensieopdrachten — NIID), to promote its interests. NIID provides the industry with information on defence needs and matériel projects, mediates in cases of compensation orders, coordinates industrial activities in certain defence technology areas, and functions as a spokesman for the industrial membership. It also serves as the secretariat for the Dutch delegation to the European Defence Industrial Group (EDIG).

National defence technology policy used to be set out in the Defence Technology Concept (DTC, Defensie Technologie Concept, TK 23400, X 2, p. 43). The DTC was part of the Integral Defence Planning Process (IDPP), which is revised annually. However, despite the name, it was more accurate to consider the DTC as a frame of reference rather than an established plan. It aimed to relate future operational tasks of the armed forces to technological needs and requirements. To this end, tasks were subdivided into basic elements called 'missions'; each mission was then translated into a specific technology need, defined in terms of requirements specified by the armed forces. To avoid duplication, the actual matériel development projects were grouped into systems.

After a hiatus of some years, in 1993 the full cycle of long-term planning started anew, but the organisation of the DTC itself remained problematic. In an explanation accompanying the 1994–95 defence budget (TK 23900, X 2, p. 44) the DTC was criticised as too oriented towards the near term and involving an overly laborious bureaucratic process. This approach was, therefore, to be dropped, and replaced by a procedure more attuned to the IDPP. The DTC appears, moreover, to have been a wholly internal MoD procedure, to which parliament had little access.

About 1% of the annual defence budget is spent on R&D, or Dfl 156 million per year. From this amount, TNO Defence Research (TNO-DO, sometimes described as the 'house-laboratory' of MoD) receives some Dfl 100 million per year as a lump sum from the MoD. TNO-DO comprises three laboratories: the Physics and Electronics Laboratory (FEL, Fysisch en Electronisch Laboratorium), the Prins Maurits Laboratory, and the Institute for Human Factors. (See Appendix). The Commission for the Development of Defence Matériel (CODEMA — see below) receives Dfl 27 million from the national defence R&D budget. Matériel projects conducted by the Air Force receive Dfl 11 million from the defence R&D budget; Army and Navy projects are funded at the levels of Dfl 4 and 5 million respectively. NATO research receives Dfl 5 million, which is spent on military technological development. TNO-DO receives a further Dfl 21 million from the Armed Forces for R&D on specific projects, some Dfl 9 million in other subsidies and Dfl 24 million from civilian sources.

Other military R&D takes place at the National Aerospace Laboratory (NLR, which does aviation and space research, with a turnover in the defence sector of Dfl 42 million/year, of which some Dfl 25 million is earmarked for projects and Dfl 1 million is core funding) and at the Maritime Research Institute Netherlands (MARIN, with a Dfl 3 million annual budget). Taken together, Dutch defence R&D amounts to over Dfl 200 million. Virtually no military research is carried out at Dutch universities.

Most *industrial* defence R&D is done in close cooperation with MoD, and it is often connected with concrete defence matériel projects. CODEMA is an arrangement for funding defence technology development at the Dutch industry, in which the Ministries of Defence and of Economic Affairs and a company each contribute one third of the cost of R&D projects. The initiative for projects often lies with industry. Proposals for funding are judged as to their military and economic merits and for their relevance to the Defence Technology

Concept. Two types of projects are supported. *Technology* development projects are directed at new technologies related to specified future defence requirements. *Matériel* projects involve the development of a prototype. CODEMA funds are used for several projects of each type, including radar technology, new materials/composites, electro-optics, artificial intelligence and simulation technology.

Dutch Defence Industry

In the period 1984–1988, the average annual turnover of the Dutch defence sector was Dfl 3.3 to 3.5 billion, accounting for about 1.2 to 1.4% of overall industrial turnover. The defence industry consists of some 100 to 125 companies, employing 15–20,000 people, or between 1.9 and 2.5% of the entire Dutch industrial workforce. Dutch military production usually takes place in rather small, specialised departments of mainly civilian companies. Parts of the electronics industry, the ammunition factories and the naval ship building industry are, however, predominantly military.

A 1994 official estimate (AMP, 1994) suggested that of the 15–20,000 employees in defence firms, some 5000 were fully engaged in military production. Employment in the defence industry was estimated to have diminished since 1988 by about 20%, or about 4000 personnel. These numbers were derived from the aerospace, vehicles, materials, electronics and ammunition sectors (AMP, 1992). Another estimate (NIID, March 1993) mentions an aggregate turnover of Dfl 3 billion and an overall employment of 14,000. It was also estimated that some 20 companies are dependent on military sales for more than 50% of their business, but that the general dependency on military sales varies from 10 to 20%. Among those firms highly dependent on military sales are found mainly systems producers; the other firms are usually sub-system producers and sub-contractors.

Some data on turnover, employment and exports of the Dutch defence industry are given in Table 1, while details of the main firms involved in defence production are given in Box 1.

Ten Largest Defence Projects Currently under Development

The largest current defence projects include some development projects, but others that should be considered as simple procurement. The Dutch Navy planned to procure Dfl 758 million of equipment in 1994; the Army Dfl 1,035 million; and the Air Force Dfl 876 million.

In the succeeding five years, the Navy, Army and the Air Force planned to spend Dfl 4,151, 5,856 and 6,576 million, respectively, on equipment. Adding in

Table 1: Turnover, Employment and Exports of Dutch Defence Industry, 1985–92

Year	Turnover[a)]	Employment	Exports[a)]
1985	1488	26000	488
1986	1525	26000	406
1987	1478	24000	475
1988	1655	25000	318
1989	1525	23000	488
1990	1519	22000	390
1991	1453	21000	366
1992	1432	20000	328

a) Millions of constant ECU (1990 base).
Source: SOT (1993); (GRIP data).

Box 1. Main firms involved in Dutch defence production

Shipyards:

The **Royal Company 'De Schelde'** (KSG): main activities are design and construction of naval craft, installation of integrated sensor, weapons and command systems, communications and navigation equipment. Has 3500 workers employed in ten business units. Annual turnover is Dfl 750 million, and the stated dependence on military sales is 25%. International cooperation includes the shared development and production of a Supply Ship (AOR: Auxiliary Oiler Replenishment Ship) and an Amphibian Transport Ship with *Bazan* of Spain, and development of an Air Defence and Command Frigate with both *Bazan* and *ARGE F-124*, a consortium of German shipyards.

The **Rotterdamsche Droogdok Maatschappij** (RDM): produces ship propulsion systems, ship-board gear for handling helicopters, and various submarine components. Has developed its own submarine for export, the Moray, and carries out maintenance and upgrading of field artillery, tanks and air defence guns. Employment was reduced from 1300 in 1991 to about 800 in 1993, with more recent plans aiming down to 500. In 1991, turnover was Dfl 112 million and production was worth Dfl 231 million. RDM's overall dependency on military sales is difficult to estimate, but is known to be decreasing rapidly. On the other hand, winning export orders for submarines by 1996 has now become vital to the survival of RDM's military activity.

Van der Giessen-de Noord Marinebouw (GNM): builds small sophisticated naval vessels, large hulls and superstructures in glass fibre-reinforced polyester. GNM has built the Dutch tri-partite mine hunters, a combined project of the Dutch, French and Belgian navies, and a series of landing craft for the R.N. Marines Corps. Employment in 1992 was 730, and the turn-over was Dfl 292 million. GNM worked with *Beliard Polyship* (Belgium) to develop a coastal waters mine hunter for the navies of Holland, Belgium and Portugal. (It was not acquired by the Dutch navy, due to the 1992 cuts.) GNM has changed its main naval focus from long-term production to short-term renovation and maintenance. Its main activities are in the civilian market.

Electronics

Van Rietschoten & Houwens Defence Systems (R&H): involved in design, development and production of complex electrical installations and computer systems, mainly for naval platforms. R&H produces systems integrators, rudder roll stabilisation units, platform automation and data-processing systems for frigates and submarines, and test and training simulators. Total R&H employment stands at 2,000, including both military and civilian production personnel. Defence turnover is buried within the gross turnover of the 'technical' part of the Internatio-Müller group, which includes R&H, other Dutch and foreign companies, and which amounts to Dfl 1,123 million, for 6,400 employees. The R&H share of this total is estimated to be about Dfl 300 million.

Hollandse Signaalapparaten (HSA): now part of the French Thomson-CSF, specialises in electronic equipment for defence applications, air and sea traffic control, and military telecommunications. Designs and builds radar, optronics and sonar, data handling and processing equipment, displays, and weapon control equipment. HSA reduced its employment from 4800 in 1988 to some 3200 personnel in 1992. Turnover in 1992 was Dfl 662 million. International cooperation includes R&D on Active Phased Array Radar Systems with *Northern Telecom* (Canada) and *TST* (Germany), production of short-range defence systems against incoming missiles (close-in weapons system), and others in cooperation with its parent company *Thomson-CSF*, such as the development of a naval version of the Crotale system.

Delft Instruments: produces image intensifiers, night vision equipment, laser range finders and related equipment. In 1992, employees numbered 1730, and turnover was Dfl 385 million, of which only Dfl 39 million was attributed to the defence branch. Due to diversification, Delft Instrument's dependence on the military market has diminished considerably, to about 10 percent.

Ammunition Factories

Eurometaal: produces medium and heavy calibre ammunition and other pyrotechnical products. Owned by the Dutch state, Dynamit Nobel AG, and Oerlikon-Contraves AG Pyrotech. The rapid decline in ammunition acquisitions by the Dutch and German armed forces has put the company in a difficult position. It has diversified into the civilian market through buying the firms Intergas and Euro Mul-T-Lock. Employment stands at around 800, down from 1200 a few years ago. Its turnover in 1992 was Dfl 155 million. Between 1991 and 1992, defence-related sales almost halved from Dfl 205 million to Dfl 118 million, while civilian turnover has increased from Dfl 2 million to Dfl 37 million.

NWM De Kruithoorn: produces medium calibre ammunition, components and heavy metal penetrators. Owned by Rheinmetall GmbH since 1975; it has developed the missile piercing discarding sabot ammunition for the 'Goalkeeper' anti-missile gun. The existing know-how in metallurgy has enabled De Kruithoorn to turn to civilian markets with its so-called 'Metal Injection Moulding' technology.

Aerospace

Fokker: Taken over by Daimler Benz Aerospace in 1993, and allowed to collapse in 1996. Produced the Fokker 50 Maritime Enforcer, the Fokker 60 Transporter for the Dutch Air Force and builds the F-16 under license, as well as various systems and equipment, and some components under subcontracts. Produced mainly for the civilian sector. In 1992, defence turnover amounted to some Dfl 300 million, employing 1,100 personnel.

Trucks, etc.

DAF Special Products: manufactures landing gear, actuators, helicopter transmissions, rotor components, armoured infantry fighting vehicles, recovery crane vehicles, recovery tanks, main battle tank components, simulators and training systems. R&D currently centred on the Multi-Purpose Vehicle, a light reconnaissance vehicle. In 1993, DAF SP was taken over by a combination of Van Halteren Holding and Liebherr, a Swiss company. DAF SP has a defence turnover of Dfl 55 million and employs 195 personnel, almost all in the defence area.

New Materials

Dutch State Mines (DSM): develops new light-weight materials: engineering plastics, composites and fibres. DSM is a multi-national company that operates mainly on the civilian market. It has a turnover of Dfl 10 billion and 25,000 employees. Its Dyneema fibres are used for ballistic protection in vests, helmets, protective shields, armour and impact plates.

Royal Nijverdal Ten Cate is an international concern with two core activities. plastics and advanced textiles. The company manufactures fibres, resin systems, specialised textiles, plastics, fabrics, prepregnated and laminated material for protective clothing, weather protection systems and anti-ballistic protection. The largest part of its production is for the civil market. Employs 4300 personnel; turnover is Dfl 1.1 billion. Defence production is centred in Ten Cate Protect, Ten Cate Technical Fabrics, Nicolon, and Ten Cate Advanced Composites.

the projections for the five years after that (i.e., to the year 2004), the figures are Dfl 10,028, 12,089 and 13,391 million, respectively.

The Navy's largest projects are as follows:

- Building eight new M-frigates, a programme which is nearly complete, at a total cost of some Dfl 3,600 million.
- Building a new supply ship: Dfl 75 million (total Dfl 78 million).
- Building an amphibian transport ship (due by end of 1997): Dfl 78 million (total Dfl 249 million).

In addition, mine-hunting and sweeping capabilities are under study, and updates to existing systems are envisaged. The NH-90 helicopter is due to replace the Lynx, and the sensor systems of the Orion patrol aircraft are being upgraded.

The Army has a greater number of smaller projects. The largest are:

- Light trucks: Dfl 48 million (total Dfl 140 million).
- Combat Net Radio: Dfl 57 million (total Dfl 390 million).
- Various logistics projects: Dfl 98 million (communications projects, Dfl 67 million, manoeuvres projects, Dfl 35 million and infrastructure, Dfl 217 million).

The Air Force is involved in a smaller number of costlier projects:

- The Mid-Life Update of the F-16 fighter: Dfl 129 million (total Dfl 1639 million until 2003).
- The recent purchase of two heavy and four light air transport planes: Dfl 71 million (total Dfl 469 million); and 13 Chinook heavy transport helicopters as well as 17 medium weight transport helicopters, at a total price of Dfl 1,226 million.
- Acquisition and refit of two commercial airliners as air tankers: Dfl 123 million (total Dfl 166 million).
- The purchase in 1995 of the Apache attack helicopter, for which a budget of Dfl 1,616 million was available.

Budgetary Trends

Past and projected expenditures on defence equipment are shown in Table 2. Expenditure on military R&D has changed little over time and amounts to about 1% of the defence budget, or about Dfl 150 million (75 million ECU). In view of the declared importance of the use of advanced technology in defence it is likely that this — admittedly relatively small — amount will not be cut and may even grow slightly.

Table 2 suggests at first sight that the defence budget has hardly been affected by the end of the Cold War. In current prices, the actual total defence budget is now at an all-time high. It is expected to decrease slightly in the coming years. Weapons procurement stands at a relatively low point, but is due to rise again in connection with the large matériel projects currently in the pipeline. Total procurement has been relatively stable, but seems set to diminish. In the years to come, however, a relatively heavy emphasis will be placed upon weapons procurement, due in part to the changed requirements of the Armed Forces for large purchases such as transport helicopters and reconnaissance vehicles. In addition, acquisition plans for the years up to 2003 show the Navy spending heavily on replacing the Tromp and Kortenaer frigates, and on buying the NH-90 helicopter and the Troika mine-sweeping system. Reductions in the defence budget are being achieved mainly by selling off surplus equipment and reducing personnel.

We should, however, be cautious over these figures and projections. There are technical disputes over the procedures for inflation correction. We are also in a period of frequent intermediate budget cuts. And the cost of UN missions has somehow to be met.

Table 2: Dutch Military Expenditure, 1986–1998 (Dfl million, current prices)

Year	Defence budget	Total procurement[a)]	Large matériel projects
1986	13766	5635	3791
1987	13854	5526	3501
1988	13723	5062	3023
1989	13966	5766	3193
1990	14201	5831	3037
1991	14206	5331	2648
1992	14087	5410	2660
1993	14092	5240	2498
1994	13415	4421	2432
1995	13614		2922
1996	13686		3158
1997	13667		3422
1998	13640		3458

a) includes maintenance, repairs, buildings, consumables.

Sources: The figures for the years 1993 and 1994 are from the 1993 and 1994 Defence budgets. The figures for 1995 to 1998 are based on projections in the MoD's Priorities Whitebook.

Table 3: Dutch Defence Cuts, 1990–1999

Year	Total cuts since 1989 (Dfl million)	Cuts against zero-growth (Dfl million)	Cumulative reduction, as percentage
1990	571	501	4.1
1991	1,024	809	6.6
1992	1,537	1,194	9.1
1993	2,776	2,306	17.9
1994	3,127	2,545	19.9
1995	3,697	3,005	23.4
1996	3,964	3,143	24.5
1997	4,355	3,404	26.2
1998	4,562	3,480	26.7
1999	4,562	3,480	26.7

Source: TK 23900, X no. 8, p. 15, 4 November 1994.

Moreover, a new government took office in August 1994. In November of that year it announced new cuts over and above those already scheduled, together with the abolition of conscription from 1998. A three-track policy was proposed of savings on overheads and support costs, intensified international coordination and cooperation, and the slowing down of major investment projects and so-called 'structural measures', which should enable the MoD to save money while staying within previous Priorities Whitebook force goals. MoD budget cuts for the years 1995–98 were projected to rise progressively from Dfl 448 to 664 per annum. The accumulating effect of cuts since just after the fall of the Berlin Wall is shown in Table 3. It seems unlikely that these will be the final cuts in the defence budget.

Policy Towards Defence and Dual-Use Technology

Government Policy Statements on the Future of the National Defence Technology Base

Defence and dual-use technology policy is not prominent on the Dutch political agenda. Insofar as such policy exists, however, it has been subject to certain reorientations in recent years.

Government defence technology policy only began to be made explicit with the release of a White Paper in 1984 by the then Deputy Minister for Defence, van Houwelingen. Even then, well before the end of the Cold War, the White

Paper linked defence technology policy to a more general industrial policy aimed at innovation and technology development. The national technological and industrial input to fulfilling military needs was to be strengthened. Domestic defence companies were to be involved in the process of military matériel choice at the earliest possible stage. Government would be willing to incur costs if this might improve chances for technological advantages to be realised by the industry, and if it would stimulate international — preferably European — cooperation. The policy for offset orders would be similarly directed (TK 19157, no. 1–2, p. 12).

According to the White Paper, defence technology policy would be aimed at bringing together operational plans for fulfilling military needs, the domestic potential of scientific and technological research in the Netherlands and the ability of domestic industry to apply new technologies in developing and producing defence matériel. Cooperation in IEPG programmes was to be encouraged[1]. These policy goals would be implemented via the CODEMA-arrangement, and coordinated by an interdepartmental working group — the Steering Group for Defence and Dutch Industry[2]. The Advisory Council on Military Production (AMP — see below) would advise on coordinating government and industry regarding defence technology policy (TK 19404, no. 1–2, pp. 17–18).

There were, however, problems in bringing together the Long Term Requirement Plan (LTBP) and the Defence Technology Concept (DTC) (see above) as Dutch industry lacked the required know-how (TK 19157, no. 5, p. 3). Accordingly, the Deputy Minister for Defence, together with the Steering Group for Defence and Dutch Industry, issued a second White Paper in 1988, on International Defence Matériel Relations, which placed a greater emphasis on international cooperation. It was considered of great importance for the armed forces that a certain national defence industrial capability be maintained that could produce competitively in order to avoid undue dependence on foreign producers and governments. On the military side, NATO-wide standardisation and common defence activities were to be actively sought; from an industrial point of view, participation in military programmes was preferred to offset orders. Here, however, for the first time, mention was made of the importance of liberalising the defence equipment market as a long-term goal. In the interim, the principle of 'juste retour' was to be kept in mind, implying a preference for return orders or proportional participation in multinational projects to lead to indirect compensation or licence production (TK 20679, no. 1–2, pp. 6, 12–13).

A White Paper on the military industry, issued in 1989, just after the end of the Cold War, addressed directly the future of the Dutch defence industry (TK 21886). The Dutch government was quick to announce deep cuts in its future defence budgets, which seriously affected expected military procurement orders. In the preamble to this White Paper, the changed international situation was described, and international overcapacity in arms production was given as the rationale for restructuring and possibly closing down sizeable parts of the arms industry. The domestic industry, according to the White Paper, would be forced to concentrate and to produce more efficiently and on a larger scale, to meet the challenges posed by the '1992' Single European Market. However, the White Paper noted that the competitive strength of the US armaments producers and of the emerging weapon producing countries was even more important.

At the contextual level, the White Paper considered it to be normal that markets wax and wane. The free-market gospel was presented as economic wisdom, according to which it was the responsibility of the entrepreneur to anticipate market developments and to react in a timely and alert manner. Individual companies that failed to adapt to the new international market situation could not be helped by the government. Mention was again made of the CODEMA arrangement, and of the need for international cooperation, preferably in IEPG projects. Free-market rhetoric was used once more to argue for the abandonment of Article 223 of the Treaty of Rome. The military industry was treated as a sector of normal industrial activity in an extensive section on the general technology policy instruments of the Ministry of Economic Affairs.

Shortly after this, a new Defence White Paper was published (TK 21991, no. 2–3, 1991, pp. 187–193). It introduced a wholly new defence policy, leading towards a substantially reshaped armed service characterised as 'smaller, more versatile [... and performing] different tasks'. The White Paper stated that MoD would consider buying nationally in the case of potentially successful, as well as demonstrably superior, companies. The Dutch defence industry was, however, advised not to depend wholly upon the MoD, which would place its own needs above those of industry.

Policy regarding military technology was also changed somewhat, although in slightly contradictory ways. 'Seen from the national military-strategic point of view, there is no need for a military industry' said the White Paper. From the international perspective, nevertheless, there continued to be a need for an Alliance military industry. This being the case, it seemed sensible to maintain part of it in the Netherlands. In particular, the industry should be maintained at a sufficient level to keep the Netherlands involved in international development and production projects, with the ultimate aim being the 'Europeanisation' of defence equipment. A certain level of indigenous knowledge would also be needed to evaluate the technical qualities of weapons systems used by the Dutch military. In this respect, a comparison between buying new defence matériel 'off the shelf' versus co developing equipment had concluded that the former was less risky and generally cheaper. That being so, there was a real risk that, in the tougher financial climate, companies might move out of defence R&D, so threatening the national defence technology base. One consequence of such a possibility might be that more government support might have to be given to the TNO-Defence Research laboratories.

There was a further reorientation of defence policy in early 1993. Two White Papers, on offset policy (TK 22826) and on priorities (TK 22975, Prioriteitennota) were issued. Industrial policy was reviewed in the former. Defence industrial policy again was treated as part of general industrial policy as defined and implemented by the Ministry of Economic Affairs. The regrettable absence of an open European or NATO defence technology market forced the Dutch government to conduct a vigorous offset orders policy: 'an effective national offset policy therefore remains a vital precondition, if a Dutch defence industry is to be viable in the present uneven field', the aim being to maintain the industry's capability to participate in international developments. The extra costs arising from international cooperative programmes would, however, be acceptable only in exceptional cases, such as if Dutch technological know-how would thereby be enhanced, if it was likely to result in specific spin-offs, or if it enabled the MoD to involve Dutch firms in repair, maintenance and upgrading work. It was considered important that Dutch companies be given the opportunity to maintain or even strengthen their position as co-producers or subcontractors. Only then would the Netherlands be able to play a role of any substance in the area of defence technology (TK 22826, no. 1–2, p. 21).

In the Priorities White Paper (TK 22975, no. 2, p. 61) yet heavier cuts in procurement and in virtually all parts of the armed forces were announced. The same argument about MoD needs prevailing over industrial requirements was repeated, together with the qualification that an indigenous military industry was still needed for the Netherlands to remain involved in international projects and to retain customer expertise. Although the MoD took care to keep industrial interests at arm's length, the formulation used this time allows the interpretation that these interests were nevertheless now considered slightly more important than they had been in the 1991 White Paper. All the same, a clear warning was given that a so-called 'structural concern' for the national industry would not degenerate into re-nationalisation of Dutch military procurement.

This 'structural concern' was to consist in attracting industrial cooperation in the earliest phases of studies on the needs and requirements for new armaments, through the industrial interest organisation NIID (Foundation for Dutch Industrial Participation in Defence Procurement). Dutch industrial capacity in electronics, marine vessel, aircraft and land transportation vehicles production and fibres for composite materials were to be stimulated in particular.

Mention of industrial interest groups leads naturally to reference to the Advisory Council on Military Production (AMP) which is given an important voice in government-industry relations[3]. Thus, the 1990 White Paper on the Dutch Defence Industry had included an annexe by the AMP strongly recommending greater government commitment to, and support for, the domestic industry, accompanied by less abrupt truncation of the defence budget. Despite this privileged platform, however, the AMP evidently did not persuade the government in 1990. This same divergence of views resurfaced in the 1991 Defence White Paper, where Dutch defence industrial interests appeared almost as an afterthought, with industry being advised not to look to MoD for its survival. In the Priorities White Paper of 1993, however, the AMP finally succeeded in exerting more influence. The White Paper contains a section in which the AMP advice is included in full. Moreover, the White Paper lists a set of industrial capacities that are to be particularly fostered[4], a list that coincides precisely with the advice of the AMP. Since, however, the government is reviewing its system of advisory councils, the future of the AMP was uncertain at the time of writing.

Dual-Use Technology

As with defence technology issues in general, so dual-use technology in particular is not a prominent political issue in the Netherlands. However, a 1985 White Paper on Defence Technology did discuss the relations between military and civilian technological development (TK 19404, no. 1–2, pp. 10–17). It stated that in a number of industrialised countries the development of defence technology had an important role to play in strengthening the national industry's competitiveness and technological capacities, and that it was common in other countries for key technologies developed for both military and civilian use to be paid for by government. The Ministries of Economic Affairs and of Defence undertook to investigate the possibilities for transferring technology developed by TNO-Defence Research to industry at large, but maintained that Dutch military requirements would remain the main focus of such R&D. The Ministries also recognised that Defence might well profit from civil R&D results. Two committees were charged with assisting with the formulation of policy regarding defence and civil technological development: the Interdepartmental Steering Group for Defence and the Dutch Industry, and the AMP. These statements on civil-military relations were, however, of a very general nature, and did not indicate any special interest with dual-use technology.

In the first post-Cold War White Paper on the Dutch defence industry, the issue of Dual-use/Dual-purpose technology was raised again (TK 21886, no. 2, 1990–91, p. 6). The Ministry of Economic Affairs was asked to take civilian applications of military technology and product R&D into account when supplying CODEMA funds to industry. It was added that Government would thus be able to contribute both to the upscaling of production, spreading risks and costs, and to the adaptive capacities of the firms. The White Paper also stated that these dual-use/dual-purpose technologies would make companies less dependent on defence activities.

In its policy on indirect offset orders, the Ministry of Economic Affairs also aimed to link defence technology cooperation projects with existing MoEA programmes in information-, materials-, bio-, and environmental-technology, and at using dual-use technology to minimise industrial dependence on military production. Indeed, dual-use technology was deemed to be of such importance that the MoEA had also already asked the Policy Studies Department of TNO to report on the area in order to enable informed discussion of policy options (Schipper, 1992). The resulting study included a survey mapping the interactions between civilian and defence industry by areas of research, technology and matériel development. It also restated the main points of the 1985 White Paper on Defence Technology on this subject, outlined above, as well as arguing that the defence R&D activities taking place at MARIN and NLR were already largely integrated with civil R&D. The study was extensively quoted in the White Paper on Offset Policy that was issued at the end of 1992.

In particular, the White Paper referred to sections of the TNO study that focused on company-oriented advice on conversion, repeating the point that the prospects for successful conversion would be greatest for companies that were not internally sharply divided into civil and military branches, and that had in-house advanced production technology, a clear insight into civilian markets, and finance available for carrying out a well-defined conversion plan. The government refused to respond to some industrial demands for clear and unambiguous choices for a limited number of high technology spearhead projects, of military or dual use orientation. In the end, therefore, the TNO study failed to initiate any serious discussion on dual-use technology. It thus fitted the general pattern in Dutch government of not giving great attention to this issue, a conclusion that is reinforced by further noting that, under the CODEMA scheme, any dual-use element is only a secondary criterion in judging the merit of industrial proposals.

Overall, then, Dutch defence industrial policy remains firmly embedded in general industrial policy, with civil and defence-funded R&D programmes being usually conducted separately. In most cases, the promotion of synergy is left to companies' human resources policies and, in the case of TNO, to the TNO Board. Only a slight shift of emphasis in government policy is noticeable, from a very limited interest in making R&D work 'both ways', to encouraging companies to turn to civilian products via the route of dual-use technologies (TK 22826, no. 1–2, 1993, p. 21).

Developments in Research Institutions

There is no obvious attempt by the government to involve a wider range of research institutes in defence activities. Since most Dutch defence technology R&D is done at TNO-Defence Research (TNO-DO), we shall focus on developments there.

As we have seen, it was suggested in the 1993 Priorities White Paper that TNO-DO might have to assume a larger share of Dutch defence R&D, to compensate for possible diminished company interest in defence technology. In fact, the MoD has already begun to increase the project-related share of its financial contribution to TNO, and to decrease the general-purpose (lump sum) share. Perhaps more significantly, in the past few years, the civilian-financed share of R&D by TNO-DO R&D has increased from some 6% in 1986, to 14% in 1992. TNO-DO has conducted R&D in areas like aeronautics, space, process safety, traffic safety, logistics, labour environment, information systems and telematics. It now considers 'dual-use' technologies as promising assets, and favours both spin-off and spin-in to military projects. One example is maritime traffic control with radar-identification, originally developed for the Navy, then used in Rotterdam harbour, and now applied in military helicopters. Another is the production of ignition materials for the Ariane rocket, based on existing explosion know-how.

Possibly the most important change in TNO-DO's R&D priorities, however, has been in the attention now paid to operations research and simulation technology. These new priorities have been formulated by a government that has been sending Dutch soldiers on United Nations missions all over the world. Meeting these new operational circumstances is now an important goal for TNO-DO research.

Participation in EUCLID and Other International Collaborative Defence Research Projects

The Netherlands is eager to participate in international defence technology projects and programmes, such as EUCLID, in order to enlarge its know-how and to strengthen its technological position. Industrial participation in the Research and Technology Projects (RTPs) of EUCLID is funded within the framework of the CODEMA arrangement, with NIID often playing a mediating role.

The Netherlands is the lead nation for six of the RTPs: advanced materials and structures, light weight armour optimisation, knowledge engineering, crew assistance, low frequency underwater sound propagation, and training system concepts for simulator based military training.

Industrial Defence Technology Capabilities

We discuss below the overall strategies adopted by firms in the face of the changed market conditions of recent years. In terms of maintenance of defence-related technological capabilities, however, we can note here that company-initiated defence R&D in the Netherlands is of a rather limited nature. There are some projects in the very few highly defence-dependent companies, using wherever possible CODEMA or EUCLID funds. In addition, the NIID has identified a number of defence-related 'industrial chains' that it believes are worth preserving, meaning by this term industrial niches that contain to some degree elements of personnel education, R&D, system builders or integrators, subsystem producers, maintenance capacity and expert customers. The niches listed include naval technology, parts of the aircraft industry, simulation, command and control systems, night vision equipment and vehicle tyres.[5]

As we have already seen, both the AMP and NIID, as representatives of industry, have criticised the government for its alleged lack of a long-term industrial vision, and for lack of support in matters like export and national matériel acquisition. They believe that TNO-DO and CODEMA subsidies should be more intentionally geared towards possibilities for industrial follow-up activities. According to AMP and NIID, national policy should be more concerned with future industrial needs than with largely symbolic gestures towards an open European defence matériel market.

Policies on International Company Relationships

The government has noted a trend, which it has neither encouraged nor discouraged, for Dutch defence companies to team up with foreign 'partners'. Recent policy statements on international cooperation have, however, given two reasons why international defence matériel projects is considered beneficial. First, there are economic and military advantages in standardisation, inter-operability, economies of scale and avoiding duplication of effort. Second, international cooperation would enhance the general political and economic cohesion among NATO partners.

In the contexts of NATO, WEAG and WEU, the Netherlands aims to achieve an open defence matériel market in the long run. In the meantime, a policy of offset orders remains an important means to provide Dutch industry with assured participation and access to new technologies. In order to ensure the enforceability of the offset agreements, it was deemed essential that in the Memoranda of Understanding (MoU) concluded between the partner countries, an industrial paragraph be included with guarantees for this participation. The

Ministries of Defence and of Economic Affairs publicise information on upcoming opportunities for participation, and promote the exchange of technical data between the involved industries once a project is agreed upon. A distinction is made between direct and indirect offsets: direct offsets involving industry in joint ventures, licensed production or co-production of the imported defence goods; and indirect offsets obliging the exporting industry to place orders with Dutch industry in other areas (TK 22826, no. 2).

On the conceptual level, we should perhaps separate cooperation in international defence matériel projects from defence matériel-related offset policy. In reality, however, they seem to merge seamlessly, an important goal of offset policy being, as we have seen, to keep Dutch industry at a technologically adequate level to participate in international cooperation projects. EUCLID is also actively used to the same end.

Major International Activities of the Main Dutch Defence Manufacturers

Dutch ammunition-producing companies have been more noticeably affected than other firms by procurement cuts which started long before the end of the Cold War. In consequence, Muiden Chemie International was taken over by BAe Defence, Royal Ordnance plc., and NWM De Kruithoorn by Rheinmetall as early as 1975. Another key firm, Eurometaal, which was nominally privatised in 1973, nevertheless had 70% of its stock retained by the state, the rest being in the hands of Dynamit Nobel. Since 1990, however, the Dutch state, Dynamit Nobel and Oerliken-Contaves AG Pyrotech (Switzerland) have held equal shares, adding this to the list of foreign-linked firms (Stichting OSACI, p. 39).

Examples of foreign mergers, acquisitions and teaming from other parts of the defence industry include KSG (Royal Schelde) which has linked with Bazan from Spain (see Box 1), in order to maintain itself as an independent naval shipyard. Other shipyards have behaved similarly. In the aircraft sector, Fokker explained its takeover in 1993 by DASA (Germany) by stating that 'The aerospace industry has been forced to consolidate and integrate by the high cost of developing new aircraft programmes and the sharp cuts in defence spending', and even this, in the event, did not prevent further losses and the eventual decision by DASA in 1996 to allow Fokker to collapse, ending a 77 year tradition of Dutch aircraft manufacture. In electronics, Philips has sold almost all its defence assets, most notably HSA, which was sold to the French Thomson CSF. In land systems, following the bankruptcy of DAF, DAF SP was sold to a combination of Van Halteren, a Dutch company, and the Swiss Liebherr LAT.

Policy Towards Conversion

Past Experience

Conversion has repeatedly been an issue in the Dutch parliament, but with a relatively low profile. There have been no moves by any recent government to design and implement a conversion policy.

If 'conversion' means switching from predominantly military to civilian production, then it has been an issue for only a few companies in the past. Dutch military production is in general concentrated in small specialised departments of companies that predominantly work in civil areas. This structure has prevented conversion from becoming a pressing issue until recently.

On the other hand, 'diversification', in the sense of expanding into new markets through companies' own efforts or through acquisitions, has been rather more in evidence. For example, HSA (Hollandse Signaalapparaten) tried in the early 1980s to start a branch specialising in the adaptation of military radar and radar screen equipment to civilian uses in airports and harbours. This branch was geographically and organisationally separated from HSA's military sector. The effort was, however, unsuccessful. One reason may have been that the nature of defence radars and electronics (naval radar and sonar) was too specialised to make conversion a viable prospect (Schipper, 1992). Another may have been the tough competition in this field. Furthermore, these efforts seem to have been largely ignored by the Ministry of Transport.

Current Government Policies on Conversion

In the 1990–91 White Paper on the defence industry, the Dutch government stated as its own role the provision of favourable economic conditions for the industry. Companies that proved unable to withstand the normal pressures of the marketplace were not to be helped by public means. Therefore, no conversion fund was envisaged. Apart from the budgetary problems that such an approach would pose for government, it was argued that such a fund would give parts of the defence industry an unfair commercial advantage over companies producing for the civilian market only. It was also considered doubtful whether the EC would approve such a conversion policy. (TK 21886, no. 2, pp. 5 6). The 1993 White Paper on Offsets was also somewhat sceptical of the prospects for conversion, taking into account the extent to which defence companies are steeped in the culture of the military. It considered conversion more a problem of organisation, management and culture than of technology. (TK 22826, no 1–2, p. 22).

Despite this formal position, the Dutch government has undertaken a two-track approach that could be considered a *de facto* conversion policy. First, companies continue to be invited to participate both in Dutch and foreign defence procurement, even though the total volume of orders is expected to diminish. This will cushion companies as they switch towards civilian business. Second, those companies wishing to enlarge the civilian share of their output are able to utilise various initiatives of the Ministry of Economic Affairs which aim at general stimulation of new technological developments. These include the BTIP scheme (Bedrijfsgerichte Technologie Stimulering in Internationale Programma's — Company-aimed stimulation of technology in international programmes) which subsidises companies participating in international programmes like EUREKA; subsidies for companies participating in European Space Agency programmes; the INSTIR (Innovatie stimulering) scheme which supports innovation; and technology development loans (the TOK — Technisch Ontwikkelingskrediet — scheme). Further schemes apply to the four priority areas of information technology, biotechnology, materials, and environmental technology. The government has also promised preferential treatment for companies that apply for the MoEA programmes for defence conversion purposes (TK 21886, no. 3, 29 January 1991, p. 4).

Actions Undertaken by Firms

There is a general feeling in the defence industry that companies are left to their own devices over conversion. Representative organisations like NIID and AMP, moreover, are primarily interested in military production, and seem not to take much interest in conversion efforts.

The NIID has, however, identified four different strategies used by companies for coping with the new market structure (NIID, 1993c):

- conversion or diversification into civilian production;
- broadening and deepening defence activities, both nationally and internationally;
- seeking national and international cooperation, for example through NIID platforms like NISP (Simulation technology), C2 (Command and Control) and in concrete projects, such as in EUCLID; also, the takeover of companies like HSA, Fokker, Muiden Chemie by foreign companies;
- matching production capacity to the shrinking market.

In practice, the first strategy has often been followed in conjunction with the fourth, as we illustrate below. We also give an example of the second. The third was implicitly discussed in the preceding sub-section.

The first strategy is being pursued by companies like RDM, KSG, Delft Instruments, Eurometaal, and MFT. It is no accident that these firms include naval shipyards and ammunition producers. The cyclic nature of military expenditure is especially severe in naval procurement, involving lengthy waits for follow-up orders. In addition, delaying or cancelling ammunition orders is probably one of the easiest ways to cut the defence budget. Ammunition cuts had in fact already begun before the end of the Cold War, and now the reduced army of the future will presumably need even less.

Hence, Eurometaal, one of the main Dutch ammunition producers, decided to initiate measures aimed at conversion in 1988, in the expectation that these might start to pay off by about 1993. It acquired smaller companies building household heating equipment and locks, and moved into the precision engineering industry. In the meantime, however, heavy cuts in military contracts forced Eurometaal also to follow the fourth strategy and to lay off hundreds of its employees. Similarly, companies like MFT (Metaalwaren Fabriek Tilburg, cartridge link production), Muiden Chemie International (ammunition, part of Royal Ordnance) and De Kruithoorn have all engaged in some form of conversion activity. MFT seems to have been the most successful, now being dependent on defence markets for only 15% of its total turnover. However, information on these cases is limited since they have been forbidden by their foreign owners in the UK and Germany respectively to discuss their business plans.

In the shipbuilding sector, the naval shipyard RDM was taken over by the Koninklijke Begemann Groep, a large holding company, at the end of 1991. One of the reasons given was that conversion activities initiated in 1990 would thus be on safer ground. RDM is now involved in energy systems, producing large vessels for the oil industry, as well as repair and overhaul of army matériel and general (military and civilian) subcontracting for other parts of the holding. But strategy four has also been forced on the company. The delivery of the last Walrus-submarine to the Dutch Navy left RDM with excess capacity in that area. No export licence was given to sell submarines to the Taiwan Navy, which precipitated a major restructuring in 1993, including sharp cuts in jobs.

Purer cases of the first strategy include the naval shipyard, Royal Schelde, which has followed a policy of diversification into allied industries for many years. In addition to its military activities, de Schelde is active today in civilian ship building, offshore equipment production, process industry equipment, environmental technology, and with the energy industry and other mechanical engineering industries. Naval shipbuilding continues, however, to be of major importance to the company. Similarly, Wilton Feyenoord seems to have exited from naval shipbuilding entirely. It now concentrates on dry-dock facilities, workshop facilities, repairs and ship conversion. To take another case, this time from electronics, Delft Instruments, a holding company which was formed from the merger between the defence electronics company Oldelft and Enraf-Nonius (a producer of precision engineering equipment), has through acquisitions in the civil sector diminished its share of military production in its total activities. In the former Oldelft part of the holding, limited real conversion is taking place through using specialised know-how for developments in the industrial R&D and space sectors. By now, medical activities and industrial precision measurement equipment are the mainstay of most Delft Instruments companies. Defence production has dropped to about 10% of the overall total.

The second strategy is well illustrated by the electronics firm Hollandse Signaalapparaten which, since its takeover by Thomson-CSF, has decided to focus almost entirely on the military market. One spin-off activity has, however, met with some success: a number of contracts were won from Nederlandse Spoorwegen, the national railway company, to support increased density of track use, and this civilian activity is now a steady though minor part of HSA activities.

Finally, in terms of strategy four, we can note that Van der Giessen-de Noord has shifted its naval division from construction to shorter-running projects like overhaul, maintenance and modification. It is envisaged that existing know-how can be retained, and that in the design department a distinct military branch will remain in place. Indirectly, also, Van der Giessen-de Noord may have profited from the denial to RDM of a licence to export submarines to Taiwan, as it itself recently won contracts from the People's Republic of China for building two vehicle ferries.

Konver

The EU's KONVER programme allocated ECU 3.6 million to the Netherlands, to support economic conversion and diversification in areas badly hit by the decline of the arms industry and military installations. 35% of this sum (ECU 1.3 million) was for employment purposes, and came from the Economic and Social Fund; the rest (ECU 2.3 million) was for structural conversion measures, taken from the European Regional Development Fund. The regions eligible for this funding were Twente, east-Zuid Limburg, the northern portion of Noord Holland and the Veluwe.

In 1993 and 1994, these regions undertook a number of projects. Noord Holland received the lion's share, some Dfl 5 million, which it spent on refurbishing dock yards for fisheries and the offshore industry, extending the civil use of a heliport, constructing beach accommodation on the Amstelmeer, and retraining former military personnel. Gelderland (Veluwe) also set up a retraining scheme, for former employees in the military electronics sector. It also investigated the civilian use of former military bases in Harderwijk, and restored tank exercise grounds in Nunspeet to their former state. In Twente, product development aid was given to companies trying to turn from military to civilian markets, and former military sites were 'revitalised' for industrial use. Finally, South Limburg has converted a former NATO emergency hospital for industrial use, and has initiated studies into regional effects of the drawdown. These include the re-use of former military sites and buildings, reduced military spending in the region, and retraining of former military personnel.

Controlling the Diffusion of Defence Technologies

Arms Export Controls

The Dutch arms export regime is best characterised by the words 'prudence' and 'international coordination'. Since no ABC weapons are produced for or held by the Armed Forces, arms export policy is concerned only with conventional weapons. It is implemented through the Export Decision Rules on Strategic Goods.

Arms exports to NATO allies are usually considered acceptable. Exports to other countries are not *a priori* unacceptable, if they concur with Dutch arms export policy criteria. Given the existing control measures, legal weapons exports usually go to a fixed set of customer countries.

Four criteria are used in Dutch arms export policy:

- The *area of tension* criterion means that requests for permits to export to countries in areas of tension will be subject to political scrutiny.
- The *human rights* criterion examines whether grave and repeated violations of human rights occur in the receiving country, and whether the arms under consideration could possibly be used for that purpose.
- When, in the 1970s, the *international weapons embargo* criterion was formulated, export policy was meant to comply with embargoes ordered specifically by the UN Security Council. Now, embargoes agreed by the European Union are also covered. Generally, Dutch weapon export policy complies with international agreements.
- The *reasonable sufficiency* criterion implies a political assessment of the needs and intentions of the receiving country. It was introduced at Dutch behest at the meeting of the European Council in Luxembourg on 28–29 June 1991. If a country appears to be arming itself in an undue manner, or trying to import quantities of arms far beyond its reasonable defence needs, the European Council can impose an embargo.

Hence, decisions on export licences are based on a political assessment of such issues as the nature of the weapons involved, the political situation in the receiving country (international or internal conflicts, human rights), embargoes, international agreements, the character of the defence needs of the receiving country, the risk of re-export, the economic and financial situation of the receiving country, precedents, the employment situation of the producing companies, agreements with third parties, and Dutch security and industrial property considerations?

The COCOM list of proscribed goods, technologies and countries served in the past as a basis for the law regulating Dutch exports with possible military significance: the Dutch list is virtually identical to the former COCOM list. The Netherlands also participates in the UN Register of Conventional Arms.

In international defence matériel development projects, Dutch policy is to define the responsibilities for any resulting exports in a Memorandum of Understanding. When negotiating offset agreements, the general arms export policy guidelines are also consistently followed. This is to prevent Dutch military technology from being exported to countries already proscribed by the Dutch export regime.

Export of Dual-Use Technologies

The Export Rules for Strategic Goods contain, in addition to the military section discussed above, a section on nuclear items and an industrial section that deals with so-called 'dual-use' goods. These dual-use goods consist mainly of key materials and equipment for the fabrication of chemical, biological and nuclear weapons.

Dutch export policy regarding chemical and biological dual-use goods has become stricter in the past few years. For instance, the 'warning-list' approach for certain precursors, which left it to the companies to decide whether the prospective importing country might intend to produce chemical weapons, has been abandoned. The Netherlands has also implemented the 'trigger' lists emanating from the Non-Proliferation Treaty and the Nuclear Suppliers Group. Following a Dutch proposal, the Nuclear Suppliers Group has agreed upon a consultation structure for dual use nuclear goods. The Netherlands also subscribes to the Missile Technology Control Regime.

The Dutch government has been extremely interested in EU-wide dual-use export control measures. The disappearance of internal European Union border controls has fuelled concerns that dual use items could leak out through the least effectively guarded external border (TK 22054, no. 1–2 and 9). Moreover, the loosening of COCOM restrictions — the lists both of prohibited countries and goods having been shortened in the final days of COCOM — caused some Dutch concern, and led to the announcement that, if necessary, the Dutch government would impose unilateral export control measures (Pouw, 1993).

Government Policy on Exports

Stated government policy on military and dual-use technology exports generally inclines in the direction of preventing exports. The constraints imposed on such exports would indeed seem to indicate that actual practice conforms to this stated policy. However, since exports are considered essential to the survival of the defence industry, and since the industry itself is considered vital for the viability of the Dutch contribution to NATO, it is clear that the government is aiming to strike a balance on this question. In recent years, the Dutch diplomatic service has become even more active in promoting arms exports in a number of countries. The Ministry of Economic Affairs has also stepped up its presence at defence matériel fairs in the Middle and Far East. Nevertheless, political support for weapon exports remains well below 'average' European or American levels.

Moreover, even though governmental support for the Dutch defence industry is not overwhelming, the government does take some interest in promoting intra-European arms trade. In a succession of White Papers, the Dutch government proposed extending European cooperation into the area of defence industry and trade policy. The (in)famous article 223 from the EEC Treaty was regularly cited as an impediment to treating civilian and defence industry alike (TK 21991, no. 2–3, p. 186).

Within the framework of a genuine European defence market, the Dutch government would continue to argue that care should be taken to give the Dutch defence industry fair access to business. Dutch companies, it has been stated, are often hindered by the strict rules applied by some countries to technology transfer. In addition, the information companies need to submit tenders is often not available. Technology and project information transfer is an important precondition for competitiveness in R&D and production cooperation programmes. In this regard, there have been some expressions of concern over signs of a tendency towards 'renationalisation' of European and US military production and procurement in the tighter post-Cold War market. Hence, the government particularly favours liberalising international military trade and production cooperation within a NATO-wide framework, and has, accordingly, endorsed both the NATO 'Code of Conduct' and the similar IEPG (now WEAG) document.

At the same time, there is some concern that any steps towards relaxing intra-European arms trade barriers might tempt companies to export to prohibited destinations through the countries with the weakest (or the least well enforced) arms exports regimes. The Dutch government therefore welcomed the European Commission's proposals of 17 January 1992 (and subsequent developments) concerning harmonisation of the widely differing rules among the countries of Europe on dual-use exports (TK 22054, no. 9, p. 11).

Appendix: Defence Research in the Dutch National Laboratories

At the **Physics and Electronics Laboratory** (FEL) research is carried out in: operations research; systems and computer models in support of government policy; systems development and information technology; collecting, selecting and processing of information; radar and communications; observation and communication using radio waves; physics and acoustics; optical and acoustic sensing; technical developments in digital and analogue electronics, video presentation, high-frequency and microwave, opto-electronics, miniaturised circuitry, high precision mechanical construction, and circuit prints using CAD/CAM; and command and control, training and simulation.

The **Prins Maurits Laboratory** works in the fields of: characterisation, identification and detection of toxic substances; protection against ballistic and chemical agents; pulse physics research; ballistics and rocket technology; weapons effects; vulnerability and effectiveness; ammunition and explosives; and explosion prevention.

The **Institute for Human Factors** (Instituut voor Technische Menskunde) carries out research in: sensory perception and physiology; human information processing and ergonomics.

Some further research is carried out in the **Medical Biological Laboratory** (MBL), the **Plastic and Rubber Institute**, the **Technical Physical Service** and the **Metal Institute**, in areas including acoustics and optics, nutrition, mechanical construction, metals and non-metallic materials, and maritime research (TK 19404, 1–2, pp. 9, 20–24).

National Aerospace Laboratory (NLR — Nationaal Lucht- en Ruimtevaartlaboratorium) works on wind tunnel testing, computational fluid dynamics, radar cross section prediction, flight testing, flight simulation, aircraft navigation, operations research, structures and materials testing, etc.

At the **Maritime Research Institute Netherlands** (MARIN — Maritiem Research Instituut Nederland) R&D includes: consultative assistance, mathematical modelling and model experiments for the shipbuilding, shipping and offshore industries and advice for governmental and inter-governmental bodies.

References

AMP (Advisory Council on Military Production (Adviesraad Militaire Productie)), 1992, Advice to the Ministers of Foreign Affairs, Defence and Economic Affairs, Contribution to the Priorities Note, 1 October 1992.

AMP, 1994, Interview with Secretary of AMP, 11 November 1993.

Dijkman, R. and Smit, A., 1993, *Moet dezelfde smid zowel zwaarden als ploegen kunnen smeden?* Groningen: Wetenschapswinkel voor Economie, Rijksuniversiteit Groningen.

Houwelingen, J. van, 1992, 'Politically influencing military technology: a policy-maker's experience', in W.A. Smit, J. Grin and L. Voronkov (eds.) *Military Technological Innovation and Stability in a Changing World. Politically assessing and influencing weapon innovation and military research and development.* Amsterdam: VU University.

Ministerie van Economische Zaken, D-G voor Industrie en Diensten, Commissariaat voor Militaire Productie, 1993, *Catalogue of Netherlands Defence Related Industries 1993/1994.* Den Haag.

NIID, 1993a, *Kiezen voor technologie,* Lezingenbundel NIID Symposium 29 October 1993, Den Haag: Stichting Nederlandse Industriële inschakeling Defensieopdrachten.

NIID, 1993b, *Almanak 1993,* Den Haag: Stichting Industriële Inschakeling Defensieopdrachten.

NIID, 1993c, *Industriële aspecten bij een veranderende defensiemarkt,* Den Haag: Stichting Nederlandse Industriële inschakeling Defensieopdrachten.

NIID, 1993d, *Nieuwsbulletin,* Den Haag: Stichting Industriële Inschakeling Defensieopdrachten.

NIID, 1994, *Nieuwsbulletin,* Den Haag: Stichting Industriële Inschakeling Defensieopdrachten.

Pouw, F., 1993, *Wapens en Dual-use goederen onder controle? Naar een Europees beleid inzake de intra-communautaire handel in wapens en dual-use goederen en de export naar derde landen,* Utrecht: Wetenschapswinkel Rechten Utrecht.

Schipper, P.G., 1992, *'Dual-use technologie: koppelingen en barrières in het civiel en defensie georiënteerd onderzoek en technologie ontwikkeling,* Den Haag: TNO Beleidsstudies technologie/economie, no. 19.

Stichting OSACI, 1990, *Bezuinigingen op de Nederlandse Defensiebestedingen. Gevolgen voor de Nederlandse Defensiebestedingen,* Bewerkte versie van het onderzoeksrapport in opdracht van de Industriebond FNV, Utrecht.

STOA, 1993, *European Armaments Industry: Research, Technological Development and Conversion, Final Report,* Brussels: GRIP (European Institute for Research and Information Peace and Security).

Company Documents

Jaarverslag 1991 De Rotterdamsche Droogdokmaatschappij BV
Jaarverslag 1992 Koninklijke Begemann Groep NV
Jaaroverzicht 1992 TNO-Defensieonderzoek
Jaarverslag 1992 Delft Instruments
Jaarverslag 1992 Hollandse Signaalapparaten BV
Jaarverslag 1992 EUROMETAAL
Jaarverslag 1992 van der Giessen-de Noord NV
Jaarverslag 1992 Wilton-Fijenoord Holding bv
Annual report 1992 NV Koninklijke Nederlandse Vliegtuigenfabriek Fokker
Annual report 1992 National Aerospace Laboratory NLR, Amsterdam.
Annual report 1991 DAF NV
Annual report 1992 Royal Nijverdal-Ten Cate NV
Annual report 1992 Internatio-Müller NV
Schelde Groep Bulletin 1993, Jaargang 3, Nr. 2
Company profile van Rietschoten en Houwens
Company profile DAF Special Products
Company profile EUROMETAAL
Company profile van der Giessen-de Noord
Company profile Dutch State Mines DSM

Government Documents

(TK = Tweede Kamer der Staten Generaal, denoting a Parliamentary paper)
TK 19157: Defensie en de Nederlandse Industrie, 1984–1985, 1986–1987
TK 19404: Defensietechnologie, 1985–1986
TK 20679: Indernationale Defensie Materieelbetrekkingen, 1987–1988
TK 21886: De Nederlandse defensie-industrie, 1990–1991
TK 21991: Defensienota 1991, Herstructurering en verkleining, de Nederlandse krijgsmacht in een veranderende wereld, 1990–1991
TK 22054: Wapenexportbeleid, 1990–1991, 1991–1992
TK 22800 H.X: Begroting 1993, hoofdstuk Defensie
TK 22826: Het compensatiebeleid 1974–1992 en de inschakeling van de Nederlandse industrie bij het defensieverwervingsproces, 1992–1993
TK 22975: Prioriteitennota, Een andere wereld, een andere Defensie, 1992–1993
TK 23400 H.X: Begroting 1994, hoofdstuk Defensie

TK 23900 X nos. 1, 2, 8: Begroting 1995, hoofdstuk Defensie; Brief van de Minister en de Staatssecretaris van Defensie, Naar een doelmatiger defensie-organisatie

Defensie Technologie Concept, Ministerie van Defensie, 1989

Endnotes

1 For an account of the difficulties in realizing international cooperation, see van Houwelingen (1992), from his experiences as chairman of the IEPG from 1984–1986.

2 This Steering Group (Stuurgroep Defensie en de Nederlandse Industrie) included representatives from the ministries of Economic Affairs, Common Affairs, Foreign Affairs, Finances, Social Affairs and Employment, Education and Sciences.

3 The Adviesraad Militaire Productie consists of representatives of industry and the Ministries of Foreign Affairs, Economic Affairs, and Defence. Its main aim is to influence defence policy in industry's favour. This it tries to achieve through issuing comments and advice on defence policy.

4 These areas were electronics, marine vessel, aircraft and land transportation vehicles production and fibres for composite materials.

5 There has been a further study, commissioned from Arthur D. Little by AMP, in cooperation with MoD and MoEA, to make a strength/weakness assessment of the Dutch defence industry, but the results are classified and no further information has been released on it.

Chapter 7
Spain

Jordi Molas-Gallart

Basic Data

Organisational Context

Paradoxical as it may seem, one legacy of General Franco's dictatorship was to be an outmoded Spanish defence structure and a weakened military industrial base. During the Franco years, the armed forces were separated into three different ministries. Although this arrangement caused coordination problems and economic inefficiencies, it suited the interests of Franco's regime. The armed forces provided the cornerstone of political support for the regime, but Franco still had to deal with and control the different political tendencies that arose within the military institutions (Payne, 1967). His defence legacy has therefore to be understood in terms of the broader internal political context.

Predictably, one of the first measures approved by the new democratic regime concerning the armed forces was the creation in 1977 of a single Ministry of Defence (MINDEF). Organisational reform since then has been a slow but continuous process.

The new Ministry of Defence was initially organised into two clearly differentiated domains: a military domain, under the military chain of command, responsible mainly for operational matters; and a political-administrative domain charged with supporting the armed forces, including, in particular, the provision of the resources needed by the military to perform their duties (Ministry of Defence 1986). In 1984, a further step towards centralisation and civilian control was taken with the integration of the Army, Navy and Air Force within the structure of the Ministry of Defence, and the creation, below the Minister of Defence, of the position of Secretary of State for Defence to administer and control both economic resources and policies for armament, procurement and infrastructure.

These measures, which effectively ended the Ministry's previous dual structure, were progressively reinforced by other minor changes. Politically, their main outcome has been to establish a clear subordination of the Armed Forces to the elected civilian authorities. Economically, decision making was concentrated in a few offices within the Ministry with responsibilities for planning, budgeting and procurement. The necessary organisational conditions for defence expenditure planning and rational decision-making were now in place. Yet organisational reform alone was not sufficient to achieve the modernisation of the armed forces, nor to attain rational and reliable planning of the resources made available to them.

The structural constraints upon the modernisation of the armed forces stretched far beyond organisational design. Until the late seventies, Spain's defence policy had been only marginally concerned with the situation of the domestic defence industry. For decades, Spain had not had anything resembling a defence industrial policy. The first step in this direction was taken shortly after the creation of the Ministry of Defence, with the establishment of a centralised office responsible for preparing, developing and co-ordinating arms procurement and defence research policies. This office, the Directorate General for Armament and Material (DGAM), came into effect in 1979, effectively becoming the principal policy making agency dealing with defence industry and technology issues. It coordinates, oversees, and plans equipment purchases, organises, negotiates and monitors all offset agreements, sets up the defence R&D policy and is responsible for certification and quality requirements. The coordination of purchasing decisions radically reduced the autonomy with which the three former Armed Forces Ministries had managed their procurement. Today the DGAM comprises five sub-directorates: strategic analysis and planning; programmes and systems; inspection and technical services; international relations; and research and technology.

Centralised procurement policies were a pre-condition for the implementation of much-needed and often promised medium and long-term procurement plans. In the early 1980s, the newly elected Socialist government committed itself to elaborate medium and long-term budget and purchasing plans, thus answering the demands of Spanish military producers. DGAM's stated policy goals were in line with this commitment: they included medium and long-term procurement planning (rarely followed) and the creation of consultative bodies to act as channels of communication with the defence industry.[1]

In addition, the DGAM oversees an 'Autonomous Organism' involved in research: the El Pardo Canal for Hydrodynamic Experiments (CEHP). The larger National Institute of Aerospace Technology (INTA) functions under the jurisdiction of the Secretary of State for Defence. These organisms are administratively autonomous, and have their own budgets to which the Ministry of Defence contributes. INTA and CEHP are the two most important government establishments involved in defence research, and before the explosion of defence R&D investment in the late eighties, INTA accounted for most Spanish military-related research. As will be discussed below, INTA's fortunes as a recipient of Ministry of Defence R&D funds reflect the changing priorities between carrying out research in State laboratories and contracting R&D out to firms.

The Spanish Defence Industry

As shown in Table 1, estimates of the volume of Spanish defence production vary widely. This can be explained by a lack of information and the absence of a generally accepted definition of defence production. In any case, defence production amounts to a small share of the Spanish economy; estimates differ only with respect to exactly how small a share this amounts to. According to a MINDEF study, the percentage of industrial manufacturing accounted for by military production was 1.02 in 1991 (down from 1.31% in 1987), with a total

Table 1: Contrasting Estimates of Spanish Defence Production

(billion 1990 ptas)

Year	Afarmade	GRIP	Oliveres
1980		189	165
1981		227	203
1982		346	313
1983	329	309	307
1984	293	372	334
1985	202	305	267
1986	206	257	240
1987	215	283	278
1988	233	308	280
1989	230	337	298
1990	208	301	237
1991	194	274	328
1992	187	241	
1993	179		
1994	173		

Sources: GRIP Database, Brussels; Oliveres (1993).

Note: Oliveres' own figures are an overestimate, as they assume all MINDEF investment to provide demand for the defence industry. He includes all R&D which is partially allocated to government research institutes, and many other investments by the Ministry of Defence that are not related to defence production. 'Afarmade' figures are based on domestic arms sales data published by the Association of Spanish Arms Producers (Afarmade) in several issues of its journal *La Voz de la Defensa*.

production value of Pesetas (Pt) 194 billion (*Jane's Defence Weekly*, 18 April 1992, p. 664). A later official estimate put total defence production in Spain in 1992 at Pt 160 billion.[2]

Most estimates show a marked fall in production after 1989–1990. The percentage of industrial production accounted for by defence products oscillates between 1 and 2%, and it is clearly declining. Differences in employment estimates are also notable (see Table 2). Yet again, they all confirm a substantial reduction in the level of defence employment. Without exception, defence-related companies are substantially reducing their workforce.

Production is concentrated in five firms which, according to MINDEF data, comprised 74% of defence production and 79% of defence industrial employment in 1992. Four of them are controlled by State-owned holdings:

- Construcciones Aeronauticas, S.A. (CASA) in aerospace.
- Empresa Nacional Bazán de Construcciones Navales Militares (Bazán), which controls the most important military shipyards in Spain.
- Empresa Nacional Santa Bárbara de Construcciones Militares (Santa Bárbara), an arms conglomerate which produces munitions, firearms, artillery pieces, armoured vehicles and other military-related equipment.

Table 2: Estimates of Employees in the Spanish Defence Industry

Year	Directly employed: Oliveres	Directly employed: GRIP	Directly employed: AFARMADE	Directly employed: Ministry of Defence
1981		47744		
1982		68492		
1983	36503	62548		
1984	36500	77412		
1985	29414	64480		
1986	30300	51448	30922	
1987	30496	49713	30496	
1988	31211	52882	31211	
1989	26659	55963	26659	33066
1990	25339	50367	25339	(average for the
1991	23521	45330	23521	period 1989–93)
1992		40797	21391	
1993			16097	

Sources: GRIP Database, Brussels; Ministry of Defence 1993b; Oliveres 1993; *La Voz de la Defensa*, Nr. 14 (September–October 1991), p. 13.

- INDRA, the state-controlled (60%) electronics holding, which has resulted from the merger between Empresa Nacional de Electrónica y Sistemas (INISEL) and the most important defence-related private electronics company (CESELSA). Hughes has a 49% stake in three of INDRA's defence-related companies: Gyconsa (missiles), ENOSA (electro-optics), and SEA, a recently created spin-off company.[3]

The only privately-controlled firm among the five biggest Spanish defence producers is the young Industria de Turbo Propulsores, S.A. (ITP). ITP was founded in 1988 in the framework of the EFA programme to develop and manufacture aircraft engine components. ITP is owned by Rolls Royce (45%) and a consortium of Spanish firms which includes SENER and Bazán.

The rest of the private sector plays a secondary role in military production, manufacturing mostly light weaponry, ammunition, sub-systems and components. The group of private firms involved in military production may be divided broadly into the specialised arms manufacturers concentrated in the north of Spain and firms producing sub-systems and components for both the defence and the civilian markets. The former constitute a cluster of small- to medium-sized firms with an intermediate technological level; they include firms like GAMESA, Explosivos Alaveses (EXPAL) and other defence operations of the conglomerate Unión Española de Explosivos (UEE), and Sociedad Anónima Placencia de las Armas. Sub-systems and components producers are usually private firms that display a diversified production pattern in sectors like electronics and communications, for instance, Amper, Telefónica Sistemas, and the Spanish divisions of Alcatel. In vehicles, the defence activities of the multinationals IVECO, Nissan and Peugeot accounted for a total of Pt 9 billion in sales in 1992.

Finally, the Ministry of Defence owns ISDEFE, a systems engineering and consulting company specialising in defence systems. Created in 1985, the firm grew very rapidly to reach sales of Pt 4.3 billion in 1992.

With the exception of private small and medium firms in the traditional arms and munition sectors, Spanish defence-related firms maintain close linkages with foreign companies. Some of the private firms operating in the electronics and communication areas are divisions of foreign companies such as Alcatel and Ericsson. Foreign firms have acquired minority shareholdings in some Spanish military producers, and new joint ventures have been created with the 'big' Spanish producers, as discussed below.

Budgetary Trends

The activity of Spanish companies is taking place against the background of a decreasing procurement budget. This contrasts starkly with the growth perspectives envisaged in the early and mid 1980s, when new long-term budgetary plans were forecasting real growth in defence budgets, as well as budget restructuring in favour of procurement outlays. Moreover, the Ministry of Defence placed new emphasis on using domestic procurement whenever possible and on obtaining offsets when local production was not a possibility. However, the anticipated rates of budget growth failed to materialise. Furthermore, when economic conditions and the end of the Cold War forced defence budgets downwards, personnel expenditure proved to be very inflexible, so that procurement bore the brunt of the cuts. Hence, instead of increasing the proportion of procurement within the budget, the 1990s have seen the opposite.

These trends (reduction in defence expenditure and a more than proportional reduction in procurement) have, however, been overturned again more recently. The 1994 budget represents a 6.3% increase in real terms over the previous year (the first time such an increase has taken place in the 1990s); the growth in equipment expenditure will be much larger (15%), and within equipment, the budgets for weapon modernisation and matériel will increase by 24%. The main acquisition programmes include the acquisition of 130 Pizarro armoured vehicles for the Army, several communications and electronic warfare systems, the modernisation of C-130 Hercules and Mirage F1, the purchase of eight new Harrier aircraft, the acquisition of new frigates, the construction of four minehunters, and the development and production of a new amphibious transport. From a low of Pt 86 billion in 1992, contracts for new defence matériel were expected to grow to Pt 223 billion in 1994.

Although the growth in the 1994 budget was largely unexpected, it left the Armed Forces lukewarm. The Armed Forces Chiefs of Staff declared to Congress on 18 October 1993 that the increase was not sufficient to meet requirements, as years of budget reductions had depleted the reserves of matériel, and had reduced operational capacity to a minimum (*International Defense Review,* 26 December 1993, p. 931).

The woes of Spanish defence producers were compounded by a sharp reduction in military equipment exports. A substantial part of the mid-1980s growth was built on the increase in arms exports, and these exports remained a key element in the industry's growth strategy. Yet the arms export boom was short lived, adding to the difficulties faced by arms exporters and compounding the pressures for a restructuring of Spanish arms production.

The SIPRI estimates in Figure 1 show a clear decline in Spanish arms exports. Such a fall is confirmed by circumstantial evidence; for instance, in 1992 Spain reported no items in the UN arms register list. However, there are discernible signs that Spain's position in the international arms market may be about to recover. Firstly, some apparently contradictory figures for defence

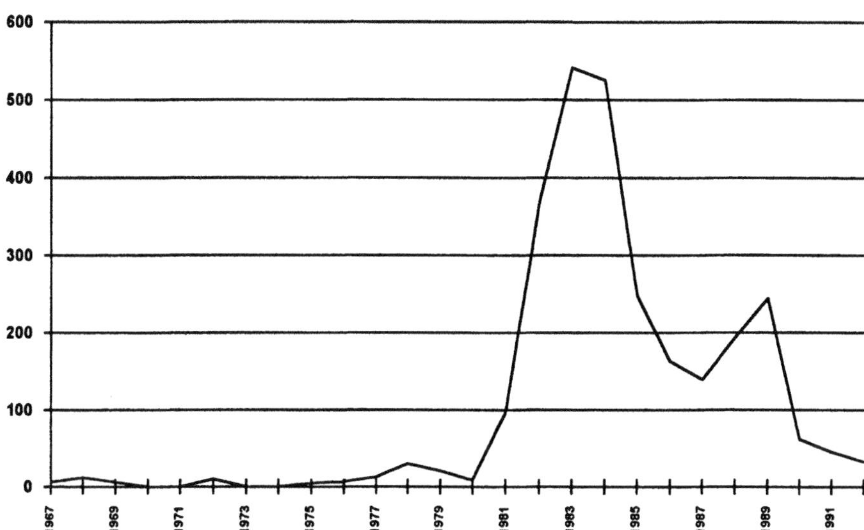

Figure 1: Spanish Exports of Major Arms Systems (1985 Million US$).
Source: Derived from SIPRI data. Data adjusted to discount re-exports of used equipment.

exports in 1992 were presented to the Senate by the Secretary of State for Defence in late 1993: these showed exports as amounting to 39% (Pt 62.4 billion) of the total 1992 defence production of Pt 160 billion. Such a figure would be very high even if compared to the 'golden age' of Spanish military exports in the early to mid 1980s.[4] Secondly, Spanish firms signed some major arms export contracts in 1992: the sale of a small aircraft carrier to Thailand and of 16 transport planes to South Korea may be worth around $400 million. Spanish arms deliveries therefore appear poised to grow again in the near future.

Policy Towards Defence and Dual-Use Technologies

When, in the 1980s, science and technology policy gained unprecedented attention in Spain, a growing proportion of the increasing budget for R&D was allocated to defence. As shown in Figure 2, Government defence R&D budgets grew very rapidly during the second half of the 1980s, reaching Pt 60.8 billion in 1992. Military R&D was still growing while the defence budget was falling rapidly in 1991 and 1992, until it finally started contracting, slightly, in 1993.

Although modest by international standards, such figures are very substantial given Spain's science and technology base. The military R&D spending occurred in an environment in which defence investment in R&D projects had previously been insignificant. Spanish research facilities could barely absorb the funds suddenly lavished upon them, and parts of the budget went unspent.

Nevertheless, the high budgets indicate the importance which the Ministry of Defence has attached to building up a technologically capable defence industrial base. At present, about 20% of total State outlays on R&D are being spent by the Ministry of Defence (and over 60% of this is earmarked for the Eurofighter 2000 aircraft). Attempts to coordinate these activities with other R&D and industrial programmes have never been successful. The Ministry of Defence now effectively manages its own research programmes and priorities with total independence from the other government bodies involved in industrial and S&T policies.

In consequence, a very substantial part of the country's R&D effort is being targeted at industries undergoing a profound crisis, due mainly but not exclusively to the fall in demand for military equipment. These are circumstances that would seem conducive to the consideration of dual-use strategies. Yet internal debate on the relationships between defence and civil technologies has been slow to appear. Although some officials and industrialists have paid lip service to the concept of dual-use technologies, there is little in the way of explicit policies to deal with the problems posed by the combination of relatively large R&D efforts carried out in an area accounting for a falling share of total economic activity. In this, as in other matters of defence industrial policy, a distinction must be made between explicit policies (usually absent or lacking in detail) and the emergence of trends in day-to-day practice that could be considered implicit policies. The implicit policies are clearer in the field of defence industrial strategies than in the area of technology and dual-use issues.

Defence Industrial Policies

Although the Defence Ministry has no explicit responsibilities for industrial policy, there is sufficient of a legal basis for the Secretary of State to argue that 'the Ministry of Defence has the responsibility to buttress the defence industry as a support and a component of the national defence system' (Ministry of Defence, 1993a). Yet, the concept that the Ministry of Defence has a role to play in the field of defence industrial policy does not find easy acceptance either in the Armed Forces or among officials within and beyond the Ministry itself. In partial consequence, Spanish defence industrial policy has been formulated in only the broadest terms. Already in the mid-1980s, the Ministry of Defence called for the establishment of a defence industry that could supply to the maximum extent possible the requirements of the Spanish Armed Forces, and spoke of using military demand to develop 'high-technology industries' (Ruiz Montero, 1989). Common and straightforward as it may seem, this approach was new for Spain. Never before had similar emphasis been placed on the need to develop a viable domestic arms industry. The main tools to achieve this goal was the Ministry's purchasing power and its consequent capacity to plan and support industrial and research initiatives in selected areas. Although the budget reductions have weakened this capacity, the main defence industrial goals of the Ministry of Defence have remained unaltered.[5]

In 1994, the Secretary of State for Defence summarised the goals of Spanish defence industrial policy as follows:

- To achieve a 'total capacity' in the maintenance of the systems and equipment used by the Spanish Armed Forces.
- To preserve present capacities for the manufacture of light and medium conventional weaponry.
- To promote industrial technological development.
- To maintain a 'sufficient' presence in specific subsectors, in line with available resources. (Medina, 1994).

Such objectives are very much in line with the ideas that informed defence industrial policy making in the 1980s. It is difficult to find official statements signalling a shift in the goals or the procedures of defence industrial policy, even though a closer look at practices emerging in the 1990s would suggest that new, implicit policies are being implemented. For example, a range of new industrial developments is receiving tacit official support, including concentration through mergers at the national level, internationalisation of research and production, and changes in the locus of defence R&D. Dual use technology and defence conversion policies, on the other hand, do not feature strongly. We discuss each of these points immediately below.

Mergers

Officials at the Ministry of Defence are aware of the weakness of the Spanish defence industrial base. One expression of this weakness is the industrial fragmentation found in most defence-related sectors. It is common to find references in statements by Ministry of Defence officials and defence industrialists to the lack of the 'critical mass' necessary to face the highly complex tasks required from advanced defence companies. So when competition heightened in the wake of world-wide reductions in defence procurement, the need for restructuring of the sector became especially acute. A slow process of concentration had taken place since the early 1960s with the gradual but slow transfer of Army plants to the INI defence company Santa Bárbara and the merger of aeronautics firms into CASA. In the 1980s, the most important target for concentration became the State electronics companies leading, in 1985, to the creation of INISEL through the amalgamation of the leading Spanish electronics firms: EESA and EISA. INISEL also became the head of the public electronics holding which operates in both the military and civilian markets. In 1986, the new INISEL group had 2554 employees; a figure that both INI and the Ministry of Defence considered still insufficient.

In spring 1989, INI proposed a complete overhaul of the defence electronics sector based on the merging of INISEL with the leading private defence electronics producer, CESELSA. The protracted negotiations stalled several times, but political pressure was key in keeping the process moving until July 1992, when the merger of the two groups was agreed. In 1993, the resulting CESELSA-INISEL changed its name to INDRA. In that same year, the total consolidated sales for the group reached Pt 55 billion, of which its 'Defence and Dual-Technologies Division' accounts for about 40%; this makes it a medium-sized competitor in the European defence electronics markets, and the third biggest defence related firm in Spain. The consolidation in the electronics sector is not limited to the CESELSA-INISEL operation. INISEL had previously established a cross-shareholding agreement with Amper (a communications equipment producer that is part of the Telefónica group). In 1989, INISEL transferred to Amper its communications business, including defence activities, in exchange for a minority share in Amper's capital (7%). As a consequence, Amper established a defence division, which has become Spain's main military communications firm (see *ABC* (Madrid), 13 April 1989; *El País* (Madrid), 14 May and 14 June 1989).

Other initiatives in the field of conventional armament and munitions have proved less successful. The attempt to link Santa Bárbara with the defence operations of UEE (the biggest Spanish private group in the conventional armaments sector) failed. That merger would have created the most important Spanish, and one of the biggest European, arms and munitions producers. Although the Spanish government was keen to merge the firms into a mixed ownership company, disagreements about the valuation of the companies' assets seemed to be insurmountable. Although the sector is sinking into ever deeper crisis, its restructuring keeps being postponed. Evidently, it does not arouse the same interest in the Ministries of Defence and Industry as did the mergers in the electronics and communications sector.

Internationalisation of Research and Production

Industrial mergers have been accompanied by foreign firms acquiring shares in Spanish defence-related producers. This is a recent trend. In fact, the 1980s had seen some high profile withdrawals, like Northrop's abandonment of its interests in CASA, in which, back in 1965, it had held as much as a 25% share. By the late 1980s, national control of Spanish defence-related firms was almost absolute with the exception of the vehicles sector. The internationalisation of Spanish defence production was taking place under mechanisms connected to the purchase of defence equipment (for instance through offset agreements) and participation in international arms production and development programmes.

The return of foreign firms to the ownership of Spanish defence-related companies has been a recent, gradual, and often unnoticed process, in which both foreign and domestic companies have an interest. Foreign firms may be attracted to invest in countries like Spain to gain access to their domestic markets. The generally sluggish conditions of military demand are forcing big defence manufacturers to seek new foreign markets, even when this implies taking some risks through investments in local companies. For the Spanish firms, alliances with foreign partners provide access to technological knowledge and to international marketing and commercial structures.

A clear pattern of alliances has emerged. A foreign firm will take a large but minority share (between 40% and 49%) in an existing or newly-created division of a big defence related-company but never as the group leader.[6] Newly-created divisions are often the result of 'spinning off' plants into new firms and, consequently, are much smaller and, at least initially, free from the risk associated with taking over shares of companies which have historically been burdened by large and almost perpetual losses. Most of these operations are connected to a specific purchase programme by the Ministry of Defence. That is, instead of seeking offset agreements, Spain has started to require the foreign firm to take a minority share in a Spanish company that will act as a contractor in the programme. This has the effect of granting the Spanish side more control over the project, and hopefully of linking the foreign supplier to the domestic industry on a longer-term basis than would have been the case in a simple offset agreement. In this way, the US-based Hughes company has taken minority shares in three INDRA firms (ENOSA, the newly created Gyconsa, and the spun-off SEA). The French Thomson Sintra took a 49% stake in SAES, a firm in the INDRA group specialising in underwater electronics,[7] while Thomson-CSF has taken a similar stake in Amper Sistemas, Amper's military communications division. Rolls Royce has a 49% interest in ITP, a company which was created to be the Spanish partner in the Eurojet consortium, in charge of developing the engines for the future EFA.[8] Another EFA-related joint venture was CESA, a joint venture of CASA and Lucas Aerospace, which specialises in hydraulic components.

Foreign partners have also joined new joint ventures independently of any specific development or purchasing programme. Santa Bárbara has been particularly active in this respect. It has set up four, mostly small, companies with foreign participation: Aeronáutica Maintenance Tooling (AMT), with Pratt and Whitney; DEFTEC, with MBB; Surgiclinic Plus, an effort at diversification into the medical equipment field in cooperation with the Italian company Cremascoli, which holds a 50% share in the venture; and ICSA, a firm set up with CASA for the development and production of composite materials, in which Aérospatiale has taken a 15% share.

The two main axes in the process of internationalisation are thus participation in international development and production programmes; and penetration by foreign partners, mainly into components and sub-systems divisions of Spanish producers. Both trends strengthen the Spanish technological base in the development and production of specific components and sub-systems.[9]

Changes in the Locus of R&D

One of the most important aspects of recent Spanish defence industrial and technology policies was the rapid growth of R&D investment in the mid- to late-1980s. While sectoral priorities have remained stable, with aerospace and electronics topping the list, important changes in the main recipient of these funds have taken place. The main beneficiaries of the first round of research expenditure increases in the late 1980s were mainly State-controlled firms. The laboratories and research institutions dependent on the Ministry of Defence were languishing with budget levels similar to, or even smaller than, those in the early and mid-1980s. Then, without any official explanation, this trend was abruptly reversed in the 1990s.

To demonstrate this conclusion, it is necessary first to estimate the percentage of MINDEF's research expenditure that is contracted to outside companies or institutions; official figures at the necessary level of disaggregation are not available. Having made such estimates,[10] Figure 2 then shows the shifting budget allocations between external firms[11] and Ministry of Defence research organisations. When defence R&D rocketed in the late 1980s, industrial firms got the lion's share of the newly available funds, while expenditure in the Ministry of Defence's own research establishments remained approximately stable. Therefore, the growth of defence R&D brought about a change in the main performers of publicly-funded defence R&D. After 1989, a further reversal returned the State-owned research facilities, especially INTA, to a key role.

Meanwhile, research contracted out to firms first stagnated and then started to decline.[12] INTA's remarkable growth (a more than 300% increase in its budget between 1989 and 1993), accompanied by the rise of current expenditure in the ministries in charge of administering R&D programmes, signalled a shift towards a more balanced distribution of R&D funds between facilities controlled by the Ministry of Defence and external firms.

This policy may be contrasted with that of other European countries, like the UK, in which the quest for privatisation and competition is opening to the market the research operations conducted by government research facilities (see UK chapter in this volume). Spain's return to direct financing of R&D in Government research organisations has to be understood against the background of the difficulties of administering and carrying out the rocketing research budgets in the late 1980s. There were cases in which the results of feasibility studies and other research projects carried out with public funds were less than satisfactory, to the extent that some of the research funds could be construed as hidden subsidies. Although never stated officially, these problems caused concern among Ministry officials, and it was felt that research carried out in government laboratories would be easier to monitor. Such opinions were gaining ground when an energetic new director was appointed to INTA, the largest of the defence research establishments. The combination of a new management able to set up attractive, achievable goals, and the difficulties encountered with some of the external research contractors, explains the picture shown in Figure 2. Although it has not been immune to budget cuts, INTA's profile in the 1990s has nevertheless grown.

INTA's main lines of research (all of them in the space field)[13] have by their very nature dual-use applications. Therefore, another consequence of reinforcing INTA's capacities has been the growing importance of research on dual-use technologies financed by the Ministry of Defence.[14] Although, again, precise data are unavailable, it seems that this outcome has been largely unintentional. Certainly, the increased emphasis on dual-use research resulting from INTA's new programmes is not a response to any explicit dual-use policy by the Ministry of Defence. In fact, as the next section will show, the problems of dual-use technology have received very little attention in Spanish defence industrial and technology policy-making.

Dual-Use and Conversion-Diversification Policies

Dual-use technologies, conversion and diversification issues do not seem to be at the forefront of MINDEF concerns. In the Ministry's report on the period of the last legislature (1989–1993), there is only one reference to any of these concepts:

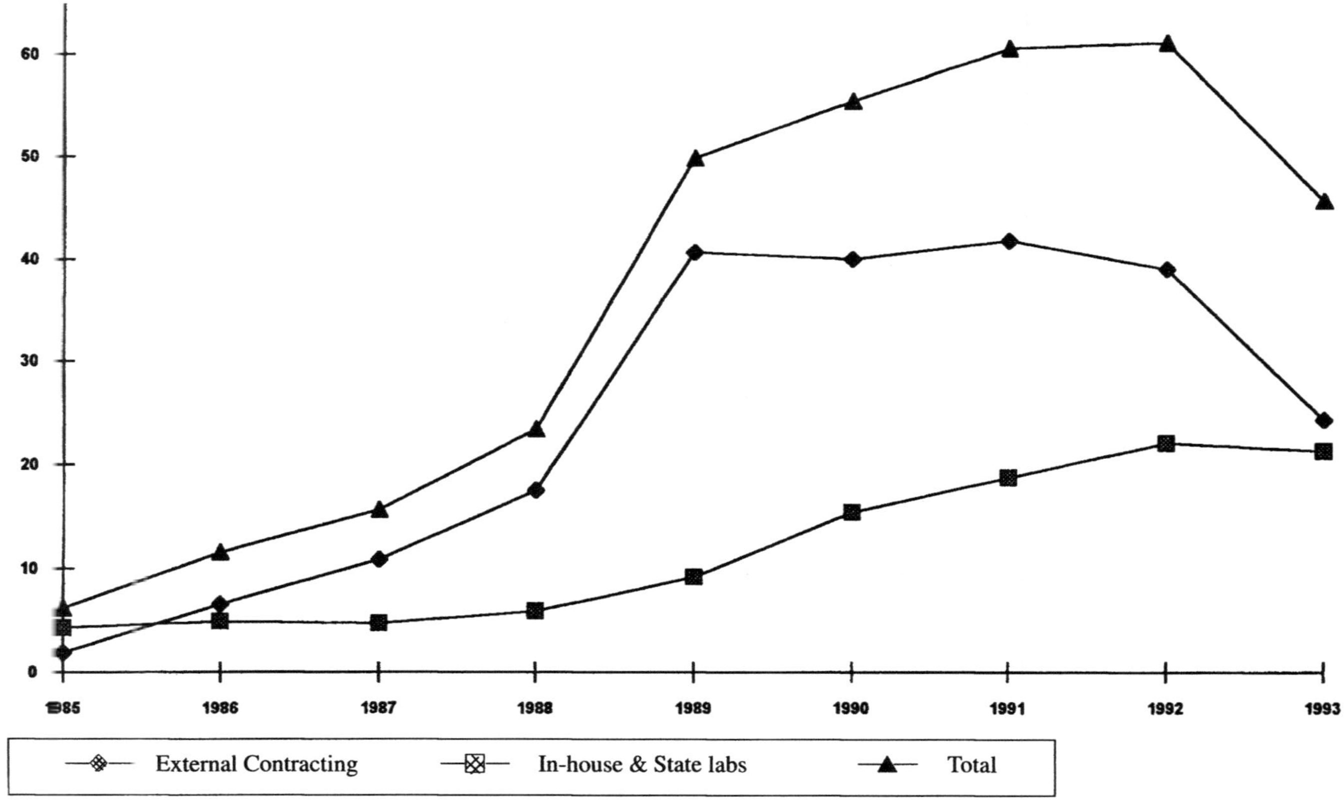

Figure 2: MINDEF R&D by Performer Billions Current Pesetas (Estimate).

Finally, the Ministry of Defence's technology policy pays special attention to those technologies that can have a dual use, military and civilian, as the best way to take advantage of the [defence] R&D resources, thus backing the Spanish industry confronting free competition in the coming years (Ministry of Defence, 1993b, p. 333).

This statement was not backed by any explicit strategy or other elaboration, although certain implicit policies can be identified in practice. Of particular relevance is the growing role, mentioned just above, of INTA (and therefore of space-related research) within the R&D activities financed by the Ministry of Defence. There are also some weak signs of dual-use activities in the strategies of individual defence firms, such as the initiatives from Santa Bárbara discussed below. Given the State-controlled nature of most Spanish military-related companies, these individual company policies cannot be decoupled from government policy. But even acknowledging this point, one has to conclude that the companies are not responding to a coordinated industrial policy from any of the ministries (defence and industry) involved in the supervision of the main Spanish military-related firms.

In fact, and despite its brief statement of intent concerning dual-use technologies, the Ministry seems more committed to another goal expressed earlier in the same report:

[Defence] industrial policy has sought to foster the national industrial base ... building up detailed knowledge of its capacities in order to make the fullest possible use of them (Ministry of Defence, 1993b, p. 325).

In other words, the Ministry is monitoring Spanish industrial capacities to identify firms that could become defence suppliers. To this end, it has long been engaged in constructing a 'Register of Firms ... of interest to the national defence.' The Ministry has contacted about 1000 firms, of which 700 have joined the Register. This is necessary in order to become a defence supplier, and so the Ministry has been able to use this resource to monitor the evolution of the defence industrial base. This pro-active stance concerning potential suppliers represents an attempt to introduce more competitiveness in defence supply, seeking out new firms active in the civilian market that may be able to offer 'value for money' to the Ministry of Defence but could be discouraged from entering the market by the complexity and the problems surrounding military procurement.

There appears also to be no policy for the diversification or conversion of specialised defence suppliers; rather the opposite as the Ministry tries to draw civilian firms into military work. There are no official data on the results of this approach, but given the concentration of military procurement in a few established defence suppliers, it is safe to assume that the success of this initiative has been so far very limited.

In general, Spanish managers are extremely sceptical of the prospects for conversion or even diversification. Javier Alvarez Vara, then President of CASA, stated that 'my opinion regarding the conversion of the military industry is clearly negative. I believe that, with few exceptions, it is simply impossible and that, besides, even attempting it would be a senseless waste of resources.' (Fundación Universidad-Empresa, 1993, p. 177). Nevertheless, CASA has a diversified production base within which, probably out of necessity, the civilian share of total sales has been growing throughout the past decade. Thus, in the same address, Alvarez Vara declared that CASA's civilian sales had grown from 15% of the total in 1985 to approximately 50% in 1992.

One can find examples of diversification attempts much more readily than examples of straightforward conversion. The process of spinning off plants and searching for foreign partners has at times been part of a deliberate diversification strategy. For example, Santa Bárbara is already claiming some success for its venture with the Italian Cremascoli, in establishing a new firm (Surgiclinic Plus) for the development and manufacture of medical and surgical equipment, to which Santa Bárbara transferred its Oviedo plant. In 1992 Surgiclinic Plus received an innovation prize for the development of a new hospital mobile bed.

Even when the new spun-off companies still have defence customers as their main market, gaining proficiency in materials and components production can place them in a better situation to exploit areas of technological convergence between civilian and military products. This is the case with ICSA, the composites firm in which Santa Bárbara holds a 85% stake, which operates in an area with clear potential civilian and military markets.

These initiatives are, however, still small compared with the size of the main Spanish defence producers. It is significant that some main producers have not managed substantially to reduce the proportion of military production in their total sales, despite the fall in the defence markets. For example, INDRA has concentrated most of its defence production in a single division, curiously renamed 'Defence and Dual Technologies,' which in 1992 accounted for 41% of total production. This is very similar to the position of its precursor INISEL in the mid 1980s. Despite the name of the division, its director stated in 1992 that the best successes in the application of technologies and knowledge learnt in the field of military applications to civilian uses had occurred when brand new subsidiaries had been created within the group to exploit this potential (Fundación Universidad-Empresa, 1993, p. 192).

Bazán's inroads into the civilian area have been similarly limited. Its modest operations in turbines for power stations and other civilian applications have been maintained, and new markets have been sought in the shipbuilding sector (such as the construction of a new fast ferry) and in other new areas of activity. For example, a new 'environment programme' has been established which has developed a system for the detection of forest fires. The success of these diversification initiatives remains to be seen, but they are in any case peripheral to the main thrust of the firm's activities, which remain firmly anchored in its military shipyard business.

Several other diversification attempts never got beyond the drawing board. For instance, the mortar producer Esperanza commissioned a study of the possibilities for diversification and conversion open to the firm. This concluded that the civilian areas that the company could attempt to enter (mainly forging) were already suffering from an excess of supply. Furthermore, any diversification attempt would require a level of investment which the firm, weakened by the decline in the munitions market, could not afford.

There are, therefore, examples of individual, and usually modest, attempts by military firms to develop civilian business. But there are no public initiatives in the field of conversion or diversification. Even more importantly, there is little debate over potential policies, and a lack of awareness of initiatives underway elsewhere.

Spain's reaction to the European Community KONVER initiative is illustrative in this respect. In 1993, seven Spanish projects were financed under KONVER to a total of Pt 2.4 billion, of which 50% was financed by the EC and the rest by four Spanish regional authorities, two firms and one local authority. The KONVER initiative passed largely unnoticed in most firms and even among officials responsible for industrial policy at the Ministries of Defence and Industry. The projects that were approved were more the result of individual initiative by some regional governments and firms than the outcome of any coordinated initiative to increase general awareness of KONVER. This explains the odd geographical distribution of the KONVER funds received by Spain; many of the Spanish projects have been located in regions with little or no dependence on military activities, while areas heavily defence-dependent received few or no funds. For instance, Catalonia is the only region receiving KONVER funds for as many as two projects, yet it has almost no defence industry. On the other hand, Madrid has only one project financed, despite being the main centre of Spanish defence manufacturing and having a large number of military facilities.

Controlling the Diffusion of Defence Technologies: Defence Technology Export Regimes

Since 1985, Spain has joined (the former) COCOM (1985), become a member of the MTCR (1989), and signed the NPT (1993). This resulted in the addition of lists of controlled dual-use items to the Spanish legislation governing exports. The process has, however, been particularly slow and has had only a slight effect on the organisational structure responsible for monitoring trade in controlled products. After Spain joined COCOM, regulations on the export of sensitive technologies began to be introduced, replacing the rather informal system that had been used until then (Fisas, 1988, pp. 123–138). Yet a list of controlled items following COCOM lines was not introduced until January 1990. It was not until early 1992 that a law was approved classifying the illegal export of controlled goods as contraband, in accordance with COCOM recommendations.

The organisation in charge of granting export licences for dual-use items is similar to the organisation that had been responsible since 1987 for licensing the export of arms and munitions: the *Junta Interministerial Reguladora del Comercio Exterior de Armas y Explosivos (JIRCEAE)* (Interministerial Board Regulating Foreign Trade in Arms and Explosives). JIRCEAE comprised representatives of the Ministries of Foreign Affairs, Industry and Trade, Defence, and Economic Affairs, and was chaired by a senior official of the Ministry of Trade (the Director General for Trade Policy). In 1988, a Royal Decree (Real Decreto 480/1988) established the basis of a new export control system. It changed JIRCEAE's name to reflect the extension of the Interministerial Board's responsibilities to cover dual-use technologies,[15] but the new Board represented the same ministries as the old JIRCEAE. Several regulations have since been introduced which specify the list of controlled technologies (following COCOM rules), and establish the procedures for obtaining licences. The whole process has evolved with little debate and negligible public interest.

Conclusion

The main characteristic of Spain's defence technology policy is the absence of an explicit formulation of strategies beyond the statement of the most general policy goals. This is accompanied by a scarcity of discussion and debate within industry, government, and the wider public on any issue related to dual-use technologies, conversion, diversification and the relationship between civilian and military technologies. Such an absence of explicit debate and of identifiable policy responses to the changing situation in the defence industries should not, however, be confused with policy inaction. Important developments which have occurred, but with little or no public announcement, include the following:

- The Ministry of Defence has adjusted the balance between the recipients of R&D funds in favour of Government research organisations under its control, and away from firms.
- Although there is a continuing emphasis on attracting foreign investors to the Spanish defence producers, the means towards this end have changed.

Instead of high profile operations involving the main defence firms, a stealthier approach has been adopted under which foreign partners are sought for new divisions of the larger companies. These divisions are smaller, specialised firms, at times brand new operations, but more often the result of 'spinning off' into new firms plants that had previously been integrated within the Spanish parent firm.

- As a result, foreign firms are becoming involved in the development and manufacture of components and sub-systems, rather than participating in the operations of the 'big' systems assemblers.
- The growth of the Ministry of Defence's R&D investment in the fledgling Spanish space sector implies a move towards an area where technological developments have an obvious 'dual use'.

There has been little debate on conversion and diversification strategies, and there is no explicit public policy in this area. Industry is left to implement its own diversification initiatives. The meagre attention paid to these issues may be partly explained by the relatively minor role of defence production within the Spanish economy. Nevertheless, the contraction of defence demand is likely to have important consequences in a few areas heavily dependent on military-related activities.

References

Fisas, V., 1988, *Les Armes de la Democràcia. Exportacions espanyoles d'armament, 1980–1987*, Barcelona: Fundació Jaume Bofill-Edicions La Magrana.

Fundación Universidad-Empresa, 1993, *Tecnologías de Doble Uso*, Madrid: Fundación Universidad-Empresa, Colección Fórum Electrónica Militar.

Medina, E., 1994, 'Chequeo a la Industria de Defensa' *Revista Española de Defensa*, January, p. 48.

Ministry of Defence, 1986, *Memoria de Legislatura (1982–1986),* Madrid: Ministerio de Defensa, Secretaría General Técnica.

Ministry of Defence, 1993a, Statement of the Secretary of State for Defence to the Spanish Senate, Mimeo, October.

Ministry of Defence, 1993b, *Memoria de la IV Legislatura, 1989–1993*, Madrid: Ministerio de Defensa, Secretaría General Técnica.

Molas-Gallart, J., 1992, *Military Production and Innovation in Spain,* Chur: Harwood Academic Publishers.

Oliveres, A., 1993, *La viabilitat ecònomica del desarmament: El cas de la indústria militar espanyola*, Unpublished doctoral dissertation, Universitat Autònoma de Barcelona.

Payne, S., 1967, *Politics and the Military in Modern Spain,* Stanford: Stanford University Press.

Ruíz Montero, J.F. 1989, 'Política General de Armamento del Ministerio de Defensa', in Círculo de Electrónica Militar, *La electrónica de defensa ante el reto de Europa,* Madrid: Fundación Universidad-Empresa.

Endnotes

1 The 'Defence Advisory Committee on Armaments and Material' (CADAM), for example, was set up in May 1982 as an advisory body to the Minister of Defence on questions of defence industrial policy. However, it has not been particularly active.

2 The estimate refers to the defence production declared by firms that are members of the Spanish Association of Arms Producers (Afarmade); the 45 member companies account for most, if not all, Spanish military production. The MINDEF/Afarmade estimate in Table 1 for 1992 gives a larger figure possibly because it includes a larger number of firms; it was published in the official Ministry of Defence report on its activities in the 1989–1993 period: Ministerio de Defensa *Memoria de la IV Legislatura.*

3 Hughes' penetration is linked to the Spanish acquisition of TOW missiles and the programme to develop an electro-optic guided TOW replacement.

4 This figure includes components and sub-systems (some of them 'exported' in the framework of international development and production programmes), and also munition and small weapons not monitored by SIPRI.

5 Economic planning of defence expenditure was authorised in the 1982 'Budget Provisions Act for Investment in and Maintenance of the Armed Forces'. The Act was intended to provide the basis for a long-term planning in Spanish defence expenditures, fixing a *minimum* annual increase in real terms for maintenance and investment credits and a *maximum* growth for defence expenditure. Despite being extended twice (in 1987 and 1990) and being still in force, its application was *de facto* frozen in 1990, when it became clear that the next procurement budgets would not bear any resemblance to the goals set up in the Act. The Secretary of State for Defence prepared a new Act for presentation to Congress in 1994. Its main objective (to provide a solid basis for defence expenditure planning) remained remarkably similar to the goals set up in the 1982 Act. Despite the noticeable

failure to provide even short-term planning at both the aggregate and disaggregate levels (Molas-Gallart, *Military Production*, pp. 114–115), the new Act was heralded as a way to achieve success in an area that has seen repeated failures. The new so-called 'Programme-Act' is designed to specify in greater detail the programmes to be developed and the years in which the planned investments will be carried out.

6 Despite persistent rumours in the late 1980s about foreign firms being interested in buying a share in CASA, the rumours never materialised. Similarly, more recently INDRA has remained wholly under Spanish control despite reports of keen interest from Thomson.

7 SAES was founded in 1990 by Inisel (51%) and Bazán (49%).

8 ITP incorporated the aircraft engine maintenance facilities previously belonging to CASA.

9 By comparison, Spanish participation in the EUCLID programme is much less significant. Although Spain participates in 9 EUCLID projects, the investment are very low: Ptas 1300 million in 1992 and Ptas 495 million in 1993. Such amounts make the EUCLID projects marginal within the research activities financed by the Spanish Ministry of Defence.

10 All of the R&D 'investment' of the Directorate General for Economic Affairs and most of the Directorate General for Arms and Matériel can be assumed to be contracted-out research. For a more detailed discussion of these assumptions, see Molas-Gallart, 1992, pp. 110–111.

11 This section includes also universities, but their role as receivers of MINDEF research funds has always been minimal in comparison with those received by State-owned firms.

12 In fairness, the technological base of Spanish industry could not handle for a sustained period the exponential growth of contracted research witnessed in the late 1980s.

13 The most important of INTA's research programmes are the development of a rocket launcher for microsatellites (CAPRICORNIO), seemingly abandoned in late 1994, an Unmanned Aerial Vehicle for surveillance tasks (SIVA), and the development of small satellites (MINISAT).

14 Most of the R&D financed by MINDEF is for the development of specific arms systems, and therefore often may have limited dual-use applications.

15 The new name was Junta Interministerial Reguladora del Comercio Exterior de Material de Defensa y de Productos y Technologias de Doble Uso (JIMDDU), that is, Interministerial Board regulating the foreign trade of defence material and dual-use products and technologies.

Chapter 8
Sweden

Björn Hagelin

Introduction[1]

Beyond the general post-Cold War re-orientation of defence and security policy that is being experienced by other west European countries, Sweden faces additional complexities arising from its traditional policy of neutrality in defence and foreign affairs.

Already during the 1980s, Sweden had experienced reduced demand for, and postponements of, matériel acquisitions, resulting in general unit cost increases. Rationalisations were made, both at the national level and within companies, to try to increase efficiency and thereby reduce costs. The peacetime (training) military organisation was also reduced. The 'peace dividend' was not realised, however, since the released resources were initially transferred to the budget for new equipment orders. This reflected the fact that since the end of the Cold War, new economic pressures have emerged, placing competing demands on the defence budget.

At the industrial level, the order of the day is restructuring. The main emphasis has changed from national restructuring, which has gone about as far as it can, with the possible exceptions of missile and electronic industries. Instead, the focus has shifted to international rationalisations and to an evaluation of which technological areas should be retained in Sweden, and which complementary technologies are to be acquired from abroad through imports, offsets and R&D cooperation.

The logic of non-alignment, aiming at neutrality in a European war, was downplayed by the government in the early 1990s. In 1994, Sweden joined NATO's PFP (Partnership for Peace) programme (see *Regeringens skrivelse 1993/94:207*). Neutrality is still official policy. Yet, at the same time, the new military situation in Europe has set off a debate about possible Swedish membership or association with NATO. Sweden is already becoming more engaged in international operations, which creates new demands for military production, organisation and training. For the first time in modern history, Sweden participated in a joint naval operation in the Baltic Sea during 1993. In March 1994, NATO troops (Danish) engaged for the first time in joint aircraft and tank peacekeeping training exercises with Swedish troops, in Sweden. During September and October 1994, Sweden participated in its first NATO/PFP military exercises.

Sweden also became a member of the EU from 1995, a position supported by all the major political parties. This will have implications for public procurement in the areas of civilian and dual-use products. EU, and possibly WEU, membership will have further consequences for the maintenance of Swedish defence technological capabilities. The traditional policy of striving to maintain an 'arm's length' distance from other countries is changing to an 'arm in arm' policy.

Basic Data

Organisational Context

A significant amount of basic and applied R&D as well as design of military systems takes place in Sweden. There is one military research organisation, the National Defence Research Establishment (FOA), and one institute for applied aeronautical research, the Aeronautical Research Institute (FFA). The Defence Matériel Administration (FMV) is the central procurement authority for military equipment, playing a key role in defining equipment requirements in cooperation with the armed forces.

A 1993 government bill entitled 'Research for Knowledge and Progress' proposed a new research policy for Sweden (*Forskning för kunskap och framsteg*). As a result, FOA's activities are becoming more specialised while, from 1994, FMV became fully funded from equipment orders instead of directly from the government's budget.

In addition, certain universities, mainly within natural and technical sciences, such as the Royal Institute of Technology in Stockholm and Chalmers Technical High-school in Gothenburg, also play a part in supporting military requirements. However, some sporadic references apart, there is no detailed information about defence-academic relations. What seems clear, though, is that they will get closer.

Sweden's Defence Industries

Acquisitions and restructuring activities during the 1980s have resulted in a high degree of defence industrial concentration (see Table 1). Celsius Industries has become the main arms producing group with around 50% of Sweden's total defence industry sales. During the 1980s it developed, through a deliberate company policy, into a large defence group. In addition to military shipbuilding, located in Kockums and Karlskronavarvet, in 1992 Celsius acquired the Bofors ordnance company[2]. In 1993 a large part of the electronics industry, formerly

NobelTech, also became part of the group under the name of CelsiusTech (Celsius *Annual Report 1992*). After the privatisation of Celsius in 1993, all of Sweden's defence industry became private.

As seen in Table 1, Swedish military firms are involved in most conventional arms technologies. There is one major company for each of the main arms categories, such as armoured vehicles and ordnance in general (Bofors), aircraft (Saab) and jet-engines (Volvo Aero Corporation, until April 1994 Volvo Flygmotor), surface ships (Karlskronavarvet) and submarines (Kockums). There is some overlap in missile technology between Bofors and Saab Missiles and in land vehicles between Bofors and Hägglunds, but in general these capacities are complementary and the companies cooperate rather than compete. The most important outstanding rationalisation is probably in electronics.

Among the few areas of production not undertaken in Sweden are production of light non-jet aircraft and helicopters (except overhaul), and long-range ground-to-air as well as air-to-air and ground-to-ground missiles. The latter missile type is not even in the Swedish arms inventory because of the air-to-ground role of the Swedish Air Force. Also, as a consequence of the transition from a heavy to a light navy, some types of surface ships are no longer produced.

Table 1 also indicates that defence employment during the period 1991–1993 fell by over 2000 people, mainly in ordnance production. The bottom had probably not yet been reached. Bofors was implementing a major restructuring program due to be completed in 1994, and several companies gave notice to employees during 1993 due to reduced orders. The number of employees at Bofors was expected to decline by about 2500 between 1991 and 1995 (*Bofors-Kuriren*, no. 2, 1994, p. 4).

The high share of defence employment in the companies listed in the table is a result of the restructuring of the defence industrial base during the 1980s and 1990s. Only in Volvo Aero Corporation was employment on defence production below 50% of total employment in 1993. After production and deliveries to Australia during 1992 of submarine sections (for assembly in Australia), defence employment at Kockums fell to just over 50% of the total in 1993. For Barracuda Technologies, producing camouflage equipment, the defence employment share increased to more than 60% in 1993.

All Swedish defence companies have been hit by reduced orders from diminishing domestic as well as foreign orders during the 1990s. Table 1 shows the same general downward trend in total defence matériel sales as in employment. The major exceptions are found in electronics, mainly CelsiusTech, and in Kockums, arising mainly from the sale to Australia mentioned above.

Table 1: Swedish Defence Firms, Production Areas, Sales (million SEK) and Employment

Group	Industries	Production areas				Defence matériel			
		A	B	C	D	1993	1992	1991	Def.sale share 1993
Celsius	Bofors AB	x				3272	3967	4288	95
	Celsius Tech Electronics AB			x		914	859	390	99
	Celsius Tech Systems AB			x		1289	1149	1284	96
	FFV Aerotech AB				x	862	1050	861	73
(Kockums)	• Karlskronavarvet AB		x			incl. below	455	506	incl. below
	• Kockums Submarine Systems AB		x			788	534	42	34
Ericsson*	Ericsson Radar Electronics AB			x		1219	1269	1407	54
	Ericsson Radio Systems AB				x	no info	–	–	–
Incentive	Barracuda Technologies AB				x	88	119	184	59
	Hägglunds Vehicle AB		x			631	659	904	91
Landsnordic	SA Marine AB	x				52	42	49	100
Saab-Scania	Saab Military Aircraft		x			1088	1058	1459	61
	Saab Missiles AB	x				614	580	860	98
	Saab Instruments AB +			x					
	Saab Training Systems AB			x		630	559	726	89
Volvo	Volvo Aero Corporation				x	977	1316	1417	27
	Volvo Aero Support AB				x	no info	–	–	–
	TOTAL					**11083**	**12511**	**13717**	

Source: *Fakta om försvarsindustrin.* Sveriges Försvarsindustriförbund, 1993.
***Note:** Ericsson Radar Electronics and Ericsson Radar Systems today make up Ericsson Microwave AB.
Definitions:
Def.sales = total invoiced company defence matériel sales.
Def.empl. = number of employees involved in defence matériel production.
Def.exp. = invoiced company defence matériel exports.
All shares are in %.
Production Areas: A = Weapons & Ammunition, B = Weapon platforms, C = Electronics, D = Other

(number) 1991, 1992 and 1993

	Employment in defence					Defence matériel exports	
Def.sales share 1992	1993	1992	1991	Def.empl. share 1993	Def.empl. share 1992	Def.exp. share of Def.sales 1993	1992
97	4554	4736	5723	90	89	37	43
100	901	1070	550	99	99	17	22
96	970	1010	1632	95	96	61	56
82	1400	1500	1435	82	80	5	3
96	incl. below	750	700	incl. below	86	incl. below	0
84	1553	845	811	56	89	4	74
66	2194	2188	2250	82	84	40	20
–	–	–	–	–	–	–	–
54	105	140	184	64	51	67	70
91	600	635	690	94	98	57	67
100	43	48	43	100	100	23	21
58	2855	3000	3500	80	75	6	5
96	406	464	496	93	95	31	74
95	530	625	804	98	99	69	62
39	1873	2083	2050	46	49	11	13
–	–	–	–	–	–	–	–
	17984	**19094**	**20868**				

Finally, Table 1 indicates that most defence companies have a high defence share of total sales. Just as for employment, this is a result of the restructuring process; those companies which decided to stay in military production have become more specialised (see also Table 7). For most of these firms, the military market is therefore their main market. In some companies there are no domestic follow-on R&D orders in their particular line of production, for instance fighter aircraft, heavy tanks, and anti-aircraft guns. Without new orders these areas of production are on the brink of being closed.[3]

International Partners

Although Sweden has officially pursued an 'independent' foreign and defence policy, there have in fact been many international contacts over the years, both official and unofficial, at governmental as well as company levels. Moreover, during the 1980s, the internationalisation of Sweden's military industry picked up sharply. One indicator of this trend is the number of foreign-based subsidiaries of Swedish defence firms, with a minimum of a 20% stake, which rose from a handful in the 1970s (*Försvarsindustrins utlandsverksamhet* 1987) to a position by 1994 where six firms had over 20 subsidiaries in 12 countries. Similarly, while there were a little over 10 companies which between 1989 and 1992 reported some 80 active manufacturing licenses abroad, 16 companies in 1994 reported 162 licenses and cooperative agreements (*KMI skrivelse* 1995).

Another indicator of Sweden's internationalisation is political. Table 2 lists Swedish bilateral inter-governmental agreements for the exchange or protection of military information and goods, as well as the most recent agreements (Memoranda of Understanding — MOUs) concerning R&D and industrial cooperation. Many countries appear more than once, most notably the USA. For several countries, a second agreement has been signed during the 1990s, in some cases nullifying its predecessor, but more usually broadening its scope. The MOUs signed during 1994 which most clearly reflect the new security and political situation in Europe are those with Poland and the Czech Republic. That with Poland is closely related to future joint peacekeeping activity and the consequent need for certain exchanges of information and goods. Several new agreements of this kind can be expected with other PFP countries.

From a military-industrial perspective, the most important new agreements are with the major military producers in Europe, such as France, Germany and the UK, together with those with such non-European states as Australia and, of course, the USA. The Swedish-French MOU states that both countries emphasise a 'selective' approach. With Australia and the UK, on the other hand, the

Table 2: Sweden's Bilateral Agreements for the Exchange or Protection of Military Information and Goods, and for R&D and Industrial Cooperation, 1952–June 1994

Year	Country
1952	USA
1961	USA
1962	USA
1964	USA
1966	Switzerland
1967	UK
1969	Norway
1970	Denmark
1974	Austria
1975	Canada
1981	USA, Belgium
1984	France, Netherlands
1985	Spain, Australia
1986	Singapore
1987	USA
1991	Germany
1992	Austria
1993	France
1994	UK, Australia, Malaysia, Poland, Germany, Czech Republic

Sources: *Sveriges överenskommelser med frammande makter*, and information supplied by the Ministry of Defence.

approach seems more open. An indication of the importance of future co-development programmes is the inclusion of common marketing and third country sales issues (see below). A feature of the new agreements is the establishment of joint committees to keep cooperation alive and active.[4]

A particularly significant development was the bilateral cooperation agreement signed between Saab and British Aerospace in February 1994, and taken further a year later, having received governmental approval. This involves international marketing of the JAS39 Gripen aircraft, common further development and production of the aircraft, and perhaps also missile cooperation. (*Svenska Dagbladet*, 12 February 1994; *JAS39 Gripen*, p. 118; and *Aviation Week*, 20 February 1995, p. 27).

The Largest Defence Projects

Table 3 lists the largest current procurement programmes at either the R&D, manufacturing or deployment stages. The table includes FMV payments received by the

Table 3: FMV Payments and Main Products

(Current millions Swedish Kroner)

Firm/group	1989–90	1990–91	1991–92	Main products
Swedish Ordnance	—	1894	2167	STRIX 120 mm mortar round
IGJAS	2080	1694	2053	JAS39 Gripen
Bofors group	1647	974	495	Anti-aircraft missile system BAMSE, anti-tank missile system BILL, STRIC C&C system
FFV group	1579	1144	1073	Torpedoes
Saab group	992	713	697	Aircraft, missiles, training equipment
Ericsson group	562	743	998	PSR-890 AEW radar, troop radio & tele system 8000
Volvo group	322	366	221	Aero engines
Karlskronavarvet	240	134	136	Smyge ship, corvettes type Göteborg
Kockums group	163	287	455	Submarines, type Gotland
HB Utveckling	117	677	170	Fighting vehicle 90
Foreign suppliers	1684	1498	1524	
Other	4493	5045	5810	
Total	13,981	15,169	15,799	

Source: FMV annual reports.
The list shows the situation before the enlargement of Celsius Industries.

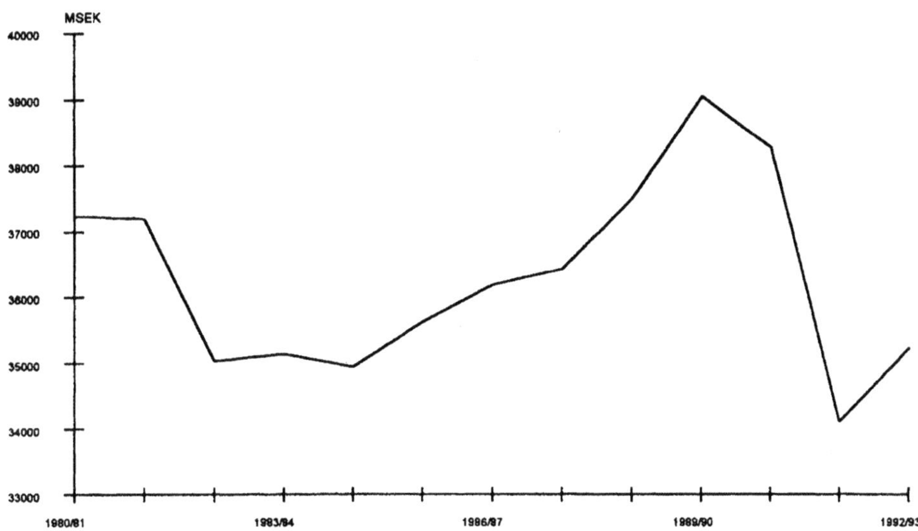

Figure 1: Military expenditures fiscal year 1980/81–1992/93 (constant 1990/91 millions Swedish Kroner).
Source: Ministry of Defence.

respective company or group for military matériel between the fiscal years 1989–90 and 1991–92 (Swedish Ordnance had then not yet been acquired by Celsius).

Some of the extra financial resources allocated in 1992 (see Figure 1) were used to order, for instance, the development of guided ammunition (the STRIX terminally-guided 120 mm mortar round) and additional equipment such as field howitzers for the Army. The intention was to increase the quality rather than the quantity of mainly Army matériel. In early 1994, the Government approved the acquisition of the German Leopard 2 Improved tank as a follow-on to the Swedish S-tank.

For the Navy, the major projects include the experimental stealth technology surface ship Smyge, the development of operational ships based on that principle, torpedoes, a ground-to-ship missile and submarines.

The JAS39 Gripen multi-role aircraft is the biggest acquisition project for the Air Force. Other major projects include the development of an Airborne Early Warning system and a new command and control system (STRIC) being developed by Bofors Electronics AB.

Budgetary Trends

Swedish official statistics generally correspond to OECD definitions. 'Defence' is defined by the *objective* of the activities performed (as defined by the performer). However, as will be illustrated below, a narrower definition of 'military'; activities can also be adopted. With regard to R&D, the 'defence' definition does not take into account whether the activities have secondary civil applications. Clearly, the line is not only difficult to draw, but is open to subjective interpretations.

As a consequence, there are no OECD statistics on dual-use technologies or products. In a 1993 report about Swedish strategic export controls, dual-use goods were defined as 'products with double use, i.e., products with an established civilian use but which also may be used, directly or indirectly, for destructive purposes' (*Kontrollen över export av strategiskt känsliga varor* 1993, p. 8). There are no specific Swedish national statistics covering such goods. Instead, in accordance with present war matériel policy, dual-use matériel is defined as war matériel only when it has both a military *and* a destructive function.

Sweden's defence expenditure actually increased during the early 1990s (see Figure 1) as a temporary result of the 1992 five-year defence plan. Earmarked financial resources were allocated in order to support development capacity and specific competence within the defence industry. Unless the next defence plan, due in 1996, adds new financial resources, defence expenditure will continue downwards.

Matériel acquisitions by the armed forces did not exceed 30% of the Ministry of Defence budget until very recently. By about 1986 that share reached 40% of the overall MoD budget as a result of the final stage of JAS39 Gripen development (Hagelin and Wallensteen 1992). Indeed, that project alone, including all types of equipment in addition to the platform, accounts for about 70% of the Air Force budget. Similarly, if coastal artillery equipment is included, the matériel share of the Navy budget is roughly 75%.

Turning to R&D data, statistics from the Swedish National Bureau of Statistics (SCB) indicate that private (business enterprise) sector R&D has declined as a share of total R&D during the last 10 years (Table 4). One obvious explanation is that public R&D has increased faster than private R&D. Another is that development expenditure in particular, not least within the military industry, has declined, although it must also be observed that the many structural changes in the defence industrial base complicate the compilation of reliable statistics over time.

Roughly 10% of Sweden's defence expenditure is used for R&D (*Forskning för kunskap och framsteg*, p. 98). Total military R&D in Table 4, defined not as a

Table 4: Swedish R&D Expenditure 1981–1991 (millions Swedish Kroner)

Year	TOTAL R&D	(of which) Business enterprise sector	MILITARY R&D						
			Total military (RRV)*	Military as % of total R&D	Military industry R&D				
					Largest military firms**	As % of total military	As % of business sector	Funds from mil. org's total	Other funds total
1981	13320	8479	889	7	796	90	9	542	254
1983	18189	11733	1426	8	1181	83	10	585	596
1985	24989	17001	2602	10	2233	86	13	1358	875
1987	30553	20401	2971	10	2652	89	13	1654	998
1989	34903	22362	3389	10	2596	77	12	1627	969
1991	36410	23000		—	2009	—	9	1851	158

Sources: SCB Forskningsstatistik; SCB, for the author; and RRV Budgetens utfall.

Notes:

* Since RRV is by calendar year, fiscal year 1992/93 corresponds to calendar year 1993, etc. Total military R&D = expenditures for army, navy and air force R&D, common defence research, operational command and control R&D, and FFA.

** The total expenditure by firms on military R&D is broken down in the final two columns into funds arising from government sources and those from other sources (including firms' own funds).

'defence objective' in OECD parlance but more narrowly as the combined R&D expenditures of the three military branches, common defence research, aeronautical research (FFA) and operational command and control R&D, increased in current prices during the 1980s. During the latter part of the 1980s it accounted for about 10% of Sweden's total R&D expenditure.

'Defence R&D' as defined in the budget bills during the last 10 years peaked in fiscal years 1986/1987 and 1987/1988 when it accounted for almost 26% of publicly-funded R&D. It then fluctuated around lower levels until it climbed to a new high of 27% in fiscal year 1991/1992 (*Forskningsstatistik* 1992, p. 45; see also Hagelin and Wallensteen 1992).

Most development work is done in industry. The largest defence firms (roughly speaking, those listed in Table 1) account for well over 50% of total spending on military R&D. Their R&D activity began to decline after 1987, however, and was sharply reduced from 1989. By 1992, total R&D by the major military companies accounted for about 30% of their combined turnover (*Fakta om försvarsindustrin* 1993, p. 5).

Military companies without major R&D orders are in future likely to seek modification and overhaul work, international cooperation, and the further development of already deployed weapon systems. Some of these undertakings will be partly privately financed. The larger military firms, in particular, are willing to risk capital for private projects, at times when government or foreign orders are few, and/or to seek outside private finance. Hence, during 1993 roughly 30% (195 million SEK) of Bofors' total R&D expenses were privately funded (*Bofors-Kuriren*, no. 2, 1994, p. 4). Similarly, within the Celsius group, about 15% of turnover is allocated to R&D, of which one quarter is private (*Annual Report 1993*).

The total magnitude of private financing in the defence industry is difficult to estimate, but may be reflected in the 'Other' column in Table 4. Part of that sum, however, is payment from abroad to Swedish firms as well as Swedish payments to foreign companies. Large projects are also often co-financed by a mixture of private and public sources. For example, a 50:50 division was used for the initial JAS39 Gripen development phase from 1982.

Arms Imports & Exports

The regional distribution of war matériel exports from 1982 to 1993 is shown in Figure 2. Although there are fluctuations, Europe has overall been the most important recipient region for Swedish war materiel, followed by Asia, whose share has, however, been sharply reduced latterly. The sharp increase for

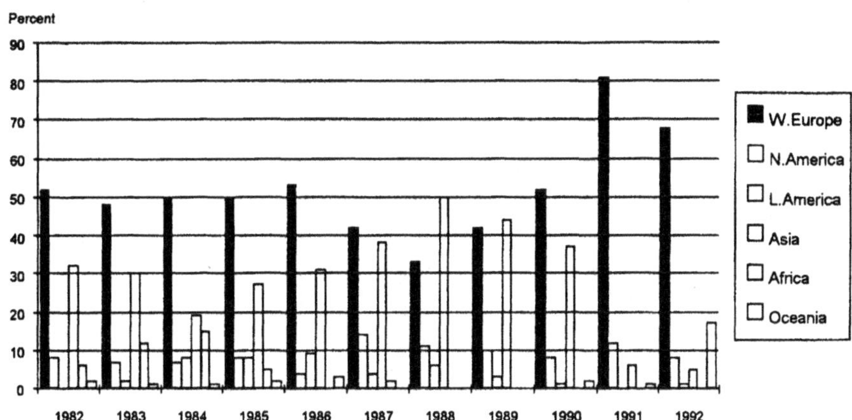

Figure 2: Regional Distribution of Sweden's war matériel sales 1982–1993.

Oceania during 1992 was mainly due to Kockum's shipment of submarine sections to Australia. For the categories used to describe exported matériel, see Table 5. In addition, Sweden has for some years had an 'assistance' programme for the three Baltic states. Since the goods under this programme have so far been defined as gifts, and not as 'war matériel', they are not included in the arms export statistics.

For Swedish industry, international Military Industrial Cooperation (what one might call the new MIC, i.e., an international 'military-industrial complex' in a general sense) is seen as a way to sustain certain advanced military R&D, define new projects and access new markets. A new phase was entered from January 1993 when a new Swedish export policy came into effect (*Lag om krigsmatériel*, 1992; *UU 1992/93).* The government's 1992 bill, outlining the principles behind the new policy, defined for the first time conditions for Swedish participation in international R&D on war matériel. It marked a watershed not only in Sweden's export policy, but also in the future political acceptance of increased war matériel sales and MIC participation.

According to the new policy,[5] Swedish war matériel sales are permitted:

- when deemed necessary in order to supply Sweden with military supplies (an argument for offsets of *quid pro quo*), or when otherwise thought desirable from a security point of view; and
- when not contrary to Sweden's foreign policy principles and goals.

Table 5: Categories of War Matériel Exported 1986–1993, and Totals

(Current million SEK. The headings were made more detailed from 1989)

Year	Small. arms/a	Artill	Ammo	Msls., torpe-does, mines	C3I	Explvs /b	Land vhcls	Ships etc	Air equ./c	Helmts etc	Traing matrls	Tools etc	Other equip./d	Total
1986			2532			90	4	24	294				299	3243
1987			3447			81	77	2	478				341	4427
1988						90	10	0	456	0			5599	6155
1989	1	1747	1662	1294	399	102	272	4	384	2	20	118		6005
1990	2	634	1008	799	334	149	130	0	188	0	65	18		3327
1991	2	206	394	1586	155	77	50	0	158	0	63	14		2705
1992	0	223	289	1166	267	71	11	490	129	0	75	32		2753
1993	1	150	287	480	1007	74	506	117	137	0	92	10	2	2863

Source: War Matériel Inspectorate.

Notes:

a) Incl. arms and ammunition for hunting and marksmanship.

b) Incl. powder and certain detonators with civilian uses.

c) Incl. parts and parachutes.

d) Incl. training aids; radars; electronic support and manufacturing equipment.

With regard to the first guideline, the government stated in the 1992 report that Sweden had 'a strong security policy need to participate increasingly in international research and development cooperation'.[6]

A particularly sensitive issue in the past has been whether the Swedish government should demand the right to veto a sale of co-developed war matériel to certain recipients ('third' countries). It was soon realised that such a veto would leave Sweden without interested partners. Therefore, according to the new policy, the conditions governing potential exports should be agreed with partners from the start. As a general rule, an end product with 'a mainly foreign identity' may be exported according to the rules and regulations of the other country(ies), but Sweden retains the capacity to intervene in the decision when strong defence policy interests are at stake.

Sales can also have specific conditions attached. Thus, while the MOUs with Australia and the UK both stipulate the need for approval by both parties for third country sales of equipment and licenses, only the UK MOU mentions that 'specific arrangements' governing such sales 'will be included in the Implementing Arrangement established for that particular programme'. This makes the Saab-BAe agreement, referred to above, particularly important as a path breaking step.

Turning to imports, one might have expected that Sweden's traditional military policy — emphasising independence and a broad indigenous military industrial base — would have led to the establishment of formal military import restrictions. This, however, is not so. Moreover, if all types of relevant technology were held indigenously, the Swedish dilemma between military-political ambitions and economic-technological reality would reduce mainly to a matter of finance. This too is not the case. For even though most conventional matériel is designed and/or manufactured in Sweden, much remains based on, and dependent upon, foreign know-how and technology. Like most other countries, Sweden has never been wholly independent in any area. In the selection of main military designs, however, Swedish-designed equipment has generally been preferred over foreign, the military arguing that the equipment can then be optimised to Swedish needs, thus costing less in the long-run than non-optimal foreign systems.

As shown in Table 3, FMV payments to foreign suppliers (i.e., government purchases from abroad) accounted for roughly 10% of total public defence payments between 1991 and 1993. This figure does not include imports by the companies themselves ('indirect imports'). Indirect imports have generally been estimated to be roughly 20% of total acquisition costs, taking overall military imports to an estimated 30% of total acquisition costs.

However, these statistics fail to reflect the strategic importance of the imported technologies or goods. Without these imports, neither Swedish industry, nor Swedish defence matériel, would be as advanced, or perhaps relatively cheap, as they have been. For economic reasons, Swedish producers increased their overseas purchases of subsystems and components during the 1970s and 1980s (*Svensk försvarsindustri* 1982). Such 'indirect imports' may be expected to increase further as a result of internationalisation processes as well as from economically and technologically more demanding military projects. In the JAS39 Gripen project, the foreign content accounts for about 40% by value.

Indeed, such is the importance attached to foreign technology that it is now explicitly linked to exports through the argument that maintenance of a strong arms industry (for which exports are crucial) is essential for making Sweden a worthwhile partner in international ventures. Such language was found for the first time in the 1992 defence export bill. And international cooperation is itself seen as necessary in order to sustain an advanced national military industrial base.

Examples of imported goods and technologies include jet engines, heavy guided missiles and electronics. All Swedish jet fighters have had engines manufactured under British or American licenses. Heavy ground-to-air missiles have been purchased from the UK and the USA. Much of the electronics used is either manufactured under foreign licenses or purchased, mainly from the USA, Japan or Germany (*Sveriges utrikeshandel i krislägen* 1989, pp. 69–71).

Policy Towards Defence and Dual-Use Technology

Future of the National Defence Technology Base

Sweden is concerned to reduce the uncertainties over obtaining advanced technologies by increasing the opportunities to participate in technology trade among the industrialised countries. The emphasis has changed from national restructuring of the industrial base (this phase is nearly complete) to international rationalisations and cooperation. Technological areas which cannot be sustained in Sweden at internationally competitive costs and technological levels are to be acquired from abroad through imports, offsets and R&D cooperation.

The traditionally broad and advanced military industrial base is likely to be further reduced if current threat perceptions do not change drastically. This is especially true with regard to development capacity and systems design leadership. In deciding what capacity should be maintained, the following criteria for defining military R&D priorities have been proposed by the Supreme Commander (*ÖB93*, p. 49):

- crucial defence importance or secrecy considerations;
- cannot be acquired through domestic networking or international cooperation;

- creates possibilities for new developments and life-extension capacity of matériel;
- decisive importance for an increase in competence of military staffs, bureaucracy, research institutes or industry;
- can offer attractive possibilities in the future which may be difficult to identify in detail in the short run;
- represents Swedish 'niches', but are also attractive for international cooperation; and
- offers possible gains from greater efficiency, rationalisation or quality increase without cost increase.

In the January 1994 budget bill, the government suggested that the most urgent future needs lie in the areas of command and control as well as 'tele-warfare'. Relevant technologies include sensors, software, C^3I, identification, and new materials (*Försvarsdepartementet* 1994, p. 87).

For both military and advanced civil technology, the USA has been Sweden's most important supplier (Wiechel 1986). Indeed, the stock phrase 'international military development' generally refers implicitly to new American or other Western technology. At the same time, the USA, together with its allies, has imposed extensive technology transfer and dual-use controls with which Sweden has had to comply. Hence Sweden's ambition of indigenously developing the most advanced technologies has in practice been tempered by a policy of becoming well informed, technologically knowledgeable and politically acceptable in order to be able to access foreign sources without impediment.[7]

In 1993 a new law was proposed for the control of 'strategically sensitive goods', including both war matériel and dual-use technologies (*Kontrollen över export av strategiskt känsliga varor* 1993). The purpose of the proposal was to sort out various existing laws and regulations, and to make administrative responsibilities clear in order to harmonise Sweden's regulations with those of the EU. This was regarded as important for future access to western advanced technology. Further amendments were proposed in a bill of March 1995.

The law regulating the export of war matériel was not thought to need change. The same was true of that part of the controls on dual-use products which depended on the 'law on weapons of mass destruction'. This law had, in 1991, translated into Swedish law several international agreements to which Sweden is a signatory (the Nuclear Suppliers Group, the Australia group, and the Missile Technology Control Regime) (SFS 1991:341 and amended SFS 1993:106). It regulates the export of missiles and missile technology, certain products in the nuclear field, manufacturing equipment for biological and chemical weapons and certain chemical and biological products which can be used for the manufacture of weapons. Technology in the form of software may also be included. This law was considered sufficient for controlling the spread of such goods and technologies, and is still in force.

Revision was, however, deemed necessary for a second set of laws, those comprising the 'law on nuclear technology' (the result of the Non-Proliferation Treaty, SFS 1984:3) and 'the high technology regulation' (SFS 1986:89 and TFS 1992:16). The goods covered included electronics, computers, telecommunications equipment, etc. The new law not only restricts *re*-exports from Sweden, which was already the case, but also regulates the *initial* export of all such products. This revision was deemed essential to enable full Swedish participation in international controls on high technology and in the free trade of high technology products among western countries. Hence, high technology products have, from 1994, been regulated by 'the law on mass destruction' administered by a new inspectorate in the Ministry of Foreign Affairs.[8]

In terms of Sweden's indigenous capacities in defence technology, the individual roles of, and relations between, institutions and organisations relevant to defence R&D are changing. The 1993 government research bill proposed a new research policy for Sweden (*Forskning för kunskap och framsteg*). It noted with regard to military R&D that international cooperation in matériel acquisitions will increase in the future, leading to fewer development orders from Swedish defence-technological organisations to Swedish companies. Instead, development decisions will increasingly be taken directly by industry in cooperation with foreign partners. Competence to direct activities and to evaluate functional criteria will grow in importance within the defence organisation, while industry will continue to need access to a broad technology base. University, technical high-school and civil research activities will become more important.

The bill made a number of proposals which are steadily being implemented:

- To increase the responsibility of the Supreme Commander and the Board for Civil Preparedness (Överstyrelsen för Civil Beredskap) in directing general, basic, defence research;
- The creation of a joint Board to increase the efficiency of, and coordination between, FMV, FOA and FFA;
- Closer links to research at the Military High-School;
- Scientific advisors to be appointed to the respective military staffs;
- Increased use by FMV of FOA, and of international competence;
- Specialisation by FOA in such areas as threat analysis, the functionality and survivability of equipment, and military-technological developments;
- More circulation of technical personnel between public and industry positions;

- To strengthen defence cooperation with academic research institutions by the establishment of special public financing of 'strategic defence research', ('scientific areas and technology of potential major military importance'), the applications for such projects to be evaluated in open competition;
- FMV to become responsible for coordinating activities to strengthen international project-oriented cooperation in defence R&D;
- FFA to receive more financial resources as part of a national program for aeronautical research.

FMV has a special advisory and expert role in the areas of military acquisitions and dual-use technology and goods. To further support military R&D preparedness, the Supreme Commander has established an 'R&D management group' (FoU-beredningen), comprising representatives from the military branches, FMV, FOA, and the Fortifications Administration. It will suggest priorities and direct activities for total defence R&D and related areas within FMV and industry (*ÖB93*, p. 48).

New national structures, so-called 'networks', are being created to link military and civil R&D organisations, embracing government, industrial and, possibly, academic institutions. A specific aim of these networks is to diffuse new technologies and innovative ideas. The means used are often personal relations, such as secondment of professors to non-academic institutions, or university Ph.D training for defence employees, as well as part-time teaching by defence experts in universities, and the shared use of equipment and installations, for instance in 'supercomputer centres' (*Svensk försvarsindustri*, 1993, p. 125). Kockums, for example, has established joint projects with the technical high schools in Gothenburg, Lund and Stockholm. The cooperation extends to employment and PhD training. Other parts of the Celsius group are also said to have established similar relationships (*Annual Report*, 1993). In addition, and although not primarily intended for military purposes, the government has allocated special financial support until 2007 for 'technology bridges' (a form of venture capital) to the university towns of Stockholm, Gothenburg, Lund, Uppsala, Linköping, Umeå and Luleå in an attempt to activate links between university research and industry applications (*Universen*, vol. 25, no. 1, 1994, p. 18).

In the choice of appropriate or 'optimal' technologies for military applications, it is becoming increasingly important to draw upon available civilian technologies and to cooperate with civil R&D institutions. One such example is the national information technology programme, focusing on developing new software for a more advanced Swedish IT infrastructure. The largest such programme is, however, the national aero-technological programme. This three-year R&D programme was launched in 1994 to support Sweden's aircraft development potential (*Svenska Dagbladet*, 30 January 1994). Together, the government and industry will supply 180 million SEK to

- create a national aero-technological R&D programme (NFFP — Nationellt Flygtekniskt Forsknings Program) involving public institutions, technical high schools and industry (meaning primarily FMV, FOA, FFA, Chalmers Technical High School, Saab and Volvo Flygmotor);
- establish an Aero-Technological Forum (NFF — Nationellt Flygtekniskt Forum) in Linköping to guide long-term policy in education, research and technology development;
- establish a new and specialised civil engineering programme at Linköping university; and
- develop links between the technical high schools in Stockholm and Linköping.

At the international level, agreements (MOUs) for regulating trade in advanced technology have in the past been directed by Sweden less to R&D than to the manufacture and/or direct purchase of foreign military equipment. More recent agreements, however, point toward a new path marked by increased R&D cooperation in Europe. Ad hoc Swedish cooperation in international military projects has been projected to increase, due to greater involvement in co-development (*Försvarsindustrins utlandsverksamhet* 1987). Hence, according to the KMI, in 1993 Swedish companies had 62 co-development or co-production agreements in force, whereas in 1994 the figure was 162 (KMI *Skrivelser*, 1995).

In the last few years, several Swedish defence companies have entered into closer cooperation with firms in Norway, France, Germany and Great Britain. For instance, Bofors has entered what has been described as a 'strategically important' set of arrangements, namely:

- An agreement with Raufoss (Norway) concerning the production of the BAMSE ground-to-air missile, which is said to lay the basis for a common Nordic defence market. Other cooperation projects with Norway includes the ARTHUR artillery locating radar, a further development of the GIRAFFE 50AT radar developed for Norwegian air defence, and possibly a new coastal artillery system;
- An agreement with GIAT-industries (France) to jointly develop the BONUS 150 mm cargo shell with sensor-fused submunitions;
- Discussions with Matra for possible further development of the Rb90 short range ground to air missile;
- An agreement with Thomson-Brandt (France) to further develop the AT4 anti-tank weapon;

- An agreement with DASA (FRG) in which Bofors participates in the development of a Target Adaptive Dispenser System (*Bofors-Kuriren*, no. 8, December 1993, p. 18; *Bofors-Kuriren*, no. 2, 1994, p. 19; *Svensk försvarsindustri* 1993, p. 66); and
- A family of air-to-ground missiles in a joint ARGE-TAURUS consortium (*Bofors-Kuriren*, no. 1, 1995, p. 5).

Swedish participation in international high-technology projects in Europe has increased during the 1980s and 1990s. In 1993, Sweden spent about 300 million SEK on EU industrial programmes, a sum which was expected to double over three years (*Svenska Dagbladet*, Europabilaga, December 30, 1993). Swedish participation in these programmes, it was said as early as 1989, aimed deliberately at strengthening its European identity, increasing its research efficiency, and preparing Swedish industry for the European market (*Sverige-EFTA-EG* 1989). One area for such co-operation has been R&D, most importantly in high technology areas such as telecommunications, information technology and aerospace (*Del av Europa — Sverige och den västeuropeiska integrationen* 1988).

Formally, there are no military EU programmes. Nevertheless, interactions between civilian and military science and technology mean that certain civil industrial projects are also militarily relevant. The Single European Act may therefore indirectly affect defence companies through their civilian activities, and create civilian capacities which could have future military applications. Space is a case in point, but many other areas have potential military use, such as telecommunications, micro-electronics, information technology and materials (*ÖB93*, p. 48). Defence is also the most probable immediate outlet for some university research areas, such as microwave technology, high speed electronics, optronics, aeronautics, light constructions, as well as naval technology (*Svensk försvarsindustri* 1993, p. 125).

Swedish military companies and groups like Saab-Scania, Volvo Aero Corporation and the Aeronautical Research Institute participate in EU aeronautical projects within the AERO programme, the BRITE/EURAM industrial and materials technologies programme, and the European Strategic Programme for R&D in Information Technology, ESPRIT.[9] Also involved in these projects are universities in Lund, Gothenburg, Uppsala and Linköping, together with firms not directly related to military R&D such as the Swedish Ceramic Institute, the Swedish Institute for Metals Research, the Institute of Optical Research, the Swedish Institute of Computer Science (SICS), the Swedish Institute of Microelectronics as well as the Swedish Telecom Administration. Some of these, such as the Swedish Telecom Administration and Swedish Institute of Microelectronics, are also involved in the DRIVE advanced transport telematics and

RACE advanced communications technologies programmes, together with, for instance, Philips and Ericsson. Among other programmes of potential military interest may be the non-nuclear energy programme JOULE, in which the Aeronautical Research Institute is involved together with the universities in Linköping, Lund and Uppsala plus the technological institutes in Gothenburg and Stockholm. Another increasingly important research field is biotechnology. Swedish universities also participate in BIOTECH (previously BRIDGE) programmes (see *CORDIS* databases).

Outside the EU framework, Sweden also participates in a large number of EUREKA projects. It has been argued that 'EUREKA is a civil project and that the participation of the neutral European countries was the price to be paid for this, (*Defense & Armaments Heracles International*, no. 74, June 1988, p. 18). At the same time, it is generally recognised that several projects can have military as well as civil applications. It was hoped during the 1980s, for instance, that Europe through EUREKA could develop technologies similar to the American Strategic Defense Initiative (*Aviation Week & Space Technology*, December 16, 1985, p. 15). Certainly, a considerable number of EUREKA projects, in such fields as automation, energy projects, robotics, metallurgy and metal treatment including die casting and corrosion, polymer manufacturing and ceramics, remote control, aircraft training systems, fatigue strength, computers, semi-conductor and chip manufacturing, laser applications, and communication systems may all be considered dual-use (*EUREKA* database).

Industrial Support Developments

The political discussions of the 1970s and 1980s did not result in any direct political support of military-industry restructuring (see below). Although it was sometimes mentioned in the debate, no serious political emphasis was placed upon argument that economic development seems to be faster in countries with lower military expenditures, as in Japan and Germany. Instead, Sweden had to consider its heritage of a broad and advanced defence industry. There was little political support for a reduced military industrial base and probably also insufficient political courage to make a decision which would result in unemployment. Instead, the government left the problem of re-structuring the military industrial base to the companies themselves. No contingency plans for reduced military orders were prepared, although some financial support was given to civilian undertakings at Saab and the then Volvo Flygmotor during the 1980s.

Two main phases and a series of industrial strategies may be distinguished in the ensuing history.

The National Phase

This really began during the 1970s and continued during the 1980s. It involved both *separation* of parts of companies by selling off peripheral activities, and *unification* through mergers and acquisition of companies. These were all important activities which not only complemented each other but also supported the political ambition during the 1980s to *privatise* public companies.

The result was fewer, but more specialised, military companies. All defence companies except Volvo Aero Corporation have a defence share of total sales above 50% (see Table 7). A high level of national concentration was achieved, which has been most dramatic for the ordnance companies. An additional development was the creation of *groupings* of defence and high technology companies. The Celsius group was the first, dating from 1977. Today it is organised into three areas, military being the most important, then dual technology support activities (Telub and FFV Aerotech), and civil activities (Celsius Invest). In addition to military shipbuilding, it acquired Swedish Ordnance in 1992. In 1993 a large part of the electronics industry, formerly NobelTech, became part of the group under the name of CelsiusTech. During 1994 Celsius bought the Swedish Dialog computer company, the British BMT Icons computer company, and acquired a majority share in Enator, a company within the civil and military IT and computer consulting business areas.

Grouping is a convenient way to concentrate technological areas and to create a single marketing organisation. For instance, Saab's four military subsidiaries (Saab Military Aircraft, Saab Missiles, Saab Instruments, and Saab Training Systems) were coordinated under one group called Saab Defence in early 1994, though this was later split into Saab Military Aircraft and Saab Dynamics. Similarly, in 1994 a new staff organisation was created in the Celsius Industries group to coordinate defence marketing activities. Other company considerations were probably to create a stronger negotiating position vis-à-vis the government for future military contracts; to consider demands by the stockholders to reduce the risk of civil financing of uncertain military undertakings; and, should it become necessary, to cut military activities, a separate military division facilitating such a decision.

The International Phase

The international market was not unimportant during the national restructuring phase. *Privatisation*, for instance, was in part a response to the requirement for public companies to be able to compete with 'expansionist' private companies on the export markets (see the chapter on Italy for a discussion of 'expansion' vs. 'withdrawal' strategies). Privatisation opened the door for Celsius to international cooperation.

Exports became an important complement to the diminishing domestic market during the 1970s and 1980s. Today, the foreign market seems to be most important for companies which do not produce complete weapon systems or weapon platforms, with the possible exceptions of Hägglunds tracked vehicles and Saab Missiles (see Table 7). In addition, *offsets* are likely to become a much more important part of Swedish defence trade in the future, beginning with the purchase of the German Leopard II tank.

We should also note that privatisation has not only been pursued in response to the need for increasing internationalisation, but that as a corollary it leads to increasing shared ownership of Swedish arms companies. Thus, about 30% of Celsius is now owned by foreign interests, and the Saab group is open to the possibility of foreign capital. How far the Swedish government is prepared to go in accepting foreign ownership in military companies is not clear. The examples of NobelTech, and Celsius itself, suggest, first, that there is still political interest in these companies and second, that even with foreign ownership the government is likely to retain a 'golden share'.

As might be expected, the preservation of technological capabilities has been easier for companies involved in dual technology fields than for firms oriented more toward military activities. In Sweden, as elsewhere, the closer to the generic research end of the spectrum, the greater has been the potential for dual use development; the nearer to specific military applications, the more restricted have been the possibilities in this regard. Only a few products or technologies have a dual-use option at the stage of application.

The activity of 'networking' reflects the intrinsically dual character of most research, as does Swedish involvement in European research projects. At the other end of the spectrum we find adaptable applications mainly in electronics and radars. Their specific applications can be decided in the final stage of the production process — or sometimes even later. For instance, in the Ericsson Defence System Giraffe radar system, the crucial component seems to be the 'black box' which distinguishes friendly from enemy aircraft. The same is true of portable telephones and Ericsson's AXE telephone switches, which can be adapted to 'open' civilian or restricted military use. Ericsson's AXE switches and digital technology has made it one of the most important telecommunications technology companies in the world. Its market share is expected to further increase as a result of de-regulation and privatisation of the telecoms market.

In between we find firms which, within either the individual company or the industrial group, have divided their activities into civil and military. This was a common strategy during the concentrations and specialisations of the last 10 years

Nobel Industries, for instance, to which Bofors belonged at the time, concentrated all non-military work in the Nobel group. Military activities including electronics went to Bofors. The organisation of Celsius Industries shows a similar division today. Also, the successful civilian aircraft undertakings by the Saab-Scania group are undertaken separately from Saab Military Aircraft. This division has been further strengthened by the creation of the Saab Dynamics group.

It follows that within larger companies or groups there is often dual technology capacity. Thus, Saab managers claim that without military aircraft production, Saab could not build civilian aircraft. This spin-off argument is repeated in the 1992 government bill on future research in Sweden (*Forskning för kunskap och framsteg*). It is, however, difficult to find unqualified support for this argument, if it is restricted to engineering matters and not extended to the levels of cross-subsidies and marketing support. Thus, Hägglunds Vehicle argues that spin-off is possible only to a very limited extent.[10] Whether this potential is used as an explicit strategy probably depends upon the company's or group's internal policy, structure and 'culture'. The Saab aircraft argument may, however, to some extent be an exaggeration formulated on political grounds. The coordination of the companies under a Saab Dynamics group also indicates that military technology is best preserved at close quarters, and that the bridging between civil and military technology within a large company should not automatically be assumed to be strong.

In electronics, the potential for dual-use technology seems more easily realisable. A 1994 study concluded that, although no formal strategy existed within the then Ericsson Radar Electronics, technology was transferred between civil and military production. Internal consulting was also found, and military engineers have taken up civil activities. Employees were encouraged to move within the company (Lorentzi & Nilsson 1994, p. 116). Similarly, Ericsson Defence Systems has been cooperating with its Radio Communications Business Area in the development of radio base stations based on the Mini-Link microwave radio links (*Ericsson annual report*, 1991, p. 55). Again, however, the creation of Ericsson Microwave AB in 1995 by merging Ericsson's radar and radio interests suggests that effective 'cross-fertilisation' has to be nourished.

International Joint Venture Policy and Actions

The number of reported joint ventures between 1986 and 1989 was higher than for the whole period from 1950 to 1986 (Table 6). These numbers should, however, be treated with caution: they probably include most of the companies' international cooperative programmes, many of which were not true joint ventures. Nevertheless, they give an indication of the upsurge of interest in international corporate activity.

Table 6: Number of New Swedish International Ventures 1950–1989

Matériel group	**1980**	**1981**	**1982**	**1983**	**1984**	**1985**	**Total 1950–85***	**Total 1986–89****
Weapons/ ammo.	0	4	2	2	15	5	32	38
Vehicles	0	1	0	1	3	1	6	9
Electronics	0	0	1	1	1	1	4	9
Total	0	5	3	4	19	7	42	56

*Number of ventures according to *Försvarsindustrins utlandsverksamhet*, 1987.
**The figures for 1989 are preliminary according to *Utlandssamverkan på krigsmatériel-området*, 1989.

Table 7: Sweden's Defence Industrial base in 1993

(1992 export position in brackets if different)

Total Sales	**Defence Share of Total Sales**			**Export Share of Defence Sales**		
	High	Medium	Low	High	Medium	Low
High	Bofors				x	
	Ericsson Radar				x	(x)
	Kockums+Karlskr.				(x)	x
	Saab Mil. Aircraft					x
	Saab Missiles			(x)	x	
		Volvo Aero				x
Medium	Barracuda Tech.			x		
	Celsius Tech. Elec.					x
	Celsius Tech. Sys.			x		
	FFV Aerotech.					x
	Hägglunds			x		
	Saab Trng Sys+Instr			x		
Low	SA Marine					x

Sources: As Table 1.
Definitions:
High total sales: >1500 MSEK, Medium: 1500–150 MSEK; Low: <150 MSEK.
High defence and export shares: >50%; Medium: 50–25%; Low: <25%.

Most of the companies engaged in international teaming during the 1980s were in the arms and ammunition sectors, rather than in vehicles, electronics or other military supplies. Most of their partners came from Europe, mainly in Germany, UK and USA. The main purpose, as stated by the companies, was to increase access to international markets. Lack of know-how in the Swedish partner, and conditions imposed by the purchaser, were also important. More than half of such undertakings in the late 1980s were attributed to foreign demands for technological cooperation as a condition of entry for the Swedish firm (*Utlandssamverkan på krigsmatérielområdet*, 1989).

There is information to suggest that the most successful joint development and/or manufacturing programmes have taken place with Norwegian and Swiss companies (Hagelin 1977, and 1989). The reasons lie in cultural, political and historical similarities and ties, security policy similarities and, to some extent, similar geographical and climatic parameters.

Principally for economic and technological reasons, Swedish participation in international projects is regarded by the government as the way of the future. In the 1992–97 defence plan, for instance, the government expressed the desire to sustain military aircraft technology by further development of the JAS39 Gripen and through international cooperation in aerospace technology (*Regeringens proposition 1991/92:102*, pp. 68 and 81). This new policy attitude is also seen in the recent agreements with Norway, France, Germany and Great Britain.

Official Policy Toward Conversion

Previous Policy

Political support for increased civilian production by arms companies has existed in Sweden for the last 20 years, at least at the level of rhetoric. A limited amount of public financial support for such activities was given to a few military producers during the early 1980s, following growing debate on the subject from the 1970s. For example, from 1972 the issue caught public and parliamentary interest as a result of two United Nations expert studies, on the *Economic and Social Consequences of the Arms Race and Military Expenditures* (1971), and *Disarmament and Development* (1972). One of the members of the second study was Alva Myrdal, Minister of State in the Swedish Ministry for Foreign Affairs, whose presence may have helped the report to generate, as it did, strong support for the link between disarmament, conversion and aid to developing nations. Swedish interest in these questions was maintained by another UN study on links between disarmament and development which began work in 1978 under the chairmanship of Mrs Inga Thorsson, Ambassador for Disarmament in the Swedish Ministry for Foreign Affairs. The report, *Study on the relationship between disarmament and development*, was presented in 1981 (A/36/356, 1981).

An additional factor which increased interest in conversion was the (ultimately unsuccessful) attempt by the Lucas Aerospace employees in Britain to convince their management that civilian production could be economically sound. A further, domestic, factor after 1972 was the decision that year to accept continued reductions in Swedish defence expenditure.

During the 1970s, therefore, there were repeated motions in Parliament for increasing civilian production by the military industries. From the beginning, such proposals met with four types of responses:

- unless paralleled by a reduction in Sweden's demand for military equipment, conversion would be contrary to the accepted principle of advanced indigenous arms production (since defence expenditures are theoretically based upon security considerations);
- conversion preparedness is a natural part of industrial responsibility;
- studies are underway; and
- Sweden is in any case actively supporting international disarmament.

The conclusion by the then Social Democratic government was that it need not, even should not, actively promote a transition toward reduced military production. Moreover, although local problems might arise, the effects on employment would, it was argued, in most cases be minimal. It was, as the Minister of Industry stated in Parliament on April 27, 1972, the responsibility of the companies themselves to secure employment (NU 1972:43, p. 2–3). Some support was, however, afforded to Saab and Volvo Flygmotor in 1980 to underpin their participation in civilian projects. These projects were in cooperation with American companies: first, the development, manufacture and sales of a new commuter aircraft (Saab-Fairchild 340). Second, the development and servicing of civilian aircraft engines and components. Both endeavours were commercially successful. The 340 aircraft project is today continued solely by Saab, and a follow-on commuter aircraft has been developed (Saab 2000).

In neither case, however, did these civilian undertakings reduce the *de facto* involvement in military aircraft and aero-engines. Diversification rather than conversion was the result. Civilian production was to 'bridge' the gap between military orders; it became a complement, not an alternative to military activities. Logically, in 1982, Parliament eventually supported indigenous development of the JAS39 Gripen multi-role aircraft.

Policy Since 1982

The 1981 UN *Study on the relationship between disarmament and development,* went further than the UN disarmament-development report 10 years earlier in emphasising the need for disarmament and conversion. It also put the chairman, Mrs. Inga Thorsson, firmly on the global disarmament map. The study emphasised the government's responsibility for the preparation for, and initiation of, a conversion process. The realisation of actual conversion, it argued, depends upon a variety of country-specific factors. The importance of using scientific and technological resources for conversion was strongly emphasised. The application of military R&D resources in civilian areas such as solar energy, environmental degradation, housing and urban renewal as well as new transportation systems, was specifically mentioned.

It was not surprising, then, that Mrs. Thorsson would prove to be one of the strongest proponents for conversion in Sweden. Her position was formulated in the study *In Pursuit of Disarmament,* Sweden's response to the exhortation by the General Assembly in 1982 that Member States should adopt measures in line with the recommendations of the UN report she herself had chaired. The first volume was presented to the Swedish government in 1984 and concluded that financial incentives from the government are needed for the defence industry to expand into civilian areas.

However, she was unable to change the political attitude toward supporting conversion. New issues came to the forefront of domestic debate. The number of parliamentary proposals for alternative civilian production was reduced. Those presented had a narrower approach than before, and requested specific assistance to individual industries, but did not lead to further actions. Only one additional study was presented on the subject, by Mrs. Maj-Britt Theorin, Inga Thorsson's successor as Ambassador for Disarmament (*En politik för nedrustning och utveckling*, 1988). It supported the conclusions of the Thorsson study. However, as with earlier studies, the members disagreed both on how to support or achieve conversion and even on the principle of conversion as such.

Accordingly, there has been no plan for conversion by the Swedish authorities. The conversion possibility was not even mentioned in the 1992 military export policy bill. Normal economic and labour programmes are generally regarded as sufficient to help Swedish industries in need. When offering assistance, the government has emphasised local and regional infrastructure and market potential rather than R&D and production capacity *per se*. In this respect, it has been argued by Hägglunds Vehicle that, although the official policy of 'non-intervention' is good, a longer-term policy would have been more supportive.

This 'hands-off' policy may, however, be changing. There is a political desire to sustain as large a part of the advanced industrial base as is economically and competitively possible. The 1992 defence decision included the preservation of 'remobilisation capacity' should the military-political situation deteriorate.[11] The importance of advanced R&D was emphasised in the 1993 research policy bill, and in 1994 a three-year R&D programme was launched to support Sweden's aircraft development potential, as well as a new IT programme. In addition, more use of military offsets is likely. The main aim is still not conversion, but rather what might be called 'adaptable specialisation' through the support of advanced, dual-use technologies.

Industry, Union and Local Attitudes to National Policy

Some military companies, for instance Karlskronavarvet and Bofors, argued for many years for increased political support for exports. They contended that Sweden's export controls impeded Swedish industry from competing on equal terms with foreign competitors. In the face of these criticisms, various relaxations of policy occurred from the early 1970s onwards, allowing Swedish companies to compete and cooperate more on the international market.

This outcome was the result partly of individual company lobbying activities, and partly of the establishment of the Association of Swedish Defence Industries in 1986. Eleven companies were founding members, and today all the defence companies belong to the Association. According to its original Director, the aim of the Association is to achieve larger defence expenditures or increasing arms exports (*Svenska Dagbladet*, 7 February 1986). It functions as an umbrella organisation in responding to government policy proposals, etc.,[12] and is the only organisation in Sweden which publishes annual and easily accessible defence industry statistics.

Today there is less industrial criticism of export policy as such. Rather, the problem from industry's point of view is perceived to be the reduced size of national and international defence markets, and the consequent lack of support for long-term development projects, which results in imports to meet Swedish equipment needs.

With regard to international military-industrial cooperation, the associated political expectations seem generally to be regarded by company managements as too optimistic. It takes time to establish good working relations, and such relations do not always lead to reduced costs. In general, for international cooperation to endure, it needs strong political support, for instance in the form of MoUs (*Svensk försvarsindustri* 1993). It also needs willing and appropriate partners. In this respect, Hägglunds Vehicle expresses preference for cooperation with companies in France or Germany in order to survive 'in a three-polar world with Europe, the USA and the Far East'.

The use of offsets[13] in Sweden has so far been rather *ad hoc*. It is claimed that the Swedish authorities have not negotiated major offsets to the same extent as has been the practice abroad (*Metallarbetaren*, November 1993). Most deals have involved 'direct offsets', i.e., military trade linked closely to a particular military project.[14] However, since both military imports and international cooperation are likely to grow, so also is the political salience of offsets. Even if they lead to sub-optimisation by side-stepping free trade, they remain a forceful competitive tool and a means of creating domestic employment. Hence, the Metal Workers Union has proposed that 'much more than today, offsets must be used as an active industry-political instrument' (*Svensk försvarsindustri* 1993, p. 129; and pp. 68, 128).

The earlier restrictive practices are already changing. Apart from the new aero-technological programme mentioned above, offsets are mentioned in the new war matériel sales policy and in import policy: FMV formulated specific and far-reaching offset conditions for the purchase of foreign main battle tanks (*Svenska Dagbladet*, January 5, 1994). Civil offsets are, however, limited to 25% of the tank offset deal. This is not because they are unimportant, but because Sweden's civil trade is already large. It is therefore easy for a foreign supplier to reach any level of specified civil trade limit. At the same time, since military trade is still within national jurisdiction, it is more important to define its content and value in detail.

Controlling the Diffusion of Defence Technology

Military Technology Export Policy

Due to the laws and regulations already in place or proposed, offsets are not likely to complicate Sweden's technology policy. How important they will be for the inflow and outflow of advanced technology depends on the government's implementation of Sweden's export policy, the willingness by FMV to take advantage of the offset possibility, and on the foreign buyer's or cooperating partner's willingness to accept far-reaching offset arrangements.[15]

As mentioned above, no need was seen for changing the 1993 export law because of new technology transfer demands, since it covers a broad range of situations and technological areas. An illustration of this point, as well as the linkage between general technological research and potential military applications, can be seen in the 'Telub Affair' (*TELUBaffären* 1981). This concerned an agreement struck in 1979 by Telub (then part of the public FFV group) with

Libya to train 96 young Libyans and two senior leaders in computer and radar technologies, telecommunications and some other related disciplines.

It later emerged that Telub's initial information to the Swedish government had been misleading and that some topics were militarily related. It also became known that some of the students had previous military training. The scheme was therefore interrupted, and the experience led the government to include in the export policy the control of military training for foreigners in Sweden. Such training can now only take place as part of an export deal for Swedish war matériel. Training abroad is still possible, however.

In addition, today the transfer of a manufacturing licence from Sweden, as well as *from a Swedish company abroad* is controlled. Only four manufacturing licences per year on average were sold between 1987 and 1993, with a peak of nine in 1990. The consequences of this for the spread of military technology are, however, more important than from direct matériel sales. In addition, the transfer of computer programmes specifically developed and designed for destructive war matériel is regarded as a form of military technology transfer and requires a government permit. A particular means of transfer is also specified in the new controls, namely transfers via modern communications technologies, as in the case of the transfer by satellite link of submarine designs from Sweden to Australia. There is thus increasing political awareness of these means of proliferation of conventional military technologies, and a certain political willingness to include them in national control mechanisms. However, serious doubts have been sown over the practical possibilities for controlling their spread, as well over the political willingness strictly to implement restrictive national controls.

The Importance of the EU

As already discussed, developments in Europe were important for both Sweden's 1993 export policy and the international military-industrial cooperation policy, as well as for the 1994 strategic goods export law.

The 1993 arms export policy was presented by the government as a more restrictive policy than its predecessor (*Dagens Nyheter*, 22 August 1992, p. 3; *Ny vapenexportpolitik* 1992, pp. 4–6). The criteria for what is to be defined as war matériel may, it was said, have to be changed more often in the future, in line with technological developments and with changes in the then COCOM and future EU classifications. It remains to be seen what arrangements will succeed COCOM, and whether they will be able to put further restrictions on what remain essentially national export policies. In the meantime, however, one important development is that arms embargoes by the EU are now regarded as unconditional restrictions by the Swedish government, which has also extended its list of war matériel and introduced the distinction between destructive and non-destructive war matériel that is used elsewhere in the EU. In addition, since Sweden's accession to the EU, member states of the EU have been added to those others (Nordic and neutral European states) to which no foreign policy constraints apply in terms of military trade and cooperation.

The Export of Dual-Use Technologies: A Policy Dilemma

Sweden's policy on this subject is ambivalent. On the one hand, Sweden has a strong tradition as the world's 'conscientious objector'. Hence, one reason for the new technology trade legislation has been to enable full participation in international controls of high technology. During the last few years Sweden has become involved in three of the major multinational control regimes in advanced technology.

On the other hand, the emphasis given to dual-use technology controls also serves to make Sweden an acceptable trading partner, thereby enabling it to sustain its own advanced industrial activities. In this respect, therefore, it favours Swedish competitiveness in war matériel globally, and in 'critical technology' trade mainly within the European-Atlantic framework. Domestic industrial interests have convinced the government that Sweden cannot afford idealistic export policies. Hence, for example, a proposal to allow the government, under the war matériel export policy, to temporarily prohibit the export of a product with potential military use even if not defined as war matériel, was not passed.

This balance between objectives has always existed in Sweden's policy. What is new is the weight of economic and technological factors. They have become much more important and decisive for Sweden's capacity to select the 'optimal' solutions. Paradoxically, national security requires increasing international cooperation in order to safeguard indigenous development of advanced military equipment. Similarly, while military exports were hitherto regarded as potential 'fringe benefits' from production for domestic demands, today they are seen as an essential prerequisite for domestic production.

Conclusion

To the extent that, in the past, Sweden has been involved in an arms race, it has not so much been with any foreign country (we can hardly portray Sweden as in competition with the former Soviet Union), as with advanced military technology itself. For a small country with big ambitions in high technology, good foreign technology relations have been a necessity. Non-alignment and a sometimes stubborn foreign policy stance may have been criticised by foreign governments in public, but in the corridors of the Foreign and Defence ministries abroad, Sweden's security and technology policies have received important support. From the Cold War perspectives of Washington and London, it was worth supporting Sweden's policies.

With the Cold War over, with more imports and less indigenous development of heavy weapons such as heavy tanks and fighter aircraft in the future, and with a narrower defence industrial base in general, the military R&D budget is likely to change. Precisely how, it is impossible to say, since it depends upon such factors as the success of government policy, industrial ambitions, foreign military threat perceptions, and international military industrial cooperation projects, as well as the definitions of the borderlines between civil, dual-use and military R&D and technologies. However, it seems likely that the electronic content of all or most future military matériel will increase, creating long-term prospects for companies such as Ericsson and the Celsius group.

To a certain extent, even a sustained peace could see a reduction or retardation of the downward financial trend. Political ambitions to create a Nordic arms market, agreed in principle between Denmark, Finland, Norway and Sweden in December 1994 (and possibly including the Baltic region in the future), should be noted. Production for future, perhaps global, UN peace-keeping forces could create new opportunities for survival of the fittest military industries. The ambition to sustain 'mobilisation capacity' will establish a spending floor. In addition, with increasing international cooperation, experience suggests that national costs do not always fall to the extent hoped for.

While military R&D may be reduced, expenditure for dual-use technology R&D may increase in order to:

- sustain and create new and competitive domestic skills,
- remain a qualified military and technological customer, and
- become a sought-after partner for international military industrial collaboration.

These very reasons do, however, throw into focus the question of how real is the distinction between military and dual-use activity. If dual-use programmes are seen mainly as supportive of military activity, how far will a real shift of policy have occurred? This is not only a statistical question, but one with implications also for democratic control of military programmes.

Any such increase in dual-use programmes is likely to affect Sweden's competitive potential as well as its participation in both military and civilian international undertakings. While it was still 'outside the EU fence', Swedish policy changes toward Europe were clearly aimed at reducing the risk of being exposed to trade barriers, and to facilitate Swedish participation in EU decision-making. Should protectionistic science and technology policies increase within the EU, or between the EU and the USA, it seems politically important to be 'inside the fence'. Sweden is therefore likely to engage in both European and Atlantic dual-use high technology projects and in international military industrial cooperation projects. Cooperation, initially as an observer and later as a member, of the WEU and its defence programmes is not implausible. These possibilities are also receiving attention in non-governmental quarters: the Swedish Metal Workers Union in 1993 explicitly referred to EUCLID priorities when discussing future technological areas (*Svensk försvarsindustri* 1993, p. 125).

Sweden's entry into the EU from 1995 now puts it within the framework of European discussions about future security and foreign policy, not least with respect to the 1996 Intergovernmental Conference of the European Union. Since Sweden's next major defence review is also due in that year, 1996 will, therefore, be an important year for the continued reshaping of Swedish policy in these fields. The outcome of all these decisions and reviews will set Swedish policy on course for its relations with the new Europe, into the next millennium.

References

Books and Journal Articles

Hagelin, B., 1977, *Västeuropeiskt militär-industriellt samarbete*, Stockholm: Centralförbundet Folk och Försvar.

Hagelin, B., 1985, *Kulorna rullar*, Stockholm: Ordfront förlag.

Hagelin, B., 1988, 'Military Dependency: Thailand and the Philippines', *Journal of Peace Proposal*, vol. 25, no. 4, December.

Hagelin, B., 1989, *Neutrality and foreign military sales,* Boulder, Col.: Westview Press.

Hagelin, B., 1994, *Arm in Arm,* Canberra: Australian National University Press.

Hagelin, B. and Wallensteen, P., 1992, 'Understanding Swedish Military Expenditures', *Cooperation and Conflict*, Nordic Journal of International Studies, vol. 27, no. 4, December.

Holmström, M. and von Sivers, T., 1985, *Tekniken som vapen,* Stockholm: Ingenjörsförlaget

Laurance, Edward J. *et al.*, 1993, *Arms Watch,* SIPRI report on the first year of the UN register of conventional arms, Oxford: Oxford University Press.

United Nations, 1971, *Economic and Social Consequences of the Arms Race and Military Expenditures*, New York.

United Nations, 1972, *Disarmament and Development,* New York.

Trade Union Documents

Svensk försvarsindustri 1993. Report. Stockholm: Metal Workers Union.

Government and Parliament Documents

Ändringar i lagen om strategiska produkter. Regeringens proposition 1994/95: 159. Stockholm: Government bill.

Del av Europa-Sverige och den västeuropeiska integrationen 1988. Stockholm: Ministry for Foreign Affairs.

En politik för nedrustning och utveckling 1988.

Forskning för kunskap och framsteg. Proposition 1992/93:170. Avsnitt 4: Försvarsdepartementet. Stockholm: Government printer. 1993.

Forskning och utveckling för totalförsvaret. SOU 1992:62 (FFU91). Stockholm: Ministry for Defence.

Försvarsdepartementet. Regeringens proposition 1993/94:100. Bilaga 5. Stockholm: Government printer.

Försvarsindustrins utlandsverksamhet. SOU 1987:8. Stockholm: Ministry for Foreign Affairs.

Historiskt vägval. Fäöljderna för Sverige i utrikes- och säkerhetspolitiskt hänseende av att bli, respektive inte bli medlem i Europeiska Unionen. SOU1994:8. Stockholm: Ministry of Foreign Affairs.

In Pursuit of Disarmament, 1984. SOU XXX. Stockholm: Ministry for Foreign Affairs.

JAS industrisamverkan 1986. DsI 1986:8. Stockholm: Ministry of Industry.

JAS39Gripen. En granskning av JAS-projektet. SOU 1993:119. Stockholm: Parliament.

Kontrollen över export av strategiskt känsliga varor 1993. SOU 1993:56. Stockholm: Ministry for Foreign Affairs.

Lag om krigsmatériel 1992. Proposition 1991/92:174. Stockholm: Ministry for Foreign Affairs.

Lorentzi, Jacob and Magnus Nilsson. *Spin-off, dual-use och omställning. Modeord eller realiteter?* FOA report A 10050-1.3. Stockholm: FOA 1994. January.

NU. Näringsutskottet. Individual reports to Parliament.

Ny vapenexportpolitik 1992. Briefing 1992:1s. Stockholm: Ministry for Foreign Affairs.

Om kriget kommit... SOU 1994:11. Stockholm: Government Printer (Statsrådsberedningen).

Press Releases.

Regeringens proposition 1991/92:102. Stockholm: Government bill.

Regeringens skrivelse 1993/94:207. Sverige och Partnerskap för fred. Stockholm: Government. 24 March.

Study on the relationship between disarmament and development 1981. New York: the United Nations. A/36/356, 5 October.
Sverige-EG-EFTA 1989. Stockholm: Ministry for Foreign Affairs.
Sveriges utrikeshandel i krislägen 1989. SOU 1989:107. Stockholm: Ministry for Foreign Affairs.
Sveriges överenskommelser med främmande makter. Annual. Stockholm: Ministry for Foreign Affairs.
TELUBaffären. SOU 1981:48. Stockholm: Ministry of Justice.
UU. Utrikesutskottet. Individual reports to Parliament.

Military Publications

Svensk försvarsindustri 1982. Report C10200-M6. Stockholm: FOA.
Wiechel, Hugo. *Försvarsindustrins elektronikberoende.* Report A 10007-M5. Stockholm: FOA.
ÖB93. Programplan för det militära försvarets utveckling 1993–1998. Stockholm: Högkvarteret.

Statistical Publications

Fakta om försvarsindustrin 1993. Stockholm: Sveriges försvarsindustriförening.
Forskningsstatistik 1992. Annual. Statliga anslag till forskning och utveckling budgetåret 1991/92. Stockholm: National Bureau of Statistics.
KMI skrivelser. Annual reports to Parliament on war matériel sales.

Papers and Journals

Aviation Week & Space Technology.
Bofors-Kuriren.
Dagens Nyheter (daily).
FFV-Nytt.
Metallarbetaren.
Military Technology.
Svenska Dagbladet (daily).
Universen (Uppsala University).
Uppsala Nya Tidning (daily).

Other

Company reports. Annual.
CORDIS (Common R&D Information Service) databases
EG/FoU Inside. Newsletter about EU R&D.

EUREKA database.

Hägglunds Vehicle. Reply to questionnaire 1994.

Visit to the Swedish National Defence Research Institute 1978. European Office of Aerospace R&D. London. Related personal notes by receiving Pentagon officer during FOA Director-General visit (declassified by relevant US authorities).

Endnotes

1 A draft version of this chapter was discussed with representatives from Sweden's Defence Research Establishrnent (FOA) and the Stockholm International Peace Research Institute (SIPRI). The author is especially grateful for comments by Elisabeth Sköns, SIPRI, who also supplied part of the text in the sections on defence industry and employment trends.

2 Bofors today consists of the formcr companies Bofors and FFV Ordnance. They merged in January 1991 under the name Swedish Ordnance, owned jointly by Nobel Industries and the state-owned FFV company. After Celsius acquired FFV and its shares in Swedish Ordnance in 1991 and the Nobel shares in 1992, the company changed its name to Bofors.

3 I deliberately eschew the term 'dependence', since a high share is not necessarily identical to high 'vulnerability'. Dependence is a relative phenomenon which may vary over time. Whether the vulnerability is high or low is a function of, among other things, alternatives and cost considerations. See discussion in Hagelin 1988, and the discussion of military imports in this chapter.

4 The importance of foreign patents for the development of new technology or applications is not known. In general, however, the input from such patents ought to add to, rather than reduce, Sweden's technological potential. Within the Patent and Registration Administration in Stockholm there has for a long time existed a special section for defence patents. During the last 10 years thc total number of defence patent applications has fallen. From July 1993 FMV administers these patents. Among those considered for secrecy classification in Sweden, foreign applications are in the majority (on the average 40 per year from the US, Germany, the UK and France compared to two Swedish applications). All applications emanating from those four foreign countries are, however, automatically classified in Sweden in accordance with the bilateral agreements.

5 There are two categories of war matériel — the first based on a functional criteria, i.e., destructive matériel ('matériel for combat' such as missiles,

bombs, grenades and complete weapon systems) and the second, related but non-destructive matériel based on its design for military use. Examples are radio and telecommunications, as well as other electronic equipment, unarmed vehicles, training matériel, and protective equipment. One result is that more war matériel than before is defined as non-destructive. As such, it will be exposed to looser controls, since foreign policy arguments against exports of such matériel have less political weight. Defence and security policy arguments — even the importance of military sales itself in order to preserve domestic capabilities in military technology — will become more important in deciding whether or not to export war matériel. For instance, in 1993 and 1994 the government permitted sales of war matériel to the following countries in the Middle East: Bahrain, Kuwait, Oman, Qatar, Saudi Arabia and UAE; and from 1995 to Estonia, South Korea and Russia. (KMI Reports, 1994 and 1995). Another illustration is the statement in the January 1994 budget bill that international MIC and exports in order to sustain competence will be supported *(Forsvarsdeparternentet* 1994, p. 83). For a discussion of the law, see Hagelin 1994.

6 An export permit

- for war matériel, or cooperation for the transfer of such matériel, *ought not* to be granted to a state with extensive and serious violations of human rights;
- for destructive war matériel, or cooperation for the transfer of war matériel, *ought not* to be granted to a state involved in (1) international armed conflict, (2) international conflict which may lead to armed conflict, or (3) domestic armed hostilities;
- *ought* to be granted for non-combat war matériel if the recipient is not involved in (1) an international armed conflict, (2) domestic armed hostilities, (3) *extensive and serious* violations of human rights, or (4) if there are no unconditional restrictions preventing such a sale.

7 Although not a member of COCOM, Sweden informally followed its embargo policy for civilian (dual-use) equipment and technology until 1967 (Hagelin 1985, pp. 19–32). Then 'Letters of Assurance' were requested by the US Department of Commerce in connection with such sales to Sweden. Several Swedish companies signed such assurances in order to acquire advanced technology (Holmström, M. and T. von Sivers 1985, pp. 44–45). In 1986 Sweden passed a national regulation controlling the *re-transfer* of advanced technology produced in western countries ('the high technology regulation'; Ministry for Foreign Affairs, Press Release, 27 February 1986). One main motive for taking this step was to secure the access of advanced

technology. In 1990 the Swedish civilian control mechanisms were expanded with the use of import certificates, by which Swedish importers promised to observe American export regulations. As a result the US Department of Commerce deleted Sweden from its control list *(Svenska Dagbladet* 12 Sep. 1990). This system was in use until 1992, when the system of import certificates ended. As a result, the role of the Swedish Board of Customs increased. Sweden was invited as an observer to the first meeting of the COCOM Cooperation Forum in November of 1992.

8 This change meant that the agencies which previously handled decisions within 'strategic' technological areas, often in cooperation with FOA, no longer do so: *Customs* (Tullverket) for exports of high technology products; *the Swedish Nuclear Power Inspectorate* (Statens kärnkraftsinspektion), *the Swedish Radiation Protection Institute* (Statens Strålskyddsinstitut), *the Ministry for Environment and Natural Resources* (Miljö- och naturresursdepartementet), *the Swedish National Chemical Inspectorate* (Kemikalieinspektionen), *the Swedish Bacteriological Laboratory* (Statens Bacteriologiska Laboratorium) and *the Swedish Board of Customs* (Generaltullstyrelsen) as well as *Customs* for the export of nuclear and other products relevant for the production of weapons of mass destruction.

9 See for instance 'Volvo Flygmotor stor aktör i europeiska samarbetsprojekt', *EG/FoU Inside*, no. 3, 1994 (March), p. 3.

10 It had been the author's intention to compile responses to a questionnaire sent out to the 10 largest military companies. However, Hägglunds Vehicle was the only company that completed the questionnaire. Saab Military Aircraft and Bofors sent positive responses. Kockums replied that, as a military firm, it is company policy not to reply to questionnaires. The other companies did not respond. The author wishes to thank Hans Wikström at Hägglunds Vehicle for taking the time to complete the questionnaire.

11 How this is to be achieved and financed is unclear. It seems likely that certain matériel will be moth-balled and stored; that ammunition and some other types of production possibilities will be preserved, thereby sustaining a national production base; and that any remaining equipment will be imported, especially if remobilisation time is short.

12 Press Release, Svenska Forsvarsindustriföreningen, 5 February, 1986, p. 2.

13 Offsets are used in both import and export deals, and for military ('direct') and civil ('indirect') benefits. It was in September 1983 that the Swedish

government advised the FMV to negotiate offsets when importing expensive matériel.

14 Author telephone interview with Dennis Harlin, FMV. Such offsets have, nevertheless, been successful, especially for Volvo Aero Corporation in the JAS39 Gripen project.

15 Sweden has been prepared to offset foreign customers for buying Swedish. Part of the offsets for Austria's purchase of surplus Draken aircraft in 1985 was in the form of technology transfer (Hagelin 1985). The same is true for Kockums' sale of submarine technology to Australia. But export offsets have not always been to the advantage of Swedish industry, since its capacity has been occupied on activities which may not otherwise have been performed. For instance, it has been said that, as a result of the deal to sell field howitzers to India, Bofors had to market Indian champagne and black-and-white TV sets on the international market *(Metallarbetaren,* November 1993; *Svensk försvarsindustri* 1993).

Chapter 9
United Kingdom

Philip Gummett

Introduction

British science and technology policy has long been dominated by defence interests. From the late 1960s until well into the 1980s, half of government expenditure on research and development (R&D) went on defence, and the percentage was even higher in earlier years. After the relative decline of recent years, the current position is as follows:

- Overall national spending on R&D in 1993 (the last year for which full figures are available) was £13.75 billion, or 2.19% of GDP. About a third of this was government funded, declining from 43% in 1985.
- Of the planned government total expenditure on science and technology (S&T — a slightly more expansive concept than R&D) in 1995–96 of £6.18 billion, £2.46 billion (or 40%) was intended for defence purposes.
- Government support for civil S&T has fallen in real terms from £3.7 billion in 1986–87 to £3.2 billion in 1995–96 (1993–94 base year), while defence S&T spending has fallen more rapidly, from £2.8 billion to £2.3 billion.
- Two-thirds of national expenditure on defence R&D is performed in industry, of which industry itself funds some 23% (£324 million in 1993); almost all the remainder (comprising research rather than development) is performed in government establishments.
- Of the UK total of 279,000 R&D personnel in 1993 (including technicians and administrative staff as well as researchers), 33,000 were in the defence sector.
- Defence R&D is planned to fall between 1987 and the turn of the century by about one-third. However, within this total, defence *research* is expected to fall by only 15% by 1998. Spending on defence as a whole, in contrast, is expected to fall by 14% in real terms between 1992–93 and 1996–97 alone.

(Sources: Cabinet Office, 1995, vol. 3, para. 1.4, Figure 4, Table 2.2, Figure 5.2, and Figure 13; Cabinet Office, 1994, para. 3.10; Ministry of Defence 1994, para. 505).

Despite both the actual recent decline, and that projected until the end of the century, this remains a heavy defence commitment. Moreover, when we consider that, by the standards of its major international competitors, British manufacturing industry itself funds relatively little R&D, we can see that its technological dependence upon the Ministry of Defence (MoD) has been great. Nor has this dependence been confined to R&D: MoD is the largest single customer of British industry and so has tremendous scope for influencing its technological performance.

In terms of the percentage of government spending on R&D that has been devoted to defence, Britain was matched during the Cold War years only by the USA, USSR and France. This was because, despite the substantial reduction in its global status since the Second World War, Britain still retained a wider range of defence commitments than most countries. These included strategic nuclear forces, the conventional defence of Europe and of the eastern Atlantic and the Channel, the direct defence of the UK, as well as Northern Ireland, the Falklands, and some other 'out of (NATO) area' activities. Naturally, the equipment requirements that accompanied these commitments were considerable, and were traditionally met as far as possible in a relatively self-sufficient way. That is, with notable exceptions at the level of major systems (e.g., Polaris and Trident missiles), as opposed to subsystems and components, Britain has preferred to do its own R&D (and production), or to do this in international collaborative programmes, rather than to pay for it indirectly in imported equipment.

Even before the end of the Cold War, the traditional assumptions that had for so long underpinned British policy were coming into question. Both the degree of self-sufficiency in defence equipment and the consequences of the associated distribution of national technological resources for industrial competitiveness became the subject of debate. In Britain, as elsewhere, the growing importance of technologies of civil origin for defence purposes gradually became clearer.

In addition, within the prevailing Thatcherite liberal economic regime, an emphasis on private ownership and on competition as a means of ensuring value for money in defence procurement became a leitmotif of policy from the mid-1980s. But competition quickly ceased to make sense at a purely national level, and steps were taken to locate British defence technological activity within a broader European framework, although retaining of course the traditional British ambivalence between Europe and the USA.

At the more specific level of defence R&D, steps were also taken to reorganise the government's own research establishments. The Atomic Weapons Establishment (which is a production as well as research organisation) was put under the management of an industrial consortium. In 1991, the main non-nuclear defence research establishments (DREs) were put under a unitary management and moved into a more remote, and more sharply contractual, relationship with the MoD in the form of the Defence Research Agency (DRA). This new arrangement has had the incidental effect of encouraging renewed attempts to link civil and military research in the form of dual-use technology programmes. In 1995 DRA was itself subject to further addition of test and operational analysis facilities, plus the Chemical and Biological Defence Establishment, and was renamed the Defence Evaluation and Research Agency (DERA).

The key features of the UK system of military R&D, as we shall show, include:

- the peculiarly British degree of separation between matters of civil and military technology;
- with respect to industry, the direct leverage of the government is limited by the fact that the entire defence industry (apart from the production of nuclear weapons) lies in private ownership;
- the strong emphasis on competitiveness among firms, and the DERA, in the supply of defence R&D and production;
- the resistance, in government, but not in industry, to the idea of defining a set of technologies that should be protected because of national security or strategic interests;
- the fact that, to an extent equalled only perhaps by France among the European countries, British technological and industrial strength depends heavily on its defence sector, so that the problems of adaptation to today's circumstances are particularly acute;
- finally, the fact that financial pressure on the DERA, and an awareness among firms of the importance of accessing a wider range of technologies, is creating new interest in dual-use technologies.

Basic Data

Organisational Context

The UK organises the development, design and production of defence equipment through an arm of the MoD called the Procurement Executive. Set up in the early 1970s, this body assumed responsibility from the former separate service and supply ministries, and from the Atomic Energy Authority, for all areas of conventional and nuclear weapons R&D and procurement. It in turn responds to operational requirements set not by the individual armed services but by the cross-service Defence Staff. It is the Defence Staff which acts as 'customer' for research programmes (broken down into 'research packages') and for development projects.

The Procurement Executive is the largest single customer of British industry, with a budget of £9.6 billion for 1995–96, of which £2.4 billion was scheduled for R&D (MoD, 1995, vol. 2, Tables 1.4, 1.5).

The relations between the Procurement Executive and the defence industry underwent a significant change from the mid-1980s. The government began, within a framework of Thatcherism, to place increased emphasis on 'value for money' in all areas of public spending, defence included. Steps were taken to shift the balance between cost-plus and fixed-price contracts; to increase the number of contracts that were awarded competitively; and to require firms to put their own money at risk over defence contracts. There were also attempts to extend these reforms to the European level.

The result was a toughening of the competitive environment for defence firms, and a growing volume of criticism by industrialists of the MoD for its alleged failure to realise the need for partnership and stability in the long-term development and maintenance of technological capabilities. It is clear that, in the perception of industry, the old relations of trust and co-operation between themselves and the MoD had been replaced by a more straightforwardly commercial relationship. The moves in 1990–92 to establish the DRA, with the intention that it operate relatively independently of the Ministry under a contractual relationship, and that it be free to compete with industry for defence research contracts, exacerbated this tension (House of Lords, 1994).

The MoD funds military R&D in order to enable the needs of the armed services for equipment and weapons to be met in a timely and cost-effective manner, and to enable MoD to act as an intelligent customer for such equipment. Note that this statement of purpose does *not* include such possible objectives as to maintain the strength of the industry, or to contribute to the national science and technology base, although official statements usually contain some reference to the desirability of these objectives, provided that they do not conflict with the primary purpose of serving defence needs. This form of words arises in part from the practice of Treasury control of public expenditure, part of which turns on ensuring, as a principle of public accountability, that funds allocated to a ministry are spent on the recognised goals of that ministry, and not for some other purpose.

The MoD distinguishes between *research* and *development*, but in a way that differs from the standard distinction of the OECD's Frascati Manual.[1] In MoD terms, work is 'development' if it is directly linked to a specific equipment project. It is 'research' if it is of a more general nature, not related to the current procurement of any specific item of equipment, but concerned rather with sustaining an underlying foundation of scientific and technological expertise on the basis of which support can be given to the selection, development, production and operation of weapon systems and equipment, and assessments can be made of the likely future evolution of military threats and the options for countering them. Research can also be conducted to support arms control initiatives (Cabinet Office 1992, para. 3.24.1). Research can be *strategic*, if long term and in an area with potential defence applications; or *applied*, if shorter term and directed towards a specific practical aim (though these distinctions are soon to be altered; see below). Included also within the broad MoD concept of R&D, and accounting for 13% of the revenue of the DRA prior to the 1995 reorganisation is *project support* (House of Lords, 1994, p. 51), which embraces various forms of assistance to MoD in specifying requirements, assessing bids, and sometimes also trouble-shooting when things have gone wrong with an industrial contract.

The MoD is overwhelmingly the main source of funds for UK defence R&D. Although the British defence industry is one of the two largest in Europe, with Europe's biggest defence firm, British Aerospace (also the world's 5th in the 1995 SIPRI listing), among its number, it spends relatively little of its own money on defence R&D, as we have seen. But industry is the main performer of defence R&D. The nuclear weapons programme apart, almost all development work, and about a third of all defence research, is done in industry.

About one-third of the R&D budget continues to be spent in the MoD's own research establishments. These comprise DERA and the AWE. DERA comprises the establishments formerly known as the Royal Aerospace Establishment (RAE), the Admiralty Research Establishment (ARE), the Royal Armament Research and Development Establishment (RARDE), the Royal Signals and Radar Establishment (RSRE), the Chemical and Biological Defence Establishment (CBDE), and some smaller research units together with important test facilities. It was set up (in its earlier form as DRA) in April 1991 as part of a general initiative to move civil service organisations into a more commercial relationship with government, while still leaving them under ministerial control.[2] Its aim is:

> to provide independent high quality, efficient and cost-effective scientific and technical services to its customers, primarily to MoD (House of Lords, 1994, Appendix 5).

More specifically, DERA supplies scientific and technical services to MoD in the areas of strategic research, applied research, operational assessments and studies, project support, the formulation of operational requirements, and equipment testing services and quality assurance. It does this partly through its own laboratories and test facilities, and partly by placing contracts with industry and universities. It also provides scientific and technical services to other government departments, and to other public and private sector customers where this supports the achievement of its main objectives. Prior to the reorganisation of

1995, DRA (as it then was) had some 5,000 qualified scientific and engineering staff. Total staff (all categories) of the new DERA is some 12,000. It is therefore a very significant scientific and technological resource, by any standard.

Initially headed by a career civil servant, in September 1991 a senior executive from the defence industry became the chief executive, in order to increase the commercial flavour of the organisation, and to press more vigorously (and with considerable success) the programme of site rationalisation and cost-cutting.

Defence Industry

Britain has an extensive defence industry, with current capabilities in all the main areas of defence equipment except for long-range missiles, heavy bombers and large aircraft carriers. Direct employment in the industry has fallen in fairly steady fashion from 405,000 in 1980–81 to 210,000 in 1993–94, with indirect employment falling over the same period from 335,000 to 185,000. The total amounts to about 10% of the manufacturing workforce. The industry also typically accounts for about the same percentage of the UK's manufacturing output. While the MoD's procurement budget is the industry's main source of income, exports are also extremely important. In 1993, UK firms won £7 billion of defence export orders, capturing over 20% of the world market (compared with a UK share in world markets in general of 9%). Actual deliveries in 1993 totalled some £3 billion (MoD, 1995, vol. 2, Tables 1.10, 1.11).

Details of the ten largest UK defence firms are given in Table 1.

These firms are the result of a lengthy process of concentration and rationalisation within the industry that began in earnest in the 1960s and has continued at accelerated pace in recent years. Its most extreme effects have fallen on the major contractors. As Lovering has put it, 'The citadels of the old Cold War arms industry underwent the most radical changes in order to become the spearheads of the new order.' (Lovering 1995, p. 105). They engaged in job shedding and rationalisation on a massive scale, with over 70,000 jobs (or about one-third of direct employment) going between 1987 and the end of 1993. By the mid-1990s, as Lovering observes, most of the core defence companies had largely completed their rationalisations, and the burden of change then fell more heavily on smaller sub-contractors and suppliers, where the effects are less easy to quantify.

The industry is dominated by British Aerospace (BAe) and GEC. These companies are themselves the outcome of substantial concentration within the aerospace and electronics sectors, just as also VSEL (Vickers Shipbuilding and Engineering Ltd) is the only remaining submarine and warship yard, and Vickers Defence Systems (not listed in Table 1; and no relation to VSEL) is the sole remaining manufacturer of main battle tanks.

Table 1: The Top 10 UK Defence Firms

Rank in SIPRI top 100 firms	Company	Industry	Arms sales 1993 $ million	Arms sales as % Total sales	Employees 1993
5	British Aerospace	Ac A El Mi SA/O	5,950	37	87,400
15	GEC	El	3,210	22	86,121
30	Rolls Royce	Eng	1,580	30	49,200
56	VSEL	MV Sh	690	99	7,329
67	Hunting	SA/O	490	31	14,538
68	Smiths Inds.	El	480	44	11,200
69	Westland	Ac	480	71	8,536
82	Lucas Inds.	Ac	390	10	48,900
85	Racal	El	380	29	n.a.
93	Vosper Thorneycroft	Sh	320	89	2,019

Source: SIPRI 1995, Appendix 13A.
Note: Data relate to 1993.
Key: A = artillery, Ac = aircraft, El = electronics, Eng = engines, Mi = missiles, MV = military vehicles, SA/O = small arms/ordnance, Sh = ships.

BAe is one of Europe's leading aerospace firms, with a wide range of products. These extend well beyond the obvious aircraft and missile activities, to include also ordnance (the result of its purchase of the former state-owned Royal Ordnance company). Until its sale to BMW in 1994, BAe also owned the Rover car company, including Land Rover. Despite its prominence in the civil as well as military sector, BAe depends crucially upon its military sales for its profitability. BAe offers a full systems integration service, which it has sought to extend into helicopters and into the naval field. It bid unsuccessfully, with Eurocopter, for the £2.5 billion Army attack helicopter contract that, in July 1995, was awarded to McDonnell-Douglas and Westland Helicopters for their Apache helicopter. And it attempted, losing finally to GEC in the summer of 1995, to purchase VSEL.

GEC which, through its Marconi companies, has long had a presence in defence electronics (especially radars and avionics), has generally functioned as a supplier of major systems rather than a full prime contractor. Its purchase of VSEL, however, offers it considerably increased potential in that regard, since VSEL is now the only major warship manufacturer in the UK, after the bankruptcy of Swan Hunter. The purchase, after a tense bidding contest with BAe, continues a process begun by GEC a few years ago of broadening its range within the defence sector, not least in naval systems. The VSEL acquisition is seen by many observers as marking the penultimate stage in manoeuvres to bring about a closer linkage, if not a full takeover, between GEC and BAe.

Rolls Royce, equally, is a monopoly aeroengine and gas turbine supplier, and one of a handful of such companies outside the United States and Russia. VSEL, likewise, is one of the few companies in the world with experience of manufacturing nuclear-powered submarines.

Since the 1980s, most major British defence firms have gone beyond national concentration, to engage in a complex set of international liaisons, taking the form of ad hoc partnerships, more enduring consortia, or even joint venture companies. To give a few examples:

- BAe, GEC and Rolls-Royce are members of the consortium building the Eurofighter 2000, along with firms in Germany, Italy and Spain. (On Eurofighter, see various chapters in Forsberg, 1994).
- BAe and GEC are linked with DCN (France) and Fincantieri (Italy) in the Horizon frigate project.
- BAe has a marketing and production arrangement with Saab over the JAS-Gripen (see chapter on Sweden), is partnering Aérospatiale and DASA in the Trigat missile, and has a variety of liaisons with all the major US aircraft and missile firms.
- BAe is also engaged in (slow moving) discussions with Matra (France) over pooling their missile interests into a joint company, having failed previously to complete a similar arrangement with Thomson-CSF. A particular problem for BAe was the insistence of the French government that the UK should fill an impending missile requirement (CASOM conventionally armed stand-off missile) from the new joint company, drawing on an existing Matra missile, while the UK government refused to interfere with a current international competition for CASOM. Relations with France were further damaged in July 1995 by the decision to meet a UK requirement for an Army attack helicopter from the US rather than from the Franco-German Eurocopter company, in association with BAe. (*Defense News*, 17 July 1995, p. 4).
- Royal Ordnance, the land systems subsidiary of BAe, began talks in 1992 aimed at merging its ammunition interests with those of France's GIAT. However, reports in September 1995 suggested that reconciling the cost structures in organisations, one of which had been subjected to the pressures of privatisation, the other of which was still shaking off its history as a state-owned arsenal, was proving difficult. (*Defense News*, 28 August 1995, p. 17).
- GEC has formed a joint venture (Matra Marconi Espace) with Matra over space interests, and another (GEC Thomson Sonar) with Thomson over sonar.

- Westland is linked to Agusta (Italy) in the EH-101 helicopter.

The British defence industry believes itself to be strong by international standards (in part perhaps because of the emphasis on competition by the MoD in the 1980s) and would welcome opening up of the European arms market. In economic terms, it is one of the most internationally competitive sectors in UK manufacturing. This is particularly true of the aerospace sector which, in the UK, is an industry divided roughly equally between military and civil production, having seen a secular decline in the military proportion from 75% in 1980 (House of Commons 1993, para. 10). As presented in a parliamentary report of 1993 (Ibid., para. 1), in 1991 the industry had a turnover of about £10.4 billion, and captured 11.7% of the world market for aerospace products, compared with 8.7% for UK manufactured goods in general; exports rose from less than 40% of turnover in 1980 to 70% in 1991; productivity rose by an average of 12.6% per year in the 1980s, faster than in UK manufacturing as a whole; in 1991–92, aerospace accounted for about 4% of Britain's manufactured output and 3.5% of manufacturing employment, but as much as 9% of exports of manufactured goods.

The centrality of the aerospace sector in general, and military aerospace in particular, to the UK manufacturing sector has led the industry to press strongly for government support. The industry argues that it is suffering particularly acutely today, first from the unusual conjunction of a recession in both defence and civil markets, and second from cuts in government support for R&D. Among other things, the industry prepared a National Strategic Technology Acquisition Plan for Aeronautics (NSTAP), in October 1992, only, however, to have the government reject the idea of increasing support for the sector (House of Commons, 1993; but see below).

Major Projects

The main equipment projects currently underway are shown in Table 2.

In addition, decisions were made in late 1994 or 1995 to:

- purchase 67 McDonnell Douglas-Westland Apache attack helicopters, at a cost of £2.5 billion;
- purchase 25 Hercules C-130J transport aircraft, and to rejoin the European Future Large Aircraft (FLA) project at the end of its feasibility phase in order to develop this option for subsequent replacement of the remainder of the transport fleet;
- participate with France and Italy in Project Horizon, to develop a new class of air defence frigate.

Table 2: Major Equipment Projects as at 31 March 1994

Project	Cost £ million	In-service date, forecast or actual
Trident nuclear submarine	11,631	1994
Eurofighter 2000	(a) 3,967	Early 2000s
EH-101 helicopter	3,925	Late 1998
Rapier missile system	2,085	1994–95
Spearfish torpedo	1,060	1994
Challenger 2 tank	933	1995
Tornado GR1 mid-life update	800	1998
ASRAAM missile	795	Late 1998
Swift & Trafalgar class submarine update	628	Phased over decade
Sea Harrier mid-life update	600	1993

Source: *UK Defence Statistics 1995* (London: HMSO, 1995), Table 1.15.
a) Development costs only.

Policy Towards Defence and Dual-Use Technology

Background

The MoD has long argued that the purpose of defence R&D is to support defence activity, and that the levels of spending have been justified purely in these terms. If Britain is to retain a high degree of autonomy in the production of defence equipment, so goes the argument, then it has to be prepared to pay directly the costs of R&D, rather than to pay them indirectly in the price of imported equipment. The MoD has also long rejected claims from various quarters that defence R&D was in some sense economically damaging, arguing that rather than defence R&D being too high, perhaps the real issue was the low level of civil, and especially industrial, spending on R&D. At the same time, the MoD has also claimed that the nation has benefited from various 'spin-offs' from work done on defence R&D programmes.

Debate built up in the 1980s. In 1983, a report on the electronics industry was written for a quasi-official non-departmental body, the National Economic Development Office, by the former chief scientist in the Department of Trade and Industry (DTI), Sir Ieuan Maddock (Maddock, 1983). Maddock argued that many of the largest suppliers of defence equipment in the UK had neglected the civilian side of their businesses. Consequently, they possessed neither the inclination nor the entrepreneurial skills to exploit the potential civil applications of their R&D. By implication, the main culprits were the major electronics companies, which had grown increasingly dependent on defence contracts and had failed to stay competitive in commercial markets: security of income from defence R&D and production led to a defence market orientation, a focus on product rather than process innovation, and a lack of concern about technology diffusion between their defence and civil divisions that left them ill-equipped for international competition.

In 1986, the tempo of the debate quickened. First, in a widely reported article, three academics identified differences of a factor of two in the concentrations of qualified scientists and engineers employed in the defence divisions of Britain's leading electronics firm, GEC, compared with that firm's civil divisions. They argued that:

> The absorption of a large proportion of the pool of skilled manpower by military R&D and production is arguably the most significant cost to the British industrial economy, especially since Britain is by common consent an under-skilled society (Kaldor *et al.*, 1986, p. 39).

Second, the independent Council for Science and Society (1986) issued a report which called for better linkage between defence programmes and the wider technology base. Third, in an enquiry into the state of civil R&D, the House of Lords Select Committee on Science and Technology took evidence on claims concerning civil benefits from defence R&D, and again drew attention to the distribution between the civil and the defence sectors (House of Lords, 1987).

In response to this growing volume of concern, the MoD acknowledged in 1987 the possibility that 'necessary investment in defence R&D may crowd out valuable investment in the civil sector', adding that:

> it would be regrettable if defence work became such an irresistible magnet for the manpower available that industry's ability to compete in the international market for civil high-technology products became seriously impaired (MoD, 1987, para. 522).

A year later, the Ministry announced that it was proposing gradually to reduce the real level of defence R&D spending during the 1990s (MoD, 1988, para. 417).

This new position did not appear to arise from any detailed study of the problem. It seemed rather to be a political response to try to head off too close an intrusion into defence affairs. From MoD's perspective, a particular concern was a major study of defence R&D conducted between 1987–89 by the cabinet's Advisory Council on Science and Technology (ACOST), the most senior science policy advisory body in the UK. From about that time, however, a number of empirical studies of the spin-off issue were actually done in the UK, but with no especially conclusive outcome.[3]

The ACOST report found that Britain kept the development of defence technologies separate from civil technologies to an unusual degree. It argued that this

> concentration on a mission of national defence contrasts markedly with the attitude of most other countries which recognise the national economic benefits to be obtained from exploiting the synergy between the defence and civil sectors (ACOST, 1989, para. 6.9).

The report recommended that MoD should use its research and contractual procedures in ways that take greater account of the nation's future technological capacity, principally by encouraging investment in a broader national technology base for defence from which both the defence and the civil sectors might benefit. The government rejected this recommendation, however, arguing that it did not see the defence budget as having an industrial sponsorship role or a responsibility for technologies unrelated to defence needs; any such steps would 'lead to muddled roles and inefficiency' (ACOST, 1989, p. 5).

Stimulated by the ACOST report, the Parliamentary Office of Science and Technology (POST) commissioned its own study from a group of academic specialists, and published its own summary and commentary. (ESRC/SPSG, 1991; POST, 1991). These POST reports reviewed the organisation, management and purpose of UK defence R&D, and examined the evidence on the relations between defence and civil science and technology, including such matters as the economic impact of defence R&D, studies of spin-off, and experience with technology transfer from the Defence Research Establishments. Among other things, they concluded that the key issue for the future was not spin-off but rather *how to manage the relationship* with civil technology. In particular, they argued that, contrary to existing practice, the UK government should regard the technological dynamism of *civilian* industries as being central to defence interests as well as to civil, and should structure policy towards publicly-funded science and technology accordingly. As part of this rethinking, there should be a process of continual strategic review of national technological requirements, embracing both civil and military interests.

The government is not obliged to, and did not, respond to a report from POST, although it is understood that this POST report and background study were read widely and at high level.

The Issue of Dual-Use Technologies Today

The ACOST and POST reports emphasised the importance of dual-use technologies to the future of defence technology and defence production. They also argued that strategic decision-making over the future of technology in both civil and military departments of government should each take account of the needs and interests of the other. The argument, as seen from the perspective of defence interests, is that the combination of downward budgetary pressure and upward technological demands forces ever greater selectivity upon the MoD; in addition, the technological lead in key areas is in any case shifting to the civil sector. Dual-use technologies offer a potential escape from these dilemmas.

The MoD has long appreciated the budgetary problem. As far back as 1982 it argued that:

> It is no longer open to Government to maintain the current level of defence R&D funding across the present wide field. Selections will have to be made, and we shall need to consider reducing the range of our defence industrial capabilities and concentrating on a more limited range of weapons technologies (MoD, 1982, para. 430).

However, there is resistance in MoD to the idea of producing lists like the US Critical Technologies List. The objection stems partly from the ruling ideology of market liberalism, which gives primacy to the supply of goods and services via the international marketplace rather than to the preservation of any particular British capability. It is also partly pragmatic, recognising that it would be difficult to construct such a list in any meaningful form, and that its contents would become ammunition for firms lobbying for governmental support. Hence the argument currently prevails that the list of technologies of which the UK absolutely must retain mastery is a very short one.

Some clues as to the contents of this list emerged in the late 1980s when MoD disclosed that it was studying the question of which technologies were to be regarded as 'strategic'. (ACOST, 1989, para. 6.4). The aim was to determine those areas where MoD, in order to act as an informed customer, needed an 'expert', 'intelligent' or 'ordinary' capability, and then to ascertain where 'critical masses' needed to be retained by public funding and where MoD could rely on the private sector.

The outcome of this review has never been published, and may in any case have been overtaken by the end of the Cold War. It is reasonable to believe, however, given the emphasis of recent procurement policy, that there remains a very short list of areas in which it will be regarded as vital to maintain a UK capability. Judging from the terms imposed upon the GEC/Siemens takeover of Plessey in 1989, one such area is cryptography. Another would be nuclear technologies, because of the centrality of nuclear deterrence to British defence policy, and because of the terms of the Nuclear Non-Proliferation Treaty. Chemical and biological defensive capabilities would probably be on the list, as would warship construction, especially nuclear-powered submarines. Finally, stealth technologies are also likely to be treated as a special case.

But even if MoD itself were more inclined to operate within a wider strategic framework, there would be another difficulty, namely, that MoD has no remit to ensure that investment in military work helps the UK to raise the general competence of the national, high technology, industrial base. Were it to try to do so, the MoD could be criticised by the Treasury for exceeding its responsibilities in the use of public finance.

As the POST study argued, however, 'This position is a matter of policy, not of inevitability' (ESRC/SPSG, 1991, p. 16). It further noted that MoD's extramural research contracts have, in the past, been used to seed advanced technologies within industry. Thus, in the mid-1960s, an important reason for the merger of the Ministry of Technology with the Ministry of Aviation (the latter being the leading element of the defence procurement system of the time) was to bring the enormous public purchasing power of the Aviation ministry to the support of the Ministry of Technology's mission of introducing advanced technologies into British industry. (Clarke, 1973). The experience of the Alvey fifth-generation computing program also shows that, where joint objectives can be identified, there is no great difficulty about running joint defence-civil programmes (Oakley, 1990).

The formal, official, UK position remains one of distinct separation between the activities and concerns of defence and civil ministries. There have, however, been some signs of change. For example, the then defence procurement minister said in September 1991:

> In the future I see the MoD making increased use of commercial off-the-shelf technology wherever we can. Our R&D will be increasingly targeted on producing military derivatives of basically civil technology, and on those areas where civil technology is not suitable or simply does not exist. In the constantly extending border area between military and civil technology there will be scope for MoD to become a more eclectic — though discriminating — patron and customer of work with potential for civil application (Clark, 1991).

Much of the evidence given in 1994 to an enquiry into the Defence Research Agency by the House of Lords Select Committee on Science and Technology dwelt on this issue. (House of Lords, 1994, pp. 31–34 and evidence, *passim*). Thus, the MoD itself claimed that 'whilst the DRA would not embark on a programme of work unless it was required for defence purposes, it recognises and is seeking to exploit the dual use potential of many of those technologies'. The DTI spoke of a markedly closer relationship with MoD/DRA since the summer of 1993 and the publication of the Science, Engineering and Technology White Paper, *Realising our Potential* (see below), although against a background of sharply declining DTI resources for actually funding joint research programmes. The Office of Science and Technology (OST — which was responsible for overall co-ordination of national science and technology policy) interpreted the terms of reference of the DRA as requiring it to give some attention to wealth creation (and not only, therefore, to defence goals). The OST also noted that its own annual review of all government-funded R&D (the so-called Forward Look exercise) would 'consider the scope for greater concerted action ... within publicly-funded S&T ... [and] the balance between civil and defence research'. Finally, the Treasury stated that there would be 'no objection in principle' to MoD and DTI jointly funding projects 'if both Departments considered this represented good value for money given other competing priorities for the use of public funds and was consistent with their objectives'. This statement continues to leave room for Treasury intervention, and keeps firmly on the table the requirement for there to be a defence objective if defence money is being spent. Nevertheless the overall effect of these pronouncements is to suggest an easing of earlier constraints. The House of Lords committee added its own weight, suggesting that the government's chief scientific adviser be empowered to expose any practices which impede closer links between civil and military science and technology.

Further policy developments have since taken place. Most notably, after the publication of the White Paper on science, engineering and technology policy (Cabinet Office, 1993), which introduced a number of important changes in the British science and technology system as a whole, a process of 'Technology Foresight' was introduced. This involved panels of experts from industry, government and the universities, organised into 15 different sectors, and supported by an elaborate and wide-ranging consultation exercise. The aim was to identify market and technological requirements and potential into the long-term future, in order to facilitate more concerted policy in British government, industry and higher education. One panel was concerned with defence and aerospace. It constitutes the nearest parallel in the UK to the activity undertaken in France by the Commissariat du Plan (see Chapter on France).

The panel identified as long term issues:

- Uncertainty about global security developments.
- Rapid growth in civil aerospace markets.
- Developments in UK defence procurement policy.
- Business process re engineering employed as a competitive weapon.
- Competitive funding of R&D.

Against that background, it offered the following key recommendations:

- Develop a technology strategy for UK defence and aerospace.
- Modify UK procurement policies to align with the technology strategy.

- Develop an improved technology exploitation process, giving higher priority to technology demonstrators.
- Ensure adequate financing to support capability in applied research and technology demonstration.
- Establish new funding mechanisms for Strategic and Applied Research.

Finally, it identified as the key technology priorities:

- Design and systems integration.
- Process technologies.
- Simulation, modelling and synthetic environments.
- Aerodynamics.
- Sensor systems and data processing.
- Materials and structures.
- High integrity real-time software.
  (Cabinet Office, 1995, vol. 1, p. 42; and Cabinet Office 1995a).

It is noticeable that the panel has returned yet again to the question of a technology strategy for defence and aerospace, despite this proposal having been rejected relatively recently by the government. (House of Commons, 1993). There are indications that MoD is now more sympathetic to this idea, but no clear outcome has yet emerged.

The panel's concern about the adequacy of funding, especially for the longer-term, echoed that of many witnesses to the 1994 House of Lords enquiry into the DRA, who feared that the pressure on the Agency to act more commercially might encourage a tendency towards the often-quoted British disease of 'short-termism'. To meet this possibility, defence research is now being reorganised into two categories: *corporate research*, aimed at maintaining and developing the defence science and technology base; and *applied research*, concerned with threat assessment, the formulation of concepts of operations, and the definition of specific equipment requirements. These categories will replace the current strategic and applied research categories. By expanding the scope of corporate research compared to the former strategic research, the aim is to give more stability to longer-term work by placing more of it under the control of the Chief Scientific Adviser's staff rather than a myriad of service customers (MoD, 1995, para. 440; House of Lords, 1994, vol. 2, qu.881). The MoD has also explained that it intends to cope with reduced funding for R&D through a combination of strategies: increased off-the-shelf procurement; increased international collaboration; greater reliance on civil-led research into new technologies; increased collaboration with industry and academia; and more efficient use of resources (Cabinet Office, 1995, vol. 2, p. 56).

Some of these strategies can already be seen in action at DERA, in the form of three specific initiatives, called Pathfinder, Strategic Alignment, and Dual Use Technology Centres (DUTCs).

Pathfinder is a scheme aimed at improving the overall effectiveness of the expenditure on defence research through better alignment and exchange between government and industry. It works by inviting firms to an annual conference at which they receive a briefing on DERA plans, following which firms submit proposals for joint research. These might involve projects where the funding comes entirely from industry, but uses DERA facilities; collaboratively funded projects; or entirely industry funded ventures with a formal link to complementary work in DERA. By offering firms the opportunity for a much earlier and more pro-active involvement in the MoD applied research programme, Pathfinder seeks to give industry a voice in determining what research is carried out to meet military requirements, and the chance to target its own research more effectively. It also encourages the possibility of spin-in from civil research to defence purposes.

The first year of the scheme (1992–93) attracted 640 bids from a wide spectrum of both large and small companies. Values of individual bids ranged from £50,000 to £7 million, with the total value of bids amounting to £90 million. Forty (worth £20 million in total) were immediately introduced into the DERA research programme, and a further 133 (worth £43 million) were still being evaluated in early 1994 (House of Lords, 1994, vol. 2, p. 4).

Strategic Alignment is less clearly defined than Pathfinder. It aims to establish good lines of communication between DERA and key firms in order to align their research programmes to mutual benefit. Thus, Rolls Royce engages in a mutual review of programmes with DERA and MoD staff, and in joint production of five-year plans, though this is probably the most advanced such case (House of Lords, 1994, vol. 2, pp. 103–4, and qu.371).

Dual Use Technology Centres are to be new centres of excellence established on DERA premises, which will draw together existing DERA capabilities that, at present, may be distributed across several locations. Their staff will come from DERA, firms and universities. The aim is to achieve critical masses of expertise and facilities in areas of interest to a wide variety of users, and to improve the interchange of people and ideas between the different sectors. The first DUTC, on Structural Materials, was launched in April 1994. A second, on Supercomputing, was opened in January 1995, in association with BAe, GEC and Cray Research. Others have been established or are under development in the fields of maritime technology, software engineering, information technology and robotics (MoD 1995, pp. 75–76).

In establishing these centres, DERA was pushing in a direction already known to be favoured by leading firms, which had already begun their own initiative on the theme of dual-use technologies. Led initially by BAe, but then transferred to the Confederation of British Industry, a series of meetings has begun with the aim of bringing together firms in different sectors, plus universities and government laboratories, in a process of alignment of their generic research programmes. An example given at one such meeting was the field of 'smart materials', which could be of interest to university scientists, materials manufacturers, military and civil aircraft manufacturers, and users in various service sectors such as health or even retailing. Another example could be 'safety critical/highly reliable software' (Coghlan, 1994). This initiative clearly overlaps with that on the DUTCs, and with the Technology Foresight exercise, suggesting a general momentum in the direction of fostering dual use technologies. Given, however, the very limited DTI funds (outside certain forms of support for civil aerospace), which will restrict their involvement to a facilitating role, much will depend on how well DERA and major firms develop these ideas, and in what directions they take them.

Policy Regarding Technology Transfer

As a historical footnote to the initiatives described just above, we can observe that in Britain one of the perceived obstacles to the transfer of technology from defence to civil applications has been the relative isolation of the Defence Research Establishments from companies, other than those deeply embedded within the defence sector. Yet much of the work of the establishments has clearly had scope for dual application, and attempts have been made at various times in the past to address the problem.

During the 1980s various schemes were aimed at opening up the DREs to a wider range of customers. One such was the launching of *Defence Technology Enterprises (DTE) Limited*, in 1985, to transfer technology from DREs to industry for civil applications. This firm, set up jointly by the MoD and a consortium of eight founder members with substantial venture capital, had rights of access to the non-nuclear research establishments. Staff, colloquially called 'ferrets', sought out promising ideas in these establishments and alerted interested companies. By 1988, 260 companies had become associate members of DTE and a number of examples of successful innovation had been recorded. The companies ranged from small non-defence firms to divisions of the major military contractors (Herdan, 1988).

In 1990, however, DTE was in effect closed down, no explanation being offered. The main reason was probably that the rate of return was lower than its venture capitalist backers normally required. In addition, however, the model of technological innovation on which it was implicitly based was probably mistaken, leaving it too late in the innovation process before the developers of the technology established contact with the users. DTE itself also lacked the capital to support development of technologies to the point where a saleable product could be offered (Spinardi, 1992).

By that time, however, other links with the civil sector were quite extensive, particularly at the Royal Signals and Radar Establishment and the Royal Aerospace Establishment, where there was a tradition of work being funded by DTI and its precursors. In addition, a 'Civil Industrial Access Scheme' (CIAS) was announced in 1988 to encourage civil industry to make greater use of the expertise that the defence research establishments could provide through collaborative work, use of facilities, and advice and counselling. Secondly, under so-called 'Research Initiatives', co-funded by DTI, scientists from a consortium of companies were able to work with defence scientists in certain fields (e.g., neural networks; silicon hybrids) in a joint programme located at a defence research establishment. Under another scheme, industrial scientists could be seconded to an establishment, or DRE scientists to a firm, for one or two years. The research establishments have also taken an active part in various collaborative programmes, both national (e.g., the Alvey fifth generation computing program) and international (e.g., ESPRIT). Within the government's LINK initiative, which aims to encourage strategic research of medium-term industrial significance and to improve the transfer of new technology into industry, MoD has joined with DTI and various research councils in sponsoring programmes on structural composites, protein engineering, and helicopters. Funds are also provided centrally by MoD for the support of university science through the joint MoD-Research Councils scheme. £33 million was spent by MoD on research in universities in 1993–94.

These schemes are now being subsumed within the new DERA initiatives described above. Other technology transfer instruments include the classical one of granting licences, of which 250 were active in mid-1995 (Cabinet Office, 1995, vol. 2, p. 28). In a more novel step, MoD also began in 1994 to make available to security-cleared companies the results of its annual review of defence research programmes, which, *inter alia*, should raise the level of information about the technology transfer potential within DERA. (MoD, 1995, para. 442). Finally, under the Agency arrangement, DERA is now able to retain some of the funds that are generated from licences and royalty payments on its patents, and these are used in part to provide incentives to staff to encourage technology transfer (House of Lords, 1994, para. 4.14).

International Collaboration

There is a strong commitment by the MoD to international collaboration and, as indicated above, an intention to move further in this direction. At April 1995, the UK was involved in international collaboration with 15 countries on 22 projects already in production or service (including the Multiple Launch Rocket System, the Sidewinder air-to-air missile and the Navstar Global Positioning System); with 10 countries on 9 projects in the development phase (including the Long Range Trigat anti-tank missile and Eurofighter 2000); and with 8 countries on 14 projects in the study phase (including the Horizon frigate, a future tank main armament and a future lightweight fighter aircraft). Across all three of these categories, 25 projects involved collaboration with France, 22 with Germany and 19 with the USA (MoD, 1995, Table 6).

In addition, the UK is active in the Western European Armament Group's *EUCLID* programme. As of May 1994, DERA was participating in 12 of the then 13 currently active CEPAs (Common European Priority Areas). Of the 28 more specific Research Technology Programmes, the UK was involved in 20, contributing some £18 million of their total cost of £90 million. DERA staff were serving on 10 of the 13 CEPA management committees. DERA has also been extensively engaged in such elements of the EC Framework Programme as BRITE/EURAM, ESPRIT, SCIENCE and MAST (House of Lords, 1994, vol. 2, pp. 7 and 228).

As discussed in the Introduction, Britain is now also committed to serious exploration of the possibilities for the WEU Armaments Agency. However, the decisions made in 1995 not to adopt the European Future Large Aircraft to the exclusion of the American rival, and to buy the US Apache helicopter rather than the Eurocopter Tiger, may have seriously dented the UK's European credentials, at least in the eyes of the French (*Defense News*, 17 July 1995, p. 4). Relations with other European countries are also coloured by the beliefs in the UK that its costs are generally lower than elsewhere, that the organisational structures required for efficient collaboration should give more management responsibility to industry, and that rigid, and often costly, work sharing schemes should be avoided.

Policy Towards Conversion

Britain is far from what might be termed the 'Japanese model' of defence R&D and production, where defence activity is managed as a small part of the work of large, technologically dynamic companies, whose main competence and markets lie elsewhere. At the prime contractor level, the UK's is overwhelmingly a specialist defence industry. Even when the defence dependence of firms is not especially high, defence affairs are typically conducted in quite distinct divisions from those concerned with civil markets. Consequently, the main strategy being pursued by Britain's leading defence firms is to reduce their size and lay off staff, rather than to diversify organically from their existing technology base into new markets. (POST, 1992). On the whole, they have focused more sharply on their core defence business, as exemplified most dramatically in the case of British Aerospace by the sale of its construction firm, Ballast Nedam, of its automobile firm (Rover) to BMW, and of the proposed merger of its space interests with Matra. At the same time, as part of their attempt to win a larger share of the diminishing world market, British defence firms are also among the most active in the general process of restructuring and concentration, within and across national frontiers, European and trans-Atlantic, that has been so much a feature of the defence sector in recent years (Walker and Gummett, 1989).

Nevertheless, there has been some diversification, as distinct from conversion. Some examples are shown in Table 3.

Many companies have also sought to alter the balance between defence and civil markets or, within the defence market, between UK sales and exports. Thus, GEC-Marconi, while remaining principally a defence company, has

Table 3: Examples of Recent Diversification by UK Companies

Company	**Diversification**
Dowty	Diversification from landing gear for Tornado into Airbus landing gear
GEC	Satellite dish production
GKN	Application of aluminium casting technology from Warrior armoured personnel carrier to components for road and railway cars
Harland and Wolff	Return to traditional merchant shipbuilding
Rolls Royce	Diversification into civil aeroengines and gas turbines, and other power generation markets
Rosyth Dockyard	Refurbishment of underground trains
Smiths Industries	Development of fuel management and flat panel displays; electronic power distribution systems for Boeing civil aircraft
United Scientific Holdings	Diversification into subsystems for civil aviation, e.g., wing-flap gear boxes
VSEL	Offshore oil and gas equipment

Source: POST, 1992, p. 7.

shifted its turnover towards civil products and defence exports. In 1990, half its turnover came from UK defence, 30% from non-UK defence, and 20% was civil. By 1995, UK defence turnover had halved, while non-UK defence work and civil turnover had both increased by 50%. Areas where its civil business have grown in recent years include civil avionics, command and control systems for police and fire services, transport systems (automatic vehicle location, traffic control, on-board guidance), and consumer products (video telephones, direct broadcast receivers, smart cards and embedded electronics). Emerging areas of civil business include car radars, head-up displays, and laser blind spot detection. (Mears, 1995). In all of these the dual-use element is clear.

While it may be right for most firms not to attempt ambitious conversion plans at plant level, many, particularly among trades unions, argue that there is more scope for government support for restructuring at the regional level. The danger for Britain is that, with such a large proportion of its technological skills tied to the defence sector, it could lose substantial numbers of skilled workers unless alternative demand appears. In the present state of the economy, it is not obvious that such demand will appear unless government plays a role, in association with industry and regional authorities.

The government has not, however, responded enthusiastically to these demands. A modest amount of direct support has been given to the development of infrastructure in the Barrow-in-Furness area, home of submarine manufacturer VSEL. This exception was justified by the government on the grounds of the region's overwhelming defence dependence and its geographical isolation, a combination of factors that it said were unique to the region.[4]

Otherwise, the government's position is well summarised in its response to a recommendation by the House of Commons Trade and Industry Committee in its report on aerospace that a study should be commissioned of whether and how the conversion of defence resources to civil uses should be assisted. The government replied that 'Decisions about defence conversion are essentially matters for companies themselves.' (House of Commons, 1993, Government reply, p. viii). Nevertheless, it went on, the government does support companies' efforts through a variety of schemes, such as general DTI schemes to encourage innovation, develop marketing skills and promote exports. More specifically, DTI has run a series of seminars, under the title 'Changing Tack'. These have been regionally focused, and have included descriptions by successful firms of their own experience of diversification, designed to encourage others, particularly small and medium-sized enterprises. DTI has also launched what the government called a 'manual' entitled *Changing Tack — New perspectives for defence suppliers*, aimed at assisting companies to plan their responses to changes in the defence market. This 34 page document offers broad advice about market appraisal and business planning, together with some contact addresses for general advisory services that might be able to assist with innovation.

The government also noted that departments other than DTI have additional schemes that might be relevant, such as the Department of Employment's training programmes. It observed that the UK has also benefited from the EC PERIFRA programme. A total of 8 mecu (£6.38m) of grant under this scheme has been awarded to 8 UK projects, five of which, attracting 5.7 mecu (£4.55m), are defence diversification projects. It added that the government was also in negotiation with the European Commission over the UK's allocation under the KONVER scheme; and concluded that it did not consider an additional study to be needed.

The government did not, however, mention criticisms that had been voiced by local authorities and regional bodies of the lack of central government support in winning PERIFRA grants; nor its continued opposition to the idea, proposed by the Labour Party, of a Defence Diversification Agency (See POST 1992).

Controlling the Diffusion of Defence Technologies

As a depository state of the Nuclear Non-Proliferation Treaty (NPT), the UK has long taken a particular interest in controlling the international diffusion of weapons of mass destruction, and it has been equally concerned about diffusion of other types of weapon. At the same time, the UK defence industry depends critically upon arms exports, while the economy benefits from the associated foreign exchange revenue and jobs. Hence, the UK finds itself promoting international controls on the sale of weapons and the diffusion of dual-use technologies, while also actively seeking to promote arms exports through, for example, the Defence Export Services Organisation within MoD, or through prime ministerial support for arms deals. The complexities of the resulting positions, with intense bureaucratic politics and ministerial interventions being played out between the arms controllers in the Foreign Office, the arms sales promoters in the MoD (offset by others in MoD who are concerned about the threat implications of diffusion of advanced weaponry), export licensing authorities in DTI, export policing authorities in the Customs and Excise Service, and the intelligence services, are being revealed in great detail, and with much press and public interest, through the Scott inquiry into the so-called 'arms to Iraq' case[5], and through the alleged association between overseas aid and arms sales in the case of the Pergau dam in Malaysia.

On the non-proliferation front, the UK took an active role in preparations for the 1995 NPT review conference, pressing strongly for permanent extension of the Treaty, and for strengthening of the safeguards system operated under the Treaty and by the Nuclear Suppliers' Group. It is also playing a central role in the negotiations for a Comprehensive Nuclear Test Ban Treaty, with the Foreign and Commonwealth Office apparently winning the argument with the MoD over whether to ban even very low level tests. In addition, the UK is an active member of the Australia Group, which meets to discuss further ways to prevent the proliferation of chemical and biological weapons, going beyond the Chemical Weapons Convention and the Biological and Toxins Weapons Convention. It is active also in the Missile Technology Control Regime, and was one of the countries that promoted the UN Register of Conventional Arms. It has also been a strong supporter of COCOM.

The arms to Iraq case notwithstanding, the official self-image remains one of strict observance of export controls. All arms exports are said to be considered on a case-by-case basis in the light of established criteria. These include the common criteria for arms transfers agreed within the EU, the guidelines agreed by the Permanent Members of the UN Security Council, and the Principles Governing Arms Transfers agreed by the OSCE. (MoD, 1995, para. 445). All internationally agreed arms embargoes are also observed. There is, however, some suggestion, with respect to the EU Regulation on Dual-Use Goods, that the UK requirements concerning end-use certificates (a matter left to national discretion by the Regulation) are not as demanding as those of some other states (Saferworld, 1995, p. 8).

This is a salutary point on which to end. The UK, with a reshaped, downsized, internationally-oriented defence industry, and a defence ministry committed to value for money in procurement matters, hopes to escape the conundrum of falling budgets and rising technological expectations through increased attention to dual-use technologies. Yet, as Mussington has observed, in such a context,

> globalisation in commercial technology markets — which is much greater than in the defence sector — contributes to the regulatory burden of policing process technologies as they spread to new locations. Thus industrial policies based on leveraging commercial technologies against reductions in defence R&D probably exacerbate technology security problems (Mussington, 1994, pp. 60–61).

The solution, in other words, is double-edged. The search for security of the defence industrial base via dual-use technologies has to deal with the fact that militarily relevant technologies are increasingly available even to countries without elaborate defence technological capabilities. The dilemma thus presented confirms once more that security is ultimately a political rather than a technological matter, but that the intelligent social control of technology continues to be a matter of the utmost importance.

References

Advisory Council on Science and Technology (ACOST), 1989, *Defence R&D: A National Resource* (London: HMSO).

Cabinet Office, 1992, *Annual Review of Government Funded Research and Development 1992* (London: HMSO).

Cabinet Office, 1993, *Realising our Potential: A Strategy for Science, Engineering and Technology* (London: HMSO, Cm 2250).

Cabinet Office, 1994, *Forward Look of Government-funded Science, Engineering and Technology 1994* (London: HMSO).

Cabinet Office, 1995, *Forward Look of Government-funded Science, Engineering and Technology 1995* (London: HMSO).

Cabinet Office, 1995a, *Report of the Technology Foresight Panel on Defence and Aerospace* (London: HMSO, ISBN 0-11-430126-3).

Clark, Alan, 1991, Speech on 'Defence and the high technology industries'. London: World Economic Forum, 4 September; available from Ministry of Defence as News Release 106/91.

Clarke, Sir Richard, 1973, 'Mintech in retrospect', *Omega*, vol. 1, pp. 25–38 & 137–63.

Coghlan, A., 1994, 'Stony ground for Britain's ploughshares', *New Scientist*, 22 January, pp. 12–13.

Council for Science and Society, 1986, *UK Military R&D* (Oxford: Oxford University Press).

DASA (Defence Analytical Services Agency), 1993, *Changes to the statistics of MoD's intramural research and development expenditure* (London: MoD, Defence Statistics Bulletin, No. 1).

ESRC/SPSG Defence Science and Technology Policy Team (editor: P. Gummett), 1991, *Future Relations Between Defence and Civil Science and Technology*, A Report for the Parliamentary Office of Science and Technology (London: Science Policy Support Group, Review Paper No. 2, ISBN 1-873230-02-8).

Forsberg, R. (ed.), 1994, *The Arms Production Dilemma: Contraction and Restraint in the World Combat Aircraft Industry* (Cambridge, Mass.: The MIT Press, CSIA Studies in International Security, No. 7).

Herdan, B., 1988, 'A UK initiative for the transfer of technologies from defence to civil sector', in P. Gummett and J. Reppy (eds), *The Relations Between Defence and Civil Technologies* (Dordrecht: Kluwer).

House of Commons, 1993, *The British Aerospace Industry*, Third Report of the Trade and Industry Committee (London: HMSO, HC 563-I); and *Government Observations on the Third Report from the Trade and Industry*

Committee (Session 1992–93) on the British Aerospace Industry (London: HMSO, HC 945).

House of Lords, 1987, Select Committee on Science and Technology, *Civil Research and Development,* Session 1986–87 (London: HMSO, HL 20).

House of Lords, 1994, Select Committee on Science and Technology, *Defence Research Agency*, Session 1993–94 (London: HMSO, HL 24).

M. Kaldor, M., M. Sharp and W. Walker, 1986, 'Industrial competitiveness and Britain's defence', *Lloyds Bank Review*, October.

Lovering, J., 1995, 'Opportunity or crisis? The remaking of the British arms industry', in R. Turner (ed.), *The British economy in transition* (London: Routledge).

Maddock, Sir Ieuan, 1983, *Civil Exploitation of Defence Technology: Report to the Electronics EDC* (London: NEDO).

Mears, A., 1995, 'Civil-defence strategies in the UK', paper presented to NATO ASI on Defence Conversion Strategies, Pitlochry, Scotland, July.

Ministry of Defence, 1982, *Statement on the Defence Estimates 1982* (London: HMSO, Cmnd 8529-I).

Ministry of Defence, 1987, *Statement on the Defence Estimates 1987* (London: HMSO, Cm 101-I).

Ministry of Defence, 1988, *Statement on the Defence Estimates 1988* (London: HMSO, Cm 344-I).

Ministry of Defence, 1995, *Statement on the Defence Estimates 1995* (London: HMSO, Cm 2800); and vol. 2, *UK Defence Statistics 1995* (London: HMSO).

Mussington, D., 1994, *Understanding Contemporary International Arms Transfers* (London: International Institute for Strategic Studies, Adelphi Paper No. 291).

Oakley, B. and K. Owen, 1990, *Alvey: Britain's Strategic Computing Initiative* (Cambridge, Mass.: MIT Press).

Parliamentary Office of Science and Technology (POST), 1991, *Relationships between Defence and Civil Science and Technology* (London: POST).

Parliamentary Office of Science and Technology (POST), 1992, *Conversion and Diversification of Defence Technology and Manufacturing* (London: POST).

Saferworld, 1995, *The EU Regulation on Dual-Use Goods: Priorities for the Transitional Period* (London: Saferworld, ISBN 0948546-29-8).

SIPRI (Stockholm International Peace Research Institute), 1995, *SIPRI Yearbook 1995* (Oxford: Oxford University Press).

Spinardi, G., 1992, 'Defence Technology Enterprises: a case study in technology transfer', *Science and Public Policy*, volume 19, no. 4, pp. 198–206.

Walker, W. and P. Gummett, 1989, 'Britain and the European Armaments Market', *International Affairs*, vol. 65, pp. 419–42.

Endnotes

1 After much debate about the quality of defence R&D statistics (see ESRC/SPSG, 1991), MoD published in 1993 the results of a major review of the basis on which these data were collected, and attempted to reconcile previous practice with that of the Frascati convention. So far, however, this reconciliation is done only for MoD's intramural R&D expenditure. See DASA, 1993.

2 The DRA was set up under an initiative which transferred a series of governmental activities into government-owned organisations that would henceforth function outside ministries. They were called 'Agencies'. The aim was to deliver a better service to customers, be they members of the public or other parts of government, by introducing a more commercial style of management, freed from traditional civil service constraints. In April 1993, DRA moved onto 'Trading Fund' status, which meant that it no longer received a block grant from MoD but instead had to recover the cost of its work item by item from its customers, 90% of whom were individual budget holders in MoD. The DRA also has to meet a target rate of return on the capital invested in it. This target is set by the Treasury, and is intended to encourage financial prudence and entrepreneurship. The Agency concept is more complex than the simple rhetoric of customers and contractors might suggest, since the ministry is not only the principal customer but also the owner, and therefore responsible for the future of the Agency.

3 These are summarised in ESRC/SPSG, 1991.

4 POST, 1992, p. 23. A study by the European Commission showed that of the top 12 industrially defence dependent regions in the EC in 1992, all but two (Bremen at number 3, and Liguria at number 7) were in the UK or France. The Cumbria region in the UK, home of VSEL, was the most industrially defence dependent region by a factor of more than two over the next ranked region. Source: Commission of the European Communities, *The Economic-Social Impact of Reductions in Defence Spending-Military Forces on the Regions of the Community*, executive summary, Doc. P/92/64, available from the Commission's UK Office, London, December 1992.

5 This case turns on the export of defence-related equipment and dual-use goods to Iraq which resulted in the trial of 3 businessmen for allegedly breaking export license terms. The trial collapsed when it emerged that one of the men was acting as an agent for British intelligence. A subsequent inquiry, under Sir Richard Scott, examined the degree to which export

guidelines were breached, whether or not they were changed without due procedure and notification of Parliament, and how it came about that ministers tried to prevent documents showing the intelligence connection becoming available to the trial judge. The resulting massive (1800 pages) report was published in February 1996. It was highly critical of government handling of the affair, and singled out specific ministers for particular criticism. Nevertheless, the government succeeded in avoiding defeat in the House of Commons in a subsequent debate on the report. See *Report of the Inquiry into the Export of Defence Equipment and Dual-Use Goods to Iraq and Related Prosecutions* (London: HMSO, 1996).

Index

After a page reference, f = figure, n = note, t = table.

Advisory Council on Military Production (AMP) 177, 179–80, 183, 186
Advisory Council on Science and Technology (ACOST) 271–2
AEG 92
AEMG (Authorisation for the Export of War Matériel) 78
Aermacchi 149, 150t, 151, 152t, 155, 164
Aeronautical Research Institute *see* FFA
Aeronautica Macchi 149
Aeronáutica Maintenance Tooling (AMT) 208
AERO programme 239
Aérospatiale 53–4, 56t, 57, 59t, 65t, 76, 103, 151, 152t, 153, 208, 268
Aero-Technological Forum (NFF) 238
Agencia Spaziale Italiana (ASI) 140
Agusta 59t, 147–8, 149–50t, 152t, 155, 163, 269
Agusta Sistemi 148
Airbus 13, 31, 40–1, 43, 46
Airbus Industrie 57
Air Division for Studies, Research and Experiments (DASRS) 146
Alcatel 201
Alcatel Bell-SDT 30t, 33t
Alcatel Bell Téléphone 33t
Alcatel Espace Défense 65t
Alenia 57t, 147–8, 149–50t, 151, 152t, 155, 162
Alenia Elsag Sistemi Navali 149–50t, 155, 162
Allied Research Association 33t
AMP (Advisory Council on Military Production) 177, 179–80, 183, 186
Amper 201, 206
Amper Sistemas 207
AMT (Aeronáutica Maintenance Tooling) 208
AM-X fighter 142, 145, 152t, 153
AM-X International 152t
Apache helicopter 174, 269, 280
ARGE F-124 171
ARGE-TAURUS consortium 239
Ariane consortium 153
Ariane launcher 151
Ariete 1 142
Armaments Agency 7–8, 76
Artemis anti-aircraft system 128
ARTHUR radar 238
ASI (Agencia Spaziale Italiana) 140
ASLP missile 59t
ASRAAM missile 270t
Association of German Industrialists (BDI) 109–10
Association of Swedish Defence Industries 248
AT4 anti-tank weapon 238
Atlantique 2 aircraft 59t
Atomic Energy Commission (CEA) 52, 64
Atomic Weapons Establishment (AWE) 262, 265
ATR aircraft 151, 152t, 153
Aussenwirtschaftsgesetz (AWG) 107–9
Aussenwirtschaftsverordnung (AWV) 107–9
Australia Group 14, 78, 159, 235, 284
Authorisation for the Export of War Matériel (AEMG) 78
AV-8B fighter 142, 146
AWE (Atomic Weapons Establishment) 262, 265
AWG (Aussenwirtschaftsgesetz) 107–9
AWV (Aussenwirtschaftsverordnung) 107–9

BAe *see* British Aerospace
Bag 156
BAMSE missile 226t, 238
Barco Electronics 131
Barracuda Technologies 221, 222t, 244t
Bazán (Empresa Nacional Bazán de Construcciones Navales Militares) 171, 184, 200–1, 212–3

BDI (Association of German Industrialists) 109–10
BDM 90
Bedrijfsgerichte Technologie Stimulering in Internationale Programma's (BTIP) 186
Belgium 25–47
  conversion policy 17, 40–4
  defence industry 28, 30t, 31–3
  defence technology policy 38
  dual-use technologies 13, 40–1, 45
  economic offsets 38–40
  European commitment 37–8
  expenditure 6t, 25–7, 32t, 35–6
  export controls 44–5
  exports 15, 28, 29t, 32t, 44–5
  organisational context 25–7
  R&D 6t, 25, 34–6, 40–1
  regional developments 40
Beliard Polyship 172
Bendix 152t
BILL anti-tank missile system 226t
BIOTECH programmes 240
Blue List, Institutes of the 89
BMF 31
BMT Icons 241
Boeing B767 151
Bofors 220–1, 222t, 226t, 230, 238–9, 243, 244t, 248
Bofors Electronics AB 227
BONUS shell 238
Bosch 94t
BPD Difesa e Spazio 17, 20, 149, 150t, 152t, 153, 155–7, 164
Breda Meccanica Bresciana 148
Bremer Vulkan 92, 93t
BRITE/EURAM programme 129, 239, 280
British Aerospace (BAe) 12, 152t, 226, 233, 265–8, 277–8, 281
  BAe Defence 184
British Aerospace Dynamics 57t
Browning 42
BTIP (Bedrijfsgerichte Technologie Stimulering in Internationale Programma's) 186
Bundesamt für Wehrtechnik und Beschaffung (BWB) 86–7
C-130 Hercules 202
CASA (Construcciones Aeronauticas, S.A.) 152t, 200, 206–8, 212
CEA (Atomic Energy Commission) 53, 64
CEHP (El Pardo Canal for Hydrodynamic Experiments) 198
Celsius group 230, 237, 241–2, 252
Celsius Industries 220–1, 222t, 243
Celsius Invest 241
CelsiusTech 221, 222t, 241, 244t
Centauro 142t
Centro Ricerche Esperienze e Studi per Applicazioni Militari (CRESAM) 146
CEPAs (Common European Priority Areas) 280
CESA 208
CESELSA 201, 206
CFM56 programme 41
CFSP (common foreign and security policy) 1
CGP (Commissariat Général du Plan) 66–76
Challenger 2 tank 270t
Chalmers Technical High-school 220, 236, 238
Chemical and Biological Defence Establishment 263
Chemical Weapons Convention 15
Chinook helicopters 174
CIEEMG (Interministerial Commission for the Study of Exports of War Matériel) 78
CIRA (Italian Centre for Aerospace Research) 140
civil-military integration 11
CMI 30t, 33t
CNES (National Centre for Space Studies) 12, 64, 75
COCOM 14–5
  Belgium 45
  France 78–9
  Germany 107, 109
  Italy 159
  The Netherlands 190
  Spain 213–4
  Sweden 250
  United Kingdom 284

CODEMA (Commission for the Development of Defence Matériel) 169–70, 177–8, 180–3
collaboration, international 2, 7–9
  Belgium 31, 37
  France 54, 57–8, 76
  Germany 102–3
  Greece 126–7, 129
  Italy 147, 151–3
  The Netherlands 182–4
  Spain 207–8
  Sweden 224–6, 243–5
  United Kingdom 268–9, 280
Commissariat Général du Plan (CGP) 66–76
Commission for the Development of Defence Matériel *see* CODEMA
Common European Priority Areas (CEPAs) 280
common foreign and security policy (CFSP) 1
Compagnie des Signaux 65t
companies, leading
  Belgium 23, 30t, 31, 33
  France 54, 56t, 57–8, 65t
  Germany 92–4t
  Greece 119–21
  Italy 147–51
  The Netherlands 171–3
  Spain 200–1
  Sweden 220–3t
  United Kingdom 266–8
Comprehensive Nuclear Test Ban Treaty 284
Computing Device 152t
Confederation of British Industry 12, 278
Consorzio Esplosivi Compositi 152t
Construcciones Aeronauticas, S.A. *see* CASA
conversion policies 16–20
  see also under names of individual countries
cooperation, international *see* collaboration, international
Cray Research 277
Cremascoli 208, 212
CRESAM (Centro Ricerche Experienze e Studi per Applicazioni Militari) 146
critical technologies 10–1, 67–72, 98, 112–4, 144, 273
CWC 159

DAF Special Products 173, 184
Daimler Benz 88, 91–3t, 96–7, 111
Daimler Benz Aerospace 57, 173
DAR (Delegation for Restructuring) 77
DASA (Deutsche Aerospace) 20, 57t, 91, 93t, 103, 134, 152t, 184, 239, 268
DASRS (Air Division for Studies, Research and Experiments) 146
Dassault 33, 54
Dassault-Aviation 56t, 59t, 65t
Dassault-Electronique 56t, 65t, 77
DCN (Directorate of Naval Construction) 52–3, 59t, 268
decline of defence industry 3
defence companies *see* companies, leading
Defence Evaluation and Research Agency *see* DERA
Defence Industry Committee (DIC) 139–40
defence industry *see under names of individual countries*
Defence Matériel Administration *see* FMV
Defence Research Agency *see* DRA
defence technology policy 10–4
DEFTEC 208
De Kruithoorn 20, 173, 184
De La Penne destroyers 142t
Delegation for Restructuring (DAR) 77
Délegation Générale pour l'Armement *see* DGA
Delft Instruments 19, 172, 186–8
DERA (Defence Evaluation and Research Agency) 12, 263, 265–6, 277–80
De Schelde (KSG) 171, 184, 186–7
Deutsche Aerospace *see* DASA
Deutsche Forschungsanstalt für Luft-und Raumfahrt *see* DLR
DGA (Délegation Générale pour l'Armement) 10, 12, 51–3, 57, 59t, 64, 66, 73–6, 79
DGAM (Directorate General for Armament and Material) 198
Dialog 241
DIC (Defence Industry Committee) 139–40

Diehl 92, 93t
diffusion of defence technologies: control of *see* export control
Directions des constructions navales (DCN) 52–3, 59t, 268
Directorate General for Armament and Material (DGAM) 198
Directorate of Naval Construction (DCN) 52–3, 59t, 268
diversification policies *see* conversion policies
DLR (Deutsche Forschungsanstalt für Luft-und Raumfahrt) 13, 88, 101
DO328 aircraft 151
Dornier 92, 93t, 151
Dowty 281t
DRA (Defence Research Agency) 262–4, 266, 274–6
DRIVE programme 239
DSM (Dutch State Mines) 173
dual-use technologies 11–4
  export policies 14–6
  see also under names of individual countries
Dual Use Technology Centres (DUTCs) 12, 277–8
Dutch State Mines (DSM) 173
DUTCs *see* Dual Use Technology Centres
Dynamit Nobel 94t, 172, 184

ECN Indret 59t
Economic Interest Groups (GIE) 54
economic offsets *see* offsets
EFIM 140, 148
EH-101 helicopter 142, 142t, 152t, 153, 269, 270t
EH Industries 152t
EJ 200 engine 153
Elettronica 147, 149–50t, 155, 165
Eleusis shipyard 121, 126t, 132
Elmer 149–50t, 155, 163
El Pardo Canal for Hydrodynamic Experiments (CEHP) 198
ELVO 120–1, 126t, 131–2
Embraer 152t
employment 3
  Belgium 31, 32t, 41, 43, 46
  France 52, 54, 65t
  Germany 87, 91–2, 101, 106
  Greece 119
  Italy 162–5
  The Netherlands 167, 170, 171t
  Spain 200t
  Sweden 221, 223t
  United Kingdom 261, 266
Empresa Nacional Bazán de Construcciones Navales Militares *see* Bazán
Empresa Nacional de Electrónica y Sistemas *see* INISEL
Empresa Nacional Santa Bárbara de Construcciones Militares 200, 206, 208, 211–2
Enator 241
ENI 140
ENOSA 201, 207
Ericsson 201, 222t, 226t, 240, 242, 252
Ericsson Defence Systems 243
Ericsson Microwave AB 243
Ericsson Radar Electronics 222t, 243, 244t
ESA *see* European Space Agency
Eseina 152t
Esperanza 213
ESPRIT (European Strategic Programme for R&D in Information Technology) 129, 239, 279–80
EUCLID (European Cooperation for the Long-term in Defence) 2, 7
  Belgium 25, 34, 37
  France 76
  Greece 129
  Italy 144, 147
  The Netherlands 182–4
  Sweden 253
  United Kingdom 280
EUREKA 76, 147, 186, 240
Eurocopter 59t
Eurofighter 2000 2, 8, 91–2, 95t, 110, 142, 142t, 152t, 153, 204, 268, 270t, 280
Euroflag aircraft 152t
Euro Hermespace 152t
Eurojet 200 152t
Eurojet Engines 152t
Eurometaal 19–20, 172–3, 184, 186–7

Euromissile 57, 57t
Euro Mul-T-Lok 173
European Community 1
European Cooperation for the Long-term in Defence *see* EUCLID
European Space Agency (ESA) 13, 40–1, 43, 46, 186
European Space Programme 31
European Strategic Programme for R&D in Information Technology *see* ESPRIT
EVG 702 supplier 95t
EVO 120, 126t, 129–31
EXPAL (Explosivos Alaveses) 201
expenditure 3, 5–6
see also under names of individual countries
Explosivos Alaveses (EXPAL) 201
export controls 2, 14–6
see also under names of individual countries
exports 4
see also under names of individual countries

F-14 fighter 27
F-16 fighter 35, 36t, 37, 39, 45, 174
F-104 fighter 145–6
F-122 frigate 96
Fabrique National d'armes de guerre (FN) 20, 31, 33, 42–3
Fabrique National Nouvelle Herstal (FN) 42
Federal Office for Defence Technology and Procurement (BWB) 86–7
FEL (Fysisch en Electronisch Laboratorium) 169, 192
Ferranti 57t
FFA (Aeronautical Research Institute) 220, 236–40
FFV Aerotech 222t, 226t, 241, 244t
FhG *see* Fraunhofer Gesellschaft
FIAT 140, 143, 147, 149
FIAT Avio 148, 149–50t, 151, 152t, 153, 155, 164
Fincantieri 268
Finmeccanica 143, 148–50, 152t, 153, 162
FLA (Future Large Aircraft) 35, 36t, 269
FMV (Defence Matériel Administration) 220, 236–8, 249
FN (Fabrique national d'armes de guerre) 20, 31, 33, 42–3
FN (Fabrique National Nouvelle Herstal) 42
FNNH 28, 30t, 33t
FOA (National Defence Research Establishment) 220, 236–8
Fokker 33t, 59t, 92, 167, 173, 184
Forges de Zeebrugge 28, 30t, 33
Forschungsgesellschaft für angewandte Naturwissenschaften 90, 101
Foundation for Dutch Industrial Participation in Defence Procurement *see* NIID
France 51–80
  Armaments Agency 8
  conversion policy 16–9, 52, 76–7
  critical technologies 10–1, 67–72
  defence industry 54–66
  defence technology policy 66–7
  dual-use technologies 12–3, 51, 67–75, 78–9
  expenditure 6t, 52, 58, 60–2, 66
  export controls 78–9
  exports 15, 54, 62, 63t, 78
  JACO/OCCAR 24n
  labour costs 4
  organisational context 52–3
  R&D 6t, 10, 51, 58, 60–1, 62, 64, 66, 76
Fraunhofer Gesellschaft (FhG) 13, 89–90, 101, 107
Fraunhofer Institut für angewandte Materialforschung 101
frigate 124 95t
Future Large Aircraft (FLA) 35, 36t, 269
Fysich en Electronisch Laboratorium (FEL) 169, 192

G-7 15, 159
GAMESA 201
GATT negotiations 73
GE *see* General Electric
GE 90 engine 152t, 153
GEC 266–8, 267t, 271, 277, 281t

GEC Marconi 57t, 281–2
GEC Thomson Sonar 268
General Electric (GE) 148, 152t, 153
Gerfault 59t
German Research Institute for Aviation and Space Technology *see* DLR
Germany 85–114
  Armaments Agency 8
  conversion policy 17, 19, 103–7
  critical technologies 98, 112–4
  defence industry 91–5
  defence technology policy 97–103
  dual-use technologies 13, 95–7, 99–100
  European context 110–2
  expenditure 6t, 92, 95–6, 100–1
  export controls 107–10
  exports 15, 92, 107–8
  JACO/OCCAR 24n
  organisational context 86–91
  R&D 6t, 87–91, 95, 97–8, 100
GFE (Großforschungseinrichtungen) 88
GIAT-industries 33, 42, 52–3, 56–7t, 58, 59t, 65t, 238, 268
GIE (Economic Interest Groups) 54
GIE Atr 152t
GIE Eurosam missile 152t
GIRAFFE 50AT radar 238, 242
GKN 281t
GNM (Van der Giessen-de Noord Marinebouw) 172, 188
Göteborg corvettes 226t
Gotland submarines 226t
Greece 117–35
  conversion policy 16–8, 130–1, 134
  declining demand/policy change 129–33
  defence market/defence industry 118–24
  defence technology capabilities 124–9
  dual-use technologies 130
  expenditure 6t, 118–9, 127, 129–30
  export controls 133
  exports 15
  R&D 6t, 127–30
Großforschungseinrichtungen (GFE) 88
Groupe de stratégie industrielle 10–3
GTK 24n
Gyconsa 201, 207

HAC helicopter 59t
Hägglunds Vehicle 221, 222t, 242–3, 244t, 247–9
HAI 120, 126t, 129–31, 130t, 134
HAP helicopter 59t
Harland and Wolff 281t
Harrier aircraft 202
Harrier Plus AV-8B aircraft 142, 146
HB Utveckling 226t
HDW 94t, 107
Helios satellite 140, 152t, 153
Hellenic Shipyard (Skaramanga) 121, 126t, 132
Hercules C-130J aircraft 269
Herstal SA 57t
Hollandse Signaalapparaten *see* HSA
Horizon frigate 8, 153, 268–9, 280
Hot missile 24n
HSA (Hollandse Signaalapparaten) 172, 184–5, 188
Hughes 201, 207
Hunting 152t, 267t

IABG (Industrieanlagen Betriebsgesellschaft) 90, 94t, 99
ICSA 208, 212
IEPG (Independent European Programme Group) 7, 37, 102, 177–8, 191
IGJAS 226t
IHI 153
Incentive 222t
Independent European Programme Group *see* IEPG
INDRA 201, 206–7, 212
Industria de Turbo Propulsores (ITP) 201, 207–8
industrial conversion *see* conversion policies
industrial policy 5–10
Industrieanlagen Betriebsgesellschaft (IABG) 90, 94t, 99
INISEL (Empresa Nacional de Electrónica y Sistemas) 152t, 201, 206, 212
Innovatie stimulering (INSTIR) 186
Institute for Applied Materials Science 89–90
Institute for Human Factors 169, 192
Institute of Optical Research 230
Institutes of the Blue List 89

Institut für angewandte Materialwissenschaften 89–90
Institut Saint-Louis 64, 90, 101
Instituut voor Technische Menskunde 169, 192
INTA (National Institute of Aerospace Technology) 198, 208–9, 211
Intergas 173
Interministerial Commission for the Study of Exports of War Matériel (CIEEMG) 78
Internatio-Müller group 172
International Atomic Energy Agency 45
international collaboration *see* collaboration, international
Inter-technique 65t
IRI 140, 147–8, 149t
ISDEFE 201
Italian Centre for Aerospace Research (CIRA) 140
Italian Space Agency (ASI) 140
Italtel 152t
Italy 137–65
  conversion policy 17–9, 154–8
  critical technologies 10, 144
  defence industry 141–2, 147–53, 162–5
  defence technology policy 142–3
  dual-use technologies 143–5, 158–61
  expenditure 6t, 140–3, 145–6
  export controls 158–61
  exports 15, 158–60
  JACO/OCCAR 24n
  military technology policy 145–6
  organisational context 137–40
  R&D 6t, 139–41, 143, 145–7, 151, 155
ITP (Industria de Turbo Propulsores 201, 207–8
IVECO 149–50t, 156, 201
IWKA 94t

JACO (Joint Armaments Cooperation Organisation) 24n
Japan 11–2
JAS39 Gripen aircraft 226–8, 230, 234, 246, 268
Joint Armaments Cooperation Organisation (JACO) 24n
joint ventures 9
  see also collaboration, international
JOULE programme 240

Karlskronavarvet 220–1, 222t, 226t, 244t, 248
Kockums 220–1, 222t, 226t, 231, 237, 244t
Koninklijke Begemann Groep 187
KONVER 3, 18–9
  Germany 19, 106
  Italy 18–9, 155, 157
  The Netherlands 188–9
  Spain 19, 213
  United Kingdom 283
Krauss-Maffei 20
Krupp 94t
KSG (Royal Schelde) 171, 184, 186–7

Labinal 56t, 65t
Landsnordic 222t
Law on Foreign Economic Relations (AWG) 107–9
leading companies *see* companies, leading
Leclerc tank 59t, 61, 102
Leopard I tank 27
Leopard II tank 95t, 227, 242
Liebherr LAT 173, 184
Link-miles 57t
Lockheed-Martin 4
Loral 4
Lucas Aerospace 108
Lucas Industries 267t
Lurssen 94t

M4 missile 59t
M5 missile 59t, 61
Maastricht Treaty 1
McDonnell Douglas MD11 151
McDonnell Douglas-Westland: Apache helicopter 174, 269, 280
Mainz Industries 94t
major companies *see* companies, leading
major programmes *see* programmes, major
MAN 94t
Mannesmann 94t
MARIN (Maritime Research Institute Netherlands) 169, 181, 192
MAST 280

Matra 54, 57t, 58, 77, 152t, 238, 268, 281
Matra-Hachette 56t, 65t
Matra Marconi Espace 268
Max Planck Society (MPG) 88
MBB 57, 57t, 92, 93t, 152t, 208
MBL (Medical Biological Laboratory) 192
MECAR 28, 30t, 33t
Medical Biological laboratory (MBL) 192
Metaalwaren Fabriek Tilburg (MFT) 186–7
Metal Institute 192
MFT (Metaalwaren Fabriek Tilburg) 186–7
MIDS (Multifunctional Information Distribution System) 152t
Milan missile 24n
Milas missile 152t
Ministry of University and Scientific Research (MURST) 140, 143–4
Mirage 2000 59t
Mirage F1 202
Missile Technology Control Regime *see* MTCR
Mistral missile 36t
Mitsubishi Heavy Industries 151
MLRS (Multiple Launch Rocket System) 152t, 153, 280
Montedison 140
MPG (Max Planck Society) 88
MRAV 24n
MRCA aircraft 142t, 145
MTCR (Missile Technology Control Regime) 15, 78, 159, 190, 213, 235, 284
MTU 59t, 92, 93t, 152t
Muiden Chemie International 184, 187
Multifunctional Information Distribution System (MIDS) 152t
Multiple Launch Rocket System (MLRS) 152t, 153, 280
MURST (Ministry of University and Scientific Research) 140, 143–4

Nationaal Lucht- en Ruimtevaartlaboratorium (NLR) 169, 181, 192
National Aerospace Laboratory *see* NLR
National Centre for Space Studies (CNES) 12, 64, 75
National Defence Research Establishment *see* FOA
National Institute of Aerospace Technology *see* INTA
Nationellt Flygtekniskt Forsknings Program (NFFP) 238
Nationellt Flygtekniskt Forum (NFF) 238
NATO 3, 37, 183, 191, 219
NATO helicopter *see* NH 90 helicopter
NATO Identification system (NIS) 152t
NATO Industrial Advisory Group (NIAG) 147
Navstar Global Positioning System 280
Netherlands 167–95
  conversion policy 17, 19–20, 185–9
  defence industry 170–6, 182–4
  defence technology capabilities 183
  defence technology policy 176–80
  dual-use technologies 13, 176, 180–1, 190–1
  expenditure 6t, 167, 169, 174–6
  export controls 189–92
  exports 15, 191–2
  organisational context 167–70
  R&D 6t, 13, 169–70, 174–5, 178–83, 192
Nettuno 146
NFF (Nationellt Flygtekniskt Forum) 238
NFFP (Nationellt Flygtekniskt Forsknings Program) 238
NH 90 helicopter 59t, 61–2, 95t, 153, 174–5
NIAG (NATO Industrial Advisory Group) 147
NIID (Stichting Nederlandse Industriële Inschakeling bij Defensieopdrachten) 168, 179, 182–3, 186
NIS (NATO Identification system) 152t
Nissan 201
NLR (National Aerospace Laboratory) 169, 181, 192
Nobel Industries 243
NobelTech 221, 241
Northern Telecom 172
NPT 213

Nuclear Non-Proliferation Treaty 15, 190, 236, 283–4
Nuclear Suppliers Group 15, 159, 190, 235, 284
NWM De Kruithoorn 20, 173, 184

OCCAR (Organisation conjointe de coopération en matière d'armement) 24n
Oerliken-Contaves AG Pyrotech 172, 184
Officine Galileo 148
offsets
  Belgium 38–40
  Italy 159–60
  The Netherlands 168, 177, 179, 183–4
  Sweden 242, 249
Olivetti 140
ONERA 53, 64
Organisation conjointe de coopération en matière d'armement (OCCAR) 24n
Orion aircraft 174
OSCE 159
OTO Melara 147–9, 150t, 152t, 155, 160, 163
overcapacity 3–4

PAN aircraft carrier 59t
Panavia 152t
Parliamentary Office of Science and Technology (POST) 272–4
PERIFRA 106, 283
Peugot 201
PFP (Partnership for Peace) 219
Philips 57t, 184, 240
Physics and Electronics Laboratory (FEL) 169, 192
Pilkington 57t
Pirelli 140
Pizarro armoured vehicles 202
planning of defence 5
Plastic and Rubber Institute 192
Plessey 92, 152t
POST *see* Parliamentary Office of Science and Technology
Poudreries Réunies de Belgique (PRB) 28, 31, 33, 40
Pratt and Whitney 33t, 148, 208
PRB *see* Poudreries Réunies de Belgique
Prins Maurits Laboratory 169, 192
Procurement Executive 263–4
programmes, major
  Belgium 36
  France 58, 59t
  Germany 95t
  Greece 126
  Italy 141–2
  The Netherlands 170, 174
  Sweden 226–7
  United Kingdom 269–70
Project Horizon 8, 153, 268–9, 280
PSR-890 AEW radar 226t
PYRKAL 120, 129–31

R&D 5–7
  see also under names of individual countries
R&H (Van Rietschoten & Houwens Defence Systems) 172
Racal 267t
RACE programme 240
Rafale 59t, 61, 77
Rapier missile system 270t
Raufoss 238
Raytheon 152t
Rb90 missile 238
RB 199 engine 152t, 153
RDM (Rotterdamsche Droogdok Maatschappij) 171, 186–7
Regulus 152t
research *see* R&D
Research and Technology Programmes (RTP) 87, 100, 147, 182, 280
Research Institute for Water, Sonar and Geophysics 90, 101
Research Society for Applied Natural Sciences 90
restructuring: by defence companies 3, 9–10
reunification of Germany 85–6
Rheinmetall 92, 93t, 101, 173, 184
Rhode & Schwartz 94t
RITA programme 34, 36t, 37
Roland Missile 24n
Rolls Royce 148, 152t, 201, 207, 267t, 268, 277, 281t

Rosyth Dockyard 281t
Rotterdmasche Droogdok Maatschappij
  see RDM
Royal Institute of Technology 220
Royal Military Academy 25
Royal Nijverdal Ten Cate 173
Royal Ordnance 184, 187, 268
Royal Schelde (KSG) 171, 184, 186–7
RTO 152t
RTPs (Research and Technology Programmes) 87, 100, 147, 182, 280
Russia 3, 110–1

Saab 17, 221, 226, 233, 238, 240, 242, 246, 268
Saab Defence 241
Saab Dynamics 241, 243
Saab Instruments 222t, 241, 244t
Saab Military Aircraft 222t, 241, 243, 244t
Saab Missiles 222t, 242, 244t
Saab-Scania 222t, 239, 243
Saab Training Systems 222t, 241, 244t
SABCA 30t, 33
SACMM 59t
SAES 57t, 207
SAGEM 56t, 59t, 65t, 77
Saint Louis research institute 64, 90, 101
SAIT-Radio Holland 30t, 33t
Salto di Quirra 146
SA Marine 244
Santa Bárbara (Empresa Nacional Santa Bárbara de Construcciones Militares) 200, 206, 208, 211–2
SCIENCE 280
SEA 201, 207
Sea Harrier 270t
SEL 94t
SENER 152t, 201
SEP 59t
SFIM 65t
Short Brothers 57t
SICS (Swedish Institute of Computer Science) 239
Sidewinder missile 280
Siemens 88, 92, 93t, 111, 152t
Single European Act 239
Single European Market 2
Skaramanga (Hellenic) shipyard 121, 126t, 132
Skyguard Aspide 142t
Smiths Industries 267t, 281t
Smyge ship 226t, 227
SNECMA 33, 42, 53, 56t, 59t, 65t, 76, 148, 152t, 153
SNLE submarine 59t, 61
SNPE 56t, 59t, 65t, 152t
Sociedad Anónima Placencia de las Armas 201
Société Générale de Belgique 33, 42
Sonaca 30t, 33t
SPADA 142t
Spain 197–215
  conversion policies 16–7, 19, 209, 211–3
  defence industry 199–208
  dual-use technologies 209, 211
  expenditure 6t, 201–2, 208–9, 210f
  export controls 213–4
  exports 15, 202–3
  organisational context 197–8
  R&D 6t, 198, 203–4, 208–9, 210f
Spearfish torpedo 270t
Stichting Nederlandse Industriële Inschakeling bij Defensieopdrachten *see* NIID
St. Louis institute 64, 90, 101
STRIC C&C system 226t, 227
STRIX mortar 226t, 227
super-technologies 2
Surgiclinic Plus 208, 212
Sweden 219–53
  conversion policy 17–8, 245–9
  critical technologies 10
  defence industry 220–4, 234, 252–3
  defence technology policy 234–5
  dual-use technologies 235, 251
  expenditure 6t, 226–30, 239
  export controls 248–51
  exports 15, 223t, 230–3, 242, 248
  organisational context 220
  R&D 6t, 220, 228–30, 234–8, 252
Swedish Ceramic Institute 239
Swedish Institute for Metals Research 239

Swedish Institute of Computer Science (SICS) 239
Swedish Institute of Microelectronics 239
Swedish Ordnance 226t, 241
Swedish Telecom Administration 239
Swift class submarine 270t

tactical air-defence system (TVLS) 95t
takeovers of defence companies 9
Technical Physical Service 192
Technisch Ontwikkelingskrediet (TOK) 186
Technologiesentrum Nord (TZN) 101
technology
  civil/military 2
  see also dual-use technologies
Technology Foresight 12
Techspace Aero 30t, 33t, 41
Telefónica Sistemas 201
telesystems 8000 226t
Telub 241, 249–50
Thomson-Brandt 238
Thomson Brandt Armement 33
Thomson-CSF 37, 56–7t, 58, 59t, 65t, 77, 152t, 172, 184, 207
Thomson-CSF Electronic Belgium 30t, 33t
Thomson Sintra 207
Thyssen 93t
Tigre (Tiger) helicopter 24n, 59t, 61
TNO-DO (TNO Defence Research) 20, 169, 179, 181–2
TOK (Technisch Ontwikkelingskrediet) 186
Tornado 146, 152t, 153
Tornado GR1 270t
Trafalgar class submarine 270t
Treaty of Rome: Article 223 1, 37–8, 158, 178, 191
Trident nuclear submarine 270t
Trigat missile 31, 36t, 268, 280
Troika mine-sweeping system 175
TST 172
Turbomeca 59t
Turbo Union 152t
TVLS (tactical air-defence system) 95t
TZN (Technologiezentrum Nord) 101

UEE (Unión Española de Explosivos) 201, 206
UHU helicopter 95t
Unión Española de Explosivos (UEE) 201, 206
United Kingdom 261–84
  Armaments Agency 8
  conversion policy 17, 280–3
  critical technologies 10–1, 273
  defence industry 266–70
  defence technology policy 270–80
  dual-use technologies 12, 270–8
  expenditure 6t, 261, 264, 270, 273, 276–7
  export controls 283–4
  exports 15, 266
  JACO/OCCAR 24n
  organisational context 263–6
  R&D 6t, 10, 261–5, 270–1, 273–6
United Nations: Register of Conventional Arms 15, 190, 284
United Scientific Holdings 281t
United States of America (USA) 3–4, 6, 10–1, 13, 73, 235

Van der Giessen-de Noord Marinebouw (GNM) 172, 188
Van Halteren 173, 184
Van Rietschoten & Houwens Defence Systems (R&H) 172
VBCI 24n
Vickers Defence Systems 266
Vickers Shipbuilding and Engineering Ltd *see* VSEL
Volvo 222t, 226t
Volvo Aero Corporation 221, 222t, 239, 244t
Volvo Flygmotor 17, 221, 238, 240, 246
Vosper Thorneycroft 267t
VSEL (Vickers Shipbuilding and Engineering Ltd) 266–8, 281t

WEAG *see* Western European Armaments Group
Wegmann 94t
Western European Armaments Group (WEAG) 7, 37, 183, 191, 280

Western European Armaments Organisation (WEAO) 24n
Western European Union (WEU) 1–2, 7, 37, 76, 183, 280
Westinghouse 148
Westinghouse Electric 151
Westland 152t, 267t, 269
WEU *see* Western European Union
Wilton Feyenoord 187

Zangger Group 159
Zobel reconnaisance vehicle 95t

For Product Safety Concerns and Information please contact our EU representative GPSR@taylorandfrancis.com Taylor & Francis Verlag GmbH, Kaufingerstraße 24, 80331 München, Germany

Batch number: 08151583

Printed by Printforce, the Netherlands